The Native Woo
of Scotland

The Native Woodlands of Scotland

Ecology, Conservation and Management

Scott McG. Wilson

EDINBURGH
University Press

Edinburgh University Press Ltd
The Tun – Holyrood Road
12 (2f) Jackson's Entry
Edinburgh EH8 8PJ
www.euppublishing.com

Typeset in 11/13 Minion Pro by
Servis Filmsetting Ltd, Stockport, Cheshire
and printed and bound in Great Britain by
CPI Group (UK) Ltd, Croydon CR0 4YY

A CIP record for this book is available from the
British Library

ISBN 978 0 7486 9284 2 (hardback)
ISBN 978 0 7486 9285 9 (paperback)
ISBN 978 0 7486 9286 6 (webready PDF)
ISBN 978 0 7486 9287 3 (epub)

Published with the support of the Edinburgh
University Scholarly Publishing Initiatives
Fund.

Contents

Acknowledgements

Figure 3.1 is reproduced here by kind permission of Blackwell Publishing Ltd. I am grateful to the Society of Antiquaries of Scotland to reproduce Figure 3.2 here. Figures 3.5, 8.6 and 9.3 are reproduced here by kind permission of the Forestry Commission. Plate 16 appears by kind permission of Seafield and Strathspey Estates/Mr Will Anderson. Plate 1 is reproduced here by kind permission of Springer. Plates 2, 8b, 8c, 9c, 9d, 12b, 19 and 25 are reproduced here by kind permission of the Forestry Commission. Plate 3 is reproduced here by kind permission of the National Library of Scotland (for upper map) and by kind permission of the British Library (for lower map). Plate 6 appears under standard licence from Shutterstock.

I wish to thank my professional clients and project sponsors over the past twenty years whose valuable support has given me the opportunity to visit so many native woodlands across Scotland in connection with research and consultancy. I would especially acknowledge here Forestry Commission Scotland, Future Trees Trust, Scottish Forestry Trust and Woodland Heritage.

Professor Chris Smout undertook a most valuable review of my first draft of the volume, helping to eliminate inconsistencies. Finally, I would like to thank my family, friends and professional colleagues who have encouraged me in the endeavour required to produce this book over the past five years.

Disclaimer

Tables

Figures

Plates

Abbreviations and acronyms

Ancient Woodland Site
Any site that has a record of carrying tree cover since 1750 (in Scotland).

Ancient Semi-natural Woodland
Self-sown woodland of native tree species on an Ancient Woodland Site.

ATC – alternatives to clearfell
CCF – continuous-cover forestry
Methods of forest management that do not involve clearfelling/restocking.

Coppice management
Coppice-with-standards management
Cyclical woodland management systems relying on natural stump regrowth.

FC(S) – Forestry Commission (Scotland)
Government forest regulatory department/public forest management body.

NVC – National Vegetation Classification
A formal system for botanical description of semi-natural vegetation types.

PAWS – Plantations on Ancient Woodland Sites
Plantations of non-native tree species on Ancient Woodland Sites.

SNH – Scottish Natural Heritage
Government (statutory) nature conservation agency/nature reserve manager.

NTS – National Trust for Scotland
SWT – Scottish Wildlife Trust
WT – Woodland Trust
Non-governmental (charitable) bodies owning/managing woodland sites.

Foreword

Dr Bob McIntosh CBE
Director Environment and Forestry, Forestry Commission Scotland

Native woodlands form a significant and characteristic element of Scottish landscapes, supporting key elements of our biodiversity and providing a context for outdoor recreation and tourism activity. They also have potential to mitigate climate change by acting as a store of carbon, and to furnish valuable woodfuel and carpentry timber. As such they command our attention. However, the longer-term historical development of native woodlands, over several millennia, has seen a steady decline in their extent and condition, through a combination of climate and soil deterioration and adverse human impacts – clearance for agriculture and development and exploitation for wood products at various times. Their extent has been reduced by around 90% since their post-glacial maximum, with only half of the surviving area believed to be in favourable ecological condition.

The Forestry Commission, from its establishment in 1919, has had an important role to play in conservation and management of native woodlands in Scotland. Earlier attention focused on the Caledonian pinewoods, with Forestry Commission reserve and research areas established at Glenmore, Glen Loy and the Black Wood of Rannoch during the 1930s and 1940s. The publication of Steven and Carlisle's famous book *The Native Pinewoods of Scotland* in 1959 encouraged further action by the Commission in pinewoods at Glen Affric, for example, and, from the 1970s onwards, action through grant aid to support native pinewood management on private estates. Over the past thirty years, since the 'Broadleaves Policy' of 1985, increased attention has been given to other types of native woodland such as the Atlantic oakwoods of the Trossachs, Argyll and Lochaber, riparian woodlands and, most recently, montane scrub above the plantation margin. Measures taken by the Commission, private landowners and charitable conservation organisations over the past half-century have arrested the decline in native woodland extent and begun the inevitably long-term processes of recovery in ecological condition and habitat restoration. However, new challenges arise from the possibility of climate change, the reality of novel tree pests and diseases in recent years and from the aspiration to realise more woodfuel, timber and income from woodlands.

Recent years have seen major advances in our understanding of the history, science and ecology of native woodlands in Scotland. Documentary and archival studies have clarified their history, as have pollen analytical techniques. Technical developments since 1990, such as those of the FC Ecological Site Classification (ESC), the National Vegetation Classification (NVC) and the concept of forest habitat networks (FHN), have been seminal. Most recently, the Native Woodland Survey of Scotland (NWSS), undertaken by Forestry Commission Scotland in partnership with Scottish Natural Heritage and partner organisations, has provided an unprecedentedly detailed 'snapshot' of the distribution, extent, composition and condition of the native woodland resource, with information outputs now available on an open-source basis. This new title by Dr Scott McG. Wilson integrates these existing sources of information into a convenient narrative reference volume which should prove valuable both to students and to practising land managers and foresters. The book benefits particularly from the author's two decades of personal field experience visiting, surveying and photographing very many native woodlands across Scotland.

Accordingly, I commend this new publication by Dr Scott McG. Wilson to all with an interest in native woodlands. In conjunction with the detailed information produced by the recent Native Woodland Survey of Scotland, it provides a sound basis from which to plan for the future conservation, expansion and utilisation of native woodland resources in Scotland.

Introduction

Objectives and scope of the book

Native woodlands are those comprising tree species that have colonised Scotland naturally since the end of the last Ice Age, 10–12,000 years BP. These include three conifers (Scots pine, yew and juniper) and some thirty broadleaves (Fife 1994; Herbert et al. 1999; Martynoga 2011; Smout et al. 2005). These now represent less than a quarter of Scotland's tree cover at ~310,000ha or 4% of the Scottish land area (MacKenzie 1999; Forestry Commission Scotland 2014). Over half our native woodlands (or 2–3% of Scotland's land area) are also regarded as being 'semi-natural' in that the trees have established naturally on their individual sites, without having been planted, although there may have been a history of management. It is estimated that native woodlands may once have covered 50–60% of Scotland's land area (Smout et al. 2005). The importance of native woodlands to Scotland is increasingly recognised, not only for their well-established biodiversity and nature conservation values, but also for their amenity and recreational values in the Scottish landscape and their potential to supply 'ecosystem services' such as soil protection, flood mitigation and carbon sequestration. It is now expected that, with careful silvicultural management, native woodlands can also meet an important element of the nation's future needs for timber products and woodfuel.

This book aims to provide a comprehensive but approachable overview of the history, ecology and management of Scotland's native woodlands. It is hoped that the level of coverage will meet the needs of three readerships: (1) those studying relevant subjects (including forestry, ecology, geography, environmental science and countryside management) up to undergraduate level, (2) those directly involved with management of Scottish native woodlands who do not come from a specialist professional background and (3) those with an informed amateur or recreational interest in Scottish native woodlands and wildlife more generally. The book is not primarily aimed at those with specialist training in woodland ecology, for whom many existing sources of detailed technical information are already available, including forestry textbooks and information bulletins issued by the Forestry Commission, Scottish Natural Heritage, non-governmental organisations (NGOs) and so on. However, they may also find this book convenient as a summary or 'ready-reference' volume.

Chapter 1 sets the native woodlands of Scotland in their international forest context, with particular reference to Scandinavia, Continental Europe and North America. Chapter 2 deals with their ecological context within the Scottish landscape – aspects of climate, elevation, geology, soils and adjoining open-land vegetation communities such as moorland and heathland. Chapter 3 summarises current understandings of the historical and ecological development of Scottish native woodlands from before the last Ice Age until the present time. This covers some controversial aspects of the subject, including the ongoing debate as to the ecological role of large herbivores in prehistory, the balance between climatic and human factors in native woodland decline and the timescales for that decline. There then follow four chapters dealing with the major types of native woodland found in Scotland: native pinewoods, oak-birch woodlands, ash-elm-hazel woodlands and, finally, the wet woodlands of alder and willow. The smaller remnants of lowland mixed deciduous woodland in Scotland, often having a wood-pasture or parkland structure, are included with the oak-birch woodlands for convenience, although some have greater affinities with lowland oak-ash woodlands in southern and eastern England. Juniper woodlands and montane juniper-willow scrub are both dealt with in association with the native pinewoods, aspen stands with the oak-birch woodlands. Chapters 8, 9 and 10 deal respectively with the conservation and management of existing native woodlands, expansion of the native woodland resource and relationships between native woodlands and plantation forests. The last are of significance due to the greater extent of the plantation forests, their developing ecological and reproductive maturity and current predictions for environmental change within which both native woodlands and plantation forests will have to co-evolve. Chapter 11 presents some ideas on the likely future development of native woodlands in Scotland, taking account of predicted climatic change, novel pests and diseases and changing economic influences. For those wishing to visit native woodlands in Scotland, Chapter 12 provides a gazetteer of interesting woodland sites that can be visited on foot under current Scottish countryside access legislation. These selected locations are intended to best illustrate major ecological types of native woodland and particular approaches to their conservation and management.

Earlier publications on Scottish native woodland

By comparison with the ecological literature for England, especially lowland England, Scottish native woodlands remain relatively under-reported. This is largely due to the longer history of botanical recording in the English lowlands, coupled with a greater volume of historical sources – the Domesday Book, court rolls and so on. As a result, certain key concepts in native woodland ecology, such as use of ancient woodland indicator species and recognition of the significance of coppicing and pollarding (Peterken 1993; Rackham 1990, 2003), were less well resolved with reference to the Scottish native woodlands. Recent years have, however, seen important advances in these areas, together with considerable attention to historical and cultural landscape dimensions, including the importance of upland wood pasture in

Scotland (Smout 1997, 2003; Smout et al. 2005). In addition, scientific approaches from the North American and Scandinavian literature, including site classification, island biogeography theory and stand dynamics (MacArthur and Wilson 1967; Oliver and Larson 1996; Pyatt et al. 2001), have been increasingly applied to native woodland complexes in Scotland, particularly those within the Cairngorms National Park.

To date, there have been few attempts to produce comprehensive guides to the native woodlands of Scotland – for example, there is no Scottish equivalent of Oliver Rackham's classic *Ancient Woodland* (2003). The closest approach to this remains Steven and Carlisle's *The Native Pinewoods of Scotland*, first published in 1959. Although that dealt mainly with the native pinewoods, there were also valuable descriptions of associated native woodland habitats, particularly the upland birch woodlands. In recent years, Clifton Bain of the RSPB has revisited the pinewoods by bicycle to update Steven and Carlisle's impressions, with outcomes reported in Bain (2013). Many other volumes on this subject have taken a primarily historical approach, inspired by Mark Anderson's *A History of Scottish Forestry*, published posthumously (Anderson 1967), which did provide considerable commentary on past ecological development of our native woodlands. Some of Anderson's perspectives are now becoming rather dated in the light of subsequent research findings, particularly in palynology (fossil pollen studies) (H. J. B. Birks 1989; Tipping 1994). More recently, Professor Chris Smout and co-authors (Smout 1997, 2003; Smout et al. 2005) have improved our understandings of documented Scottish woodland history with reference to specific regions, including Badenoch and Strathspey, Breadalbane, Argyll, Lochaber, the Loch Lomond oakwoods and so on. Scottish native woodland types have been dealt with to some extent by noted English-based woodland ecologists such as Oliver Rackham, George Peterken and John Rodwell (Peterken 1993; Rackham 1990, 2003; Rodwell 1991a), but there has continued to be a perception, rightly or wrongly, that they have received lesser emphasis in field sampling work and that they are therefore not always satisfactorily described by resulting woodland classification schemes. A particular issue has been the need to distinguish the semi-permanent birch and aspen woodlands of upland Scotland (Worrell 1995, 1999) from the more transient birch woodlands occurring in England and Wales. In recent years there have been a number of illustrated publications by the Forestry Commission and Scottish Natural Heritage dealing with conservation management and expansion of specific native woodland types (Forestry Commission 2003) that have been assigned priority conservation status. Of particular value for woodland managers are the updated Forestry Commission companion guides *Managing the Pinewoods of Scotland* (Mason et al. 2004) and *Managing Native Broadleaved Woodland* (Harmer et al. 2010). These complement earlier Forestry Commission bulletins such as Evans (1984), which tended to adopt a more 'production-oriented' approach to silvicultural practice in broadleaved plantations. Finally, there have been several 'coffee-table' style books (e.g. Miles and Jackman 1991) adopting a photographic approach, usually highlighting charismatic veteran trees and wildlife species, but sometimes suffering from historical inconsistencies.

CONSERVATION STATUS OF SCOTTISH NATIVE WOODLAND

While commentaries on the declining extent and condition of native woodland resources in Scotland were recorded from the fifteenth century onwards (Smout et al. 2005), it was not until the early twentieth century that professional attention was devoted to their conservation. Field visits to Scotland by eminent British and Continental European forest ecologists between the wars indicated native pinewood stands and acid Atlantic oak woodlands to be of particular botanical interest (Tansley 1939). Pinewoods at the Black Wood of Rannoch, Glenmore and Glen Loy were acquired by the Forestry Commission prior to the Second World War and thereafter managed to an extent as 'forest reserves'. After the war, the establishment of the Nature Conservancy (later to become Scottish Natural Heritage) saw declaration of further National Nature Reserves within native pinewoods including, most notably, Beinn Eighe in Wester Ross (Laughton Johnston and Balharry 2001). Some of these areas had sustained heavy fellings as part of the wartime timber supply effort. Recognition also increased for the Atlantic oakwood ecosystems of the west coast, with declaration of reserves, for example, at the Ariundle and Taynish Oakwoods, and similarly for the upland ash woodlands, as at Rassal. Many reserves were managed essentially on a 'non-intervention' basis, while others were the setting for early experiments in ecological restoration, particularly the native pinewoods at Beinn Eighe (Laughton Johnston and Balharry 2001). Many less prominent native woodlands also acquired some measure of recognition and, after 1981, protection as Sites of Special Scientific Interest (SSSIs). These approaches to conservation, based on reservation and protection of 'special sites', were inspired by earlier experiences within the wilderness and wildlife conservation movements of the United States and the British colonies. However, most native woodland remnants in Scotland, throughout this period, remained under the ownership of either the Forestry Commission, whose main purpose was coniferous afforestation, or private landowners, whose main interest was livestock production or the fostering of red deer and grouse for sport shooting. As such, many native woodlands continued to be subject to adverse impacts from over-grazing by sheep and deer (Fraser Darling 1955) or were converted to coniferous plantations. The post-war decades saw continued losses of native woodland cover in Scotland to alternative land-uses, particularly plantation forestry. Although those may not have represented such a significant fraction of the resource as was lost to agriculture and development in England, it became clear that action was needed to ensure their continued survival. In particular, it became essential to conserve native woodlands less as 'island reserves' and more as robust and functional ecological systems at the landscape scale, inevitably traversing ownership and management boundaries.

Many would date the current raised profile of native woodland conservation in Scotland to the publication in 1959 of Steven and Carlisle's *The Native Pinewoods of Scotland*. At an international level, this pioneering book represented one of the earlier attempts to promote research and active conservation within a particular natural forest ecosystem. Again, it was perhaps inspired by conservation experiences overseas, for example in the Californian redwood forests and the Western Ghats in

British India. The relatively small extent and number of the native pinewood remnants allowed Steven and Carlisle to adopt a site-specific inventory approach, rarely feasible elsewhere. Each site was described in systematic detail, with mapping and some photography. While their book focuses mainly on the pinewoods themselves, it does place these firmly within the context of the wider Scottish native woodland spectrum, including, particularly, adjoining upland birch woodlands. Other influential Scottish publications of the post-war years, such as those by Frank Fraser Darling (1947, 1955), highlighted the extent to which past climatic and human influences had led to decline of the various native woodland types in the wider Scottish landscape over preceding millennia. McVean and Ratcliffe in the early 1960s made valuable proposals, together with predictive mapping, as to those native woodland types that should naturally occur across the country, based on evidence from existing remnants, climate, elevation and soils (McVean and Ratcliffe 1962). The establishment of the Native Woodlands Discussion Group (NWDG) in 1974, followed by a major native pinewood conference held at Aviemore in 1975 (Aldhous 1995), were early signs that the emphasis was shifting from 'passive preservation' of existing Scottish native woodland remnants towards the active conservation and landscape-scale expansion of Scottish native woodlands as functioning, inter-connected ecosystems.

The last two decades have seen increasing levels of activity in the study, conservation and expansion of native woodlands in Scotland. A major stimulus for this was the 1992 UN Convention on Biological Diversity (CBD), under which governments committed to the protection and enhancement of biodiversity at the habitat, species and genetic levels. This led to the UK Biodiversity Action Plan (Department of the Environment 1994) under which the main Scottish native woodland types became subject to Habitat Action Plans (HAPs) and several animal and plant species depending upon these became subject to Species Action Plans (SAPs). Such plans provided a more robust policy basis for public funding of their conservation and expansion. Changes in forestry policy from the mid-1980s onwards (Forestry Commission 1985) had already justified the provision of public-sector financial support for establishment of new woodlands composed of native tree species and for improved management of the existing native woodland remnants. Initially, activity focused on the higher-profile native pinewoods, but more recently a range of other woodland types have been emphasised, including Atlantic oak woodlands, upland birch-aspen woodlands, ash-elm-hazel woodlands and riparian wet woodlands. The recently completed Native Woodland Survey of Scotland (NWSS) (Nelson 2010; Forestry Commission Scotland 2014) provides an extremely valuable update on the current extent, distribution and condition of Scotland's native woodlands.

Scientific advances

Important advances in the science of Scottish native woodlands during this period have included (1) development of more detailed schemes for habitat classification of remnant native woodlands, including the Peterken stand-type classification (Peterken 1993) and the National Vegetation Classification (NVC) (Rodwell 1991a), and (2) development of computer-based predictive modelling tools, including the Ecological Site Classification (ESC) (Pyatt et al. 2001) and the Macaulay Institute Native Woodland Model (NWM) (Towers et al. 2004), aimed at defining the most appropriate native woodland communities for targeted ecological restoration on specific sites. These approaches developed upon the basic framework for Scottish native woodland potential set out by McVean and Ratcliffe (1962). Much work conducted in connection with Scottish native woodlands today forms part of the wider agenda of 'restoration ecology' (Humphrey et al. 2003; van Andel and Aronson 2012), which is also being applied to upland open habitats such as moorland and heathland and to wetland and riparian ecosystems. Techniques for the establishment of new native woodlands by planting and natural colonisation have been developed in practice over recent years, but not all have been successful and this remains an important area of 'work in progress'. A natural tendency among nature conservation managers to adopt cautious, low-impact methods has frequently proved over-optimistic, and more interventionist forestry methods are sometimes still essential. On the other hand, realistic timescales for native woodland restoration are often much longer than can be readily accommodated within 'target-driven' public-funding mechanisms, and this can pose serious challenges for those seeking to adhere to fundamental ecological principles within financially sustainable woodland restoration work. Having said that, as we enter the new millennium, remnant native woodlands in Scotland are probably in the best ecological condition that they have been in for at least the past century. While new challenges from climate change, pest and disease incidence and rising demands for timber and woodfuel are now emerging, there is a sounder platform of knowledge from which to evolve sustainable management models specific to the Scottish native woodland resource. Of particular significance will be the developing interrelationships between native woodlands and more extensive plantation forests created in Scotland over the past 300 years. While plantation forestry has often been seen as an alternative, and sometimes conflicting, land-use to native woodland conservation, the likelihood is that the future will see increasing convergence and intermingling of productive woodland types, as these expand as an element of the overall Scottish land cover.

Ownership and management of native woodland

Alongside the increasing pace of native woodland research, conservation and expansion activity described above, the last two decades have also seen important changes in ownership and management patterns for the Scottish native woodland resource. New categories of ownership have emerged during this period, including the advent of large-scale land ownership by conservation charities/NGOs in the Scottish uplands and smaller-scale woodland ownership by local communities and private individuals. By contrast with the previously dominant major public- and private-sector owners – the Forestry Commission and the large sporting and agricultural estates – native woodland is often now the reason for ownership and the focus of ownership attention. This has brought benefits: a greater diversity of management approaches, greater emphasis on the conservation significance of native woodlands, and, in some cases, access to additional sources of funding and personnel to support native woodland management and expansion. On the other hand, there have been less desirable trends towards extensive woodland management with inadequate field input by relevant specialists, and greater day-to-day reliance on non-specialist desk-based managerial staff. A major objective of this book is to make available to these interested, but non-specialist, woodland managers a single source of information on the subject of native woodland in Scotland to which they can refer for background information. While it inevitably represents a summary of the knowledge available in many key areas, it is hoped that those with more detailed information requirements will find a starting point within these pages, leading them on to further readings wherever required.

CHAPTER ONE

International context

1.1 Overview

Native woodlands in Scotland do not exist in isolation – they form part of extensive natural forest ecosystems or 'biomes' occurring across continents. This chapter sets the native woodlands of Scotland within their international forestry context, and explains how their relationships with major forest biomes have influenced their formation and development.

For a territory of relatively small geographical extent, Scotland is unusual in possessing native woodland types that represent at least two, and arguably three, major forest biomes. The majority of Scottish native broadleaved woodlands – those of oak, ash, elm, hazel and alder – form part of the temperate deciduous forest biome (Peterken 1996; Rohrig and Ulrich 1991), which extends throughout the British Isles and most parts of western Europe north of the Alps, including southern parts of Scandinavia. There are similar forests in parts of eastern North America and the far east of Asia – China, Japan and Korea. These forests are adapted to deal with a seasonal climate by shedding their leaves in the autumn and growing a new set in spring. The native pinewoods, together with closely associated birch, aspen and juniper woodlands, form part of the boreal forest biome (Andersson 2005), which extends eastwards across central and northern parts of Scandinavia and Russia, before resuming across Alaska and Canada. The dominant tree species in the boreal forests are evergreen conifers, such as pines, which are adapted to deal with severe winter conditions. Although their leaves are retained, tree growth is negligible in winter due to low temperatures and limited sunlight at high latitudes. Some native woodlands along the western seaboard of Scotland have affinities to the European temperate evergreen forest biome (Ovington 1983) also occurring in parts of Ireland, Portugal and Spain – these are 'oceanic' forests where winters are milder and trees do not need to shed their leaves, but instead can keep growing all year round. Atlantic oakwoods, where evergreen holly is common in the understorey, naturally have common features with this biome, and that has been accentuated by recent introductions of *Rhododendron* from Eurasia and a range of evergreen conifers from the equivalent temperate evergreen forests found on the Pacific coast of North America (Orians and Schoen 2013).

1.2 LINKS WITH NATIVE WOODLANDS IN ENGLAND AND WALES

There is little surprise that strong similarities are to be found between the native woodlands of Scotland and those of England and Wales, our closest neighbouring territories. This applies mainly to the broadleaved native woodland types, as Scots pine forest is not believed to have occurred naturally in England and Wales for many thousands of years (although in some areas there are very old Scots pine plantations). Native broadleaved woodland types found in upland Scotland – acid oak-birch woodlands and more fertile ash-elm-hazel woodlands – occur in similar upland areas of Wales and northern and south-western England, similarly with the wet alder-willow woodland types of river valleys and fens, found throughout the British Isles. There are fewer persistent examples to be found in England and Wales of upland birch-aspen-rowan and juniper scrub woodland types – these, together with the native pinewoods, appear to be particular features of Scotland's closer links with the Scandinavian boreal forests. In woodlands in the milder upland climates of England and Wales, these species are often outcompeted over time by oak, ash, hazel and other broadleaved trees.

Lowland England, and more southern and eastern parts of Wales, support mixed deciduous woodlands dominated by oak and ash, naturally having an understorey of hazel and/or field maple. In the past, many such woodlands would also have had a significant elm component. There are also native woodlands of lime and hornbeam in some parts of south-east England and East Anglia, reflecting forest types found in warmer lowland areas of Continental Europe (Linnard 2000; Peterken 1993; Rackham 2003; Rodwell 1991a). Many of these lowland woodlands have been heavily modified by past forestry management for oak and ash timber, the coppicing of understorey species such as hazel and field maple, and the planting of non-native tree species including beech, sycamore, sweet chestnut and conifers. However, there remain isolated examples in a 'nearer-to-nature' condition, such as the New Forest (Peterken 1993, 1996). Historically, similar lowland oak-ash-elm woodlands also occurred extensively in central and eastern Scotland, particularly within the Central Belt and the Tay, Clyde and Forth Valleys. However, most of these were removed long since, when the fertile land on which they once stood was converted to agricultural production or urban development. There are some surviving remnants of these woodland types, many in the form of ancient wood pastures and parklands, deliberately maintained around medieval castle sites, such as at Cadzow, near Glasgow, and Dalkeith, near Edinburgh (Smout et al. 2005). Oak is the dominant tree species today, with ash and elm occurring locally.

1.3 LINKS WITH NATURAL FORESTS OF CONTINENTAL EUROPE

The native woodlands found in Scotland are, to a large extent, north-western oceanic outliers of the major temperate deciduous forest types found throughout mainland Europe, ranging between the Alps/Pyrenees and southern Scandinavia (see Plate 1). Similar forests are found in other parts of the world with a seasonal climate, but where winter conditions are not excessively cold and summer conditions are not so dry as to cause trees to stop growing during a typical year. Other major temperate deciduous forest areas are the eastern United States (the Appalachian and New England forests) and those found in mid-latitude parts of eastern Asia (China, Japan, southern Korea). There are smaller areas of forests of similar type in New Zealand and Chile. The acid oakwoods of the Atlantic coast and Highland margins in Scotland resemble similar oak-dominated woodlands occurring on acidic soils in parts of southern Sweden and Norway, Ireland, Brittany and north-western Spain. The more lowland oakwoods on moderately fertile sites in Scotland, with bluebell and bracken, are similar to those of west-central France. The upland ash-elm-hazel woodlands of Scotland have similarities to those occurring in river valleys and on limestone soils in montane areas such as the Vosges and Jura in eastern France, the foothills of the Pyrenees in south-western France and parts of northern Italy. Some phases of temperate deciduous woodland vegetation in Scotland, notably the Atlantic hazel woodlands, are not found widely elsewhere. The native pinewoods of Scotland, although having stronger links to the boreal pine forests of Scandinavia, also have ecological similarities to the montane and sub-alpine pine forests of the Massif Central in France and the central mountains of Spain. Those are coniferous forests which occur as 'inliers' within the temperate deciduous forest biome, due to colder climates at higher elevations. They are also in some senses 'outliers' from the boreal forests further north in Scandinavia. Due to the compression of altitudinal ranges close to the Atlantic Ocean, the native pinewoods can occur at much lower elevations than montane Scots pine forests in mainland Europe. Genetic studies have shown that some of the native pinewoods, especially those near sea level in the far north-west Highlands, may be more closely related to the montane Scots pine populations of central France and Spain than to those of the Scandinavian boreal pine forests (Aldhous 1995; Forrest 1992). The same is likely to have been true of the Scots pine once found naturally in Ireland, which, it is conventionally believed, became extinct at least a thousand years ago. The genetics of Scots pine will be discussed in more detail in Chapters 3 and 4, in connection with the development of native woodlands in Scotland before, during and after the last Ice Age.

There are certain important natural forest types found in Continental Europe that are not represented naturally within Scotland – these include the classic beech, spruce and silver fir forests of the montane and sub-alpine areas, rich valley woodlands of lime and sycamore and the lowland forests on heavy soils of the European Plain, dominated by lime and hornbeam (see Table 1.1). These will be discussed later within the present chapter.

1.4 Links with Scandinavian and Russian boreal forests

Although we have seen that the strongest ecological links of Scotland's broadleaved native woodlands are to the temperate deciduous forests of England, Wales and Continental Europe, the native pinewoods have equally strong ecological connections to the boreal forests of Scandinavia. The boreal forest biome is the most extensive in

TABLE 1.1 Typical altitudinal zonation of forests in central Europe. Partly after Jahn, in Rohrig and Ulrich (1991).

ALTITUDINAL ZONE	ELEVATION	FOREST ASSEMBLAGE
ALPINE	>2250m	ALPINE HEATH KRUMMHOLZ SCRUB
UPPER SUB-ALPINE	1800m-2250m	ALPINE LARCH
LOWER SUB-ALPINE	1275-1800m	NORWAY SPRUCE
MONTANE	650-1275m	BEECH - SILVER FIR
FOOTHILL/ COLLINE	300-650m	OAK-BEECH-SCOTS PINE
LOWLAND PLAIN	0-300m	OAK-LIME-HORNBEAM (OAK-BIRCH ON POOR SOILS) (BEECH ON EMINENCES)
RIVERINE and HOLLOWS	0m	ASH-ELM-ALDER-WILLOW

the world and stretches in a belt around the northern hemisphere between the northern limit of the temperate deciduous forests and the southern limit of the Arctic tundra. There are no boreal forests in the southern hemisphere as the continental landmasses of South America, Southern Africa and Australasia are further from the pole. Boreal forests are composed of a relatively small number of hardy tree genera (families of related species) that can withstand cold climates, including pines, spruces, larches, birches, rowan and aspen. The exact species occurring vary between the boreal forests of the Eurasian landmass (Scandinavia and Russia) and those of the North American landmass (Alaska, Canada and northern parts of the United States), but the structure of these forests is very similar. In Scandinavia and western Russia, the boreal forest is divided into 'light forest' communities, dominated by Scots pine, birch, rowan and aspen, and 'dark forest' communities, dominated by Norway spruce with smaller components of other conifers (Andersson 2005). 'Light forest' tends to dominate on infertile, freely draining soils (see Plate 6), whereas 'dark forest' develops over time by colonisation of Norway spruce onto sites with richer, moister soils. The native pinewoods are western oceanic outliers of the 'light forest' types found in western Norway and southern Sweden, but tend to have more broadleaved species such as birch, alder, rowan and aspen. Some ecologists therefore regard them as being a transitional type, known as 'hemi-boreal' (meaning half-boreal) forests.

Another difference between Scottish native pinewoods and the 'true' Scandinavian boreal forests relates to the role of fire in stimulating natural regeneration. Only the drier, eastern native pinewoods in Scotland, such as those of Deeside and Speyside, experience such natural fires regularly. The western pinewoods, with higher rainfall and thicker ground vegetation, regenerate mainly by the formation of occasional gaps by windthrow – a feature more comparable to the montane pine forests further south in mainland Europe. A considerable number of the wildlife species that still occur in northern Scandinavian boreal forests became extinct in Scotland before the end of the last Ice Age (e.g. wolverine) or have become extinct in more recent millennia due to habitat loss and hunting pressure (reindeer, brown bear, lynx, wolf, beaver) (Yalden 2002). This means that, in biodiversity terms, native pinewoods in Scotland represent a depauperate (depleted) oceanic outlier of the boreal forests of Scandinavia and Russia.

1.5 Links with North American natural forests

Native woodlands in Scotland share many tree genera with natural forests, not only in Eurasia, but also in North America. These include pine, oak, ash, elm, birch and aspen, occurring in both the boreal and temperate deciduous forests of North America. However, there are different species representing each of these genera on either side of the Atlantic and important differences in the way that the structure of these forests has developed. In eastern North America there is a better developed ecological transition zone or 'ecotone' between the boreal and temperate deciduous forest biomes than in Europe, where the Baltic Sea 'masks' the transition from one biome to the other. The area around the Great Lakes and in northern New England is dominated by the 'northern mixedwoods' (Byrd Davis 1996), where elements of the boreal and temperate deciduous forest biomes merge together. In some ways this is comparable to the 'contact zone' between the native pinewoods and the broadleaved native woodlands in Scotland. Further east in Russia, and further west in North America, the drier continental climates prevent the widespread development of temperate deciduous forests, and the southern boundary of the boreal forest is marked by a transition to steppe grasslands.

Another important ecological relationship between the forests of Scotland and those of North America relates to the temperate evergreen forests of the Pacific Northwest (northern California, Oregon, Washington and British Columbia). Although the two territories share no individual tree species naturally, they do share a very similar climate. For that reason, foresters in Scotland have been interested to introduce many of the highly productive conifer species found in the Pacific Northwest, including Douglas fir, Sitka spruce, redwood, western hemlock, western red cedar, grand fir, Pacific silver fir and noble fir (Macdonald et al. 1957; Wilson 2011b; Wood 1955). These introduced tree species grow more quickly than the native species found in similar climates within Scotland, such as Scots pine, oak and ash, and some can be grown in wet, exposed areas of western Scotland that native tree species cannot utilise (Anderson 1961). Hence, many plantation forests in Scotland today, having been created over the past 150 years, are composed of 'exotic' species from North America.

1.6 Links with European temperate evergreen forests

We have seen that the two main forest biomes to which native woodlands in Scotland belong are the temperate deciduous forests and the boreal forests. However, some of the broadleaved native woodlands along the west coast of Scotland, although dominated by oak, also contain a large amount of the evergreen holly in the understorey. This represents a transition to a third forest biome – the temperate evergreen forests (Ovington 1983). Forests of this type develop in areas where the winter is sufficiently mild that some trees can keep growing without risk of frost damage, and hence benefit from retaining their leaves all year round. Because of the oceanic influence, these forests do not experience significant summer droughts, and as a result there is no need for a dry season growth pause. Temperate evergreen forests can be composed mainly of conifers, as in the Pacific Northwest of North America and north-west Morocco, or mainly of broadleaves, as in the Atlantic coastal forests of western Europe. Those in the southern hemisphere, mainly in Chile and New Zealand, tend to be more mixed. As we will see in Chapter 3, the examples of temperate evergreen forests found along the western edges of Europe are in effect remnants of more extensive areas of this ecosystem which existed before the series of glaciations that have occurred over the past two million years. In the far south-west of Ireland, around Killarney, native oak woodlands are found with much holly as in western Scotland, but also naturally occurring yew and strawberry tree (an evergreen broadleaf) (Cross 2012; Tansley 1939) – two other species typical of the European temperate evergreen forests. Yew occurs locally in Scottish woodlands of this type (for example in Glen Etive and at Loch Lomond) but is held by some authors to be an ancient introduction (Dickson 1993). Similar woodlands are found in western Wales, Cornwall and Brittany, although lacking strawberry tree. In north-west Spain and Portugal, we find similar Atlantic oak woodlands (Rohrig and Ulrich 1991), but here with naturally occurring strawberry tree and *Rhododendron*. Some ecologists therefore recognise a type of west-coast temperate vegetation that they term 'Hiberno-Lusitanian' (meaning Irish-Spanish). Although not native in Scotland, Ireland, Wales or Cornwall since the last Ice Age, *Rhododendron* has been very widely planted in west-coast gardens in these regions over the past 150 years, and has spread outwards into some adjoining native oak woodlands. This has effectively increased representation of the temperate evergreen forest biome, and that is probably also being encouraged by changes in the climate of western Britain towards a milder, wetter oceanic regime (Ray 2008). As was mentioned earlier in this chapter, foresters in Scotland have tended to favour introduced conifer species, particularly Sitka spruce and Douglas fir, which originate from the temperate evergreen forests of the Pacific Northwest of North America. As these species mature, and reproduce from seed, they are contributing to the expansion of temperate evergreen forest vegetation in western Scotland.

1.7 Tree species and forest types missing from Scotland

So far as we know, there have been no extinctions of tree species in Scotland since the last Ice Age. There are, however, several tree species that failed to recolonise Scotland naturally after the last Ice Age, when they might have been expected to. Some of these species did, however, manage to recolonise southern Britain before the English Channel was flooded by global sea-level rise, fed by glacial meltwaters, 7,000–8,000 years BP. Others have arrived since, with varying degrees of human assistance. Lime-hornbeam woodland occurs naturally in some lowland parts of south-east England, and may have been more abundant before human modification of woodlands began seriously, 5,000–6,000 years BP. Lime still occurs naturally as far north as the Lake District on limestone soils, but not into Scotland. Field maple occurs widely in southern England and Wales, but not in Scotland (Peterken 1993; Rackham 1990, 2003; Rodwell 1991a). In the case of beech, there is some uncertainty as to when actual recolonisation was accomplished, either naturally before opening of the English Channel, or afterwards with assistance from prehistoric human settlers, who might have brought beech seed (known as 'mast') to feed their livestock during their first winter in Britain. The species certainly did not become abundant until 4,000–5,000 years BP. Natural beech woodlands occur in many parts of southern England, especially on chalk and limestone hills such as the Chilterns, South Downs and Cotswolds (Wilson 2010). Sycamore, although possibly introduced at an earlier date, has become widespread only since the 1500s as a result of planting and natural colonisation. While lime, hornbeam and field maple may not be climatically suited to Scotland, due to lack of summer warmth required for reproduction (Piggott and Huntley 1978), there is little doubt that beech and sycamore woodlands could have developed quickly in many parts of Scotland had these species been able to colonise northwards naturally after reaching southern Britain. It is believed that beech was only prevented from doing so, over the past 3,000 to 4,000 years, by human clearance of woodlands for agriculture. Beech and sycamore are shade-tolerant tree species, allowing their seedlings to establish themselves under the canopy of existing native woodlands, eventually becoming dominant as older individuals (e.g. of oak or ash) die naturally. This happens today where beech or sycamore seeds into oak woodlands from nearby planted trees. Beech and sycamore have been introduced to Scotland over the past 400–500 years (Smout et al. 2005) and have become important, probably permanent, elements of many otherwise 'native' broadleaved woodlands.

There are also a number of tree species, absent from Britain as a whole since the last Ice Age, which occur naturally in Continental Europe. The most important of these are Norway spruce, European larch and European silver fir, all of which are believed to have occurred in Britain during Pleistocene interglacials (West 1970, 1980). These species have been deliberately introduced, or perhaps we should say 'reintroduced', to Britain over the past 300–400 years, but are still regarded by most ecologists as 'exotic' species. The same applies to *Rhododendron*, which was apparently present in the British Isles during previous warmer interglacial periods.

Finally there are a range of tree genera (families of species) that have become extinct from Europe as a result of the series of glaciations over the past two million years, but which are still found today in various parts of America and Asia, and which have been introduced by 'plant hunters' and foresters over the past 200 years. This is certainly true of the genus *Tsuga*, represented today by the common forestry species western hemlock (West 1980). Other coniferous genera, now restricted to North America and Eastern Asia, will also once have occurred in Europe (Mai 1989).

CHAPTER TWO

Ecological context

2.1 Overview

In order to fully understand the different types of native woodland that occur within Scotland, it is essential to see how they fit into the wider ecology of the Scottish landscape. This chapter will present information in four main areas: (1) how climate and elevation affect the development of native woodlands; (2) how geology and soils act as 'mediating factors', influencing how native woodlands develop locally within any particular regional climate; (3) how native woodlands relate to adjoining open-land habitats; and (4) classification and description of the different types of native woodland found in Scotland. As well as providing a framework within which to consider native woodlands at the landscape scale, it is also intended that this chapter should allow the reader to take any individual native woodland site with which they are involved and place it within the wider context in terms of its environment and species composition.

2.2 The influences of climate and elevation

Climatic factors are the most important natural determinants of native woodland distribution in Scotland and affect both the structure and species composition of the woodlands themselves. Although a large fraction of the original native woodland cover of Scotland has been removed or modified by past human activities, we can still see clearly the effects of climate when we examine the spatial and altitudinal distribution and structure of surviving native woodland remnants in Scotland. Climatic factors also have a very powerful influence on the feasibility and progress of native woodland restoration and expansion efforts. Current concerns over predicted climate change also highlight the need to have a good understanding of the climatic requirements and tolerances of Scotland's native woodland types.

Climate affects the development of native woodlands in a number of ways (Kimmins 1997), the most important of which are:

- provision of warmth required for plant growth
- provision of moisture required for plant growth
- regulation of light required for plant growth
- risk of damage to vegetation from extremes of heat or cold

- risk of damage to vegetation from strong winds and flood events
- effects on the prevalence and impacts of insects, fungi and bacteria.

Plants, including trees, need sufficient warmth, moisture, soil nutrition and light to survive and to grow by means of photosynthesis, fixing atmospheric carbon to form their vegetative tissues. Most plants can withstand, by means of a growth pause, regular seasons or occasional episodes when these factors become insufficient for growth. However, the average annual climate must be adequate to allow for positive net growth. Different tree and plant species have different requirements in terms of each of these major variables, and this is the main mechanism by which the climate of any area will determine the species composition of native woodlands. For example, Scots pine has much lower requirements in terms of warmth than does ash, and hence native pinewoods tend to occupy colder sites than upland ash woodlands. Few plants will continue positive growth when the temperature falls below 5°C, and so only days when this temperature is exceeded can be counted as part of the growing season (Pyatt et al. 2001). Similarly, the amount of growth that can be achieved is regulated by the supply of light of the correct wavelengths to power photosynthesis (known as 'photosynthetically active radiation' or PAR) (Kimmins 1997). Hence the further north one travels, the shorter the growing season becomes regardless of summer warmth and day length.

The climate of Scotland is generally regarded as a cool moist or cool temperate one, with a very strong moderating influence from the Atlantic Ocean. Climatic moisture supply is, therefore, rarely a limiting factor on tree growth at present, although there is a distinct climatic gradient between the wetter oceanic conditions of the west coast and the drier, more continental conditions of the east coast (over a relatively short distance of ~300km). This is sufficient to influence the structure and development of native woodlands on either side of the Scottish Highland mountains, and to result in local ecological adaptation within tree populations across the country. It may also have significance for the regional impacts of predicted climate change (Ray 2008). Excessive rainfall, especially if concentrated in very intensive episodes, can become a limiting factor on tree growth through the mechanisms of flooding, landslips and soil erosion. While these are rather localised and infrequent events in Scotland at the present time, they may become much more of a problem in the west under future climate scenarios.

By comparison, climatic warmth can be a much more significant limiting factor on tree growth, especially at higher elevations in Scotland. Although the overall winter climate of Scotland is much milder than that of boreal forest regions of Scandinavia and Russia, or within alpine conifer forests of mainland Europe, there is a very strong dependence on altitude, with harsher 'Arctic-Alpine' climatic conditions experienced over the hills and mountains. This tends to establish a natural 'treeline' in Scotland (an upper limit for woodland development) usually between 450m and 650m above sea level (asl), depending locally upon latitude, slope aspect and exposure. This is a much lower limit than would apply in the Alps, for example, where forests extend up to 2,000–3,000m altitude. The main reason for this difference is the very high average wind speeds encountered in Scotland, which accentuate the thermal limitations on tree growth through an exposure or 'wind-chilling' effect. Strong winds can also cause mechanical damage to woodland vegetation, and where that is sufficiently frequent or severe, they have the effect of depressing the natural treeline to lower altitudes, especially on slopes more exposed to the prevailing south-westerly winds. In extreme cases, the treeline can be depressed to near sea level, and trees exposed to very severe wind regimes tend to adopt a stunted and misshapen stem form in response. Below the natural treeline, climatic warmth and exposure continue to have marked effects on the structure and composition of the native woodlands that can develop. Light levels also vary between north- and south-facing slopes, due to the low angle of winter sunshine at northern latitudes (Scotland ranges from 55° to 59° North). This has local effects on warmth and growing-season length and can lead to different types of woodland developing on either face of glens running east to west.

Below the natural treeline, native woodland structure and composition in Scotland is determined by a combination of climate, soils and anthropogenic factors. Soils will be discussed later in this chapter, while woodland history is the subject of Chapter 3. Climate and soils impose a basic structure of altitudinal bands of different types of native woodland. The way in which these are described and classified by ecologists is dealt with later in this chapter, as this is one of the key tools that native woodland managers use when studying existing native woodlands and planning their restoration. However, at a simplified level, a 'typical' hillside slope in the Highlands of Scotland naturally has the following woodland types (see Table 2.1):

Upper slopes: Montane scrub woodland (juniper, dwarf birch and willow)
Upper midslope: Native pinewood, with birch, aspen, rowan and juniper
Midslope: Upland birch woodland (over blaeberry and heather)
Lower midslope: Oak-birch woodland (over bracken, bramble and bluebell)
Slope foot: Ash-elm-hazel woodland, often with some oak
Valley bottom: Riparian ash-alder woodland and alder-willow woodland.

Of course, the position is more complex and variable than this. In southern Scotland, native pinewoods do not occur naturally, so upland birch woodland extends further up the slopes. In the north-west Highlands, native pinewood locally comes down to the coast (as at Shieldaig). Many areas have had certain types of native woodland or individual native tree species preferentially removed by past human activities, or tree species like beech and sycamore introduced, sometimes many centuries ago. This is most likely to have happened where sites were accessible for farming or forestry management, much less so on very steep and remote sites. Where slopes are cut into (incised) by side valleys, ash-elm-hazel or alder woodland types can reach further up the main slope where sheltered by landform topography. In some parts of the country, boundaries between native woodland types are quite distinct, whereas in others, different types of oak, birch, ash and hazel woodlands merge together to form a habitat mosaic. Where areas of particularly fertile or wet soils occur, this can also modify local patterns.

TABLE 2.1 Altitudinal zonation of native woodland vegetation in Scotland (within and outwith Caledonian Pinewood Zone). Partly after Rodwell (1991a) and Peterken (1993).

ALTITUDINAL ZONE	ELEVATION	NVC WOODLAND TYPES (CPZ)	NVC WOODLAND TYPES (non-CPZ)
ALPINE	>900m	NONE PRESENT	NONE PRESENT
SUB-ALPINE	600-900m	W19, W20 JUNIPER-BIRCH-WILLOW SCRUB	W19, W20 JUNIPER-BIRCH-WILLOW SCRUB
MONTANE	300-600m	W17 UPLAND BIRCHWOOD W18 NATIVE PINEWOOD	W17 UPLAND BIRCHWOOD
FOOTHILLS	150-300m	W18 NATIVE PINEWOOD W11/17 UPLAND OAKWOOD W7 SLOPE ALDERWOOD	W11/17 UPLAND OAKWOOD W9 UPLAND ASHWOOD W7 SLOPE ALDERWOOD
LOWLAND (INFERTILE/ CONVEX)	0-150m	W11 OAK-BIRCH WOODLAND W18 NATIVE PINEWOOD *(W16 ACID OAK WOODLAND)*	W11 OAK-BIRCH WOODLAND *(W16 ACID OAK WOODLAND)*
LOWLAND (FERTILE/ CONCAVE)	0-150m	W10 OAK-ASH WOODLAND W8 ASH-ELM WOODLAND W4/W7 BIRCH-ALDERWOOD	W10 OAK-ASH WOODLAND W8 ASH-ELM WOODLAND W4/W7 BIRCH-ALDERWOOD
RIPARIAN and BASINS	0m	W1-W7 WET WOODLAND	W1-W7 WET WOODLAND

Recent years have seen increasing scientific and popular discussion of the likely impacts of human-induced climate change (Broadmeadow and Ray 2005; Read et al. 2009), arising from emissions of carbon dioxide (CO_2), a 'greenhouse' gas, from burning fossil fuels. While it is possible to make reasonable model-based predictions for global climatic trends, it is much more difficult to apply these at regional scales (e.g. for Scotland). However, work carried out as part of the UK Climate Impacts Programme (UKCIP) over the past ten years has suggested some key directions of climate change for Scotland that may affect native woodland development and conservation in future. It is predicted that both our summers and our winters will become warmer by 2–4°C during the coming century, and that snow and frost events will become less severe and less frequent on average. Rainfall, especially in the summer, may decrease significantly in the east of Scotland, while the west coast could become even wetter. This represents an increase in the climatic gradient already experienced across Scotland (see above). Windstorms and flood events may become stronger and more frequent, although this is subject to considerable uncertainty (Green and Ray 2009; Ray 2008). These trends could have major implications for native woodland types. Generally, existing types would be expected to occur further up the altitudinal range than was discussed earlier, to retain cooler and moister conditions optimal for their growth. This might cause problems for some native woodland types, including montane scrub and native pinewood, that already occur at higher elevations, as they may no longer be able to find a climatic niche in Scotland where they remain competitive. Especially in eastern Scotland, some native tree species may suffer summer drought stress, growing more slowly than at present. Other species, such as holly, spruce and *Rhododendron*, may expand in the west coast woodlands (Ray 2008). As a result, Scotland may tend to 'weaken its ecological links' with the Scandinavian boreal forest biome, but 'strengthen its ecological links' with the European temperate evergreen forest biome (see Chapter 1). Introduced tree species, such as lime, sweet chestnut, beech and sycamore, may spread further in a warmer climate as they will produce more seed.

A particular issue with a changing climate is the potential for pests and diseases to become more prevalent and damaging as the climate warms (Green and Ray 2009). This is one aspect of the impact of climate change on biodiversity more generally. Organisms which have the capacity to migrate in response to climate change should find suitable conditions elsewhere. This would apply to many mammals, birds and insects, and also to short-lived plants which can spread fairly quickly by annual reseeding. However, longer-lived static organisms, such as trees, cannot do this within a single generation, and may therefore begin to experience climatic stress. This tends to make trees more vulnerable to a range of insect, fungal and bacterial pests, which will also become more common and active within a warmer climatic environment. As a result, pest impacts could be one key mechanism by which climate change drives changes in native woodland composition. At present, Scots pine in the native pinewoods is under threat from *Dothistroma* needle blight (Brown and Webber 2008), a fungal pathogen that spreads more easily in warm, moist climatic conditions. Ash in Scottish native woodland is now under threat from *Chalara* ash dieback, and larch and juniper from the fungus-like pathogens *Phytophthora* spp.

When wishing to know the climate for any particular native woodland site or potential habitat restoration area, it is usually possible to obtain this information from published (including online) weather maps, many of which can be handled within a Geographical Information System (GIS) – an important new tool for native woodland management (Heywood et al. 2011) (see Plate 2). It is also possible now to obtain maps of predicted future climate, based on computer modelling of climate-change scenarios (Ray 2008). Those with a long-term management involvement with any particular woodland site will sometimes establish a private weather station to provide localised refinement of published climate data.

2.3 THE INFLUENCES OF GEOLOGY AND SOILS

Among natural determinants of native woodland development, geology and soils are second only to climatic factors. Whereas climate usually acts at the regional or landscape scale, geology and soil influences are normally active at the stand or site scale within wider climatic zones. For this reason they should be seen partly as mediating or adjusting factors, which help to determine the types of native woodland that will develop on individual sites within a wider landscape subject to a particular regional climate.

In the Scottish situation there is currently no volcanic activity and a very limited degree of seismic activity, which rarely disturbs vegetation cover. This is due to the current arrangement of the tectonic plates, which places the British Isles well away from active faults and 'hotspots' on the Earth's crust. There are periodic and localised landslip events, which can result in vegetation cover being disturbed, but these tend to be 'top down' events caused by heavy rainfall episodes, rather than 'bottom up' events triggered by seismic activity. The overwhelming importance of geology for native woodland development is then its role as the soil parent material. Geology influences rooting depth, particle size, drainage and fertility of soils (Fitzpatrick 1980; Pritchett and Fisher 2000), all of which have direct effects on stability, structure and composition of native woodlands.

When considering geological features of any particular site for native woodland development, it is essential to distinguish underlying 'solid geology' or 'country rock' from any overlying superficial 'drift' deposits of glacial (ice age) or fluvial (river deposit) origin. Where these are present, they, rather than underlying geology, determine soil types. In terms of geology, Scotland has several distinct provinces (Gillen 2013) (see Table 2.2):

1. The **Highland zone** (north of the Highland Boundary Fault, including the Western Isles) mainly comprises ancient hard rocks of varied origins. These strata include Lewisian gneiss, Torridonian sandstone, Cambrian quartzite, intrusive granite, Moine schist and Dalradian shale/limestone. These rocks are typically slow to weather and, in many (but not all) cases, produce inherently infertile soils. In some areas these rocks were uplifted, long after their original formation, into the high Caledonian mountains, which underwent subsequent erosion by ice and water, forming the gentler mountain chains we observe today (Grampians, Cairngorms, NW Highlands).
2. The **Southern Upland zone** (the rounded hills of the Borders, Dumfries and Galloway) comprises sedimentary (or weakly metamorphosed) rocks of a shale/slate type originating from the Ordovician and Silurian periods. These rocks underwent some later uplifting during the process of geological collision between England and Scotland. These rocks weather more quickly than those of the Highland zone and produce soils of low to moderate fertility, depending on local composition. Small areas within this zone, including Merrick and Criffel, comprise intruded granitic masses of younger ages, producing shallower, infertile soils.
3. The **Central valley zone** represents the area between the Highland Boundary Fault and the Southern Upland Fault – effectively a large trench that was at one time flooded by the sea. The bed of the trench accumulated sedimentary deposits, first of Devonian (Old Red) sandstones and later of Carboniferous (coal-bearing) sandstone and limestone. Igneous rocks erupted through these beds in ancient times, forming the various hill ranges of central Scotland. While this zone contains a wide variety of rocks, they generally produce the more fertile soils in Scotland, supporting the lowland arable farmlands of the Mearns (in Angus), Fife, East Lothian and the Merse (Berwickshire). The Old Red Sandstones in upland fringe areas (such as the Kincardineshire hills north of Fettercairn) are rather less fertile, whereas some of the igneous rocks (for example those of the Kinnoull and Moncrieff Hills, east of Perth)

TABLE 2.2 Main geological formations of Scotland and their soils. For access to comprehensive geological mapping, refer to the British Geological Survey at <www.bgs.ac.uk>.

Geological Period (youngest to oldest)	Principal Strata	Category	Main Regions of Occurrence	Inherent Fertility	Typical Soil Types Formed
Tertiary	Basalts	Igneous	West Highlands, Inner Hebrides	High	Brown earths
Cretaceous	Chalk and greensand	Sedimentary	West Highlands (very localised)	High	Brown earths
Jurassic	Kimmeridge clays	Sedimentary	East Sutherland (localised)	High	Brown earths, Gleys
Triassic	New Red sandstone	Sedimentary	Inner Moray Firth, Inner Solway	Poor–Medium	Sandy brown earths, Podzols
Permian	Desert sandstones/breccias	Sedimentary	Ayrshire, Dumfries, Isle of Arran	Medium	Brown earths (some Podzols)
Carboniferous	Sandstone/coal measures	Sedimentary	Ayrshire, Fife, Central Valley	Medium	Brown earths, Gleys
Carboniferous	Limestone	Sedimentary	Fife, Central Valley	Medium–High	Brown earths, Gleys
Carboniferous	Basalt (and associates)	Igneous	Fife, Central Valley, East Lothian	Medium–High	Brown earths
Devonian	Old Red sandstone	Sedimentary	Central Valley/Moray Firth/Orkney/Borders	Poor–Medium	Sandy brown earths, Podzols
Devonian	Basalt (and associates)	Igneous	Fife/Angus/Perth, Argyll, Lanark	High	Brown earths
Silurian	Shales (and associates)	Sedimentary	Borders, Dumfries & Galloway	Poor–Medium	Upland brown earths, Ironpans
Intrusive	Granites	Intrusive	Highlands, Dumfries & Galloway	Very Poor–Poor	Podzols, Ironpans, Peaty podzols
Ordovician	Shales (and associates)	Sedimentary	Borders, Dumfries & Galloway	Poor–Medium	Upland brown earths, Ironpans
Cambrian	Quartzites	Sedimentary	North-west Highlands	Very Poor	Rankers, Podzols, Ironpans
Pre-Cambrian	Dalradian limestones	Metamorphic	Grampian Highlands, Argyll, S. Hebrides	Medium	Upland brown earths
Pre-Cambrian	Dalradian schists and shales	Metamorphic	Grampian Highlands, Argyll, Buchan	Poor–Medium	Upland brown earths, Ironpans
Pre-Cambrian	Moine schists and quartzites	Metamorphic	Central and North-west Highlands	Very Poor–Poor	Ironpans, Peaty podzols, Peats
Pre-Cambrian	Torridonian sandstone	Sedimentary	North-west Highlands	Very Poor–Poor	Podzols, Ironpans
Pre-Cambrian	Lewisian gneiss	Metamorphic	North-west Highlands, Hebrides	Very Poor	Rankers, Peats, Ironpans

and Carboniferous limestones are strongly base-rich, supporting ash-elm-hazel woodland. In the raised area between Edinburgh and Glasgow, the Carboniferous rocks are overlain by thick deposits of fine-textured glacial tills, producing heavy soils.

4. The **Mesozoic sedimentary zone** comprises a number of smaller areas with younger sedimentary rocks from the Permian, Triassic, Jurassic and Cretaceous periods. These softer rocks (called an overburden) once occurred across the Scottish landscape, but have been removed by later erosion from more exposed upland areas, leaving underlying harder strata exposed. Soft rocks continue to form the solid geology of the southern half of England, and have survived in a few parts of Scotland, such as the Dumfries area and the Moray Firth coastlands. A common rock type is the New Red (or 'desert') sandstone of Permo-Triassic age, but there are smaller patches of Jurassic clay in east Sutherland and some very small remnants of Cretaceous chalk on Skye and on the Morvern peninsula. These rocks tend to produce relatively fertile lowland soils, although the New Red sandstones in parts of Morayshire can produce coarse and nutrient-poor sands.
5. The **Tertiary basalt zone** includes several areas along the western seaboard and islands – Skye, Eigg, Mull and the Ardnamurchan peninsula. Parts of Northern Ireland are similar. These are much younger igneous basaltic rocks from the Tertiary period, produced when the continental landmasses of North America and Europe pulled apart, forming the Atlantic Ocean. The same process is still active today in the volcanic landscapes of Iceland, which now sits over the mid-Atlantic ridge. The basaltic rocks produce inherently very fertile soils, but steep and unstable slopes.

Superficial drift of glacial origin occurs across large parts of Scotland where it has not been removed by water or wind erosional activity (Gillen 2013). Drift has been deposited during several glaciations over the past two million years and mainly comprises solid rock materials pulverised by the passage of glaciers. It can be deposited either directly when the glacier melts and its rock content is dropped *in situ* or, more frequently, it is washed out from underneath the glacier and re-sorted by meltwater activity at the end of the glacial period (Gillen 2013). The most recent period of drift deposition was at the end of the last glaciation some 10,000–12,000 years BP. Since that time many deposits have been removed by erosive action where they remained exposed, but a large portion have become 'protected' under a covering of soil and vegetation. While the chemical weathering rate of the drift is usually higher than that of the solid rock from which it formed, it can be poorer than the 'country rock' type which it now overlies, having been transported a considerable distance. Some deposits of till are dominated by fine textured material which has been compacted or 'indurated' by 'freeze-thaw' cycles at the end of the glaciation, producing a dense hard layer at the base of the soil which is impervious to rooting and impedes drainage. Locally, there are more recent floodplain deposits from rivers (Edwards and Ralston 2003), which can range from coarser 'fluvioglacial' gravels, through sand banks, to finer silt and clay beds. All of these drift substrates have implications for the subsequent formation of overlying soils.

When seeking to determine the geology for any particular woodland site, relevant information should generally be obtained from geological maps of suitable scales, readily available from the British Geological Survey (including online). Maps are available of both underlying solid geology and overlying drift. Additional information can be obtained by digging a soil pit (see below), especially as regards superficial drift deposits. An undiggable indurated layer, often of a pale greyish-yellow 'biscuity' colour and texture, may be found at the base of the pit (from around 30cm depth in some areas), and pebbles, gravel or stones found within the soil itself often derive from superficial drift deposits. If these stones are of a smooth, rounded shape, these are likely to have been transported by water, not ice.

Soils are vitally important to the development of native woodlands due to their functions in providing support, moisture and plant nutrients required for growth. Even where the climate is inherently suitable for a wide range of tree species, poor soils may narrow this down to a smaller number and limit their establishment and growth rates. Soil fertility, in particular, is a key determinant of, and limitation on, native woodland development in Scotland, reflecting the prevalence of infertile solid geologies. Many soils in Scotland are seasonally water-logged, impairing their ability to provide physical resistance to windthrow and reducing plant nutrient availability.

Soil types are usually described in terms of a soil classification system. There are a variety of these – some traditional schemes, such as the Soil Survey of Scotland classification, describe soils with reference to typical examples found at named geographical locations (e.g. Countesswells, Arkaig). Others, particularly those used in North America, Russia and tropical regions (Pritchett and Fisher 2000), emphasise the physical and chemical processes by which soils have been formed over time. Of most value for native woodland planning are schemes such as the GB Forestry Commission soil classification (Kennedy 2002; Pyatt et al. 2001) which focus on pedological development, current structure, drainage and fertility of soils. There are six main categories of soil likely to be encountered (Fitzpatrick 1980) within native woodlands in Scotland and areas where native tree planting is contemplated, these being (see Plate 4):

1. **Brown earths** – these are the best soils for woodland growth, with an absence of impervious layers, water-logging and other barriers to rooting. The soil depth is usually at least 60cm and often up to 1m, providing good support. The colour of the soil is normally brown, red or yellow, reflecting the fact that aeration is good and that iron is remaining in the oxidised state. The soil near the surface may be darker, incorporating organic matter, but there should not be a thick build-up of leaf litter and humus on the soil surface. Texture can vary from clay to sand, but is often a well-structured loam (mixture of particle sizes), maintained by the activity of earthworms. Fertility (nutrient supply) from brown earths varies widely, but is normally adequate for a range of trees. Brown earths in Scotland usually support birch, oak and ash woodland types. Brown earths are found throughout Scotland, mainly on plateau and lower valley slope sites, many long

having been cleared of woodland for agriculture. Brown earths found in upland areas may show some signs of podzolisation.

2. **Podzols** – these are infertile soils that have been stripped of their nutrients by downward movement of water through the soil profile over long periods of time. They often form over geologies that have a coarse particle size, such as sand or gravel, containing minerals with a rather low content of plant nutrients. High rainfall is also a contributory factor, speeding up formation of podzols. They can be recognised by the development of a series of layers of different colours. There will often be a thick black mat of organic material (humus) on the soil surface, which is slow to decompose and 'locks up' plant nutrients. Certain types of acid vegetation, such as heather, blaeberry and some conifers, produce leaf litter which is difficult to break down due to its chemical composition. Birch, on the other hand, produces fertile litter which can 'improve' the soil. Beneath the humus there is a grey, ash-like layer ('podzol' means 'ash' in Russian), from which iron, nutrients and organic material have been leached out (eluviated). This can vary in thickness from a few millimetres to up to a metre in extreme cases. Lower in the profile there is a strong reddish-brown or black layer where organic matter and iron from above are deposited (illuviated). This can take the form of a thin black layer, known as a hardpan, which limits rooting. Unfortunately plant nutrients such as calcium, potassium and magnesium are not redeposited, and are washed downwards out of the soil, depleting its fertility. Podzols in Scotland usually support native pine, birch and juniper woods of boreal type. Podzols are common in the East Highlands and Cairngorms, being associated with granite and Moine schist geologies and fluvioglacial gravels.
3. **Gleyed soils** – these are soils which are water-logged for all or part of the year, but which show a fairly wide range of fertility levels. Many gleyed soils have a fine clay texture which makes it difficult for water to drain away – this can be throughout the profile or only at some depth in the soil, impeding drainage. Gleyed soils can usually be recognised by their greyish colour, due to the poor aeration and the resulting reduction of iron compounds. Soils that are weakly gleyed retain their brown colour near the surface, but may show orange and grey mottling deeper down where aeration is poorer. Gleyed soils where the water comes primarily 'down from above' (as rainfall) are called surface-water gleys. Those where the water comes primarily 'up from below' are called ground-water gleys and usually occur in areas of flat, lower-lying land. The poor aeration in gleyed soils makes it difficult for many trees to take up nutrients, even if these are relatively abundant in the soil. Species such as ash, alder and willow are able to do this and are usually dominant on fertile gleys. Infertile gleys can support wet birch-willow woodlands, locally with Scots pine. Gleyed soils are found throughout Scotland, particularly in upland areas with high rainfall and also over poorly drained drift deposits in the Central Belt.
4. **Ironpan soils** – these are special cases of the podzol and gleyed soil types, which occur on upland moorland and heathland sites. The soil is normally very infertile, and it is uncommon for woodland to develop naturally over ironpan

soils. A thin, hard layer of iron is redeposited in the soil profile at a point where there is a change in moisture and aeration conditions (Fitzpatrick 1980). This can be caused by a 'wet blanket' of peat at the surface, sitting on drier mineral soil below, or it can occur where an indurated layer at the base of the soil profile holds up moisture, with drier soil below. Trampling and compaction by livestock over a long period can encourage formation of an ironpan soil in upland areas with high rainfall. The presence of an ironpan prevents drainage of moisture, creating a gleyed layer, and, if well developed, also prevents effective rooting. Ironpan soils are unsuitable for the creation of new native woodland unless the pan is first disrupted. Ironpan soils are found in upland areas of Scotland in the Highland and Southern Upland geological zones, often in areas with heather moorland.

5. **Peaty soils** – these are soils which have at least 30cm of wet organic matter at the surface, accumulated from the slow decay of plant remains deposited from vegetation. There are a number of different types of peaty soils, largely depending on the peat depth. Deep peats form in blanket and raised bogs, while peaty gleys (with shallower peat) form on wet upland moorlands. Peat tends to be found in situations where the rate of decay of plant material is slowed down by a cold, wet climate or excessive ground water. Peaty soils can form over a long period of time on sites that formerly supported native pinewood and upland birch woodland, leading to gradual loss of woodland cover. Normally, peaty soils are not suitable for native woodland development, although there are localised examples of stunted pine and birch bog woodland. Peaty soils are particularly extensive in the far north of Scotland, in areas such as Sutherland and Caithness (the 'Flow Country'), supporting wetland habitats.
6. **Ranker and skeletal soils** – these are soils which are incompletely developed due to being relatively recently formed or due to the weathering rate of the underlying rock being exceptionally slow. They are usually infertile and often incapable of supporting native woodland. Large areas of the far north-west Highlands, with Lewisian gneiss geologies, have peaty ranker soils. A special case of the skeletal soils are the beach sands, as at Culbin and Tentsmuir. Man-made soils over old land-fill sites and mining spoils can also be considered in this category, as they are usually still immature.

Information about the soil type on a particular woodland site can be collected from a number of sources. There are Soil Survey of Scotland maps available from the James Hutton Institute, Aberdeen, which provide the local 'soil series' or 'soil association', but these groupings can contain a number of different soil types that commonly occur together. Some older Forestry Commission forests have good soil maps, based on detailed surveys. However, in many cases it will be necessary to carry out a fresh soil survey to collect more local information. For a small site this may consist of a single soil test pit, to a depth of 70–100cm. For larger sites, it may be necessary to dig several pits to capture variation in soil conditions across the area of interest. Details of each layer in the soil profile are described from a soil pit, including depth, structure, texture and colour (using the Munsell scale). This should allow the soil to be assigned to one of the major categories discussed above (Kennedy 2002). Ground vegetation can also be used to 'indicate' soil conditions and that technique will be covered in more detail in Chapter 9, in terms of planning native woodland expansion.

2.4 Relationships with other habitat types

By comparison with major forest territories in Scandinavia, Continental Europe and North America, remnant native woodlands in Scotland are now highly scattered and fragmented. This was not always the case – as will be seen in Chapter 3, which deals with woodland history, Scotland once had native woodland cover over perhaps 50–60% of its total land area (Smout et al. 2005). Fragmentation has occurred through processes of human clearance, combined with climatic and soil deterioration, over the past 5,000 years. The relatively few surviving individual native woodland remnants exceeding 100ha are mostly of native pinewood, upland birch woodland or upland oak woodland. The average native woodland patch is much smaller, and a significant proportion of the total resource is accounted for by patches less than 10ha in extent. The degree of fragmentation is highest for the woodland types of better soils – the lowland mixed deciduous, upland ash-elm-hazel woodlands and alder-willow woodlands – many of which are long linear features following river valleys. This means that most native woodlands in Scotland now have a strong interaction with other adjoining habitat types – the so-called 'edge effect'.

These habitats fall into two categories: (1) semi-natural habitats and (2) man-made habitats. The former include moorland, heathland, wetland and some grassland ecosystems, which are usually subject to some human influence (e.g. grazing or burning) but are composed of self-sown native plant species, which regenerate themselves without human assistance. Most native woodlands are themselves 'semi-natural' habitats, as they have been modified by human activity and continue to be subject to its influence to varying extents. Scotland has few, if any, woodlands that can be considered truly natural, in the sense that they were never subjected to human modification. Man-made habitats have been created by human activity and require its continued influence to maintain their current formation and structure. These include arable land, improved pastures and recreation grasslands, plantation forestry and developed land. Some ecologists argue that the distinction between semi-natural and man-made habitats is artificial – that moorland and heathland, for example, came into existence as a result of human clearance of woodland in prehistory (Edwards and Ralston 2003; Fraser Darling and Morton Boyd 1969; Simmons 2000; Smout 1993). Some recent commentaries, for example by Fenton (2008) and Tipping (2008), have suggested that many open upland habitats in Scotland arose naturally. Many recent man-made habitats have developed semi-natural elements, such as ground vegetation within plantation conifer forests. Nonetheless, these two categories have different ecological implications.

Many semi-natural open-land habitats that occur in Scotland are recognised to be of conservation significance at an international level. In certain cases this may exceed the ecological value of any new native woodland that could conceivably be created there now. For example, boreal Scots pine-birch forest occurs in a vast area across Scandinavia and Russia, whereas Scotland holds much of the world's resource of heather moorland. A range of animal and plant species, some rare, are dependent upon these open habitats. The range of plant species occurring on – and the large stores of carbon locked up within – Scottish blanket and raised peat bogs means that draining these for woodland establishment is now considered to be ecologically inappropriate. When considering ecological management of semi-natural habitats in Scotland, one has to decide what the target or 'desired future condition' should be. Often it will be a native woodland habitat, but in some situations it could still be moor or heath. Both moor and heath are usually dominated by the *Calluna-Vaccinium* ericoid sub-shrubs (these include heathers, blaeberry, cowberry, etc.) – the difference being that moorland or 'mire' habitats are, at least seasonally, water-logged, whereas heaths are usually free-draining. Both may develop over infertile soils as a result of human woodland clearance, burning and livestock grazing over millennia. To assist ecologists in studying and managing semi-natural habitats, the National Vegetation Classification (NVC) has been developed over the past thirty years. The key types of open-land habitat of conservation significance in Scotland are mires and heaths (NVC M and H communities) (Rodwell 1991b), upland grasslands (NVC U communities) and wetland/freshwater habitats. There are much smaller areas of neutral and calcareous grasslands (NVC MG and CG communities) in Scotland that might still be considered partly semi-natural. The boundary between native woodland and these open semi-natural habitats is usually fairly gradual and 'ecologically porous'. There is often an ecotone between the two, such as juniper-birch scrub establishing on heathland adjoining a native woodland. Many animal and plant species can move between these adjoining habitats, and some open-land habitats, such as heathland, are relatively 'permeable' for migrating woodland species (Watts et al. 2005). Ecologists and site managers often have to deal with issues that arise from creating artificial boundaries between semi-natural habitats – for example fencing of woodlands to keep out deer or burning of heathlands to remove woody scrub and promote heather. With the exception of grazing impacts and uncontrolled fires, originally started by land managers, there are limited threats to native woodlands arising from adjoining semi-natural habitats.

Man-made habitats are regarded somewhat differently as they are usually treated as of lower conservation significance and they often have an abrupt boundary with the native woodland habitat. Many species that occur within native woodlands cannot easily migrate between native woodland habitat patches by crossing arable or developed land. This means that man-made habitats are much more effective in ecologically fragmenting landscapes, for woodland-dependent species, than are semi-natural habitats such as heathland. Plantation forestry may offer better opportunities in this regard (see below). A number of factors associated with man-made habitats can pose direct external threats to adjoining native woodland. These include various forms of pollution from agricultural chemicals (pesticides, herbicides and fertilisers), industrial chemicals (including on abandoned brown-field sites), light, noise, disturbance by vehicles, fires, fly-tipping, straying pets and invasive garden plants. In addition, there is often pressure for further expansion of built development and recreational grassland at the expense of native woodland, although many woodlands have a degree of legal protection due to designation and planning controls (see Chapter 8).

Attention is increasingly focused on 'ecological enhancement' of adjoining man-made habitats so that they pose less of a challenge to native woodlands and offer greater opportunities for native woodland expansion and for migration of woodland species. The aim is to make them more similar to semi-natural habitats and to increase their habitat permeability for particular species of conservation interest (e.g. dormouse). In the case of plantation forestry in Scotland, this can be attempted through the processes of restructuring and diversification that will be discussed in Chapter 10. That approach can also offer a more efficient and reliable route to native woodland habitat expansion than new planting or natural colonisation of native trees onto open ground. Recreation grassland habitats such as parkland and golf courses can also be amenable to improvement through vegetation management approaches – riparian corridors and canal banks offer the opportunity to create networks of semi-natural habitats (Fowler and Stiven 2003). More heavily modified man-made environments – such as urban development, transport infrastructure, industrial sites and intensive arable land – pose greater challenges, usually tackled through 'defensive measures' for threat mitigation and native woodland protection.

2.5 Ecological classification of native woodlands

For purposes of scientific survey and ecological management, it is valuable to be able to place native woodland habitats into a classification of types based on their species composition and the site conditions that they normally require. Such a scheme of classification should be no more complex than is required for its intended purpose. There have been a variety of attempts to do this over the past century, each with its advantages and disadvantages. Earlier systems of classification, devised between 1900 and 1960, took a mainly botanical approach and were really intended for use by ecological researchers. They adopted many features of earlier phyto-sociological (plant community) classifications from Continental Europe (e.g. the 'Montpellier school') (Braun-Blanquet 1932). These systems assume that groups of plant species, including trees and herbs, form 'semi-permanent associations' that are more than 'marriages of convenience'. In the 1960s, McVean and Ratcliffe produced a classification of 'potential natural' native woodland cover for Scotland, emphasising the historical woodland cover of the country and the most appropriate types for future restoration (McVean and Ratcliffe 1962). During the 1970s, George Peterken, a prominent English-based woodland ecologist, developed a system of 'stand-type classification' (Peterken 1993) that dealt mainly with the tree and shrub components of existing woodlands and was intended, to a greater degree, to inform active management of these, rather than as a tool for detailed botanical studies. Finally, the last three decades have seen the development of the woodland section of the National Vegetation Classification (NVC), edited by Professor John Rodwell at the University of Lancaster (Rodwell 1991a).

TABLE 2.3 Main native woodland vegetation types found in Scotland. For more detailed information on community composition and site types, see Forestry Commission (2003), Forestry Commission Scotland (2014), Peterken (1993), Pyatt et al. (2001) and Rodwell (1991a).

FC Woodland Habitat Type	Chapter Coverage	NVC Communities	Peterken Stand Types	Main Native Trees	Main Soil Types	Soil Moisture Regime	Soil Nutrient Regime	Ground Vegetation
Montane scrub	Chapter 4	W19 (juniper), W20 (willow)	Scrub types	Juniper, dwarf birch, montane willows	Rankers Podzols Ironpan soils	Slightly Dry to Very Moist	Very Poor	Upland acid grasses, heather, blaeberry, ferns, wood sorrel
Native pinewoods	Chapter 4	W18	Group 11	Scots pine, juniper, downy birch, silver birch, aspen	Podzols Peaty podzols Peaty soils (shallow)	Slightly Dry to Very Moist	Very Poor	Heather, blaeberry, upland acid grasses
Upland birchwoods	Chapter 5 (W4 wet birch woodlands are covered in Chapter 7)	W11 and W17 (W4 on wetter sites)	Group 12	Silver birch, downy birch, aspen, juniper, hazel, rowan, oaks	Brown earths Podzols Peaty soils	Slightly Dry to Wet	Very Poor to Medium	Acid grasses, mixed grasses, heather, blaeberry, bracken, bluebell
Upland oakwoods	Chapter 5	W11 and W17	Group 6 A/B (locally Group 3A/D)	Sessile/pedunculate oak, silver/downy birch, hazel, holly, rowan, aspen, cherry	Upland brown earths Podzolic brown earths Podzols (weakly dev.)	Slightly Dry to Moist	Poor to Medium	Upland acid grasses, blaeberry, mixed grasses, bracken, bluebell, ferns
Lowland mixed deciduous woodlands	Chapter 5 (W8 lowland ash woodlands are covered in Chapter 6)	W8 and W10 (very locally W16)	Group 1 Group 6 C/D (locally Group 3A/D)	Ash, wych elm, hazel, pedunculate oak, silver/downy birch, holly, rowan, aspen, cherry	Brown earths Gleys (not peaty) Limestone soils	Slightly Dry to Moist	Medium to Very Rich	Dog's mercury, ferns, soft herbs, calcareous grasses
Upland mixed ashwoods	Chapter 6 (W7 ash-alder woodlands are covered in Chapter 7)	W9 (W7 on wetter sites)	Group 1 (locally Group 3A/D)	Ash, wych elm, rowan, hazel, cherry, sessile oak, aspen, holly	Brown earths Limestone soils Gleys (not peaty)	Slightly Dry to Moist	Medium to Rich	Bramble, ferns, mixed/calcareous grasses, dog's mercury, soft herbs
Wet woodlands	Chapter 7	W1 to W7	Group 7 (locally Group 12A)	Alder, willows, ash, downy birch, aspen	Surface-water gleys Ground-water gleys Peaty gleys	Moist to Very Wet	Poor to Very Rich	Stinging nettle, meadowsweet, sedges, soft grasses, rushes

Note. NVC woodland communities W12–15 are not included above as these relate to beech and yew woodlands, which are not considered to be native within Scotland. Similarly with Peterken stand types 2 (with field maple), 4 and 5 (with lime), 8 (with beech), 9 (with hornbeam) and 10 (with suckering elm).

This combines study of the tree and shrub layers with more detailed botanical survey and classification of the ground vegetation. However, this classification was developed by computerised statistical analyses of British woodland vegetation survey data, rather than observation of permanent vegetation associations in natural forests, as had been the case with classical European schemes. A framework for description and comparison of the main native woodland types of Scotland in terms of the Forestry Commission woodland habitat types (Forestry Commission Scotland 2014), Peterken stand types and NVC (woodland section) is presented in Table 2.3. Information to allow an individual woodland to be allocated to the appropriate NVC community must be collected by vegetation survey in the field. Ideally this should be carried out by a systematic and quantitative method, such as the collection of plant abundance/frequency data in quadrat samples (Pyatt et al. 2001; Rodwell 1991a). Where that is not possible, a careful field vegetation description for a whole site unit can be used, but may not provide a reliable allocation.

CHAPTER THREE

Historical development

3.1 Overview

This chapter will describe the historical development of native woodlands in Scotland from before the last Ice Age until around 1960. Over at least the past 5,000 years, Scotland's native woodland cover has progressively retreated in the face of increasing human impacts, coupled with phases of climatic deterioration (Simmons 2000; Smout 1993, 1997, 2003; Smout et al. 2005). The aim here is to provide a summary of our current historical understandings, sufficient to support the chapters which follow on the individual native woodland types. However, readers with an interest in greater historical detail are directed to the previous literature on this aspect, notably by Anderson (1967), Smout (1993, 1997, 2003) and Smout et al. (2005). Smout's publications provide copious historical sub-references.

3.2 Research methods for woodlands in prehistory

With the oft-quoted exception of Roman authors' cryptic and dubious accounts of the forbidding '*Caledonia Silva*', we lack contemporary reports of woodlands in Scotland before the Anglo-Norman period, beginning from around AD 1130. For the following 500 years, through the medieval, Renaissance and early modern periods, written records for woodlands in Scotland remain scarcer than those for England, especially lowland England. Only for the period after ~1680, when agricultural and landscape 'improvements' on the lowland estates begin, do we start to have more systematic descriptions of woodland extent and type. Map evidence only begins from the later 1500s onwards, with the Pont maps (reproduced by Blaeu in Amsterdam), and attains greater detail with the military surveys by Roy, following the Jacobite risings of the mid-1700s. These map sources display a considerable degree of inaccuracy and omission, especially in less accessible areas. Private estate maps can be much better. Hence for the vast majority of the time period of interest to us, we must rely on archaeological methods, examining macrofossils (wood, leaves) and microfossils (pollen).

Although there are a variety of techniques of potential application to the study of woodlands (and other ecosystems) in prehistory (O'Connor and Evans 2005), the major materials examined are the macrofossil remains of trees (wood and occasional leaf imprints) and microfossil remains (mainly pollen, but also stomata). Taken together, these can yield significant information about tree species' presence and relative abundance in prehistory. When used in conjunction with radiocarbon dating of macrofossil remains, peat and lake-sediment stratigraphy and dendrochronological (tree-ring) dating of wood, we can begin to reconstruct the development of woodland ecosystems over longer periods of time. Early approaches to the analysis of pollen remains, working at landscape scales, took inadequate account of the differential pollen production and dispersal rates achieved by each tree species and the scope for confusion between the pollens of certain native tree species. However, more recent 'small-basin' studies provide much more reliable indications of local woodland composition surrounding pollen-collecting hollows (Shaw and Tipping 2006; Tipping and Davies 2006). The advent of radiocarbon dating, as a spin-off from atomic physics studies (1940–60), has been one of the most significant advances, providing accurate dates for macrofossil remains such as bog-oak but also derived dates and firmer chronologies for sediment and peat layers, within which microfossil plant remains are usually found. Dendrochronological dating, developed first with reference to oak preserved in Irish peat bogs, relies upon annual relationships between weather and tree-ring width (Crone and Mills 2002; Sansum 2005). Trees often grow more slowly in years whose summers are cooler or drier. As these annual variations in the growing environment are usually synchronised at regional scales (e.g. Ireland, Scotland, south of England), we can build up relative ring-width dating sequences based on samples overlapping in time.

3.3 Forests in Scotland prior to the Ice Ages

During the past two million years (known as the Pleistocene or Quaternary era), Scotland, along with Scandinavia and other parts of northern Europe, has been subject to at least four major episodes of glaciation, covering much of the country in thick ice-sheets and exterminating vegetation cover (Ehlers et al. 2011; Gillen 2013). These 'glacial' periods typically lasted three or four times longer (~80,000 years) than the warmer 'interglacial' periods between them (~20,000 years), and hence determined very long-term forest development. They have caused extinctions of a significant proportion of tree species. Unfortunately, repeated advance and retreat of ice cover has also eliminated most fossil remains of forest vegetation from Scotland, and for evidence we have to look to the nearest available unglaciated areas, in the English Midlands and the East Anglian plain (West 1970, 1980). This makes for uncertainty as to how to interpret developments in Scotland.

Prior to the onset of this period of climatic instability, Europe enjoyed a more benign climate that allowed the development of relatively stable and diverse forest ecosystems, more similar to today's tropical forests. Over much of the past 50–100 million years, since the evolution of flowering plants, major parts of Europe have been submerged. Those areas above sea level saw the development of diverse forest cover of a type known as 'Arcto-Tertiary' which included both conifer and hardwood genera and extended northwards towards the pole (Mai 1989). Climate was generally warmer, moister and with rather weaker seasonality than today – rather comparable to modern climates in parts of south-east Asia or the southern United States. Land bridges were maintained with the North American continent, originally across both the north Atlantic and the north Pacific, latterly the Pacific only. This implied that the same key families (genera) of conifers and deciduous trees are found on each major landmass in the northern hemisphere, but with diversity at the species level. With progressive changes in the arrangement of tectonic plates, a ring of continental landmasses formed around the northern pole, isolating it from warm ocean currents. This, together with fluctuations in solar output and the Earth's orbital path, caused changes in climatic regime, with formation of polar ice and redistribution of rainfall patterns at lower latitudes. In tropical areas, a drier climate led to forest retreat and the formation of open semi-wooded savannahs in some regions. Comparable processes are believed to have taken place in Europe, with some areas having similar ecosystems to modern Kenya, for example, with populations of large grassland herbivores. As in similar parts of the world today (e.g. the Kenya Aberdares), the upland regions such as Scotland may have retained more extensive canopy forests.

As average climate became progressively cooler, fluctuations in the Earth's orbit (known as Milankovich cycles) were sufficient to cause periodic expansion of ice cover from the polar regions over surrounding continental landmasses. This was associated with reductions in global sea level in excess of 100m. The climate of much of northern Europe, including Scotland, became repeatedly unsuitable for forest growth (Bradley 2014). Animal populations were also periodically displaced during periods of glacial advance. Conditions in southern England were less extreme during glacial episodes, with a lack of thick ice cover, but any vegetation on areas free of ice would have been of an Arctic tundra type. The range of many tree species became restricted to 'glacial refugia' in southern Europe, in areas such as Spain, Italy and the Balkans. However, east-west orientation of the major mountain chains of southern Europe (e.g. Alps and Pyrenees) made such 'retreat' more difficult, and there was progressive extinction of more sensitive tree species, including a number of the more shade-tolerant conifers such as hemlock (*Tsuga*) (West 1970). As a result of this process, known as 'barrier extinction', the tree species diversity of Europe is much lower today than in climatically similar areas of North America and eastern Asia, where mountains run primarily north-south. Warmer 'interglacial' periods between the glaciations saw re-advance of forest vegetation and its associated animal species, and also allowed some of the earliest colonisations by, and ecological influence of, humans in Great Britain (e.g. Boxgrove man in Sussex). Human impacts may have included some clearance of forest vegetation by burning and regulation of the numbers of larger herbivores (e.g. elephant, rhino) by hunting pressure. It is unclear how this might have affected the course of forest development, but a mosaic of forest and savannah is considered rather likely.

We have no firm evidence for human presence within Scotland during previous interglacial periods and little direct evidence for the nature of any forest vegetation. However, we are able to draw some inferences from fossil remains found in areas around the southern North Sea, including East Anglia, which were not fully glaciated. For this region, R. G. West of the University of Cambridge developed a scheme of four sub-stages of natural forest development within each of the interglacial periods (West 1970, 1980) (see Table 3.1). A comparable pattern of development is likely to have been followed in forested parts of Scotland. The driving forces behind this cyclical

TABLE 3.1 Development of forest vegetation during past interglacial periods, based on fossil evidence from unglaciated regions. Partly after the scheme of West (1970, 1980).

Interglacial Sub-stage	**Interval Occupied (after deglaciation)**	**Climatic Regime**	**Soil Development**	**Vegetation Assemblage**	**Main Tree Species**	**Holocene Equivalent**	**Impacts of Human Activity in the Holocene**
Pre-temperate	0–5,000 years	Continental cool dry	Immature structure, but high base-cation fertility	Light-demanding pioneers into dry tundra heathland	Scots pine, hazel, birch, aspen, juniper, rowan	Boreal phase	Vegetation only weakly modified Possibility of anthropogenic fire impacts Faunal extinctions
Early temperate	5–10,000 years	Oceanic warm moist	Maturing structure with good overall fertility	Medium-tolerant hardwoods with some localised pioneers	Oak, ash, elm, hazel, birch, rowan, Scots pine	Atlantic phase Early Neolithic	Beginnings of localised forest clearance Assisted colonisation by useful trees?
Late temperate	10–15,000 years	Oceanic cool moist	Declining fertility, locally impeded drainage	Shade-tolerant hardwoods and diverse evergreen conifers	Beech, sycamore, lime, hornbeam, spruce, fir, hemlock	Sub-Boreal phase Late Neolithic/ Bronze Age	Accelerated soil fertility/drainage decline Agricultural clearance Arrested succession
Post temperate	15–20,000 years	Oceanic cold wet	Generally impoverished with peatland expansion	Wet oceanic moorland with residual depleted woodland	Spruce, pine, birch, alder, *Rhododendron*	Sub-Atlantic phase Iron Age to the present day	Introduction of shade-tolerant trees Plantation forestry Muirburn Climate change?

pattern of forest succession are (1) improvement of the climate following glacial retreat, with soil development processes under earlier forest vegetation; (2) progressive colonisation by more shade-tolerant tree species; and (3) later deterioration of the climate as onset of the next glacial period approaches, with accompanying declines in soil fertility due to leaching by heavy rainfall and accumulation of acidic plant litters.

As will be discussed later in this chapter, the development of native woodland in Scotland during the present interglacial (known as the Holocene) shows both similarities to and differences from the previous patterns described above. While the pre-temperate and early-temperate sub-stages preceded major human influence, the record of human modification of woodlands during the mid-Holocene has accelerated soil fertility decline and tree species succession towards the post-temperate condition. This pattern of sub-stages has also been considerably modified by progressive extinction of shade-tolerant tree species from Britain with successive glaciations. These included fir (*Abies*), spruce (*Picea*) and hemlock (*Tsuga*). This has particularly affected the late-temperate and post-temperate sub-stages when those species would be expected to become dominant.

3.4 Woodlands in the Boreal phase

As with the end of any individual cold winter, the end of the most recent Ice Age was rather a hesitant and messy affair, with at least one major reversion to colder conditions (known from evidence in Scotland as the 'Loch Lomond readvance'). Perhaps because of these rapid climate fluctuations (over ~3,000 years), coupled with pressure from small bands of nomadic Palaeolithic human hunters, many of the larger mammals of the late Ice Age period were driven to extinction (mammoth, woolly rhino, musk ox). As conditions finally stabilised, around 10,000 years BP, the landscape that was left behind was a mixture of bare glacial debris (coarse broken rock, gravel and sand) together with arctic tundra vegetation of low-growing plants. Climatic and landscape conditions might have been similar to northern Scandinavia or Russia today. Rivers would have been broad, shallow and fast flowing over stony beds. Soils were young and poorly developed, but with some intrinsic fertility from recently exposed broken rock fragments.

This landscape provided an ideal environment for the spread of 'pioneer' tree species, including juniper, birch, aspen and, later, Scots pine (H. J. B. Birks 1989) (see Figure 3.1). These species all have the ability to colonise bare ground over large distances, with light seeds and pollen transported mostly on the wind, often over the surface of winter snow-pack. These tree species also share the characteristic of being 'light-demanders' which cannot regenerate naturally under their own shade. This promotes the onward colonisation of the forest edge out onto open land. Hazel also formed part of natural woodland that developed at this time and may have been significant as a human food source. The tree species making up these forests had to migrate into Scotland from the areas where they had found glacial refuge. It is believed that most would have spread across from mainland Europe and Scandinavia, assisted by the fact that the English Channel and southern North Sea had not yet been flooded

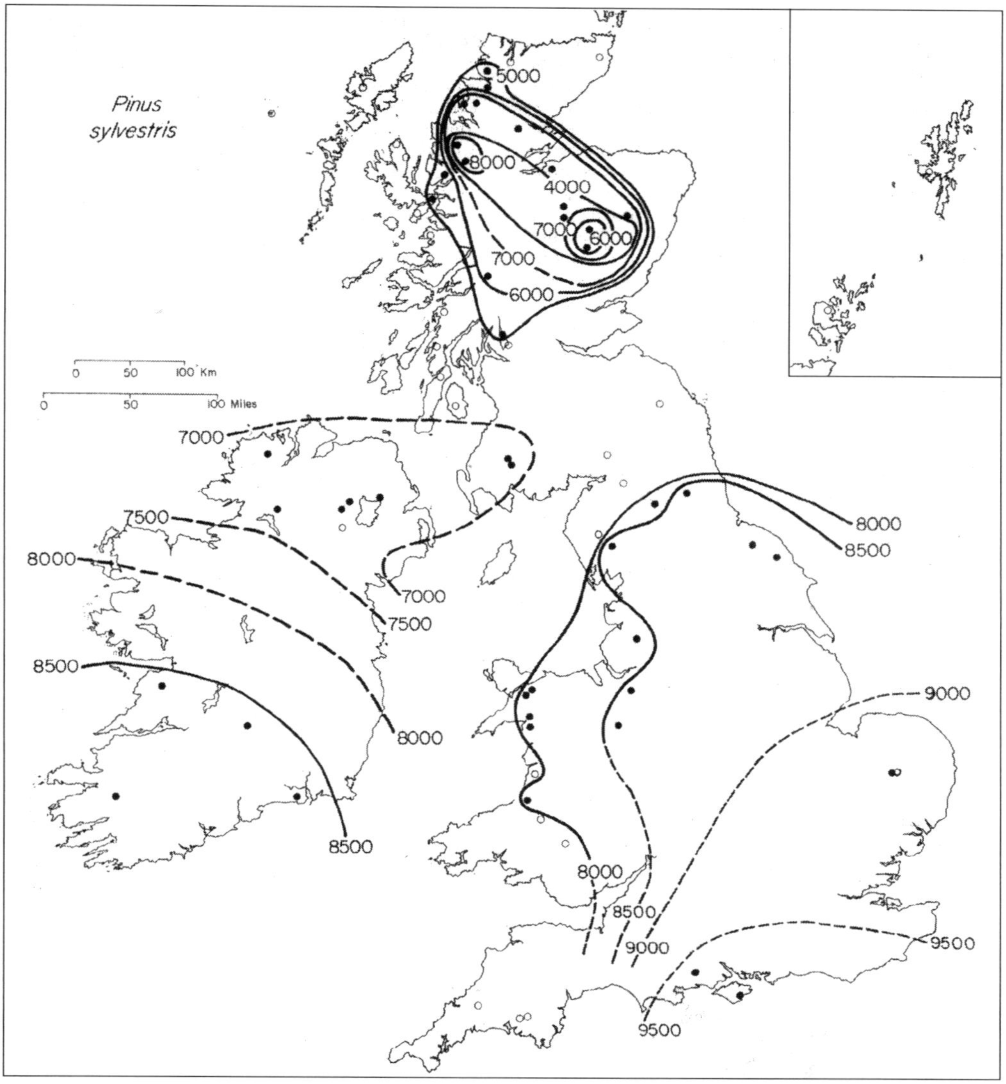

FIGURE 3.1 *Pollen isochrone map for Scots pine in the British Isles The isochrones are based on data from the sites indicated by dots and are shown as radiocarbon years* BP. *Sites where there is no pollen-analytical evidence for local presence are shown as open circles. Reproduced from H. J. B. Birks (1989), 'Holocene isochrone maps and patterns of tree-spreading in the British Isles',* Journal of Biogeography *16: 503–40, with kind permission from Blackwell Publishing Ltd. Copyright: Blackwell Publishing Ltd/*Journal of Biogeography, *1989.*

by global sea-level rise – that was not completed until around 7,000–8,000 years BP. Pollen evidence shows successive waves of tree species spreading northwards and westwards from points of arrival on the south and east coasts of England (H. J. B. Birks 1989). It is also possible that there were small glacial refugia along the Atlantic coasts of Scotland and Ireland, on land now long since submerged. During the Ice Age, the Atlantic Ocean will have acted as a heat store, keeping the coastal fringe areas freer of ice. Early pollen records for Scots pine in north-west Scotland suggest that it may have recolonised from 'oceanic' refugia to the west, 9,000–10,000 years BP, and we will see in Chapter 4 that there is some genetic evidence to support this. As woodlands which these tree species formed were similar to those of the present-day Scandinavian boreal forests described in Chapter 1, this earliest developmental phase is known as the 'Boreal phase'. It is noticeably similar to the 'pre-temperate sub-stage' noted for previous interglacials in West's scheme. The major animal species of the boreal forests, such as wolf, lynx, brown bear, beaver and elk, would have been present in Scotland (Yalden 2002). There is not thought to have been significant ecological modification of woodland by humans at this early period, so successional development of the vegetation followed a naturally determined course.

The woodland types that had developed first during the Boreal phase persisted longest in more climatically exposed and infertile areas of upland Scotland, to become the native pinewoods, upland birchwoods and montane scrub of today, which we will examine in detail in Chapter 4. In more sheltered lowland areas, improving climate and soils, together with progressive colonisation by additional tree species, led to major changes in woodland ecosystems in the late Boreal phase. Native woodlands were now moving into their next major phase of development.

3.5 Woodlands in the Atlantic phase

The 'Atlantic phase' of native woodland development in Scotland was similar to the 'early-temperate sub-stage' described for the previous interglacials by West. It is often seen as the natural 'high-point' or 'climatic maximum' of native woodland in Scotland, before human impacts became significant. It lasted roughly between 7,500 years BP and 5,000 years BP (Peterken 1993) – by the end of this period humans had begun to clear woodlands for livestock grazing and agriculture on an increasing scale (Simmons 2000; Smout 1993). Climate during this phase was generally warm and moist, having more in common with west European lowland areas of England and France than with the boreal forests of Scandinavia. The name 'Atlantic phase' reflects the moderating influence of the ocean in reducing risks to vegetation both from very severe winter cold and from climatic drought in summer. This allowed native woodland to develop across perhaps 50–60% of the Scottish landmass, with a natural treeline in the range 600–800m as in the central Highlands. The higher mountain tops and particularly wet boggy areas in the lowlands would not have supported woodland cover. While open pine-birch-aspen-juniper woodlands persisted at the higher elevations, the lowlands and mid-slopes were rapidly colonised by a range of deciduous (or 'hardwood') species (see Figure 3.2).

Native woodland that developed in the early part of the Atlantic phase was dominated by 'medium-tolerant' hardwoods. These are species that can regenerate within patchy woodland but are still not able to regenerate easily under heavier canopy shade. Hazel was inherited from the Boreal phase, but was now added to by oak, elm, alder, rowan and ash (H. J. B. Birks 1989). These species are believed to have colonised northwards from mainland Europe through England during the later Boreal phase, progressively replacing earlier pine-birch-hazel forests found there. While ash, alder

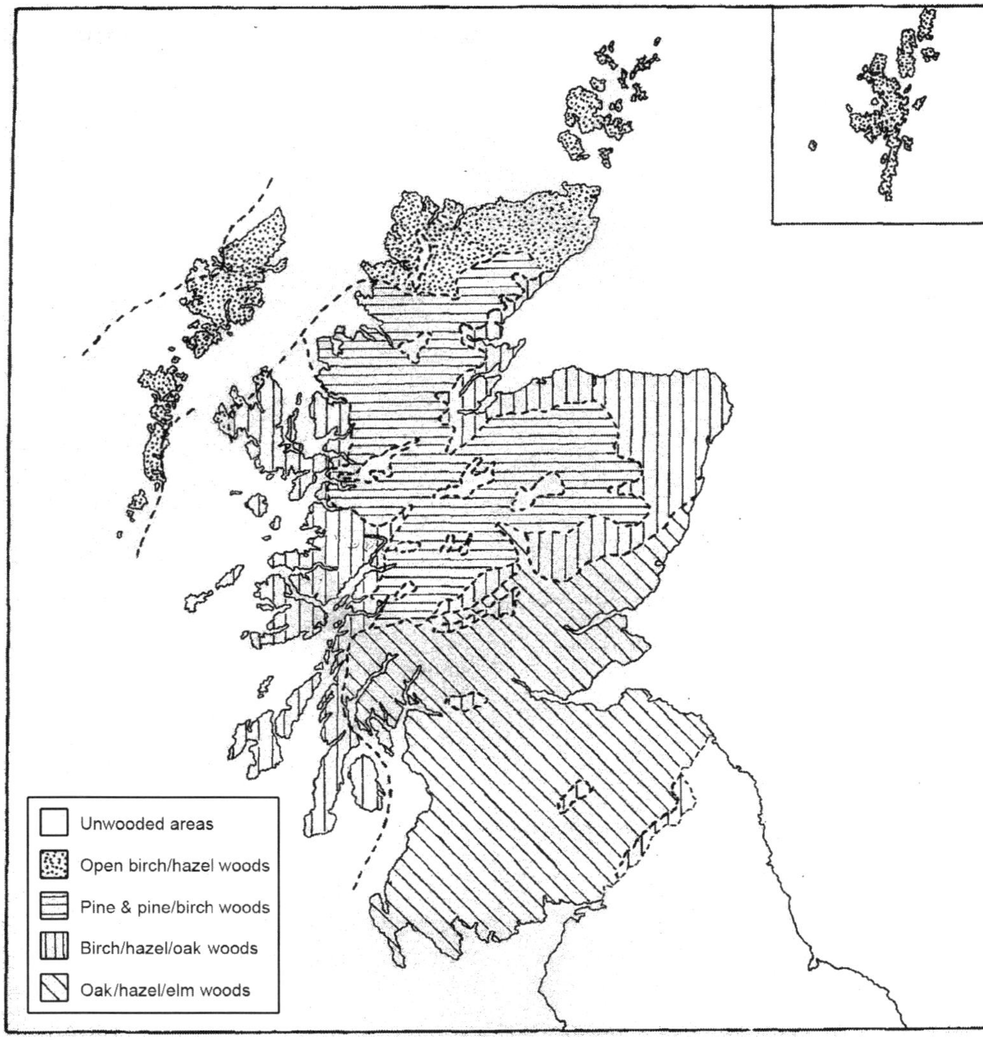

FIGURE 3.2 *Distribution map of woodland types in Scotland at 3000 BC. Reproduced from R. Tipping (1994), 'The form and fate of Scotland's woodlands',* Proceedings of the Society of Antiquaries of Scotland *124: 1–54, with kind permission of the Society of Antiquaries of Scotland/R. Tipping.*

and elm can spread by windblown seed, oak requires assistance from mammals or birds to carry its heavier acorns forward – these include the jay, red squirrel and wild boar. Therefore its rate of advance was rather slower. Birch, rowan and aspen continued to be present within lowland woodlands, but only as a temporary 'successional' element. For example, if a windstorm created a clearing in oak woodland, birch, rowan and aspen might colonise there first, but would then be replaced over time by oak, ash and elm. Birch survived for longer on poor, sandy soils where oak woodland would remain far more open and where ash and elm could not thrive. Pine became restricted to higher ground, other than locally in the north-west.

Lowland areas of Scotland are thought to have carried extensive areas of fairly dense woodland cover, dominated by oak and elm in the canopy, with an understorey of hazel (Tipping 1994). Ash would have occurred more locally, especially where moist fertile soils favoured it or where the canopy remained more open. We will see later that there is some discussion amongst woodland ecologists as to how natural oak forests actually functioned, as it might have been difficult for oak to find enough light to regenerate. Little lowland oak woodland survives, and almost all remaining examples are plantations, deer parks or landscape elements whose structure has been heavily modified. In upland areas it is thought that natural oak woodlands might have had a more open structure, with greater components of ash, elm, birch and hazel. These woodlands developed into today's Atlantic or upland oakwoods (see Chapter 5), but it is likely that they were rather more species-diverse at that time, prior to human impacts, and before declines in their soil fertility due to prolonged high rainfall. At the upper limit of these woodlands, there was, in many areas, a more gradual natural transition into native pinewood than today, with extensive mixed pine-oak stands. Those exist in both North America and Continental Europe, but few convincing examples survive in Scotland today. On fertile sites, such as over limestone and base-rich basalt rocks, ash, elm and hazel would have been the dominant species (ash was an Atlantic phase coloniser). These woodlands later developed into the upland mixed ashwoods found today (see Chapter 6), with rather less change in their basic ecology.

During previous interglacials, the 'late-temperate sub-stage' of woodland development had seen a progressive transition toward more shade-tolerant hardwoods, including beech and alder. In the Holocene, there is evidence for this natural pattern being reflected to some extent. Alder was one shade-tolerant hardwood which expanded naturally into Scotland during the Atlantic phase. However, as a specialist of wet woodland sites, it remained relatively localised, finding a place within floodplain and springline woodlands of ash, birch and willow (see Chapter 7). Beech reached southern England between 4,000 and 6,000 years BP (Wilson 2010), but initially spread only slowly. It is likely that increasing human disturbance of existing woodland for agriculture later gave beech the opportunity to expand more rapidly. Lime, hornbeam and field maple colonised England naturally and came to dominate many lowland broadleaved woodlands there by 5,000 years BP (Peterken 1993; Rackham 2003). The sycamore (also a form of maple) occurs naturally as far north as the Paris basin, and was deliberately introduced to Britain at some time prior to 1500. Despite the arrival of these additional, more shade-tolerant hardwoods, they did not form 'late-temperate' woodlands as far north as Scotland. In some cases, this may have been due to insufficient climatic warmth – for example, lime does not readily set seed north of the Lake District in today's cooler climate (Piggott and Huntley 1978). Only with deliberate plantings of lime, beech and sycamore as part of estate improvements since 1600 have these species become a common feature.

During the early Atlantic phase of native woodland development in Scotland, small populations of humans were increasingly present. These were the Mesolithic hunter-gatherer peoples, rather small in number and operating mainly on the coastal and island margins and along the major river valleys, such as the Dee. As the landscape became more wooded, these people were unable to travel large distances overland to find game as had their nomadic Palaeolithic ancestors on the open steppes of the late-glacial and Boreal phases. Mesolithic people would have hunted game and collected fruits and nuts in woodlands around seasonal hunting settlements and caught fish in nearby rivers. There is evidence for this lifestyle from a number of archaeological sites, notably Star Carr in North Yorkshire (Simmons 2000). Other than in the immediate vicinity of hunting settlements, it is unlikely that this level of human activity had lasting impact on native woodlands. It is quite possible that Mesolithic people used fire to some extent to clear woodland vegetation and create 'game lawns' which would attract game for easier hunting. We know that Stone Age people did this elsewhere, for example in Australia. Today, pine-birch woodlands in Scotland can be burned in the winter/early spring, but the dense, moist, broadleaved woodlands of the lowlands are very difficult to burn. It is just possible that the warmer, drier climate in the past made this easier. Such burning could have modified the structure of woodlands and increased browsing pressure on a localised basis. People may also have assisted the spread of fruit- and nut-producing tree species, such as hazel and cherry.

3.6 The 'Vera Hypothesis' and Scottish native woodland

As indicated earlier, there is strong debate among ecologists as to how the lowland woodlands of the Atlantic phase functioned in terms of their natural regeneration. We have seen that oak, as a 'medium-tolerant' hardwood, is often now unable to regenerate successfully under a dense canopy shade, including that cast by mature oaks. It would therefore be expected to be excluded over time from closed-canopy woodlands of this type, being replaced by more shade-tolerant species such as alder, lime, elm, maple, sycamore and beech. However, we know that oak certainly remained a dominant tree species within lowland woodlands in Scotland throughout the Atlantic phase (Peterken 1993; Tipping 1994), and has done so until the present day in surviving remnants. In part, this may have been because other more shade-tolerant tree species had not yet reached Scotland by natural colonisation, but that still leaves the issue unresolved as to how oak itself could regenerate under its own shade. The same issue puzzles woodland ecologists in England, and other parts of lowland western Europe, where oak remained dominant, despite the established presence of shade-tolerant competitors (e.g. beech), over a much longer period of time.

Recently, a Dutch forest ecologist, Dr Frans Vera, has put forward a controversial new theory as to how European lowland oak woodlands persisted (Vera 2000). He argues that, even before the influence of human animal herding began, wild populations of large herbivores could have kept the structure of primeval woodlands more open and patchy, allowing opportunities for oak to regenerate into larger canopy gaps. The animal species involved would have included wild ox (aurochs), European bison and wild horses (tarpan). We know from observations in many savannah ecosystems overseas, for example in East Africa, that larger browsing and grazing animals such as elephant, rhino, buffalo and bison help to retain woodland with an open structure within a grassland mosaic. There is also quite good evidence that woolly mammoth and woolly rhino had a similar effect on dry, cool Pleistocene steppes of Europe – an ecosystem actually known as 'mammoth steppe'. However, these are climatically marginal ecosystems where development of closed-canopy woodland is restricted by drought. In denser forests in moister areas elsewhere, large herbivores do not appear to have this effect – for example in the Congo rainforests, openings known as 'bais' are much more localised and probably only occur due to very specific swampy soil conditions.

Vera proposes that European lowland oak woodland, prior to the onset of major human impacts, would have operated in a centuries-long cycle of oak growth and regeneration, driven by the large herbivores present. At any one time, a significant proportion of the area would be open grassland, maintained as such by browsing pressure. Within these areas, clumps of spiny, unpalatable shrubs, such as blackthorn, would periodically become established, usually from seeds dropped by birds. These clumps would then expand until they reached a diameter too large for the browsing animals to reach into their centre. As the oldest shrubs in the middle of the clumps matured and died back, a gap would be created in the centre, into which acorns could be introduced, for example by jays. The remaining spiny shrubs in a 'doughnut ring' around the young oak sapling would protect it from browsing until it became sufficiently large to be out of much danger. Vera calls this surrounding shrub ring 'mantle and fringe vegetation'. Kirby (2004) has attempted to test this model for the conditions of Britain.

There is no doubt that we can see this process in action in present-day lowland wood-pasture habitats. While there are few good examples of this in Scotland, there are a number of well-known locations in England, such as Hatfield Forest and the New Forest, where this mechanism for oak regeneration is active. However, these are situations in which a high density of domesticated herbivores – cattle and ponies – is maintained by human husbandry. It is unclear whether in a natural situation, during the Atlantic phase, such large densities of herbivores could have co-existed with natural predators such as wolves. If the number of herbivores became too low, the forest would gradually 'close up', eventually reverting to the traditional 'closed-canopy' model after Peterken (1996). Pollen evidence from woodland areas of this time period does not give clear determination as to how open lowland woodlands actually were before human clearance began. While some pollen from grasses and other plants of open land is usually found, it is at a relatively low level, suggesting that only a minor portion of the landscape was open. It may be that Vera's model was active in some areas, while other parts of the landscape had extensive tracts of closed-canopy oak-elm-hazel woodland. At the present time, the balance of opinion among woodland ecologists remains in favour of a general predominance of closed-canopy forest during the Atlantic phase (Mitchell 2005), but perhaps with rather more open ground than had once been imagined (Kirby 2004).

If Vera's model does not find complete support, we must look for other mechanisms by which oak could persist in lowland broadleaved woodlands, as it clearly did. There would have been a natural process by which small gaps formed as a result of the death and collapse of individual canopy trees or storm damage to the woodland. In present-day woodlands of this type, small gaps tend to close up rather quickly due to growth of more shade-tolerant tree species like ash, sycamore and beech. This means oak 'misses its chance' to regenerate unless the gaps are made larger for some reason. Some biologists suggest that oak in the past may have been more shade-tolerant than it is now, at least during its seedling and sapling phases. A number of tree species, notably ash, are more shade-tolerant when young, allowing them to regenerate in the understorey of existing woodland, but become light-demanding once in the canopy. One mechanism which could account for a change in the behaviour of oak is the recently increased incidence of insect pests, particularly various moths. These lay eggs on the leaves of mature oaks, which hatch into caterpillars the following spring. These can rain down on to the young regenerating oaks seedlings below, defoliating them. The reduction in leaf area of the seedlings effectively reduces their shade-tolerance. There is also some evidence that mildew impacts on oaks increased early in the twentieth century, again effectively reducing their shade-tolerance (Rackham 2003). Unfortunately we have too few examples of oak woodland in Scotland where natural regeneration processes can be observed – most have been modified by management for timber or as parklands over recent centuries (these are cited in Chapter 5). However, regeneration of oak into open birch-conifer woodland does occur, assisted by jays (Worrell, 2014).

Vera (2000) does not suggest that his model be applied to upland or 'montane' woodlands. As we move from a lowland to an upland or montane environment in Britain, it is very likely that natural woodland structures would have been more open, due to climatic, soil and topographic factors – especially at their upper limits. It is also less likely that there would be large numbers of herbivores present naturally within these woodlands, due to lower amounts of food and harsher climates, at least during the winter months. Many Atlantic and upland oak woodlands that we find today in Scotland appear denser than they should be naturally, as a result of management as industrial coppices between 1650 and 1850, which we will look at in more detail later in this chapter. This management aimed to promote a dense stand of even-aged oaks, restricting other tree species. While oak does not regenerate readily in these 'semi-natural' upland oak woodlands of today, it might have been able to do so in natural upland woodlands of the Atlantic phase, due to a more diverse canopy structure.

3.7 ARCHAEOLOGICAL EVIDENCE IN WOODLANDS

For the period of human settlement, native woodlands actually provide one of the most fruitful contexts for archaeological investigation in Scotland. By comparison with agricultural fields, plantation forests and developed land, they represent areas that have seen much less disturbance of soil profiles during the past 5,000 years. Hence buried artefacts, especially the remains of settlements, are often better preserved. However, by comparison with upland moorland and heathland or lowland farmland, the official monuments record for native woodlands is rather sparse. Excavators have tended to avoid native woodlands due to their remoteness, rough terrain, dense vegetation and lack of imminent threat to any remains. This is beginning to be remedied by increasingly active woodland archaeological survey. Some of the key types of archaeological remains that can be found are (Ritchie and Ritchie 1991; Ritchie and Wordsworth 2010):

- **Prehistoric, Roman and early medieval settlements and ritual monuments.** These include remains of stone and timber buildings (long-houses, round-houses, hut-circles, halls, hill-forts, monasteries, temples, marching camps), burial cairns, barrows and stone circles dating from 8,000 through to ~1,000 years BP. Sites may have been much less wooded at the time any structures were erected and used. It would be unusual for early farmers to build their settlements within dense woodlands or to erect stone circles hidden from sight. Many landscapes were probably a mosaic of woodlands and patches of open land.
- **Medieval and early-modern farm buildings and field systems.** These include the largest category of archaeological remains found in Scotland, arising from the normal agricultural uses of the land from the Middle Ages through to the 'clearances'. The clearances should be seen as a process of agricultural change and land abandonment over the whole of upland Scotland during the period 1750–1950, rather than, conventionally, as a single acute episode in the Highlands in the period 1820–50. Many remains are foundations of smaller stone buildings – shielings, blackhouses and cottages – together with associated systems of dykes, walls, sheep-fanks and so on. Some are isolated, while many are in small 'clachan' settlements. 'Ridge-and-furrow' cultivation traces, within woodland, are an indication that the site has not always been so wooded, having seen active cultivation during medieval times.
- **Industrial, military and infrastructural remains.** Generally dating from the past 400 years, these include abandoned mine-workings (see Figure 3.3), ironworks (e.g. the well-known charcoal-burning furnaces of the west Highlands), charcoal

FIGURE 3.3 *Historical mine-workings in native woodland, Galloway. Copyright: Dr Scott McG. Wilson.*

pits, sawmills, railways (e.g. the small steam railways built to extract timber during World War I and larger railway lines closed during the 'Beeching cuts' of the 1960s), wartime pill-boxes and other defensive installations. Some charcoal pits and bloomeries date back 400+ years, but most are from around 1700 onwards.

There is increasing interest in the various archaeological remains found in native woodlands and in public interpretation of the historic environments that they represent. A number of localities have created historical woodland trails to cater for tourist visitors – for example at Kilmartin Glen in Argyll (dealing with prehistoric remains), the Antonine Wall (Roman remains), Argyll and Lochaber (oak coppice, charcoal, tanbark and iron working) and Strathnaver (pre-clearance agricultural landscapes). Remains are found in both native woodlands and more recent conifer plantations, where forest management is now being adapted to avoid damage to archaeological sites.

3.8 Woodlands in the Neolithic and Bronze Ages

As the Atlantic phase (or early-temperate sub-stage) drew to an end between 4,500 and 5,000 years BP, humans were having an increasingly significant impact on the native woodland cover of Scotland. Although there are clear indications of underlying climatic and soil deterioration toward the conditions of the late-temperate sub-stage experienced in previous interglacials, these are augmented by increasing evidence of human clearance and modification of woodlands in prehistory (Simmons 2000; Smout 1993, 2003). The major categories of human impacts were (see Table 3.2):

- Clearance of upland woodlands by fire, to facilitate livestock grazing
- Clearance of woodland around settlements for pasture and crop growing
- Favouring of certain tree and shrub species (e.g. fruit/nut producers)
- Utilisation of timber for construction and the smelting of metallic ores
- Deflection of the natural successional development of native woodland
- Deliberate/accidental introduction of non-native trees (e.g. beech).

The people we are dealing with now are those of the Neolithic and, later, the Bronze Age cultures. They differed from their Mesolithic predecessors both in their greater numbers and in their development of farming techniques, allowing them to stay at a single location throughout the year. Both increased their ecological 'footprint' as compared with earlier hunter-gatherers. Earliest farming systems consisted mainly of following herds of semi-domesticated sheep, goats and cattle that were attracted into an area by the creation of open grazing land within a still largely wooded landscape. In summer these would be encouraged to use higher pastures, allowing lower land to be used to grow winter forage, and later food crops for human consumption. This system, known as 'transhumance', developed later into the traditional 'shieling' system of livestock agriculture in Highland Scotland. Early cultivation was of the 'shifting' type, with subsequent woodland recovery, but introduction of arable farming methods and bronze metal-working technology from

Table 3.2 Development of Scottish woodlands during the Holocene. Partly summarising and interpreting information previously presented by Dickson (1993), Smout (1993, 1997, 2003), Smout et al. (2005) and Tipping (1994).

Archaeological Period	Climatic Phase	Approximate Dates	Colonising Tree Species	Main Woodland Types	Approximate Woodland Cover
Palaeolithic	Late Glacial Pre-Boreal Boreal	~14,000 years– ~10,000 years BP	Juniper, birch, hazel, aspen	Juniper scrub Birch-hazel woodland	Open landscape with woodland increasing from <10% to perhaps 30–40% by end
Mesolithic	Boreal into Atlantic	~10,000 years–6,000 years BP	Scots pine, wych elm, oak, alder	Birch-hazel woodland Oak-elm-hazel woodland Pinewood expanding	Heavily wooded landscape with cover increasing from 30–40% to 50–60% or more at climax
Neolithic	Atlantic into Sub-Boreal	~6,000 years~4,300 years BP	Ash	Pinewood maximum Birch-hazel woodland Oak-ash-hazel woodland (Elm sees serious declines)	Still a well-wooded landscape with growing clearings – cover declining from 50–60% back to perhaps 30–40% by end
Bronze Age	Sub-Boreal	~4,300 years–~2,700 years BP		Oak-ash-hazel woodland Birch-hazel woodland Ash-alder woodland Pinewood retreating	Partially open landscape with significant but fragmenting native woodland cover (~20–30%)
Iron/Roman/ Dark Ages	Sub-Atlantic	~2,700 years–~900 years BP		Oak-ash-hazel woodland Birch-hazel woodland Ash-alder woodland Pinewood retreating	Open landscape with residual native woodland (~10–20%) on difficult sites (wet/ steep)
Medieval/ Renaissance/ Early Modern	Sub-Atlantic [variation between Medieval warm (1050–1300) and Little Ice Age (1450–1850)]	~900 years–~300 years BP	Beech, sycamore, lime, larch, Norway spruce, silver fir (all with human assistance)	Remnant native woodland of similar types to today, but somewhat more extensive Early plantations in 1600s	Open landscape with residual native woodland (~5–15%) but becoming locally treeless
Modern/ Industrial	Sub-Atlantic (latterly with some evidence for anthropogenic climate warming/ instability)	~300 years BP to present	Pacific Northwest and Far East Asian conifers (all with human assistance)	Relict native woodlands Industrial oak coppices Plantation forestry Urban/amenity woodlands	Open landscape with sparse native woodland (~5%) and increasing plantation forestry (rising to 15% today)

the Mediterranean and Near East enabled more intensive land-use and more rapid increases in the human population.

There is some evidence that land usage by Neolithic and Bronze Age people was initially concentrated on the 'lighter land' that was easier to cultivate with the stone and bronze tools available to them, including areas of sandy soils near to the coast and some upland areas. Areas that are now considered remote and marginal, such as the Northern and Western Isles and the coastal fringes of Aberdeenshire and Caithness, saw more intensive settlement at these early times due to better maritime communications and abundance of land that was relatively easy to bring into production. These areas contain some of the most impressive prehistoric monuments in Scotland, such as those of Orkney. The probable method of forest clearance was a combination of burning and livestock grazing, preventing tree regeneration over a long period of time. Large areas of open woodland, grading into 'pasture woodland', are thought to have developed, rather than treeless upland 'sheep walk' pastures of the type found today, for example in the Scottish Borders. Native woodlands on steeper slopes, and on lower ground with heavier soils, tended to be left less disturbed at this time. Direct felling activity would have been restricted to woodlands within easy reach of the settlement, from which timber and woodfuel could readily be retrieved for domestic use. Areas cleared of woodland in this way might then be used for arable and vegetable crops or for cultivation of hazel and other fruit- and nut-producing shrubs. The landscape is likely to have taken on a 'patchwork' appearance, with areas of cleared land surrounding settlements, bare uplands above extensive open wood pastures on the slopes, and heavier woodlands in the valley bottoms and on lowland plains.

An important long-term impact that human clearance had on the ecology of Scotland was depletion of original soil fertility. As woodland was cleared, soils were directly exposed to heavy rainfall, which caused more rapid leaching of their nutrient capital, especially over the acid geologies with slower weathering rates. Burning of vegetation, particularly if repeated frequently, could also have led to loss of soil nutrients through the process of volatilisation into the atmosphere. The vegetation types that replaced woodland in the Scottish uplands were dominated by acid grasses, together with the ericoid sub-shrubs, including the heather species, blaeberry and cowberry (Fraser Darling 1955; Fraser Darling and Morton Boyd 1969). These are known to produce litter that is very rich in secondary aromatic compounds, which are both slow to decompose and also directly acidify the soil when percolated through the profile by rainwater infiltration. All of these effects would have accelerated the process of podzolisation (see Chapter 2) and made it much less likely that woodland, certainly mixed broadleaved woodland, could recover naturally. Heavy pressure on upland soils by the hooves of grazing livestock can also cause the formation of a compacted layer at the soil surface, promoting ironpan soil development.

Within those large parts of the landscape that retained woodland cover of some sort, human populations were also influencing the species composition of that woodland. Species that were valued for particular purposes, such as timber production, might be either selectively exploited over time, or favoured to ensure continuing supplies. Scots pine and oak are likely to have been considered especially useful for timber. Fruit- and nut-producing species such as cherry, hazel and blackthorn could have been managed as a productive resource, especially within reach of settlements. Hazel, birch and willow were utilised to produce small-diameter material for a wide variety of building and manufacturing purposes. Some tree species were of considerable potential value as sources of winter livestock fodder – in Scotland, these included ash and elm. These may have been managed by the combined processes of pollarding (cutting the stem off above browsing height) and stripping of resulting foliage to provide seasonal fodder supplies (H. H. Birks 1989). Species that were potentially toxic to livestock (for example yew) may have been selectively removed. The possibility that additional tree species were introduced should not be ruled out – either deliberately, to harvest useful products (this may apply to the wild cherry or 'gean' in Scotland), or accidentally, when seed was transported as fodder.

During the earlier Neolithic period woodland clearance was mainly pursued to create the opportunity for agricultural food production, with firewood and shelter-building using the harvested material as 'by-products'. As the Neolithic gave way to the Bronze Age, and especially during the Iron Age, more durable and effective cutting tools, coupled with new demands for charcoal for smelting, led to increased pressure on native woodlands. During this period, many parts of the Scottish landscape changed from a mainly wooded character with patches of open land appearing, to a primarily open character with patches of native woodland remaining. This threshold is reached when local woodland cover falls below 25–30%, and is of major significance for the biodiversity that the landscape will support. When patches of woodland become isolated, animal species that depend on woodland conditions can no longer move between them and will decline in numbers over time. In addition, the patches of remaining woodland were significantly manipulated by human activities – grazing, coppicing and pollarding.

3.9 Woodland retreat – human and climatic factors

Scotland has seen a reduction of total woodland cover, over the past 5,000 years, from at least 50–60% of the land surface to a minimum of 5–9%, prior to the extensive reforestation activity over the last century (Smout et al. 2005). This reflects the trends in much of the British Isles and western lowland Europe, but the declines in Scotland were earlier and more severe than in some other regions. It is thought that at least half the original native woodland cover of Scotland had already been removed by the Roman period (2,000 years BP) and that woodland cover had reduced again to ~15% by the Anglo-Norman period (1,000 years BP). There is continuing debate as to how this retreat of native woodland cover came about. Some ecologists place more emphasis on the ongoing natural processes of climatic and soil deterioration, while others place their major focus on human-induced clearance of woodland by burning, grazing and tree-felling activities.

Until the 1950s or 1960s many ecologists believed that native woodland decline in Scotland was primarily caused by human over-exploitation. These ideas were often presented in the simplified terms of a 'lost Eden', where if only we had been more careful, Scotland would still possess valuable forest resources. Frank Fraser Darling's famous reference to upland Scotland as a 'wet desert' was highly influential in post-war ecological thinking, and similar ideas were carried over into Mark Anderson's *A History of Scottish Forestry* (1967). There was also a tendency to believe that most of the woodland had survived until relatively recent times and had then been removed rapidly during specific phases of over-exploitation – for example by invading Romans, marauding Vikings, Cromwell's armies of the 1650s or rapacious English and Irish timber merchants of the late 1700s. To an extent these ideas were based on misconstrued written references to woodland exploitation in Scotland after 1600, but they also reflect experience from other parts of the world with better written records of historical land management. For example, there has been a long-held belief (rightly or wrongly) that the once extensive temperate evergreen forests of the Mediterranean basin (Italy, Greece, Crete, etc.) were removed in antiquity by over-exploitation for agriculture, shipbuilding and fuel. In southern England, it was assumed that much of the temperate deciduous woodland remaining by Anglo-Saxon times had then been removed by over-exploitation over following centuries. Similar stories are available for lowland parts of France, Germany and Scandinavia. More recently, British colonial foresters had seen the devastating effects of over-exploitation in the extensive natural forests in parts of North America, Asia and Africa. By contrast, areas with a similar climate to Scotland, where human impacts had apparently been less significant (e.g. Norway and parts of North America), had retained their woodlands. There was therefore a seemingly logical basis to the inference that human impacts had indeed been the major cause of long-term woodland removal in Scotland over past centuries.

During the past fifty years attention has tended to focus on natural changes in climatic and soil conditions as the primary causes of deforestation in Scotland (Dickson 1993; Simmons 2000; Smout 1993; Tipping 1994). One major factor in this shift has been the increasing use of the palynological (pollen analysis) techniques that were described earlier. These have generally pushed back the timescale for major native woodland decline in Scotland to the Neolithic and Bronze Ages, between 3,000 and 6,000 years BP, indicating that the landscape has been primarily open during the past 2,000 to 3,000 years. Some ecologists and archaeologists have questioned whether the relatively smaller numbers of people present in Scotland during the Neolithic and Bronze Ages, with the simple tools available to them, could have cleared so much native woodland. Impacts would be expected to be smaller in Scotland than in areas which had much earlier concentrated civilisations (e.g. the Mediterranean, the Near East, India).

Evidence from a variety of sources, including pollen records, lake sediments, peat cores and polar ice-cores, has suggested that there were natural changes in the climate and soils of the British Isles from around 4,400 years BP onwards (Chambers 1993; Edwards and Ralston 2003; Simmons 2000; Smout 1993), which may have contributed to native woodland decline. Initially there was a short climatic period, during the Neolithic when the climate became markedly drier, allowing woodlands (particularly of Scots pine) to expand onto areas of the landscape that had become peat-covered during the wetter Atlantic phase. Scots pine certainly saw its maximum natural extent during the Holocene before 4,500 BP. This was followed, after about 1,000 years, by further changes, when upland climates especially became colder and, again, much wetter. This was associated with serious declines in soil conditions, with more rapid peat formation, podzolisation and nutrient depletion, causing woodland thinning and retreat (Tipping 2008). For previous interglacials, these trends would be viewed as clear signs of natural transition toward West's post-temperate sub-stage (West 1970). To a large extent we are still living within this generally cool, wet 'sub-Atlantic' climatic phase, although there have been other shorter-term climatic fluctuations within the past 2,000 years.

A major difficulty in deciding between human and climatic causes of woodland decline in Scotland, and similar areas of north-west Europe, is that the two appear to be synchronised. The onset of the wetter climates of the 'sub-Atlantic' phase appears to occur at the same time as late Bronze and Iron Age farmers began to clear woodland in lowland Scotland more rapidly. There is no doubt that, combining pollen and archaeological evidence, we can see that woodland retreat occurred at the same time that human settlement increased in particular areas. This should not be seen as a surprise, however. Where climatic and soil deterioration led to some upland areas of Scotland becoming unattractive or non-viable for agricultural production, people would move into new areas of more sheltered landscape, accelerating the clearance of woodlands there. In upland areas which were abandoned, a combination of poor climate and soils, together with resistant ericaceous vegetation types, prevented the recovery of woodland. The challenges of dealing with deterioration in climate and soil fertility would encourage transfer and adoption of new technologies such as the use of iron tools, while resource conflicts promoted wider use of timber for fortified settlements (such as the vitrified forts of Scotland) and for the construction of shipping. All of these factors make for the complexity in historical study.

It is safe to assume that some native woodland retreat would have occurred in Scotland without human impacts, especially in the more marginal upland areas, over the past 4,000–5,000 years. In many areas of lowland and mid-elevations in Scotland, however, there is no reason why native woodland cover should not have persisted until the present, had it not been cleared for farming and timber exploitation. It is also likely that alternative tree species (e.g. beech), more suited to a changing climate, might have been able to colonise upland Scotland naturally, and more rapidly, through more extensive, less fragmented woodland cover retained in the lowlands. That process had certainly allowed adaptation of woodland cover during the late-temperate and post-temperate phases of previous interglacials. The blame for woodland removal must then be shared between a deteriorating environment for tree growth and human impacts. These factors must be taken into account to ensure success when attempting ecological restoration of native woodland cover, as will be discussed in Chapter 9.

3.10 Woodlands in the Iron, Roman and Dark Ages

The Iron Age in Britain is conventionally dated from around 600 BC, and had, at least until recently, been associated with the settlement of the British Isles by Celtic-speaking peoples originally from central Asia. While some archaeologists would now question whether any large-scale migration of peoples (rather than adoption of ideas, technologies and fashions) took place at this time, the beginning of iron use does mark a turning point. The new, tougher metal made for better axes to fell trees and better ploughs to cultivate the heavier soils of the lowlands. This, together with deteriorating climate and soil conditions in the uplands, appears to have led to a refocusing of settlement and agricultural activities to the valley bottoms and lower slopes. This certainly implies that the remaining woodland cover of Scotland – estimated at 20–30% – came under renewed pressure. It also led, perhaps for the first time, to land resource competition and resulting conflicts. Settlements became more aggregated, very often a sign of insecurity, and indeed fortified. While the brochs of the Hebrides and Northern Isles were mainly of stone (though perhaps with wooden floors), the *crannog* settlements of Highland lochs and the vitrified and palisade hill-forts of the eastern Highlands and Southern Uplands used much wood. The vitrified forts in particular used massive amounts of interlaced timber to cause melting and fusing of stones, to form a smooth *glacis* slope. This, taken together with the demand for wood and charcoal for iron-smelting, created a context where semi-industrial pressures were imposed on native woodlands. Iron Age agriculture is believed to have placed great emphasis on cattle rearing, and there is little doubt that much of the remaining upland native woodland in southern Scotland was cleared during these centuries. Only in the remotest and least accessible areas of the country would larger tracts of unmodified native woodland have remained by 2,000 years BP.

This brings us to the point in time where the Romans made an appearance on the Scottish scene, having invaded southern Britain in AD 43. The Romans were themselves an Iron Age culture, but with greatly increased appetites for the industrial-scale smelting of a wider variety of metal ores, firing of pottery, heating of villas and bath-houses, and construction of timber-built military fortifications, track-ways, bridges, amphitheatres and other structures. This was certain to have placed very considerable demands on the woodland resources of more heavily occupied regions in Britain. In the south of England, there may well have been significant development of industrial coppice working (e.g. using the introduced sweet chestnut in the south-east and beech in the Cotswolds), and indeed substitution of coal-firing for metal working and villa heating (e.g. in the Forest of Dean, the south Wales valleys and the Cotswolds). However, in Scotland it does not appear that Roman settlement ever became sufficiently well established to promote this kind of 'woodland industry', but cutting timber and woodfuel from the local native woodland resource was doubtless common. Military logistics are thought to have accounted for a proportion of the Roman woodland exploitation in the Southern Uplands and Perthshire, in terms of both woodfuel and building timber, with some woodland also perhaps cleared to deter ambush attacks by local tribes along roadways. While Roman impact on native woodland in Scotland may have been locally acute, it is not realistic to regard it as a decisive contribution to the long-term declines in woodland cover across larger parts of the country.

The Romans entered a Scotland which had already lost possibly half or more of its original woodland cover. The Roman period is of significance in that it yields the first written descriptions of woodland cover in Scotland, and Britain more generally. These are derived from narrative accounts written by commentators describing Roman military campaigns (e.g. Tacitus). This should give us pause for thought as to how much reliance we place on these sources – there may have been an incentive to exaggerate the wildness and impenetrability of the landscape campaigned through to add honour to victories and explain away defeats. Reports and maps from the various Scottish military campaigns (spanning AD 71–221) do make mention of a large highland area of forbidding woodland known as the '*Caledonia Silva*' from which the local tribes could emerge at will to offer battle. Similar descriptions emerged from Roman campaigns in Germany, which certainly remained more heavily wooded at this time, and from Wales. The first Roman invasion of Scotland ended with the major battle at '*Mons Graupius*' which has been tentatively identified with the Bennachie hillfort in Grampian. The Romans appear to have won that battle, but decided to 'quit while they were ahead', retreating southwards to defend permanent boundaries along the Antonine Wall and, later, Hadrian's Wall. There has long been discussion as to whether the *Caledonia Silva* referred to a specifically defined forested area, or was a more generalised reference to a still heavily wooded and unapproachable region in the central and eastern Highlands. It cannot, however, be taken to mean that Scotland as a whole was still heavily forested – we have too much other evidence that it was not.

After the Roman departure from Britain in AD 410, we enter the period known as the 'Dark Ages', for which written records are scarce. To a large extent, the following six or seven centuries were economically similar to the pre-Roman Iron Age, certainly in the less Romanised parts of Britain. Accordingly, the level of human impact on woodlands, at least in the uplands, appears to have reverted to its former level. In the lowlands of southern England, where the Roman 'villa economy' had been more fully developed, there is at least some evidence for woodland recovery onto now abandoned agricultural and even urban land. This process is known as 'old-field succession' and has occurred on a much larger scale in the north-eastern United States over the past 200 years, as settlers moved 'out west'. During the early post-Roman years, marginal farmland areas (including the Cotswolds, Chilterns, Downs and Weald) may have experienced localised woodland recovery (Peterken 1993). These woodlands (known by ecologists as 'ancient secondary woodlands') contain a combination of native tree species and Roman or later introductions such as sycamore, sweet chestnut and box. They can still be distinguished from 'ancient primary woodlands' on archaeological and botanical grounds, due to the lower diversity of plants having recolonised and the presence of underlying field boundaries and cultivation traces. In Scotland, there is some evidence for this kind of post-Roman woodland recovery (Smout 1993), but it would be more difficult to detect it from study of upland woodland vegetation. There may have been some recovery of woodland in the areas surrounding the Roman roads, forts and fortifications that had placed unusual pressure on the resource. During the period up to around AD 1100, the preceding gradual attrition of Scottish woodland cover probably continued, with only localised impacts associated with invasions and settlement by Northumbrian Angles (AD 600–800) and Scandinavian Vikings (AD 800–1000).

3.11 Historical research sources

For the period prior to AD 1130 we have seen that there is little written evidence available and that reliance has to be placed on archaeological methods. After the beginning of the Anglo-Norman period in Scotland (from around AD 1130) a wider variety of manuscript sources do become available to us. Although, throughout the medieval period, these certainly remain sparser than equivalent sources for lowland England, they do add significantly to the picture we can assemble of native woodland extent, type and utilisation (Ritchie and Wordsworth 2010; Smout 1997, 2003; Smout et al. 2005). In the early medieval centuries, ecclesiastical and royal records are the major sources for woodlands. By 1600, monastic sources disappear but records for some major private landed estates become available, together with survey maps by Timothy Pont in the later 1500s and General Roy in the mid-1700s (see Plate 3). The eighteenth century sees an increase in official governmental records and the Statistical Accounts, which together with private estate records and maps are the major sources during the nineteenth century. Published travel accounts become significant sources from the later eighteenth century.

It is quite rare for written records to deal with native woodlands in Scotland as their major focus of interest prior to the twentieth century. This means that there is often a considerable amount of work to be done to find and extract information relevant to native woodland research from a background of less relevant material relating to rural economics, landed estates, finance, law and inheritance. Early maps do not present a comprehensive picture of native woodlands, having been drawn mainly for military purposes. Very early material may be written in Latin, French or antiquated versions of lowland Scots and English that require specialist interpretation. In addition, it must be remembered that the purpose of written records was not usually to inform future objective research. Very often it was to persuade, sometimes to mislead, the likely readership. For that reason all documentary historical research must be done with a critical 'historian's eye'.

A major distinction in historical records relating to woodlands is between primary sources and secondary sources. Primary sources are first-hand accounts of the conditions and management of a particular woodland or of woodlands across a given area, written or drawn within living memory of the period described. Older primary sources were often not published, and include private correspondence, estate papers, monastic archives and official court records. Later primary sources, such as military map surveys, government records and Statistical Accounts, were published. Primary sources often have the advantage of being more authentic, but are less accessible and more demanding to interpret. Secondary sources are collations and reinterpretations from primary sources and oral reports, prepared at a later date (very often for the purpose of publication). Secondary sources include published books and journal articles (from the eighteenth century onwards), recent internet resources and official publications (e.g. research reports). Secondary sources are usually more accessible and easier to interpret, but carry different risks – as to how carefully the primary material was collected, selected and reinterpreted.

Another distinction between historical records is whether they have been indexed (this may not always have been by the original author). Indexing makes it much easier (and less time consuming) to find the information sought. Published books and articles are very often 'internally' indexed as to topics covered, with page numbers. Public records and county archives are usually 'externally' indexed as to document type and subject matter, but the original may still need to be examined to assess its relevance. For example, an 'estate survey' listing from the 1740s may describe woodland management and have a good estate map, or it may only be an account ledger of rentals due and received from tenants. County archives are usually indexed by place name (often by parish), overall theme (e.g. estate management) and sometimes by the names of landed estates/families. Official, monastic and published sources, together with 'deposited' private estate papers, can be examined free of charge at public libraries and county archives, sometimes with a need for an advance appointment to view, based on prior examination of excellent online indexes now available. Private estate papers retained by the estates' own archives are very often unindexed and may require considerable time and expertise to access by private arrangement and then to interpret effectively.

Some major types of written records relevant to native woodlands are:

- **Medieval monastic, royal and baronial court rolls, cartularies, terriers and ledger books** – these are very important sources on the management and utilisation of native woodlands during the period AD 1100–1600, but they tend to be rather demanding to interpret and may well require specialist linguistic and historical document interpretation skills.
- **Map surveys** such as those by Timothy Pont in the late sixteenth century (published later in Amsterdam by Blaeu) and by General Roy in the mid-eighteenth century. These indicate woodland cover, but may give an incomplete or partial impression of position and extent. Ordnance Survey maps become a vital source after the mid-nineteenth century. Many maps are available online from the National Library of Scotland.
- **Official records for the period 1700–1900** – these cover an important period for the industrial exploitation of woodlands in Scotland and include the records of the Commission for the Forfeited Estates (land seized by the authorities after the Jacobite risings of 1715 and 1745), two rounds of Statistical Accounts of Scotland (collated by parish ministers during the period 1790–1850) and annual Agricultural Census records. These records tend to be rather easier to interpret than those from before ~1700 on both linguistic and presentational grounds.
- **Private estate papers** – for the period ~1600 onwards, many private estates kept records of legal, economic and managerial aspects of estate life, including maps, woodland plans and wood product sales accounts. These can be very useful for the purpose of woodland history research, but are often incomplete. Some estate papers (or 'muniments') have been gifted (or 'deposited') into county or national archives, for example when a family had no living heirs and estates were sold off. Others were retained by the private owners themselves – the largest Scottish

estates such as Atholl, Argyll, Seafield and Buccleuch have well-organised archival sections, but many smaller estates may have lost their records in fires or discarded them long since. Some types of private estate papers, such as maps, are easier to interpret, but long-hand legal correspondence can be very demanding. There are also some archived papers relating to private businesses such as tree nurseries, timber merchants, sawmills, and factors' and landscape architects' practices that can be relevant, particularly if there is a likelihood of past woodland planting.

- **Published books, articles and research reports** – these are amongst the most accessible sources, available from public libraries and, recently, over the internet. Some early examples of relevance to woodland history research are the 'travel reports' from the 1770s by James Robertson, Johnson and Boswell and Thomas Pennant. A number of similar, often aristocratic travel diaries and memoirs followed over the next two centuries, together with motor-touring guides over the past century. These accounts are often rather opinionated and may be intended to flatter the authors' hosts with reports of well-managed property or convey an exaggerated sense of adventure to an 'armchair' readership. Some are also rather generalised, dealing with conditions of whole Highland districts 'at the stroke of a pen', whereas others deal with specific estates and localities with greater care and attention. From the early twentieth century, works of academic history and scientific ecology become available, including papers in various journal series (e.g. *Journal of the Royal Scottish Arboricultural Society*, now *Scottish Forestry*), published books and official reports (FC, SNH, ITE, etc.).

3.12 Living archaeology – veteran and modified trees

Another important source of information for the management of Scottish native woodlands over more recent centuries is what can be termed 'living archaeology', or the detailed study of the structure and form of surviving trees (Ritchie and Wordsworth 2010; Smout 1997, 2003; Smout et al. 2005). While there may be occasional examples of older individual trees (for example, the Fortingall yew in Perthshire is suggested to be several thousand years old, and there might be a few lowland parkland oaks dating back 700–900 years), almost all Scottish trees are less than 550 years old, most very much less. However, those trees dating from the period 1500–1800 can provide much valuable information for a period when many native woodlands were subject to poorly documented customary management. Major methods for 'living archaeology' in woodlands are:

- **Study of veteran and ancient trees** – these are usually individual trees that have survived to extreme old age due to a combination of chance events, environmental conditions and human management systems. In many situations, the longest-lived trees are actually those growing slowly on unproductive sites or those artificially modified by coppicing or pollarding. Well-grown timber trees on productive, accessible sites were typically harvested at 100–200 years old for optimum timber value. Hence many veteran trees display indicators of their 'difficult' history in terms of decay, deadwood, poor stem form and an uneven, heavily branched crown (Rackham 1990, 2003). Most, but by no means all, have a larger than average stem diameter for their species (Harmer et al. 2010). Veteran trees can provide information about the species composition and regeneration of woodlands when they were younger, although care must be taken to interpret this information, as shorter-lived species may have since completely disappeared, exaggerating the importance of remaining oak especially. The actual age of veteran trees varies by species – veteran status typically occurs at 250–500 years in Scots pine, 400 years and over in oak, 200–500 years in sycamore, 200–300 years in beech and ash, and 100–200 years in birch. The age of veteran trees can sometimes be estimated from their 'diameter at breast height' (dbh) (White 1998), although this technique is less reliable in the more variable growing conditions of upland Scotland than in lowland England. Dendrochronology (see below) can also be used under certain circumstances, but may be impaired by heart rot. The location of veteran trees can indicate settlement and land-use patterns over recent centuries as some were planted or encouraged along field boundaries and near farmsteads. Veteran tree information is available from the Ancient Tree Forum.

- **Study of modified trees** – these are trees, very often also veteran trees (see above), which have been modified by past human management. The main management systems involved are wood pasture (possibly with tree fodder lopping), coppicing, pollarding and, locally, tapping of pine resins. These practices typically change the structure of trees in terms of stem form and branching pattern, and may shorten or extend their lifespan. Most such practices declined as commonplace active management systems during the nineteenth century, but were a common feature between 1500 and 1800. Industrial oak coppicing persisted in some cases until the 1930s. With the natural processes of tree ageing and mortality, the stock of modified trees in Scotland will inevitably decline over coming decades and their study should clearly be prioritised while they remain available.
- **Dendrochronology** – also known as tree-ring dating (Crone and Mills 2002; Mills and Crone 2012). We saw earlier in this chapter that this technique can be applied to archaeological samples such as prehistoric oak preserved in peat bogs. It can also be applied to standing trees using the technique of Pressler increment coring or to felled trees by means of ring counting. Timber samples in historic buildings can also be studied by Pressler increment coring. At a basic level these techniques can help to estimate the age of trees where the heartwood has not been subject to decay. More sophisticated analytical techniques, using reference samples, can also be used to study patterns of growth over time, illuminating past climate change and silviculture. For pine and oak in particular, sawn samples may be related to a region of origin (e.g. Scotland, France, the Baltic) based on growth patterns. Professional expertise/advice is required when taking Pressler increment cores from veteran or ecologically valuable trees to avoid damage/disease ingress.

3.13 WOODLANDS IN THE MIDDLE AGES AND RENAISSANCE

For convenience, the period in Scottish native woodland history between AD 1130 and around 1660 is taken as a whole. It is estimated that due to continued clearance, the woodland cover of Scotland began this period around the 15% mark, and ended it between 5% and 10%. During that period, many aspects of customary woodland management in Scotland might have changed rather little from Iron Age and Dark Age conditions. However, the advent of written records, together with evidence from surviving native woodland remnants, makes it possible to look in rather more detail at three categories of native woodland management during this period (Dickson 1993; Smout 1997, 2003; Smout et al. 2005):

1. **Hunting forests and deer parks** (Fletcher 2011; Gilbert 1979) – these were areas, incorporating surviving native woodland, that were protected for use by royalty, nobility and the bishops as hunting grounds (primarily for red deer and wild boar). These were located in many of the more accessible parts of Scotland, including the Borders, Galloway, Stirlingshire, Renfrewshire, Perthshire, Angus, Aberdeenshire and Moray. Some were large wild upland areas with a variety of land-cover types (e.g. Glen Finglas in the Trossachs) (see Figure 3.4); others were smaller, more 'manicured' lowland deer parks around castles such as Dalkeith, Cadzow and Lochwood. In these areas there was often a strict protection regime in place aimed at retaining the native woodland by controlling grazing and felling by the ordinary people of the area. This could be compared

FIGURE 3.4 *Upland wood pasture of late medieval origin, Glen Finglas. Copyright: Dr Scott McG. Wilson.*

with modern conservation and national park management, both in Europe and in the developing countries. As a result, some of these forests and parks survive, still containing veteran native trees dating from the period 1450–1650, some of which may originally have been planted.

2. **Working woodlands** – these were areas of native woodland that were managed, or at least regularly utilised, by ordinary people, to produce timber, woodfuel and also meat, leather and wool from livestock under wood-pasture systems (see Plate 5). These would have included much of the surviving accessible woodland in the lowlands, coastal fringes and lower slopes of the Highland glens. Compared to lowland England, there is weaker written evidence for organised woodland management in Scotland prior to 1600 – especially for 'high-forest' timber production and rotational coppicing. It was certainly pursued to some extent, for example on monastic and crown lands in south Scotland. There are also reports of periodic supply of oak and pine timber for castle, cathedral and ship construction. There is also a growing body of what might be termed 'circumstantial' evidence for customary, informal management of woodlands by way of wood-pasture systems. To what extent these represented 'sustainable' silvo-pastoral systems remains uncertain, but it is likely that action was taken to retain and perpetuate the local woodland resources.
3. **'Waste' woodlands** – these were the remoter and less accessible areas of native woodland remaining in the Southern Uplands and Scottish Highlands, which were not regarded as being of practical economic value. They were too far from settlements and markets for woodland products to be profitably extracted and utilised. Some of these woodlands disappeared entirely, replaced by upland grazing land, especially areas of the Southern Uplands under monastic sheep-grazing systems. Other areas, such as the native pinewoods and upland oakwoods of the Highlands, survived, but were under varying degrees of pressure from seasonal livestock grazing, muirburn and sporadic harvesting of timber, mainly for local usage.

3.14 Woodlands in the age of industrial exploitation

The period between 1650 and 1850 saw fairly intensive industrial exploitation of the two major categories of native woodland in Scotland – native pinewoods (for building and naval timbers) and upland oakwoods (for iron-smelting charcoal and tanbark) (Lindsay 1975, 1977; Smout 1997, 2003, 2005, 2006; Smout et al. 2005). Alder woodlands were also exploited on a smaller scale during this period for gunpowder charcoal. These pressures reflected increased demands from military and civilian industrial markets and exhaustion of the English and Irish wood resources.

The more accessible native pinewoods saw an increased rate of felling to meet the demands of building, including naval construction, between 1680 and 1830. Timber was usually extracted by flotation down rivers to the Scottish coastal ports (e.g. Inverness, Aberdeen, Garmouth) and then onward by sea transport to final markets in the Lowlands or in England. This put pressure on those native pinewoods with

FIGURE 3.5 *Modern production of charcoal within a native woodland. Image: Forestry Commission/Isobel Cameron. Crown copyright.*

better access to larger rivers and lochs (e.g. those in Strathspey). The more land-locked woodlands were usually less affected. Scottish supplies became critical, including for the Navy, during and after the Napoleonic Wars (1793–1815) when alternative Baltic and North American pine supplies were blockaded or subject to tariffs. A variety of Scottish, Irish and English landowners and timber merchants were involved and standards of forest management varied greatly. Natural regeneration was often satisfactory in the eastern Highlands, aided by temporary stock exclusion, whereas this period of heavy felling contributed to the steep decline of some of the more westerly pinewoods.

Many upland oakwoods were coppiced on a 20- to 25-year rotation throughout the 200 years between 1650 and 1850 for the production of charcoal (see Figure 3.5) for iron-smelting and tanbark for leather curing. Oak was the favoured species and other components such as hazel, birch and ash tended to be removed as 'barren timbers'. Industrialised smelting began in the far north-west (Letterewe) during the early 1600s, but most intensive coppicing and smelting was focused on the woodlands of Argyll, Lochaber, Loch Lomond, Perthshire and the Trossachs between ~1700 and ~1860. A number of major iron furnaces were established (see Figure 3.6) at coastal locations to which iron ore could be brought in by ship and from which pig iron and tanbark could be exported as a return cargo. Ownership of the woodlands remained in the hands of the Scottish 'lairds' but coppicing and smelting leases were often granted to Cumbrian ironmasters and Irish tanners. Productive coppices were usually enclosed and the traditional forms of Highland wood-pasture management were excluded to protect the valuable growing stock of oak. Failing oak coppice stools were replaced by plantings

FIGURE 3.6 *Site of historical iron furnace at Bonawe, Argyll, managed by Historic Scotland. Copyright: Dr Scott McG. Wilson.*

of oak (Tittensor 1970), leading over time to a regularly stocked, even-aged structure within large areas of the upland oak woodlands, which persists until the present time. Gunpowder charcoal was a specialist user of alder coppice, for example at Roslin Glen in Midlothian.

There has been much debate as to whether these forms of industrial exploitation were responsible for a significant proportion of long-term native woodland decline in Scotland. Both came to an end by the late nineteenth century as iron-built shipping, coke-fired iron-smelting and chemical tanning became dominant. In the case of upland oakwoods, it is likely that coppice management acted to conserve many from removal and over-grazing, although at the expense of structural and species diversity.

3.15 Native woodland in Victorian/Edwardian times

The century between 1815 and 1915 saw steadily reducing levels of industrial exploitation of native woodland resources across Scotland (Anderson 1967; Smout 1997, 2003; Smout et al. 2005). To some extent this period is seen as a quiet or 'dark' episode in the history of these woodlands during which they were left under-managed and in process of steady, but poorly recorded, decline. A number of causes can be identified:

- Reduced demands for timber, charcoal and tanbark due to changes in industrial processes (iron shipbuilding, coke-firing of ironworks, etc.) and greater affordability of overseas timber supplies, from Scandinavia and eastern North America in particular, due to changes in tax regimes.

- Declines in traditional wood-pasture, pollarding and coppicing systems following on from massive depopulation of the Highlands during the 'clearances' period, prior to the mid-1800s; progressive loss of 'folk memory' and practical skills associated with these forms of woodland management, compared with Scandinavia and other parts of Europe.
- Introduction of extensive sheep-rearing systems and lowland sheep-stock from the 1790s onwards in many Highland districts; increased year-round grazing pressure on the remaining native woodland resource, with reduced labour-availability to manage and distribute that pressure, leading to a hiatus of natural tree regeneration in many upland areas.
- Reservation of significant areas of the Scottish Highlands as sporting estates from the 1840s onwards. Management for large populations of red deer and grouse led to declines in natural tree regeneration (especially in the native pinewoods) due to over-grazing and localised losses of woodland area by deliberate felling and uncontrolled muirburn.
- Focus of forestry attention on plantation woodlands on some large private estates, which had been expanding since around 1680. While the native pinewoods of Strathspey and Deeside remained a productive forestry resource, the introduced plantation species including larch, Douglas fir and Norway spruce became the major productive forestry resource in Scotland during the later nineteenth century. The productive management of hardwood species in Scotland declined markedly, with abandonment of most oak coppices and importation of tropical and temperate hardwoods. Beech and sycamore also expanded in places.

It is not clear how much native woodland area was lost in Scotland between 1800 and 2000. Smout et al. (2005) infer that the minimum of woodland cover as a whole was reached during the late nineteenth century (at ~6%, of which half was native), but the figure has now rebounded to 16–18%. Until the last thirty years, almost all of this re-expansion had been by plantation of introduced species, and this must have masked some level of continuing decline in native woodland extent. What is certainly true is that many forms of land management applied within surviving native woodlands, since around 1840, have impeded natural regeneration – particularly of Scots pine and oak – leading many woodlands to develop an unbalanced age-class distribution. Deer browsing is the key continuing challenge to regeneration, especially in the native pinewoods (Forestry Commission Scotland 2014).

Another important aspect of Scottish native woodland history during Victorian and Edwardian times was the rise of the 'romantic' or 'picturesque' literary and artistic movements. The works of authors such as Sir Walter Scott and John Ruskin, together with that of artists such as John Everett Millais and Edwin Landseer, contributed to the later emergence of nature conservation and the advent of landscape/wildlife tourism in Scotland. The royal family's acquisition at Balmoral on Deeside was very influential.

3.16 NATIVE WOODLAND DURING THE TWO WORLD WARS

The first half of the twentieth century was a difficult and perilous period for the native woodland resources of Scotland, but also saw the first signs of the conservation movement that has shaped their development over the last sixty years (Fowler 2002). The factors already described for the nineteenth century continued, particularly neglect of native woodlands, decline of silvicultural management for timber or coppice, and widespread over-grazing by sheep and red deer. With the exception of the native pinewoods of the eastern Highlands, there was little effective regeneration.

To these long-standing factors were added two new acute impacts – emergency fellings during the two world wars (1914–18 and 1939–45) and subsequent replanting/under-planting with introduced tree species. During the First World War, the depleted condition of Britain's existing woodland resources, coupled with the submarine blockade of timber imports, saw a recurrence of the supply problems encountered during the Napoleonic Wars. However, the demand on this occasion was primarily for small-dimension timbers, particularly for mining, given the use of iron and steel for shipbuilding. Although extensive forestry plantations were established between 1920 and 1940, these remained too young to prevent similar supply problems recurring during the Second World War, on a greater scale. On both occasions, the government instigated emergency programmes (Anderson 1967) of devastation felling, primarily within the native pinewoods and the older plantations of Scots pine, larch, spruce and firs. These were carried out by specialist timber corps employing Canadian lumberjacks during both wars and also by the Women's Timber Corps ('lumberjills') during World War II. Some of the larger felled native pinewoods, for example in Glenmore and Abernethy on Speyside, were satisfactorily restocked after the two world wars by a combination of natural regeneration and replanting. However, others, for example at Glenfeshie and Mar Lodge, suffered loss of woodland area due to natural regeneration failure in the presence of large populations of red deer, maintained for sporting purposes. Wartime felling was a less significant and much more localised factor in deciduous native woodlands.

Following the First World War, the Forestry Commission was established in 1919 to create a national strategic reserve of timber against future supply interruptions. The Commission adopted ideas for expansion of the forest resource in Scotland that had been advocated earlier by prominent private landowners, notably Lord Lovat. As the emphasis was on speed, to create a reserve of potential mining timber as quickly as possible, attention focused on establishment of plantations of fast-growing conifer species. Many of these were created on bare land using Sitka spruce and lodgepole pine, two species from the Pacific Northwest that were capable of growing on the infertile, wet upland soils of Scotland, which had not carried significant tree cover for many centuries. Application of highly mechanised deep cultivation techniques and mineral fertilisers, especially after the Second World War, aided rapid establishment. However, in many areas where native woodlands remained, attempts were being made to convert them into conifer stands, using introduced Sitka spruce and western hemlock, in the expectation of greater productivity. This was accomplished by a combination of felling and replanting (especially in the western oak woodlands) and under-planting (applied both in native pinewoods and in oak woodlands). As will be discussed in Chapters 8 and 10, this had important implications for the future conservation of these native woodlands.

CHAPTER FOUR

Native pinewoods and montane scrub

4.1 Historical development

Native (or 'Caledonian') pinewood and montane scrub habitats in Scotland are both direct descendants of 'pioneer' woodlands that first developed during the Boreal phase, after the end of the last Ice Age, 8,000–10,000 years BP. During the intervening period they have undergone significant changes to their distribution, extent and composition, forming the native woodlands of these types observed today. The native pinewoods have attracted particular attention from many previous authors (Aldhous 1995; Bain 1987, 2013; Bunce and Jeffers 1977; Forestry Commission 1994, 1998; Mason et al. 2004; Steven and Carlisle 1959). The last three references provide fuller accounts of their distribution, ecology and management than is feasible here.

The montane scrub woodlands of Scotland form an important ecotone (ecological transition) between the upper edge of the native pinewoods and the open montane heathland and moorland habitats higher on the Scottish hills (Gilbert et al. 1997; Pearsall 1971). They are composed primarily of juniper, dwarfed forms of Scots pine, downy birch and willows (see Plates 7a and 7b). In the early Boreal phase, such scrub (then also including hazel) may have occupied much of the land area of Scotland, but later, as the climate improved, it became restricted to higher altitudes (600–800m) by expansion 'from below' of more competitive tree species. Over the last 5,000 years, montane scrub has also been severely restricted 'from above' by natural climatic deterioration and human modification. The latter has occurred mainly in the forms of poorly managed moorland burning and increased red deer and livestock browsing.

It has been suggested that the total area of native pinewood surviving today may be as little as 1% of its maximum Holocene extent (Mason et al. 2004), around 6,000 years BP. This may exaggerate the maximum extent of native pinewoods, but there is no question that in the late Boreal and early Atlantic phases, pine-birch-aspen-hazel woodland types occupied much of the northern Scottish landscape below 600m asl, with areas of montane scrub widespread above this. With the expansion of competitive broadleaved tree species from lower altitudes throughout the Atlantic phase, native pinewoods became restricted to an altitudinal zone above these. In the eastern Highlands this now ranges from 200–550m asl, whereas in the more exposed west Highlands 100–400m is more typical. Occasional native pinewoods reach sea level in the north-west Highlands, as at Shieldaig (see Plate 7c). There have been major climatically driven fluctuations in the past natural distribution and extent of Scots pine – by around 5,000 years BP it had expanded outwards onto some previously peat-covered ground, only to retreat from there by 3,000 years BP (see Smout 1997; Smout et al. 2005; Tipping 1994). It has also retreated from higher ground over several millennia, with the upper limit of fully developed native pinewood in the Cairngorms falling back by at least 100m from its Holocene maximum. More isolated Scots pine populations arising in central and southern Scotland, as with those of England and Wales, were displaced by temperate deciduous trees during the Atlantic phase, although it is possible that very small remnant Scots pine populations survived until later in some areas.

Within the present natural range of native pinewoods in the Scottish Highlands, their actual extent has been reduced by climate change and possibly by the growing human impacts over the past 5,000 years (see Chapter 3 for further discussion). The effect has been to confine their distribution to thirty to forty substantial pinewood remnants (Steven and Carlisle 1959), with a similar number of isolated satellite fragments (Forestry Commission 1994, 1998). Within surviving native pinewood areas, both species composition and natural regeneration dynamics of the pinewood ecosystem are partly modified. While birch and smaller components of aspen, rowan, alder and juniper remain as associated species, the species diversity of native pine woodland is thought to have been reduced by selective browsing of oak, hazel, holly, bird cherry and other hardwoods. Artificially high populations of red deer, sheep and goats have also interrupted the natural regeneration dynamics of Scots pine since at least 1800 (Oliver and Larson 1996), resulting in many stands becoming 'geriatric populations', lacking younger age-cohorts (Mason et al. 2004).

4.2 Historical distribution

Evidence from pollen analyses suggests that Scots pine expanded into Scotland during the Boreal phase (7,500–9,500 years BP), initially from refugia to the north-west (H. J. B. Birks 1989). Separate routes of colonisation from the south and east must have existed, as for pine in England. During the period since the early Atlantic phase, some 6,000 years BP, the land cover of native pinewoods (together with associated montane scrub habitats) has been dramatically reduced. The major causes of that decline have been deterioration in climate and soil conditions at higher altitudes, increasing competition from deciduous trees at lower altitudes, and increasing human impacts. How much can be said about the spatial pattern and temporal phasing of this native pine decline? This should be considered separately (1) for the Scottish Highlands within today's Caledonian Pinewood Zone (CPZ) and (2) for the Central Belt and Southern Uplands.

The Caledonian Pinewood Zone (CPZ) has been defined with reference to thirty to forty major pinewood remnants recorded by Steven and Carlisle (1959), but also contains forty to fifty smaller fragments subsequently recorded by the Caledonian Pinewood Inventory (Forestry Commission 1994, 1998). It also contains much ground with comparable climates and soils to those within the native pinewoods, which is currently open heath and moor. Some of this ground is likely to have carried native pinewood in the past, but in most cases probably not for millennia. From pollen evidence, much native pinewood disappeared between 3,000 and 5,000 years BP, following a briefer episode of more continental climates when it was permitted to spread onto formerly water-logged peatlands (Aldhous 1995; Tipping 1994). It is not realistic, based on available evidence, to map this decline in pinewood cover, even on a century-by-century basis, over the intervening period. It is, however, believed that many of the existing pinewood remnants have continued to decline in extent over more recent centuries, particularly those in the wetter western Highlands where regeneration following exploitation was less reliable. There is reliable evidence that those in the Argyll and Lochaber areas (e.g. Black Mount, Glen Coe, Glen Orchy) were reduced in extent by exploitation and climatic factors between 1600 and 1900 (Smout et al. 2005; Smout 2006). This leaves open the question as to whether any discrete areas of native pinewood, which had survived into the historical period, have since disappeared from the landscape. One approach to investigating this is to combine evidence from place names (*guisachan* = pine in Gaelic) with documentary references to pinewood fellings and so on. Gaelic place names can be taken to refer to the past 1,500 years, after the language was introduced into Scotland from Ireland. It should be noted that use of the name *guisachan* may refer to bog deposits of pine. There are a few localities where relatively recent disappearance of native pinewood (during the period 1600–1900) is at least suspected – caused by a combination of exploitation for timber and the deteriorating climates of the 'Little Ice Age' period (~AD 1450–1850). Were all such cases of suspected recent pinewood removal confirmed, they would certainly not double the actual extent of native pinewood surviving today.

For areas outside the Caledonian Pinewood Zone, there is very little palaeoecological evidence for the presence of pinewood within the past 5,000 years (Aldhous 1995). A raised bog near Stirling does appear to have carried Scots pine for a short period ~4,000 years BP, when the climate became temporarily favourable (Dickson 1993). Pinewoods which once developed in the Southern Uplands (e.g. in Galloway) had disappeared, through natural competition, before 5,000 years BP (Aldhous 1995), as the climate warmed into the Atlantic phase. Later climatic cooling did not enable any return of Scots pine to these areas, perhaps due to increased human and livestock impacts in the intervening period. However, pollen analyses might not detect very small pinewood remnants in Border 'cleuchs' – some such may just have survived into the Iron Age and post-Roman period, as suggested by Welsh-language literary sources (Linnard 2000).

4.3 Current geographical distribution

The Caledonian Pinewood Inventory (Forestry Commission 1994, 1998) records those eighty-four populations of Scots pine that are believed to be self-sown descendants of the post-glacial natural forest cover. These can be arranged into a number of major geographical pinewood groupings, as follows:

- **Strathspey** – the largest assemblage of native pinewoods in Scotland, including the major populations at Glenfeshie, Rothiemurchus, Glenmore, Abernethy and Kinveachy, with much smaller fragments at Glen Tromie and Glen Avon. A wide range of management approaches are being applied under a spectrum of ownerships – public agencies, charitable conservation organisations and private sporting estates.
- **Beauly catchment** – the second largest pinewood assemblage, after the Strathspey pinewoods, including four major native pinewood glens: Glen Strathfarrar, Glen Cannich, Glen Affric and Guisachan/Cougie. These woods form a particularly important ecological grouping and are mostly under restoration and conservation management at present.
- **Deeside** – the major pinewoods at Mar Lodge (Glen Derry, Glen Quoich and Glen Luibeg) (see Plate 7d), Ballochbuie (on Balmoral Estate), Invercauld, Glen Tanar and Birse (Glen Ferrick). Red deer are a significant factor, influencing regeneration levels within many of these.
- **Great Glen** – native pinewoods along several glens draining eastwards into the Great Glen, including the major examples at Glen Moriston, Glen Garry, Loch Arkaig/Glen Mallie, Glen Loy and Conaglen/Ardgour. There are also a number of much smaller pinewoods, such as Glen Loyne, Glen Nevis, Glen Shiel and Glen Buck. Certain of these pinewoods have been affected by replanting with exotic conifer species.
- **South West** – isolated pinewoods in the Crianlarich, Tyndrum and Bridge of Orchy areas, including those at Black Mount, Coille Coire Chuilc and Glen Falloch. Other smaller fragments include those at Glen Orchy, Glen Etive and Glen Kinglas. Glen Falloch is the most southerly of the surviving native pinewoods recognised on the inventory.
- **Perthshire** – two major pinewoods in the upper reaches of the Tay catchment: the Black Wood of Rannoch and the Old Wood of Meggernie in Glen Lyon. The Black Wood of Rannoch is one of the best-studied of the native pinewoods, surveyed since the 1940s.
- **Wester Ross** – several pinewoods in catchments draining mainly westwards into the Atlantic. The most significant are those at Achnashellach, Beinn Eighe, Coulin, Shieldaig and Rhiddoroch, with additional smaller fragments. Some of these woods are believed to be genetically highly distinct from others, perhaps arising from separate oceanic or Irish glacial refugia (Aldhous 1995; Forrest 1992).
- **East Sutherland** – the important native pinewoods at Amat and Glen Alladale in Strathcarron, draining east into the Moray Firth, together with the smaller Glen Einig and Strath Oykel fragments, which are the most northerly surviving pinewood remnants on the inventory.

In addition to these 'inventory pinewoods' there are a large number of Scots pine plantations within the Caledonian Pinewood Zone, some of which have been established using local planting stock. A small proportion are over 200 years old and can be difficult to distinguish from the natural pinewoods. The most significant from an ecological point of view are the old Seafield Estate pine plantations of mid-Strathspey, which form part of an extensive pinewood complex with the native pinewoods at Abernethy and Kinveachy.

The recent Native Woodland Survey of Scotland (NWSS) (Forestry Commission Scotland 2014) records some 88,000ha of native pine woodland within the Caledonian Pinewood Zone, of which 22% (~20,000ha) represents semi-natural pinewoods on ancient woodland sites and the remaining 78% (~68,000ha) represents forestry plantations of Scots pine. In practice there is some overlap (e.g. old plantations that have 'naturalised').

4.4 Current ecological distribution

We have already seen that native pinewood surviving at the present time occurs below ~600m asl. The highest elevations recorded are in the Cairngorms, where it is believed that climatic warmth and wind exposure are the main natural factors determining the treeline altitude. Further west, their altitudinal limit is depressed to 300–400m asl, here primarily by exposure. Native pinewood can develop from sea level upwards, but is more often outcompeted by deciduous woodland below 150–200m asl, other than on the exposed north-western coast. Montane scrub woodland occurs in a band above the upper limit of the native pinewoods in the Highlands and of upland oak-birch woodlands elsewhere in Scotland. In extreme cases scrub may extend up as far as 800–900m asl, but it usually fades out lower.

Within its zone of climatic suitability, native pinewood tends to dominate on slopes with colder climates – north-facing round to east-facing – as well as on level and undulating plateaux and valley-bottom sites (Steven and Carlisle 1959). Obvious examples of the preference for north-facing slopes are evident at the Black Wood of Rannoch, Old Wood of Meggernie, South Loch Arkaig, Glen Garry and Glen Strathfarrar, where north-facing pinewoods are opposed across the valley by south-facing upland oak-birch woodlands. In most cases it is likely that the natural forest composition reflected these site preferences, as deciduous tree species would have outcompeted Scots pine on the warmer south-facing slopes with better soils. Oak has often been cleared from warmer slopes for agriculture, at a later date, leaving Scots pine to stand on cold north-facing slopes with poor soils. The preference of native pinewood for east-facing slopes is much less distinct. In the far west, aspect is a less significant factor due to the greater overall wind exposure. Montane scrub woodland can potentially be found on all aspects, but some of the better-developed examples are found on south-facing slopes, particularly those at Ben Lawers in Perthshire.

Native pinewoods are now found almost exclusively over infertile Precambrian and Cambrian hard-rock geologies – mainly the Moine series – together with intrusive granites. A very few, notably the southernmost pinewood remnant at Glen Falloch, stray onto the generally more fertile Dalradian series. Several are found over coarse fluvioglacial gravels of valley bottoms, for example at Abernethy and Glen Tanar.

Native pinewood is found today predominantly over freely draining podzolic soil types in the eastern Highlands and over poorly drained peaty gleys and peaty podzols in the western Highlands (Mason et al. 2004; Steven and Carlisle 1959). A minor proportion of native pinewoods and much of the montane scrub woodland occurs over rankers and skeletal soils at higher elevations. All of these are inherently infertile soil types on which more demanding tree species cannot compete. While occasional examples can be found of Scots pine attempting to colonise deep peat soils (for example at Inshriach Forest) (see Plate 8a), it does not seem to form fully developed bog woodlands, tending to 'arrest' at the scrub stage. Well-developed ironpan soils do not usually develop within native pinewoods but are certainly found in close proximity to some of the western pinewoods and may well act as a serious constraint on their potential for expansion. Few semi-natural pinewoods (as opposed to old pine plantations) occur on upland brown-earth soils or surface-water gleys. The litter decomposition of Scots pine and of associated ericaceous pinewood understorey vegetation is typically too slow to allow brown soils to persist in the long term.

4.5 Stand dynamics, structure and regeneration

As a light-demanding pioneer species, Scots pine (*Pinus sylvestris*) tends to form stands with simple, single-storey structures. Seedlings of Scots pine cannot survive under full shade from a canopy of mature Scots pine, but can establish where there are gaps in the canopy or only partial canopy cover. It has been suggested that Scots pine found within the Caledonian pinewood ecosystem of Scotland forms a distinct variant (*Pinus sylvestris var Scotica*) from that found elsewhere in Europe, which can be distinguished by crown architecture, bark and needle colour (Steven and Carlisle 1959). Other native species that can be found in the canopy of native pinewoods (Steven and Carlisle 1959; Mason et al. 2004) are silver birch (*Betula pendula*), downy birch (*Betula pubescens*), rowan (*Sorbus aucuparia*) and aspen (*Populus tremula*). These are also all light-demanding species, and are usually only present on a temporary 'gap-phase' basis, other than around the edges of the pine woodland. In the understorey, there is locally a shrub layer of juniper (*Juniperus communis*). Alder (*Alnus glutinosa*) may occur along streams and river banks running through native pinewoods and is more shade-tolerant. Very occasionally there may be some oak (*Quercus* spp.), holly (*Ilex aquifolium*), hazel (*Corylus avellana*) or bird cherry (*Prunus padus*), but these species have more often been removed in the past, either by deliberate management or by preferential browsing. Attempts to restore them are in progress (Ogilvy et al. 2006), most notably at Glen Affric.

In the boreal forests of Scandinavia, Scots pine often regenerates over large areas following forest fires, forming extensive even-aged stands (Andersson 2005). Even before human management became a significant factor, widespread fires were probably much rarer in Scottish pinewoods, due to the moister climate in Scotland. Some fires do occur 'naturally' in the drier, eastern pinewoods of Strathspey and Deeside and can promote prolific pine regeneration. However, when human-induced fires occur in wetter, western pinewoods, they are often destructive, particularly where the peat is consumed, and may prevent or delay pine regeneration. In most native pinewoods, the main mechanism for natural regeneration is believed to be gap formation by windthrow and age mortality of groups of canopy trees. This creates a 'window of opportunity' during which pine seedlings can establish and grow rapidly to replace the canopy (Oliver and Larson 1996). Pinewoods with an open canopy across a larger area may have patches of regeneration present at any time, without gap formation.

The major issue affecting native pinewood natural regeneration at present is lack of seedling establishment and recruitment. This has a number of causes, including an unsuitable seed bed due to competing ground vegetation (heather, grass and mosses), together with heavy deer browsing of pine seedlings. From the 1840s onwards, many native pinewood areas were managed to hold high populations of red deer (*Cervus elaphus*) for sport shooting. In some cases there were also larger numbers of sheep grazing these woodlands, until thirty to forty years ago. This resulted in many native pinewood remnants developing a 'geriatric' age structure, consisting exclusively of over-mature 'granny pines', with little or no seedling regeneration, even where canopy gaps were readily available. The over-mature pines usually range from ~250 years old up to ~550 years old in extreme cases (Mason et al. 2004). From tree-ring data (from increment cores or cut-stumps) (Crone and Mills 2002), there often appear to be well-defined age-cohorts of trees, having regenerated at specific times in the past when conditions became temporarily favourable. This may have been due to climatic conditions, fires or reduction of grazing pressure for military and economic reasons – for example during the Jacobite wars of 1689–92, 1715 and 1745–6. Scots pine typically lives for 250–300 years before natural mortality commences. This can reduce seed source availability by reducing the number of potential parent trees – even before death, pines may produce fewer seeds in their latter years. For these reasons, it is sometimes necessary for woodland managers to artificially promote natural regeneration either by reducing the numbers of browsing animals or by protecting pine seedlings by fencing until they can grow clear of the reach of browsing animals.

4.6 Botanical interest

The characteristic range of plant species found within the native pinewoods of Scotland reflects their affiliations to the boreal forests of Scandinavia. The native pinewoods all fall within the National Vegetation Class W18 (Rodwell 1991a) (see Chapter 2). A small number of the ericoid sub-shrubs, together with a few acid-loving grasses, dominate the vegetation in almost all pinewoods on the Caledonian Pinewood Inventory. Ling heather (*Calluna vulgaris*), bell heather (*Erica cinerea*), cross-leaved heath (*Erica tetralix*), blaeberry/bilberry (*Vaccinium myrtillus*) and cowberry (*Vaccinium vitis-idaea*) are the common ericoids present, while wavy hair-grass (*Deschampsia flexuosa*) and the sheep's fescue (*Festuca ovina*) represent the fine grasses. All of these species are specially adapted to deal with acid, infertile soil conditions by maximising the efficiency with which they extract plant nutrients from the soil. However, the ericoid sub-shrubs are known to produce leaf litter, rich in secondary aromatic compounds, which is rather slow to break down. The balance between these species is usually dependent on levels of canopy shading and the fire and browsing history of the site. The *Vaccinium* species are slightly more shade-tolerant than heathers and grasses and will, as a result, become dominant in pinewoods with a more complete canopy. However, where the canopy is more open, the heathers and grasses become more competitive and will generally dominate the *Vaccinium* species over time. Woodland managers sometimes wish to increase the cover of *Vaccinium* to provide food for populations of the capercaillie (Moss and Picozzi 1994) – this can be encouraged by temporarily reducing competition from heather by controlled burning (as at Glen Tanar) or cattle grazing (as at Abernethy).

Those native pinewoods on wetter sites, primarily in the western Highlands, tend to have a more open canopy structure with a wider range of grass and rush/sedge (*Juncus*/*Carex*) species present. The purple moor-grass (*Molinia caerulea*) can become dominant over significant areas of wet ground within pinewoods, with the deer-grass (*Trichophorum cespitosum*) and the cotton-grasses (*Eriophorum vaginatum*/*angustifolium*) also found in open areas. Some pinewoods accumulate a considerable cover of mosses, over both the ground and deadwood – *Sphagnum* spp. are often dominant, with a range of other common mosses also found. Dense ground cover of *Molinia* or mosses can restrict natural regeneration of Scots pine seedlings – this is a major problem in some pinewoods. Where Scots pine stands develop a lush vegetation of mixed soft grasses such as the bents (*Agrostis* spp.), Yorkshire fog (*Holcus lanatus*) and creeping soft-grass (*Holcus mollis*), this can be due to nutrient enrichment by livestock or deer or can be an indication that the pine stand is actually a long-established plantation.

The native pinewoods also host a number of rarer, more specialist plant species of conservation importance. The best known of these are the wintergreens (*Pyrola* spp.), chickweed wintergreen (*Trientalis europaea*) and twin flower (*Linnaea borealis*), but creeping lady's tresses (*Goodyera repens*) and lesser twayblade orchid (*Listera cordata*) are also characteristic. These species rarely occur outside the native pinewoods unless they have been accidentally or deliberately introduced (for example in soil carried along with transplanted pine seedlings). There are also specialist pinewood moss and lichen species, such as *Ptilium cristacastrensis*. Chickweed wintergreen in particular can persist on former native pinewood sites long after Scots pine itself has been removed. It can therefore be used to confirm sites within the CPZ that have previously carried native pinewood and might therefore be priorities for pinewood habitat restoration work (see Chapter 9). This makes it a potential example of an 'ancient woodland indicator species' of specific relevance to Scottish upland sites (see Chapter 8).

4.7 Wildlife and biodiversity

The native pinewoods are well known as the habitat for a range of mammals, birds and insects, representing some of the most characteristic biodiversity present within Scotland (see Plates 8b to 8d). Of the mammal species, the wild cat (*Felis sylvestris*), the pine marten (*Martes martes*) and the red squirrel (*Sciurus vulgaris*) now have a particular dependence on areas of surviving native pinewood habitat, having become frequently excluded from other woodland types by human hunting pressure, loss of habitat area and, in the case of the red squirrel, competition from the introduced North American grey squirrel (*Sciurus carolinensis*). There are a number of other wild mammal species that make some seasonal use of native pinewoods, such as the red deer (*Cervus elaphus*), the fox (*Vulpes vulpes*) and the badger (*Meles meles*), although the majority of their time is spent in other habitats. Rivers and streams running through native pinewood areas support local populations of the otter (*Lutra lutra*) and the water vole (*Arvicola terrestris*). Many of these species are under legal protection and active conservation measures at present. Carnivorous mammals, such as wild cat and pine marten, were extensively persecuted during the last 200 years in an attempt to preserve stocks of game birds for shooting. A number of mammal species formerly present within the native pinewoods have become extinct in Scotland over the past few thousand years, mainly due to hunting pressure and reductions in habitat area. These include the wolf, the lynx and the brown bear, which continue to be present in similar forests in mainland Europe. While lynx and brown bear have been extinct for at least 1,000 years, wolf survived into more recent centuries (Yalden 2002). Some ecologists have considered the possibility of reintroducing lynx and wolf. Beaver and wild boar, both extinct from Scotland for several centuries, may have used pinewood to some extent but strongly prefer deciduous woodland. Other large mammals such as the reindeer, the elk and the wild ox (aurochs) may have been present in Scotland for a period of time after the last Ice Age but are longer extinct (Yalden 2002). Elk survive in Scandinavia, and small populations of wild horse and Heck cattle (akin to aurochs) exist in Europe.

Of the birds, the capercaillie (*Tetrao urogallus*) (a large forest grouse) is the most closely associated with the native pinewoods. The species actually became extinct in Scotland prior to 1800 due to climate change and hunting pressure but was reintroduced in the late 1830s from Scandinavia (Moss and Picozzi 1994). Numbers have fluctuated since that time and are currently thought to be unsustainably low, despite a legal moratorium on shooting the bird over the past decade. The main cause appears to be a run of cold, wet springs, reducing breeding success, but disease and collisions with forestry deer fences may also be contributory factors. Techniques for marking fences to avoid capercaillie mortality are being implemented at present. The closely related black grouse (*Tetrao tetrix*) uses a mosaic of pinewood, montane scrub and heathland habitats around the edges of the native pinewoods. A number of birds of prey, including the osprey (*Pandion haliaetus*), golden eagle (*Aquila chrysaetos*) and goshawk (*Accipiter gentilis*), make considerable use of native pinewood habitats as part of larger hunting ranges. The osprey returned to Scotland in the 1950s after many decades of absence, re-establishing itself first in the large native pinewood at Abernethy Forest in Strathspey (now owned by the RSPB). Smaller birds of the native pinewoods include the endemic Scottish crossbill (*Loxia scotica*). Native pinewoods host a range of important insect species such as wood ants and deadwood beetles which require conservation.

4.8 JUNIPER, BIRCH, ASPEN AND ROWAN IN THE NATIVE PINEWOODS

The main tree species that occur along with Scots pine within the native pinewoods are juniper, silver birch, downy birch, aspen and rowan. These are all species which formed part of the pioneer natural forests that colonised Scotland during the Boreal phase (7,500–9,500 years BP). They also form part of the boreal forests found in Scandinavia today. Hazel (*Corylus avellana*), which, from pollen evidence, was quite common in the native woodlands of Scotland during the Boreal phase, is now largely absent from native pinewoods (but was recorded in the Rothiemurchus pinewoods as recently as the 1770s). This may be because soils within these forests have become progressively less fertile since the Boreal phase – hazel generally occurs today in woodland with better soils. Hazel also prefers warmer temperatures than occur within many Scottish native pinewoods today – summers in the Boreal phase may well have been warmer and drier.

4.8.1 Birch and rowan in the native pinewoods

The upland birch woodlands of Scotland will be covered in detail in Chapter 5, as the National Vegetation Classification (NVC) treats them as oak woodland variants (Rodwell 1991a). However, the presence of birch and rowan is also very significant within the native pinewoods, although they usually occupy a minority of the woodland area at any one point in time. Birch tends to colonise openings within the native pinewoods at first, being replaced later by regenerating Scots pine. As a deciduous tree, birch sheds its leaves each autumn, and the leaf litter from birch is believed to improve the soil (Miles 1985). Birch litter breaks down more quickly than that of Scots pine, heather or bilberry, helping to release nutrients back into the soil in a form that is available to plants. Over time, this helps to maintain the fertility of the soils within the native pinewood ecosystem, preventing long-term declines in productivity. Where forestry management has removed birch, this is generally unhealthy for the pinewoods. Birch also supports a range of fungi which would not exist in pure Scots pine stands. Rowan and aspen often occur together with birch within the pinewoods.

4.8.2 Aspen in the native pinewoods

Aspen is rather a scarce tree in Scotland but occurs as a permanent component of the native pinewoods and upland oak-birch woodland habitats (Mason et al. 2004; Rodwell 1991a). It has noticeable population concentrations, particularly within the extensive pinewoods of Strathspey, Deeside and the Beauly catchment. Aspen also occurs in a number of areas that are now dominated by coniferous plantations or open heathland, but which probably once carried native pinewood – for example in parts of east Sutherland. Aspen in Scotland, at the present time, mainly reproduces asexually (by clonal suckering) as it can only set seed after unusually warm, dry summers (Worrell 1995). As with hazel, climatic conditions within the Boreal phase were probably much more suitable for aspen to reproduce sexually than they are today. Most aspen occurs in small stands consisting of only one distinct clone (or a few). There are some larger, multi-clonal aspen woodlands (particularly adjoining the Strathspey native pinewoods) which apparently have twenty to thirty different clones represented among several hundred aspen stems. This clonal reproduction system makes aspen a tough and persistent component of Scotland's native woodlands. Aspen supports an important range of specialist biodiversity species which depend on it alone. These include the aspen hoverfly, feeding on decaying aspen wood, the aspen bracket fungus and the aspen bristle-moss (Cosgrove and Amphlett 2002; Parrott and MacKenzie 2009; Wilson 2009).

4.8.3 Juniper in the native pinewoods

Juniper occurs as a localised understorey shrub within the native pinewood ecosystem. It can take either the prostrate form (a low-growing bush) or the fastigiate form (a thin, columnar-shaped, small tree). It is rather more common in the eastern pinewoods (e.g. Strathspey) than further west.

4.9 MONTANE SCRUB – DWARF BIRCH, JUNIPER AND WILLOW

As mentioned above, the montane scrub habitats of Scotland usually occur beyond the upper limit of the native pinewoods at 600–900m asl. In parts of Scotland where native pinewood is absent, montane scrub can be found above upland oak-birch woodland or non-native conifer plantations. Although the extent of montane scrub is now much less in Scotland, as compared, for example, with Norway, it is probably rather under-recorded by botanical surveys because of its small stature and inaccessibility (Forestry Commission Scotland 2014). There are several well-known sites where it has been observed over time, as at Ben Lawers in Perthshire and on the Cairngorm plateau. However, increasing amounts are now being recorded in association with higher elevation conifer plantations, for example in Galloway. As grazing pressure from hill sheep flocks has declined, montane scrub is now recovering locally in those montane areas where muirburn for red grouse and red deer browsing are less severe.

The main shrub species within the scrub are juniper, which can extend well beyond the upper edge of the pinewood zone, downy birch in its dwarfed form (ssp. *tortuosa*), true dwarf birch (*Betula nana*), mountain willow (*Salix arbuscula*) and downy willow (*Salix lapponum*). In a few places, stunted and contorted Scots pine is also found, resembling the characteristic *Krummholz* treeline woodland familiar from European and Scandinavian mountains. The Creag Fhiaclath site in the Cairngorms is especially well known for this (Mason et al. 2004). Where juniper is dominant, the scrub may reflect the NVC W19 juniper woodland community (Rodwell 1991a). Where willow dominates, the scrub may reflect the NVC W20 willow scrub community, sometimes with greater woodrush dominant beneath the willow. Dwarfed forms of birch can be common in either case, usually *Betula pubescens* ssp. *tortuosa* at lower elevations, with *Betula nana* coming in higher on the hillside and plateaux.

Montane scrub has an ecological importance well beyond its current limited extent in Scotland. It provides a natural ecological transition between woodland and open heathland and moorland habitats. As such it serves as habitat for a number of bird species which prefer to operate at the interface between the two, most notably the black grouse. The shelter provided by the woodland, albeit only a few metres tall, also helps to protect a number of rare plant species. Ben Lawers is a famous botanical site for the study of montane and Arctic-Alpine vegetation communities.

The condition of much of the montane scrub in Scotland is poor, due to a history of heather burning to promote new growth for livestock and red grouse and excessive browsing by red deer and grazing by hill sheep (Gilbert et al. 1997). Heavy trampling by hill-walkers can also damage the vegetation on a more localised basis, as can colonisation by natural regeneration of introduced conifer species where montane scrub adjoins plantations. Due to harsh climates and infertile soils found in montane scrub areas, recovery of vegetation from impacts is often very slow. As a result of the accumulating loss of montane scrub over a long period, there are few locations in Scotland where it is now possible to observe the natural transition from native pinewood through montane scrub to sub-alpine heath. By contrast, in the mountains of Norway there has been far better retention of these natural ecotones. Efforts are currently under way by Forestry Commission Scotland, SNH and Trees for Life to promote conservation and recovery of montane scrub woodland in Scotland, both in association with native pinewoods and as part of naturalisation of forestry plantations.

4.10 Historical management

There is good documentary evidence for organised management for timber production within certain of the existing native pinewoods over the past 300 years and an increasing body of evidence from both archaeological and veteran tree studies that suggests a much longer history of less formalised management for timber, wood pasture and non-timber forest products (Aldhous 1995; Anderson 1967; Mason et al. 2004; Smout 1997, 2003, 2006; Smout et al. 2005; Steven and Carlisle 1959).

4.10.1 Management for timber production

The best evidence for organised forestry management within the native pinewoods, for periods prior to 1900, refers to those in mid-Strathspey (Abernethy, Glenmore, Rothiemurchus and Glenfeshie) and on Deeside. During the period 1780–1830, these pinewoods were intensively harvested to supply markets for building and naval timber throughout Great Britain, especially during and after the Napoleonic Wars. Both local landowners and timber merchants from further south were involved. Timber was apparently harvested across significant areas on an exploitative system, leaving only inaccessible or poorly formed stems. Some material was sawn locally, but considerable amounts were exported as 'round timber' by flotation down the major rivers, notably down the River Spey to Garmouth. Much discussion has surrounded the extent of pine regeneration after these fellings. As mentioned above, most 'natural' pine stands existing today tend to consist of stems established before ~1830, with a lengthy regeneration pause prior to recent conservation interventions. It appears that an organised approach was taken to securing localised natural regeneration during the period 1680–1830, probably involving periodic exclusion of livestock by a combination of temporary fencing and careful herding/shepherding. Increment-coring studies have found evidence for episodes of regeneration, consistent with such efforts. Planting may also have been employed to supplement natural regeneration. After 1840, increasing numbers of sheep and red deer prevented natural regeneration. In native pinewoods in the west Highlands, felling from 1600 to 1800 seems to have been more exploitative and regeneration efforts less determined, certainly less successful. As a result, timber harvesting contributed to losses of area in some western pinewoods, in combination with the poorer climates during the Little Ice Age period.

4.10.2 Traditional management systems

In those parts of the native pinewoods that were not subjected to organised forestry management prior to the twentieth century, informal utilisation by the local population was the norm. As in other parts of the world, this was a mixed picture, combining long-term over-exploitation of the resource with localised attempts at conservation. Most of the pinewoods probably had a relatively open structure from prehistoric times onwards, with a prevalence of older, heavily branched trees of poor form. The ground was used, at least seasonally, for the pasturing of domestic cattle under informal wood-pasture systems. These would restrict, if rarely completely prevent, natural regeneration of Scots pine in the more accessible areas, but had a lesser effect on pinewoods further from settlements or on inaccessible slopes. Whether any deliberate attempt to foster natural regeneration was made is uncertain. Pine trees were also harvested on a sporadic basis for local construction and fuel, with some evidence for modification of individual trees to make 'pine candles' for lighting. This would have created small openings that could have allowed gap-phase regeneration where livestock numbers were sufficiently controlled. From the 1840s onwards, cattle were replaced by much larger numbers of hill sheep and red deer in most areas.

4.11 Towards pinewood conservation and expansion

4.11.1 The century prior to Steven and Carlisle

During the century from 1840 until the publication of Steven and Carlisle's book *The Native Pinewoods of Scotland* in 1959, the majority of native pinewood remnants continued to decline in both extent and, particularly, condition. This was due mainly to a combination of woodland neglect, persistent over-grazing by hill sheep flocks and intensive browsing by red deer maintained for sport shooting. There were some exceptions, again primarily the pinewoods of Strathspey and mid-Deeside, which remained under more active and effective forestry management with extraction of timber to market by steam railway. With the emergency timber demands of the two world wars, a renewed episode of heavy felling in the more accessible pinewoods was followed by forestry replanting, often with non-native species such as Sitka spruce and lodgepole pine. Some of the pinewoods of the Great Glen group, such as those in Glen Garry and Glen Mallie, were extensively replanted with spruce by the Forestry Commission. This was also the case, to a rather lesser extent, in the Beauly catchment (Glen Cannich, Cougie and Glen Affric) and at Glenmore in Strathspey. Fire damage, especially associated with wartime military training, affected some of the Great Glen pinewoods. However, on the positive side, botanical field tours in Scotland between 1910 and 1940, mainly by English and Continental European ecologists, led to increasing recognition of the wider scientific interest of the native pinewoods. This stimulated the Forestry Commission to designate a number of experimental reserves within those pinewood areas that they owned, including the Black Wood of Rannoch, Glenmore and Glen Loy (Coille Phuiteachan). These became the subject of long-term research and monitoring from the 1930s onwards, and were protected to some degree from wartime emergency fellings and, to a large extent, from under-planting, although introduced species were planted in areas adjoining some of these reserved areas. Silvicultural trials within the Glenmore pinewoods and long-term ecological monitoring at the Black Wood of Rannoch have been of particular significance in informing conservation management in the native pinewoods (Mason et al. 2004). After the last war, the Nature Conservancy established a nature reserve within the Beinn Eighe pinewoods of Wester Ross, also serving as a focus for pinewood regeneration studies (Laughton Johnston and Balharry 2001).

4.11.2 The impact of Steven and Carlisle

Surveys leading to publication of Steven and Carlisle's book drew attention to the fact that many of the native pinewood remnants lacked natural regeneration, and were reducing in extent due to a combination of mortality, grazing and burning. Being the 'first of its kind', at least in the context of Britain, the book achieved a significant impact on policy-makers in both the forestry and nature-conservation 'camps'. There was an increasing commitment at least to protection of the existing pinewood remnants, and later to more active conservation and expansion work. This was a reaction delayed by fifteen years, with most of the increased conservation effort following establishment of the Native Pinewoods Discussion Group and organisation of a scientific symposium, held at Aviemore in 1975. Action for the native pinewoods, both on the national forests and on private estates, under new grant-aid mechanisms, was concentrated on two aims: (1) securing natural regeneration by fencing and deer control and (2) expansion by new planting within the Caledonian Pinewood Zone. These have now been pursued over thirty to forty years, with clear results beginning to show.

4.12 PINEWOOD REGENERATION – DIVERGENT APPROACHES

By the mid-1980s, the large hill sheep flocks were disappearing from many native pinewood areas for wider agro-economic reasons. However, red deer numbers continued to increase across many areas of the Highlands and were seen as the major challenge to the regeneration of the native pinewoods. Current estimates are for between 300,000 and 350,000 red deer across Scotland. Roe deer and introduced sika deer also present a more localised challenge to pinewood regeneration. Two major approaches to addressing this problem are (1) reduction of deer numbers by humane culling and (2) exclusion of deer from regeneration areas by forestry fencing. Deer culling has been successfully implemented at a number of pinewood locations within the Caledonian Pinewood Zone where management is focused predominantly on habitat restoration – for example the SNH reserve at Beinn Eighe, the RSPB reserve at Abernethy Forest, the National Trust for Scotland's Mar Lodge Estate and the private Glenfeshie Estate. Regeneration has improved significantly at these sites recently. However, the very low deer population necessary to permit native tree regeneration (around five deer per square kilometre) makes this approach difficult to reconcile with continuation of commercial deer stalking on Highland estates. A suggested move to 'Continental style' forest deer hunting has found limited favour in Scotland to date. Those estates that try to combine pinewood conservation with sporting usage (e.g. the National Trust for Scotland's Mar Lodge property on Deeside) have found it difficult to secure pine regeneration by deer culling alone. Many properties with a sporting or commercial forestry interest continue to employ deer fencing, often coupled with a supporting regime of sport stalking. Fences pose a number of practical issues in terms of installation, maintenance and repair after severe weather, and also create a localised risk of bird-strike mortality for the capercaillie. Fencing is a proven, reliable method of protecting pine regeneration where it has already established, but is less effective at encouraging fresh regeneration, as complete exclusion of deer browsing allows strong growth of competing vegetation. There is also a philosophical objection on the part of many nature conservationists and upland ecologists to the artificial fencing of landscapes into segregated management units.

4.13 Expanding pinewood area by new planting

In order to accelerate the expansion of the native pinewood cover in Highland Scotland, approaches based on encouraging natural regeneration have been supplemented by promoting the establishment of new native pinewoods by planting on private estates under forestry grant-aid schemes. A significant issue that arose early in this process was that of genetic conservation. Many plantations of Scots pine have been established within Scotland over the past 300 years. Those within the Caledonian Pinewood Zone have often employed locally sourced planting stock from the native pinewoods, but others, especially since the last war, used non-local stock. A proportion of the latter derived from German and other Continental pine populations. There are varying scientific opinions as to whether use of non-local planting stock represents a conservation threat to native populations in their vicinity, once cross-pollination begins as the planted trees mature. It must be remembered that most native populations of Scots pine within Scotland are originally descended from mainland European ancestors, due to the migration routes of post-glacial recolonisation. However, genetic and monoterpene resin studies have produced evidence for genetic differentiation between the different populations in the native pinewoods (Aldhous 1995; Forrest 1992; Mason et al. 2004). In the cases of some of the western population groups, these differences were of greater magnitude and may suggest western, oceanic glacial refugia for these populations. This inherited genetic diversity, although not always significant for present-day ecological adaptation, is worthy of conservation as a component of forest biodiversity. There is also a clear east-west gradient of adaptive variation across Scotland, such that if pine from an eastern Highland seed source is planted in the far west, it tends to fail, whereas west Highland seed sources grow slowly if planted in the east. For these reasons, even if mechanisms were only partially understood, it was decided to sub-divide the Caledonian Pinewood Zone into seven 'biochemical zones' (Mason et al. 2004) with seed for new planting schemes to be taken from native populations within the same zone as the planting site. More controversially, stands of planted pine of non-Scottish origins have been removed from the vicinity of some native pinewoods, most notably at Glen Affric.

Establishment of new pinewoods by planting onto exposed upland sites has not always proved straightforward. Sites involved have not carried woodland for millennia in some cases and soil deterioration and vegetation changes have occurred since. Traditional forestry site preparation by cultivation, drainage, and herbicide and mineral fertiliser application has become unpopular with nature conservationists, leading to adoption of 'minimum-intervention' approaches. However, these have sometimes left young pine plantations struggling in water-logged, infertile and poorly aerated soils, with strong heather competition. As a result, establishment has been patchy.

4.14 Recent developments in pinewood management

Recent years have seen more emphasis on active conservation management within existing native pinewood remnants and associated maturing Scots pine plantations (Mason et al. 2004). Aided by effective deer-control measures, regeneration is improving at many sites. Key techniques include:

- Diversification and naturalisation of stand structure, especially in maturing Scots pine plantations, but also in even-aged naturally regenerated populations, in order to improve future opportunities for distributed natural regeneration and increased biodiversity values.
- Continued removal of introduced conifers (and locally *Rhododendron ponticum*) from native pinewoods, followed by deer fencing to protect young Scots pine naturally regenerating onto the cleared ground.
- Management of pinewood ground vegetation by controlled burning and introduction of conservation cattle grazing to improve ground conditions for natural regeneration of Scots pine and to promote increased *Vaccinium* cover in support of resident capercaillie populations.

- Restoration of lost species diversity, both by encouragement and planting of minority tree species (e.g. birch, aspen, holly, juniper) and by trial reintroduction of extinct animal species (elk, wild boar, cattle).
- Development of sustainable systems for harvesting of sawn timber and woodfuel from native pinewoods in support of rural development and renewable energy initiatives, also contributing to much-needed structural diversification and natural regeneration in pinewood stands.
- Management of the potential threats posed by disease to Scots pine and juniper populations in Scotland. The fungus-like pathogen *Phytophthora austrocedrae* is now seriously affecting wild juniper populations in some parts of Scotland. The needle-cast fungus *Dothistroma septosporum* poses a serious but as yet unquantified threat to Scots pine within native pinewoods. The effects to date have been more severe on plantations of introduced Corsican pine (*Pinus nigra v. laricio*) at Culbin and lodgepole pine (*Pinus contorta*) across upland Scotland (see Figure 4.1). However, the disease has been found in native pinewoods and it may become necessary to restrict planting of nursery stock in these areas and to implement 'ventilation' thinning of thicket stage regeneration. Some commentators suggest that it is now inappropriate to plant Scots pine in areas where natural regeneration can be expected to occur, both to limit risks from disease and to favour natural woodland processes – RSPB proposals for pine planting at Abernethy have proven controversial.

FIGURE 4.1 *Stand of lodgepole pine affected by* Dothistroma *blight. Copyright: Dr Scott McG. Wilson.*

CHAPTER FIVE

Oak, birch and aspen woodlands

5.1 Historical development

This chapter will deal in detail with the native oak and birch woodlands of Scotland. These include extensive upland birch and upland oak woodlands occurring primarily on relatively infertile soils, but also smaller remnants of lowland mixed deciduous woodland over soils of moderate fertility. The recent Native Woodland Survey of Scotland (NWSS) (Forestry Commission Scotland 2014) identified upland birch woodland as the most extensive native woodland type in Scotland (~91,000ha), slightly exceeding the native pinewoods in area. Upland oakwoods and lowland mixed deciduous woodlands are less extensive at ~19,000ha and ~23,000ha respectively. Of the lowland mixed deciduous woodland, half is oak-dominated woodland and half ash-dominated. The latter category is covered with upland mixed ashwoods in Chapter 6.

Although many of the principal tree species now found within the birch and oak woodlands, including oak, birch, rowan and hazel, had first colonised Scotland during the Boreal phase (H. J. B. Birks 1989), oak woodland did not mature in Scotland until the Atlantic phase, from around 7,500 years BP (Dickson 1993; Tipping 1994). The populations of oak present naturally within Britain today mainly survived the last glaciation in refugia within Spain and Portugal (Iberia) (Hubert and Cottrell 2007). A western route of colonisation along the Atlantic seaboard is therefore probable (H. J. B. Birks 1989). Oak is a moderately shade-tolerant, and heavy-seeded, tree species, and hence was unable to expand as rapidly as the pioneer species such as birch and aspen. Oak also prefers greater climatic warmth and better developed soils. Its main mechanism of post-glacial spread was transport by wildlife, particularly jays and squirrels, carrying it into landscapes of pre-existing open-canopied pine-birch-hazel woodland.

Between 7,500 and 5,000 years BP, oak-dominated woodlands steadily displaced boreal pine-birch-hazel woods from lowland and southern Scotland. Only in the far north and west did pine-birch-hazel woodlands persist at lower elevations after 6,000 years BP (Tipping 1994). Oak woodlands had also displaced pine-birch-hazel woodlands throughout England and Wales, locally reaching 450m asl in Cumbria, leaving insufficient 'climatic space' for pine to persist, even on the hilltops. Areas of Scotland where oak woodland became dominant had, and generally still have, brown soils, and this preference, together with climatic factors, limited its spread. There is little evidence for oak being able to colonise areas that had already developed podzols, ironpan soils or ericaceous vegetation, which are typical of today's native pinewoods. The notable role of birch and hazel in woodlands of the earlier Boreal phase may have been significant in preparing the soil conditions necessary for oak to spread later (Miles 1985). Early oak woodlands were of oak-birch-hazel, with ash-elm not expanding in Scotland until the Atlantic phase (H. J. B. Birks 1989; Tipping 1994).

The oak woodlands of Scotland had a fairly short period of natural development between initial expansion and the onset of significant human woodland clearance and modification during the later Atlantic phase. This is the period that ecologists often call the 'post-glacial maximum', 'climatic woodland climax' or '*Urwald*/wildwood' and it may not have lasted much more than 2,000 years. Early human impacts would have modified the structure of woodlands more than their extent, opening the canopy by use of burning and influence of grazing, with localised felling. Oak woodlands on the lighter coastal soils would have been affected early, followed by those in accessible upland areas. Oak-elm woodlands on heavier lowland soils would have remained intact longer (Dickson 1993; Smout 1993; Tipping 1994).

5.2 Historical distribution

During the Atlantic phase (7,500– 5,000 years BP), oak- and birch-dominated woodlands occupied the majority of the Scottish land area below 200m asl (Tipping 1994). Certainly in areas south of the Great Glen, only 'special sites' would have carried other native woodland types (or open habitats) below that contour. Very fertile sites in valley bottoms or over limestone/basic igneous geologies carried richer ash-elm-hazel woodlands, but with oak remaining as a component – these woodland types are dealt with in Chapter 6. Wetter sites (raised bogs, fens and riparian margins) carried either open habitats or alder-willow woodlands, with birch present in many cases (to be covered in Chapter 7). In the far north-western Highlands there are areas of exposed land below 200m asl, in Caithness, Sutherland and Ross, where birch-hazel-rowan woodland is found today with no pine or oak present – these areas are beyond the climatic tolerance of oak. In many parts of the country, upland birch woodland extends above the altitudinal range of oak, into the 300–600m zone. There are some instances of oak itself extending above 300m in Scotland, for example Craigendarroch Wood at Ballater, reaching close to 400m asl. However, these may be plantations onto old birch or pinewood sites.

Within the range of oak woodland in Scotland there are significant ecological differences between (1) the upland oak woodlands of acid soils in the exposed western districts and inland at higher elevations and (2) the oak-elm-hazel woodlands of heavier soils in the eastern and central Lowlands, predominantly below 150m asl (Rodwell 1991a; Peterken 1993). These differences may, however, have been less pronounced in the Atlantic phase than today, as decline in soil fertility in the 'acid soil' areas had not proceeded so far. In some localities these oak woodland types do merge.

While oak woodland remains fairly abundant in many 'Atlantic' west coast and Highland margin districts, it has been extensively removed from its former ranges in the Borders, the eastern Lowlands and the Central Belt and from many parts of the eastern and central Highlands. Only a small proportion of the original total area remains, and much of this has been heavily modified by management. By contrast with the record for the native pinewoods, it appears that natural climatic and soil deterioration have played a secondary role in the retreat of oak and birch woodlands in Scotland. The removal of the oak woodlands particularly has been mainly a product of human clearance for agriculture and unsustainable levels of browsing and grazing by their livestock. While there was much local variation in the timing of oak and birch woodland removal, the following pattern is suggested by archaeological and palaeo-ecological evidence (Dickson 1993; Ritchie and Ritchie 1991; Simmons 2000; Tipping 1994):

Neolithic – removal of oak-birch woodlands from lighter soils in the north-east lowlands and islands, particularly in those districts with good coastal/riverine access. These areas have the most abundant Neolithic remains. The key mechanism was livestock browsing with some localised clearance by fire and/or felling.

Bronze Age – widespread attrition of oak-birch woodlands in the more accessible parts of the uplands by seasonal livestock browsing and some targeted 'slash and burn' or tree felling to enable agricultural land-uses nearer to fixed settlements.

Iron Age/Roman – major impacts on oak-elm-hazel woodland of heavier lowland soils, initially near to settlements and transport corridors, with concentrated impacts on some upland oakwoods for agricultural purposes. Initial felling to produce timber/fuel becomes a more significant factor.

Medieval onward – continued removal of oak from the upland margins (especially in the Borders for sheep husbandry) and progressive elimination from eastern/central lowland areas by exploitative harvesting and agricultural land-take (Smout 1997, 2003; Smout et al. 2005).

5.3 Current geographical distribution

Oak and birch woodlands are found today in Scotland only in those areas that have escaped the processes of removal identified above. The reasons for such survival are basically two-fold: (1) inaccessibility/unsuitability for timber harvesting and agricultural conversion and (2) deliberate retention/protection for utilitarian woodland values. While some of the least accessible upland oak and birch woodlands on steep slopes, together with birch woodlands on rough lowland terrain in the far north, might have been thought unprofitable for agriculture of any sort, this is a less important factor than in the native pinewoods. Much semi-natural oak and birch woodland which survives today in Scotland does so mainly as a result of human 'decisions' to retain woodland cover over time. These retentions were almost always accompanied by some modification of the woodland structure and species composition, as will be discussed later in the chapter. Having said this, there are several clearly identifiable geographical concentrations of retained oak-dominated woodland (Roberts et al. 1992):

- **Argyll, Lochaber and Wester Ross.** The largest areas of oak woodland in Scotland are the Atlantic oakwoods of the west Highlands, many of which were managed during the period 1650–1850 as industrial oak coppices (see Plate 9a). Their regular structure continues to reflect that history of use. These woodlands are developed on acid soils and have few other tree species present, birch, rowan and holly being local exceptions. There are major complexes of acid Atlantic oak woodland in Argyll, Lorne, Morvern, Ardnamurchan, Lochaber and Wester Ross.
- **Southern Highland margins.** There are also extensive, formerly coppiced, upland oak woodlands along the margins of the Highland Boundary Fault, for example at Loch Lomond, Loch Katrine, Comrie/Drummond and Killiecrankie. These tend to be somewhat less acid sites and the woodlands contain more birch and hazel. The Aberfeldy, Pitlochry and Blair Atholl areas contain some of the most significant upland silver birch woodlands, although these may be partly artificial.
- **Dumfries and Galloway.** There is also a notable concentration of upland acid oak woodlands in Dumfries and Galloway, particularly at Glentrool, Wood of Cree, Carsluith, Castramont, Kirkconnel, Hannaston and Lochwood Castle. These also have a history of coppice working.
- **Aberdeenshire and Moray Firth.** There are a number of oak woodlands in north-eastern Scotland, including those at Spinningdale in Sutherland, Drummondreach on the Black Isle, Cawdor in Nairnshire, Elgin in Moray, Craigdarroch in Ross-shire and Dinnet and Craigendarroch on Deeside. These woodlands are a mixed group in terms of their ecology and management history. Some may have been restocked with oak over the past 300 years and some are transitional to the lowland oakwoods.
- **Clyde Valley and Central Belt.** These include surviving remnants of the lowland mixed deciduous woodland of better soils, much of which was removed in prehistory. The valley woodland complexes on the River Clyde between Lanark and Glasgow are the most extensive and natural of these, with smaller examples found at the Ayr Gorge, Roslin Glen, the River Avon gorge at Linlithgow, Callendar Wood at Falkirk and Methven Wood near Perth. Some of these woodlands are transitional towards the richer ash-elm woodland type. Finally, there are the old deer parks or wood pastures at Cadzow (Lanark) and Dalkeith (Lothian). These last are heavily modified remnants of the natural oak-dominated woodlands of plateau sites in the Scottish lowlands, and may include some late-medieval oaks planted to enhance the parklands for hunting.

5.4 CURRENT ECOLOGICAL DISTRIBUTION

The oak-dominated woodlands of Scotland occupy primarily lowland and upland margin (or 'foothills') sites in Scotland below 300m asl. Upland birch woodlands can extend to between 300–600m asl without oak. Climates within these altitudinal zones vary considerably, with four sub-climates being clearly identifiable (Pyatt et al. 2001):

- The **warm-wet** (and some **warm-moist**) 'Atlantic rainforest' climates of the west Highland coast, with very high rainfall throughout the year and a distinct lack of severe frost conditions in most winters. This climate is experienced by the coastal oak woodlands in Argyll, Lochaber and Wester Ross.
- The **cool-moist** and **cool-wet** conditions of the upland fringes of the Scottish Highlands and Southern Uplands. This is the climate experienced by most upland birch woodlands, and also by birchwoods at lower altitude in the north-western Highlands (e.g. in Sutherland) where oak is beyond the limit of its climatic tolerance. Some upland oak woodlands also experience this climate in more inland areas such as Galloway, Stirlingshire, Inverness-shire and Perthshire.
- The **warm-moist** conditions of the eastern lowland districts of the inner Moray Firth, the Lothians, the Clyde Valley, Berwickshire, Fife, Angus and Aberdeenshire. These conditions apply to most lowland oakwoods such as Cawdor and Dalkeith. Eastern areas such as Berwickshire may suffer significant summer moisture deficits, especially in dry years, and are now transitional to the warm-dry climates of eastern England.
- The **cool-moist,** more continental, climates of parts of the eastern Highlands, for example the valleys of the Rivers Spey, Don and Dee at mid-elevations. Significant winter frost is experienced in most years. Upland birch predominates over oak in many of these areas, for example around Aviemore, but there remain small pockets of upland oakwood, for example at Dinnet and Ballater (Craigendarroch). The natural climatic limits on oak in these areas are still open to ecological debate.

Oak and birch woodlands occur over a range of geological types within Scotland, but the Dalradian metamorphic rocks of the western and southern Highlands, the Ordovician and Silurian shales of the Southern Uplands and the red sandstones of the eastern lowlands are predominant. These are primarily rock types of low to moderate fertility. Upland birch woodlands, without oak present, extend on to the Moine schists and intrusive granites of the northern Highlands with inherently lower fertility. Lightly stocked, stunted birch-dominated woodlands occupy very poor Precambrian rocks.

Almost all oak-dominated woodland in Scotland occurs over brown-earth soils, but these include some very acidic brown earths with noticeable leaching of soil nutrients (see Chapter 2). There is considerable discussion among ecologists as to whether oak woodland can persist where soils develop into classic podzols. In some cases, in very high-rainfall areas with a history of intensive oak coppicing and birch removal, oak is found on sites with a bleached soil E-horizon and a dense ground vegetation of the ericoid sub-shrubs (Rodwell 1991a). These conditions would usually be regarded as more characteristic of native pinewoods. It may be that, unless birch and hazel were maintained within these woodlands, oak would gradually decline due to soil infertility. The oak woodlands of drier areas in lowland Scotland are developed on heavier brown-earth (and a minority of surface-water gley) soils that are much more resistant to this type of nutrient depletion. In these situations even artificially pure oak woodland is likely to be able to persist indefinitely. Upland birch woodland occupies a much wider range of soils, such as acid brown earths, podzols, flushed peats and rankers.

5.5 Stand dynamics, structure and regeneration

Oak woodlands in Scotland have either the sessile oak (*Quercus petraea*) or the pedunculate oak (*Quercus robur*) dominant in the canopy or mixtures of these two (Rodwell 1991a; Peterken 1993). These are two very similar oak species that can hybridise readily. They can sometimes be distinguished by their leaf shape and acorn stalk length, but there are many intermediate and hybrid forms, which makes this problematic. In England and other parts of Europe, the sessile oak prefers freely draining and upland soils and the pedunculate oak prefers heavier lowland soils, but this distinction is much less clear in the conditions of Scotland. Some ecologists have argued that the sessile oak is the only native oak in Scotland, with the pedunculate oak having been introduced over recent centuries. Even if both species are accepted as native, it is certainly known that pedunculate oak was preferred for plantings within oak woodlands during the period of industrial coppicing activity (Tittensor 1970; Smout 2005). The two birch species – silver birch (*Betula pendula*) and downy birch (*Betula pubescens*) – both occur within upland oak woodlands and also form upland birch woods elsewhere. These species do not readily hybridise in Scotland and there is little doubt that silver birch prefers free-draining soils at lower elevations, with downy birch found more on upland gleys and peaty soils (Worrell and Malcolm 1998).

Other tree species found frequently within upland oak and birch woodlands are rowan (*Sorbus aucuparia*), holly (*Ilex aquifolium*) and aspen (*Populus tremula*). Yew (*Taxus baccata*) is found locally in association with some upland oak woodlands in the southern Highlands, but its native status in Scotland is disputed. Scots pine (*Pinus sylvestris*) and juniper (*Juniperus communis*) occur in some upland birch woodlands, but rarely together with oak. Hazel (*Corylus avellana*) occurs frequently in the more lowland oakwoods, and is also common in birch woodlands of the far north-west. It is likely that hazel has been deliberately removed in the past from some coppiced oak woodlands – by contrast with lowland England, oak was the preferred species for coppice in Scotland, with hazel often regarded as a 'barren timber' (Smout 1997, 2003; Smout et al. 2005). By comparison, holly has expanded naturally due to its greater shade-tolerance. Ash occurs as a minor component in some richer lowland oak woodlands across Scotland. Elm was previously a significant component of lowland mixed woodlands but has been drastically reduced by several outbreaks of Dutch elm disease (Rackham 2003). Introduced sycamore (*Acer pseudoplatanus*) and beech (*Fagus sylvatica*) can colonise oakwoods where elm has failed.

We saw in Chapter 3 that there are ecological difficulties in understanding how oak woodlands in Scotland could have been perpetuated naturally. The role of gap formation by natural mortality and windthrow was certainly most important, but there may have been a significant influence from browsing and grazing animals even before human wood-pasture management became commonplace (Vera 2000).

Unfortunately, there are few oak woodlands within Scotland today that are successfully regenerating. Many of the former industrial oak coppices have a dense, even-aged pole-timber structure, which is rather artificial and does not admit sufficient light for seedling oak regeneration. Most oak stands remain too immature (at 100–150 years since the last coppicing cycle) for natural gap-formation by windthrow or mortality of canopy trees to have become significant. Oak in Scotland only produces abundant acorns or 'mast' at most every five to ten years. Browsing by deer and livestock is often too persistent for regenerating oak seedlings to survive in these woodlands, and this is also common in wood pastures and deer parks in the lowland situation. Some form of human intervention, in the forms of deer culling, fenced replanting or deliberate protection of seedlings, is normally required to secure oak regeneration. By contrast, in the absence of heavy deer browsing and sheep grazing, birch and rowan can usually regenerate fairly successfully in open woodlands and on surrounding open land. Although birch is more light-demanding than oak, it produces seed much more frequently and larger numbers of wind-dispersed seed allow birch to regenerate more widely beyond the existing woodland edge. Jays and squirrels can carry acorns out of oak woodlands into more open areas, where they too can establish (Worrell 2014).

5.6 Botanical interest

Oak and birch woodlands in Scotland are associated with a number of relatively simple vegetation communities. These basically correspond to the NVC communities W17 (upland acid oak-birch woodland), W11 (upland oak-birch woodland of medium fertility sites), W10 (lowland oak woodland of medium to high fertility sites) and W4 (wet birch woodland) (Rodwell 1991a). The W4 type will be covered in Chapter 7 on wet woodlands. Aspen woodland is currently not recognised as a distinct type within the National Vegetation Classification. Richer lowland mixed deciduous woodlands with a significant component of ash, corresponding to NVC W8, will be dealt with in Chapter 6 alongside upland mixed ash woodlands (W9). NVC W8 occurs locally in Scotland, mainly in lowland river valleys. There is some discussion among ecologists as to whether NVC community W16 (lowland acid oak-birch woodland) occurs in Scotland – a few dry, acid sites around the inner Moray Firth and in East Lothian arguably belong to that type rather than to W17/W11. With the exception of W4, oak and/or birch can be found in all these communities – under Scottish conditions, upland birch woodland variants of communities W17 and W11 can be semi-permanent, rather than successional to oak woodland, as is usual in England and Wales.

Where birch is dominant over oak in the canopy, the ground vegetation tends to be of a more light-demanding grass or grass-bracken type, whereas a dense cover of oak favours the more shade-tolerant plants, including blaeberry, woodrush, ferns and bramble. While not particularly rich in vascular plants, oak and birch woodlands in Scotland do support some species of individual conservation importance such as the small cow-wheat (*Melampyrum sylvaticum*). However, most conservation attention is focused on the acid 'Atlantic' oakwood (NVC W11/17) habitats of the west coast (known at the European level as 'old oak woodlands of the British Isles with hard fern'), for their associated lower plants (mosses, lichens and liverworts) and fungi (see Plate 9b). These woodlands are sometimes referred to as 'Scotland's rainforest' due to their climate and very high species diversity in epiphytes. A number of existing botanical publications (e.g. Phillips 1994) assist with field recognition and identification of these species, which can be demanding, and it is not intended to deal with these in detail here. Many require a stable, moist and shaded habitat, and this can impose conservation constraints on woodland operations that might open up old coppiced oak stands to encourage increased natural regeneration (Harmer et al. 2010; Harmer and Thompson 2013; Thompson et al. 2003).

5.7 Wildlife and biodiversity

Oak and birch woodlands in Scotland provide valuable habitat for a number of mammal species, including badger, wild cat, pine marten and red squirrel, but are not as strongly associated with these 'charismatic' mammals as are the native pinewoods. However, Scottish oak woodlands in particular are of noted conservation importance for their migratory bird species and a wide range of invertebrates, including butterflies, moths and deadwood beetles.

Among the birds, the black grouse (*Tetrao tetrix*) makes use of woodland-edge habitat associated with upland birch woodlands in a similar way to that adjacent to native pinewoods. The pied fly-catcher (*Ficedula hypoleuca*) (see Plate 9c), spotted fly-catcher (*Muscicapa striata*), wood warbler (*Phylloscopus sibilatrix*) and song thrush (*Turdus philomelos*) are examples of smaller bird species that are particularly noted within Scottish oak woodlands. The fly-catchers and the wood warbler are migratory insect feeders (over-wintering in Africa) which depend on the high populations of caterpillars and adult invertebrates within Scottish oak and birch woodlands in summer. Habitat conditions for bird species are usually best when there is good structural diversity, creating suitable conditions for nesting and feeding. A variable structure in woodland increases the number of ecological niches for invertebrates, enhancing biodiversity and ensuring food availability. Relatively few birds and invertebrates are adapted to closed-canopy woodland conditions, at least in Britain, where such habitats had become uncommon due to the long history of woodland management by coppicing and wood pasture. However, cessation of active management in oak coppices over the past century, coupled with coniferous under-planting in some cases, has artificially created extensive areas with dense canopies.

Invertebrates are also a valuable element of biodiversity in Scottish oak and birch woodlands (Chinery 2012). Oak supports an unusually high diversity of invertebrate species – some 400. Important groups include butterflies, moths, beetles and ants. The chequered skipper (*Carterocephalus palaemon*) and the pearl-bordered fritillary (*Boloria euphrosyne*) are the two most significant butterfly species for conservation in the Atlantic oakwoods (see Plate 9d). Lochaber is the main population centre for the chequered skipper within Britain. Again, a key requirement is structural diversity, with emphasis on openings or glades in the woodland, allowing growth of food plants, including grasses and violets. The argent and sable moth (*Rheumaptera hastata*) and the square spotted clay moth (*Xestia rhomboidea*) also use oak and birch woodland. Beetles are a key invertebrate group in oak and birch woodlands. These divide into two groups: those associated with living trees in mature woodland and those that are dependent on the deadwood resource. A diversity of deadwood (or 'saproxylic') beetles on a site is a good indication of ancient woodland cover, as these species require a continuity of suitable dead and dying trees. Due to the history of coppice and forestry management, the deadwood resource in many oak woodlands in Scotland is currently limited. An important exception are veteran trees found within some oak woodlands that have been managed as wood pasture and parkland – these contain a high proportion of standing deadwood, vital for beetle species. While the narrow-headed ant is essentially restricted to native pinewoods, the Scottish wood ant (*Formica aquilonia*), hairy wood ant (*Formica lugubris*) and shiny guest ant (*Formicoxensus nitidulus*) are found in upland oak-birch woods.

5.8 Birch and aspen woodlands in Scotland

Birch- and aspen-dominated woodlands in Scotland (see Plates 10a and 10b), lacking significant amounts of oak, fall into four major categories, reflecting ecological and historical development (Rodwell 1991a; Peterken 1993). These are:

- **Natural upland birchwoods** – these are 'permanent' upland birchwoods growing on sites that are climatically unsuitable for oak. Sites of this type occur extensively between sea level and around 400m asl in the far north and west of Scotland (Wester Ross, Caithness and Sutherland) and also in various other locations across the remainder of the country at 300–600m asl, above the local altitudinal limit of oak. Some upland birchwoods are found on sites that could potentially carry Scots pine, but where that species has never colonised or has been removed by human activity. There are concentrations of upland birchwoods in the Southern Uplands, Highland Perthshire and the Cairngorms/Grampians. Downy birch (*Betula pubescens*) very often dominates in this type of birch woodland. At lower elevations in the north-west, downy birch is found together with hazel, whereas at higher elevations inland, downy birch and rowan dominate with a little hazel and sometimes silver birch. Ground vegetation within these woodlands is similar to that of the acid or Atlantic oak woodlands (NVC W17). Aspen and juniper are localised associates, throughout the upland birchwoods. Birch-juniper woodlands above 400m asl tend towards montane scrub types discussed in Chapter 4, often being found in association with remnant native pinewoods.
- **Wet birchwoods** – these are birchwoods developed on sites that are unsuitable for the growth of oak or Scots pine due to poorly drained soils, and which are also too infertile for alder or willow woodland. They can occur at any elevation below the treeline. Downy birch (*Betula pubescens*) dominates in this type of birch woodland (NVC W4). Typical situations are basin mires and fens, receiving run-off from surrounding land surfaces, and raised bogs that have been subjected to artificial drainage. There are many woodlands of these types in central

and southern Scotland. Some birch woodlands, usually of low stature, can be found around the margins of blanket bogs, but they do not usually spread out on to the wet peat surface. Birch can also be found in some riparian woodlands, often with alder and willow. The vegetation found in wet birchwoods will be discussed in more detail in Chapter 7.

- **Successional birchwoods** – these are 'temporary' birchwoods that occur where there is no obvious climatic or soil factor that makes the site inherently unsuitable for oak. Many occur within areas where oak would be expected to be dominant (NVC W11). Silver birch (*Betula pendula*) is most common in these woodlands, but downy birch is also found. Oak may be absent due to a history of past human removal, with only birch surviving (or having recolonised the site following clearfelling). These woodlands include many of the attractive 'silver birchwoods' of Perthshire, Strathspey, Deeside and the inner Moray Firth. It is assumed that, given sufficient time, oak might recolonise, but this may take centuries in some cases. During this ecological succession, a competitive light-demanding vegetation of grass and bracken develops, which makes it difficult for oak to recolonise, even where a seed source is present. Grazing by red deer or sheep may also play a part in restricting oak regeneration. While the other types of birchwood are mainly of interest for nature conservation, the silver birch found within successional birchwoods can be valuable for production of fine timber for furniture and flooring, along the lines common in Scandinavia (Worrell 1999).
- **Clonal aspen stands** – these are stands dominated by aspen, but very often with some birch and rowan also present (NVC W17). Many occur along edges of forestry plantations and agricultural fields and along the embankments of roads and railway lines (Wilson 2009; Worrell 1995). The clonal reproductive habit of aspen allows it to persist for some time where conditions prevent seedling regeneration. Some sites where aspen dominates are likely to be too exposed or infertile for the growth of oak, especially in the north. Aspen is also associated with native pinewoods.

Both aspen and birch woodlands are important for a range of associated biodiversity species including fungi, bryophytes and invertebrates.

5.9 Historical management – wood pasture

For most of the period since the emergence of the oak-birch woodlands of Scotland, the majority may have been functioning as some form of informal upland wood pasture (Quelch 2000–1; Stiven and Holl 2004). We saw in Chapter 3 that there is considerable debate among ecologists as to how open these oak woodlands were prior to human influence, and as to how significant browsing by natural large herbivore populations was in determining their structure and natural regeneration systems. What is certain is that once human influence became established in many upland areas of Scotland, these woodlands began to be opened up by a combination of livestock grazing and burning across the wider landscape, and clearance for agriculture on a localised basis.

By contrast with the native pinewood areas, the soils within the oak-birch woodlands were often of sufficient fertility to support a combination of shifting cultivation and livestock husbandry over several centuries. The oak-birch woodland retained within the prehistoric 'cultural landscape' (H. H. Birks 1989) would have been predominantly on steeper slopes that could be used by livestock, at least seasonally, but were unsuitable for cultivation. Its density would have varied from accessible ground near settlements cleared of woodland to near-intact woodland canopies in the more inaccessible areas, but most would have been partly open pasture woodland. Tree species harmful to livestock, such as yew and elder, might have been removed, whereas those species producing edible nuts and fruit, such as hazel, were likely favoured. Abandoned former pasture woodland is still recognisable by a higher proportion of ancient veteran trees with a multi-stemmed canopy structure, created by pollarding.

In some parts of the country, oak-birch woodland was largely removed during prehistory, where rates of browsing, grazing and burning exceeded regeneration. Once the period of historical records is reached, there is evidence for deliberate regulation of woodland usage to preserve remaining cover, primarily as a source of timber supply and as a location for hunting by the medieval elites (Smout 1997, 2003; Smout et al. 2005). Many remaining examples of upland pasture woodland, for example at Glen Finglas in the Trossachs, have survived because they were incorporated into royal hunting forests centuries ago. This imposed restrictions on the levels of livestock browsing and woodfuel collection that local populations were permitted to undertake, preserving remaining woodlands. The model of the hunting forests, protected from most economic uses, is reflected in today's woodland nature reserves. The relatively few major areas of oak-birch woodland surviving in the lowlands were preserved through the medieval period as sources of construction timber (e.g. Cawdor) or as enclosed deer parks (see below). During the period 1650–1850, the value of upland oak coppices rose dramatically for charcoal and tanbark production (to supply iron-smelters and leather tanners) (Lindsay 1975, 1977; Smout 1997, 2003, 2005; Smout et al. 2005). This led to oak woodlands being physically enclosed in many parts of Scotland, to protect coppice regrowth from livestock browsing and unauthorised fuel-wood harvesting. Where these areas had earlier developed an open, pasture-woodland structure, a combination of natural regeneration and deliberate tree planting was used to increase stocking to the levels optimal for industrial coppice production. From the early to mid-1800s on, the amount of oak woodland under active wood-pasture management steadily declined, with increasing segregation of open grazing land from enclosed productive coppice woods and plantations.

5.10 Historical management – deer parks

We saw earlier that much of the lowland oak woodland cover of Scotland was cleared in prehistory, in favour of agricultural land-uses. However, some areas of this type of woodland had survived into the medieval period. One of the main mechanisms by which remnants of this type of woodland were retained within the landscape was as part of deliberately enclosed parklands around the medieval castles (Fletcher 2011;

Gilbert 1979). Although partly used for livestock production, the main purpose of these parks was to provide a convenient and secure area for deer hunting – they were in effect miniature versions of the more remote upland royal hunting forests referred to previously. In order to be able to use oak woodland for hunting on horseback, it needed to have an open structure through which it was possible to ride safely, but which offered sufficient shelter to hold deer within the park (see Plate 10c). This was normally accomplished by retaining a population of large, widely spaced trees (initially oaks, but later beech, sycamore and lime). The structure and species composition of the native woodland originally found on these sites was therefore significantly modified over time. A fence or 'pale', usually of wooden stakes, was constructed around the park to prevent deer from escaping and to exclude unauthorised livestock and potential predators (including human ones).

During the reigns of the medieval kings of Scotland in the period AD 1100–1500, the establishment of deer parks in Scotland was pursued at a number of locations, following the model set earlier in England. Some prominent surviving examples include Hamilton High Parks in Lanarkshire (also known as the 'Cadzow Oaks'), Dalkeith Park in Midlothian and Cumloden Deer Park/Knockmans Wood in Galloway. These sites each contain large numbers of veteran oaks, some of which may actually date back to the original establishment of the deer parks. There are also a number of smaller populations of similar veteran oaks elsewhere, for example at Darnaway Forest in Moray, Lochwood Castle in Dumfriesshire and Drum Castle on Deeside, which may well be fragments of former deer parks, largely lost to agriculture over later centuries. There are likely to have been many other examples, now completely lost. It is unclear in most cases whether the deer park was created from surviving native woodland on the site (e.g. by some form of 'thinning') or by organised tree planting onto open land. In many cases it may well have been a combination of both techniques. As time went on, there was a tendency for the deer-hunting purpose of many parks to decline, in favour of a 'designed landscape' form, aimed mainly at enhancing the appearance of the castle/house surrounds (McGowan and Dingwall 2011). This often involved the planting of individual trees or groups of trees into a landscape, with considerable use of non-native species such as beech, sycamore, lime, pine and larch within formal layouts, from the early seventeenth century. More naturalistic landscape styles were adopted after 1750. Some medieval deer parks were converted into designed landscapes between 1600 and 1850, for example Pollok Park near Glasgow and the 'policies' of Scone Palace and Drummond Castle, near Perth.

As well as being of historical importance and considerable landscape amenity, the surviving medieval deer parks (and remnants of these) are of great importance for nature conservation as they contain among the oldest living trees in Scotland. Trees in woodlands managed for timber production over the past 200–300 years were normally harvested by 150–200 years old in the case of oak, whereas many individuals in deer parks are at least 400–500 years old (e.g. at Dalkeith and Cadzow), and a few possibly older. This makes them very valuable for deadwood invertebrates, which depend on the standing deadwood which only appears in oak at such ages.

5.11 HISTORICAL MANAGEMENT – COPPICING

Coppicing is a traditional management system in British woodlands (Rackham 1990, 2003; Peterken 1993), aimed at producing a regular supply of small-diameter wood products for fuel, fencing and rustic building materials. Individual trees are 'stumped back' to produce a coppice stool from which a number of stems can then regrow. Many British native hardwoods, with the exception of beech and in some cases birch, coppice fairly readily. Cutting can be repeated on a regular basis, known as a 'coppicing cycle'. This can vary in length from a few years for fast-growing willow and poplar species on a good site, up to 20–25 years for oak on poor soils in western Scotland. In a formal coppicing system the woodland is divided into the same number of equal cutting areas (also known as 'coupes' or 'haggs') as there are years in the coppicing cycle. This allows for the working of one coupe per year, and an even flow of coppice material for the intended applications. The classic underwood coppices of southern England were typically managed on 7–20-year rotations (Rackham 2003), to produce coppice poles of 3–10cm diameter, meeting the requirements of specific craft industries. Coppice regrowth needs to be protected from browsing by livestock and deer for a period after each cutting cycle, and this was traditionally achieved by temporary fencing or 'dead hedging' using brash material from the felling. Successful coppicing becomes more difficult where there is intensive browsing pressure that cannot be well controlled.

We have limited information as to the use of coppice systems in prehistory, but there is some archaeological evidence for the resulting small-diameter wood products, for example in wetland track-way and round-house construction. It is likely that as the woodland cover of the landscape as a whole declined, throughout the Bronze and Iron Ages, organised woodland cropping in the form of coppice became more essential. The Romans operated a coppicing system to produce 'faggot-wood' for fuel for metal working and hypocaust heating systems (Rackham 2003). There is strong documentary evidence for the application of coppicing systems in medieval England, primarily using several native species, to produce woodfuel, thatching spars and 'wattles' for the traditional 'wattle-and-daub' rural construction system. Beech and chestnut coppices provided much of the woodfuel requirements of London prior to the widespread adoption of 'Tyne coals' from the sixteenth century on. Many English coppices were managed under a variant of the system known as 'coppice-with-standards', where a number of widely spaced trees, very often oak or ash, were allowed to grow on to semi-maturity. These 'standard trees', although they tended to reduce the productivity of coppice underwood immediately below their canopies, produced valuable larger timbers for farm building and similar uses.

In Scotland, there is rather weaker historical evidence for prehistoric and medieval coppice management (Smout 1997, 2003; Smout et al. 2005). It may well have been undertaken on royal and monastic estates, which were often 'early adopters' of land-management innovations from further south. In rural areas, small roundwood was certainly harvested from native woodlands near settlements. Upland birch woodlands in particular were noted suppliers of material for everyday craft and manufacturing uses in rural areas until around 1900. This may have amounted to 'informal' coppicing, for example of birch and hazel, wherever browsing was kept under sufficient control to permit regrowth. Where the transhumant or 'shieling' system was adopted (Smout 1997, 2003; Smout et al. 2005), with livestock being driven to summer pastures at higher altitudes, woodlands on the lower ground should then have enjoyed some relief from browsing.

From the late sixteenth century onwards, there was a rapid increase in demand for woodfuel for metal working, particularly for the smelting of iron ore and the casting and forging of ironwork (Lindsay 1977; Smout 2005; Smout et al. 2005). A particular impetus was the invention of the cannon and its widespread adoption for naval warfare during and after the Spanish Armada. Traditional sources of woodfuel in lowland England, such as the Weald and the Forest of Dean, had been in use for these purposes since Roman times and were heavily depleted by 1600. Attention switched to alternative sources of supply, initially in Cumbria and Ireland, but these too rapidly started to show signs of strain. From around 1610, Irish and Cumbrian ironmasters and timber merchants began to look to the Atlantic oakwoods of Scotland as potential new fields of exploitation for charcoal. These had the advantage of easy access from the sea, allowing the import of iron ore and labour and the export of manufactured 'pig iron' or cast ironwork. Earlier medieval 'bloomeries' were replaced by larger industrial 'furnaces' from the seventeenth century. The first noted example of such activity was in the Letterewe oakwoods on the north side of Loch Maree around 1611 (Smout et al. 2005), but over the next two centuries several 'furnaces' were established down the western seaboard of Scotland through Wester Ross, Lochaber, Lorne and Argyll. This became a major industry requiring large amounts of coppiced oak to produce charcoal for the smelting process. Another major upland oak coppice product was 'tanbark', rich in natural tannins, which was stripped from the oak logs and sent south to the Central Belt and to Ireland to cure cattle hides into leather.

It was essential for the 'furnace' proprietors to ensure an ongoing, and reasonably sustainable, source of suitable charcoal to meet their requirements. Exhausting the woods could only imply failure of their enterprises in the longer term. In some cases they may have found surviving oakwoods of sufficient density to meet their needs, but in other areas only partly exhausted upland wood pastures remained. Here it is known that woodlands were enclosed to exclude livestock and considerable planting may have occurred, using acorns collected locally, or often imported from England. By contrast with traditional coppicing in England, oak was preferred over hazel and ash, due to the superior charcoal produced and the added value obtained from the tanbark. In these northern areas, oak grows relatively slowly and the coppice rotation had to be extended to 20–25 years to produce the diameter of material required for these markets. This meant that extensive areas of oak woodland in the western Highlands were brought under organised industrial coppice management between 1650 and 1850, thereby preserving them from over-grazing and depletion. These woods were also the focus of the charcoal-burning activity itself, as it was easier to carry that lighter product to the furnace by pack-horse than the original coppice wood itself (Lindsay 1975). Not until around 1860, with increased adoption of coal-tar tanning agents and coke-fired iron-smelting, did industrial coppicing in Scottish oak woodlands finally begin to decline.

The two centuries of industrial coppicing activity not only preserved and reinforced many of the oak woodlands of Scotland, it also modified them in terms of both structure and species composition. Non-oak species (including ash, hazel, birch, rowan, aspen and holly) were frequently removed as so-called 'barren timbers', leaving more space for a monoculture of coppiced oak (Smout et al. 2005). Imported oaks were transplanted into the woods to replace these species and any 'exhausted' oak coppice stools, changing the genetic composition of the oak populations and the balance between the sessile and pedunculate oaks in some cases (Tittensor 1970). The regular cycle of oak coppicing across large areas, coupled with its relatively sudden end (within one or two cycles), created a legacy of artificially even-aged oak stands (now standing between 80 and 150 years since their last cutting) with a single-storey oak canopy and a higher density of stems than in natural woodland.

5.12 Historical management – timber from high forest

Although much of the lowland oak woodland in Scotland had been cleared during prehistory, several distinct areas had survived into the medieval period. These were an important and valued source of oak timber for construction purposes – including the roofs of castles and cathedrals – and for shipbuilding. Although Scotland began to import oak, pine and spruce 'deal' timber from the Baltic region during the late medieval period, home supplies of oak remained of considerable importance (Mills and Crone 2012). Such large timber was used in the major towns, which mostly had reasonably good access from the sea, as well as for castles and country houses. Hence those remaining lowland oak woodlands which were close to the coast or to navigable rivers were particularly prized. Documentary evidence suggests that a number of major oak woodlands, under royal or aristocratic ownership, supplied large-dimension timbers for building projects (Smout et al. 2005) such as the roofs of Stirling and Edinburgh Castles and the construction of the *Great Michael* warship at Leith during the sixteenth century. Examples include Darnaway Forest in Morayshire, Cawdor Forest in Nairnshire, Dalkeith in Midlothian, Kincardine Castle in Perthshire and the Torwood area close to Stirling. It is possible that timber supplies were also obtained from other lowland oak woodland areas that have since largely disappeared, such as the Forest of Plater in Angus. Oak woodlands in remoter parts of the Highlands and the Southern Uplands were less important for this large-dimension timber trade as the trees were smaller and of poorer stem form and were much less readily transported to the locations of major commercial demand. It was easier to import good timber from Scandinavia or mainland Europe from a fairly early date.

There is limited evidence for deliberate silvicultural management of oak woodland to produce large-dimension construction and naval timbers in Scotland before around 1500 (Smout et al. 2005). Most harvesting of large oak stems in the forests mentioned above essentially took advantage of what had arisen naturally, with legislation and contractual documents mainly dealing with regulation of tree felling and avoidance of over-exploitation. There is evidence that some areas were cropped several times at intervals of 100–150 years (Mills and Crone 2012), which suggests that, at the very least, browsing was regulated so as to permit successful natural regeneration. There may well have been more determined efforts to secure regeneration by rudimentary stand tending and even perhaps by planting. In England, the coppice-with-standards system allowed for the production of large numbers of small timber stems of oak, which were certainly quite suitable for normal rural building works – barns, houses and smaller church roofs. However, these would not have been satisfactory for larger construction projects, including major shipbuilding and large-span sawn roof-trusses. There are mentions of larger-diameter English oaks being 'reserved' for these demanding applications, such as the replacement of cathedral roof-trusses and the construction of warships. These were often growing in royal forests and those owned by the nobility. Whether it was possible to sustain such efforts over a sufficient period of time, in the face of competing shorter-term demands on the forest for hunting, livestock grazing, charcoal and woodfuel, is uncertain. Some traditional oak-producing forests in England, such as the Forest of Dean, had certainly been depleted by over-cutting by 1600 (Rackham 2003). By around 1660, serious shortages of oak timber for naval use were being reported by commentators such as John Evelyn in England, and similarly in Scotland (Smout et al. 2005). Scotland began to run short of home-grown oaks of larger dimensions by around 1400, with increasing imports from the Baltic (Mills and Crone 2012). In response to this challenge, private estates began to plant oak, both within existing woodlands and on bare land. In Scotland, oak plantations were created in several areas such as Perthshire, Angus, East Lothian and Berwickshire and were actively managed, especially for naval timbers, until the market for oak ships' timbers collapsed in the 1860s.

5.13 Major oak woodlands lost since AD 1130

Compared to the position within the native pinewoods, it is rather easier to identify some key areas from which oak woodland has apparently disappeared from the landscape since the start of the period for which we have some written historical records (AD 1130 onwards). Two examples serve to illustrate different pathways by which this could happen.

5.13.1 The Ettrick Forest

Perhaps the best known example of a 'lost forest' in Scotland is the Ettrick Forest, which once occupied a large area in the central part of the Southern Uplands – centred on the upper catchments of the Ettrick and Yarrow rivers, but possibly extending into the catchments of the Teviot, the Tweed and even the Clyde. This area was certainly partly wooded in the Anglo-Norman period and was recorded as a royal hunting forest. Upland oak-birch woodland would have been the dominant type, with more localised ash-elm-hazel and alder woodland types along the valley bottoms. The name Ettrick Forest still appears on modern maps, but only fragments of native woodland actually survive within the area today (see Plate 10d), in side valleys or 'cleuchs'. A fundamental question that we need to ask is 'how extensive was the woodland cover within the medieval Ettrick Forest?' The term 'forest' in that period referred more to the Anglo-Norman legal status of the area as a royal hunting preserve than to the actual extent of tree cover. Some modern Highland 'deer forests' are virtually treeless. It is likely that an area such as the Ettrick Forest would have consisted of a mosaic of closed-canopy woodland, open pasture woodland with some cultivation and rough grassland, heathland and wetland. During the medieval period, several large Cistercian abbeys and monasteries were established on the Borders (Melrose, Jedburgh, Dryburgh, Kelso) which ran extensive commercial sheep flocks on the surrounding hills. These would inevitably have imposed additional grazing pressures around the margins of the Ettrick Forest. Later, even before the monarchy moved to London in 1603, the Scottish kings granted on long-term lease, or sold, large parts of the Ettrick Forest area to local noblemen and farmers, in return for rental payments, feus or services rendered. These new landowners and tenants cleared more of the surviving native woodland and introduced larger numbers of sheep, which prevented future native woodland regeneration. Many Border hills that may once have carried the upland oakwoods of Ettrick are now bare of trees. A similar fate befell many of the smaller oak forests of lowland Scotland, for example those of Fife, Angus and the Mearns, including the Forest of Plater near Kirriemuir.

5.13.2 *The Torwood*

The Torwood was a significant area of oak-dominated woodland during the medieval period, lying to the south of Stirling. It straddled a Roman road leading to Stirling Bridge and was guarded by a castle, remains of which survive to the present day. The forest was an important source of timber for Stirling and surrounding areas and was doubtless used for hunting as well. There are reports of William Wallace hiding out in the Torwood during the Wars of Independence (~1300) and a tree in which he was reputed to have concealed himself survived there until the end of the eighteenth century. Significant parts of the Torwood remain as woodland today – however, most are now composed of mixed forestry, with significant modern plantations of introduced conifers, beech and sycamore. There is some surviving ancient oak woodland within the Torwood, notably at Wallacebank Wood. It is believed that the composition of the woodland has been changed progressively by private landowners over the last 300 years. This process continued into the twentieth century, with conversion of many native oak woodlands into conifer 'Plantations on Ancient Woodland Sites' (PAWS), especially in Stirlingshire, Argyll and Lochaber.

CHAPTER SIX

Ash, elm and hazel woodlands

6.1 Historical development

This chapter deals in more detail with the ash, elm and hazel woodlands of Scotland. By contrast with the native pinewoods, upland birch and oak woodlands, these are woodland types of generally more fertile sites within those climatic regions where they occur. They are therefore naturally restricted to a smaller proportion of the land surface of Scotland, where the fertile soil conditions that they require occur. The recent Native Woodland Survey of Scotland (Forestry Commission Scotland 2014) has identified ~12,000ha of upland mixed ashwood and it is believed that a similar amount of ash-dominated woodland is captured within the lowland mixed deciduous woodland category. Some ash-alder woodland is included within the Forestry Commission Scotland wet woodlands category.

Hazel was present as a very significant component of the native woodlands of Scotland during the early Boreal phase, while ash and elm were later arrivals, colonising during the late Boreal (elm) and early Atlantic (ash) phases (H. J. B. Birks 1989; Peterken 1993; Tipping 1994). During the Boreal phase with its cooler, drier climate, hazel is known to have occurred in mixture with birch, aspen and juniper in more open scrub woodland types, associated with immature but base-rich soils. It still occurs today in birch-dominated woodlands along the far north and north-west coasts of Scotland, and on some of the Hebridean islands, where ash and elm do not thrive due to unfavourable climates and infertile soils.

As the climate improved and soils continued to mature in less exposed parts of the country, medium-tolerant tree species expanded – particularly oak, ash and elm. These species each have somewhat different ecological requirements, which helped to determine which became dominant on any given site during the Atlantic phase. Both ash and elm require fertile soils, particularly favouring those sites with good supplies of base cations – calcium, magnesium and potassium. Oak can grow well on a wider range of soil types, many too infertile for ash and elm. This might lead one to expect that oak would be found everywhere that ash and elm occur, but this is not so. Young ash and elm are more shade-tolerant than oak, and can regenerate under its shade, whereas it cannot regenerate under theirs. Elm remains more shade-tolerant than oak throughout its life-cycle, whereas ash becomes more light-demanding when mature, having reached the canopy (known by ecologists as a 'sprinter strategy'). Where soil conditions favoured ash and elm, they were able to achieve dominance over oak, restricting it to a more minor component of the stand. This led to the development of ash-elm woodlands with sparse oak on a range of fertile soils on colluvial valley slopes and over base-rich limestone and igneous rocks. In these richer woodlands hazel functioned as a medium-tolerant understorey shrub, producing fewer nuts than in open hazel scrub situations, instead relying on vegetative reproduction strategies (Rackham 2003). Atlantic hazel woodlands occur on some western coastal and island sites (Coppins and Coppins 2012), where climatic exposure limits the development of ash and elm. In these woodlands, hazel functions as a light-demanding shrub dominant, regenerating well from abundant nuts.

Once human impacts on native woodland in Scotland became significant, the extent of ash, elm and hazel components began to decline. As the fertile sites were highly desirable for agriculture, much lighter upland mixed ash woodland was cleared in prehistory. As a result, a significant proportion of surviving woodlands of this type are found on steep and rocky sites, particularly over limestone, having thus escaped deliberate clearance for cultivation or browsing by cattle and sheep. Lowland mixed deciduous woodlands, with oak present, often survived until the Iron Age or later due to the difficulty in cultivating heavy clay soils with more primitive plough technologies. Some examples have survived until the present day on steep valley-side slopes in the lowlands (e.g. the Clyde Valley woodlands).

6.2 Historical distribution

Compared to the more extensive native pinewoods and upland oak-birch woodlands, it is more difficult to assess the maximum extent that was reached by ash, elm and hazel woodlands prior to the onset of major human clearance. Rather than covering large, continuous tracts of the Scottish landscape, these woodlands would always have occupied a patchwork of smaller areas scattered across those parts of the country where climates and soils were most favourable. It is, however, likely that their maximum total extent was significantly less than for either of the other two major categories of woodland dealt with so far – native pine and upland oak-birch.

From the Atlantic phase onwards, mixed ash woodlands will certainly have been the most common woodland type on fertile sites in the uplands, to ~200m asl (Dickson 1993; Roberts et al. 1992; Rodwell 1991a; Tipping 1994). In many cases these will also have contained elm and hazel as significant sub-components. Where side-valleys provide sufficient topographical shelter, upland mixed ash woodland can persist to higher elevations than might be expected (locally above 300m asl in Scotland). The well-known 'cleuch' woodlands of the Scottish Borders are of this type. Where fertile soil conditions are combined with a higher degree of climatic exposure, for example on Mull and Skye, ash and elm can locally drop out of the picture, leaving the pure 'Atlantic' coastal hazel woodlands.

There are essentially two reasons for inherent soil fertility reaching the levels necessary for ash and elm woodlands to thrive: direct access to base-rich geological parent materials, and gradual accumulation of soil nutrients by downslope (colluvial) movement in soil solution. Base-rich geologies are found in fairly restricted areas of

Scotland, including the Dalradian limestones of Highland Perthshire, the Durness limestones in Wester Ross, the Tertiary basalts of Ardnamurchan, Morvern, Skye and Mull, and the Devonian basalts and andesites of the hills between Stirling and Dundee. Scotland lacks significant extent of soft younger limestones of the type found in southern England (the Cotswolds, the Chilterns, etc.). However, sites with nutrient accumulation from downslope movement in solution – so-called 'receiving sites' – are fairly common in many glens and valleys cutting through geological strata of even low to moderate fertility – for example the Dalradian metamorphic rocks, the Old Red Sandstones and the Ordovician/Silurian shales. Nutrient accumulation tends to occur in a distinct belt along the lower slopes of valley-sides, below the midslope province of upland oak woodland, but above the floodplain where wet woodlands dominate (see Chapter 7). In some cases this is associated with a discrete 'springline' along which alder may occur together with the ash.

In more lowland areas ash and elm could only ever have formed a major component of woodlands where there were soils of unusually high fertility. Mixed ash woodlands survive today along the steep sides of valleys cutting through the more fertile geologies of the Central Belt and Ayrshire. Almost all examples on more level ground would have been cleared in prehistory for cultivation. Most lowland areas of Scotland with soils of moderate fertility carried oak-dominated 'lowland mixed deciduous woodland' (see Chapter 5), but these originally contained significant components of elm in the canopy and hazel in the understorey, particularly on heavier soils (Tipping 1994) (see below for more detailed discussion on elm occurrence in Scotland). Outbreaks of Dutch elm disease during past centuries have seriously depleted the elm resource of Scotland, and in some cases hazel has been removed in the past by foresters. These trends have favoured artificial dominance of oak in many woodlands. There are few Scottish examples of those ash-hazel stand types found (with field maple) in coppice woodlands on heavy clay soils in lowland England (Peterken 1993).

6.3 Current geographical and ecological distribution

At the present time, native ash, elm and hazel woodlands are concentrated in distinct geographical regions and ecological contexts within Scotland (Peterken 1993; Roberts et al. 1992; Rodwell 1991a). Ash-dominated examples correspond to either upland mixed ashwood or lowland mixed deciduous woodland (Forestry Commission Scotland 2014). The main regions and ecological contexts where these woodland types occur are:

- **Atlantic fringe.** There are woodlands along the extreme Atlantic fringe of Scotland where hazel is generally predominant (Coppins and Coppins 2012), with ash and elm often absent as soil fertility is lower and sites are more exposed. Good examples occur on the Inner Hebrides, for example at Ballachuan on the Isle of Seil, Aros on Mull and Tarskavaig on Skye. Soils at these locations are usually shallow and only moderately base-rich.

- **West-coast lowlands.** There are a number of notable ash-elm dominated woodlands in Lochaber, Wester Ross and on the Isles of Mull and Skye which are associated with discrete outcrops of base-rich geologies. These occur on coastal slopes and undulating terrain, rather than only in incised valleys. Most are associated with the Tertiary basalts of the Morvern peninsula (as at Lochaline) and the Isle of Mull (Kilninian, Ulva Ferry), with smaller examples over the same geology on Skye. Further north, there are examples on the hard Durness limestones of Cambrian age, most importantly at Rassal Ashwood in Wester Ross.
- **Eastern uplands.** Ash-dominated slope woodlands also occur in a restricted area near Perth, Stirling and Dundee, formed of highly base-rich igneous rocks of Devonian age – mainly andesites and basalts. The best examples are on the Glencarse, Kinfauns, Kinoull and Moncreiffe Hills to the east and south of Perth. Some are developed on very steep slopes, verging on cliffs, where soil depth is restricted by downwash.
- **Upland valleys.** Ash-elm woodlands occur on the side slopes (and sometimes the floor) of upland valleys incised through a broad range of metamorphic strata. The best known examples are in two areas: Highland Perthshire and Argyll over Dalradian limestone rocks, and the Borders over Ordovician/Silurian strata. While local seams of base-rich strata such as the Dalradian limestone favour this woodland type, it can occur in valleys cut through less fertile strata. Nutrients are transported downslope in soil solution, accumulating on the 'colluvial' lower slopes, and on the 'alluvial' valley floors, over a long period of time. Upland ashwoods (NVC W9) are often found 'sandwiched' between upland oak-birch woodlands (NVC W11) on the middle and upper slopes and wet woodlands (NVC W7) on the valley floor. Some of the best examples of this woodland type are found in the Loch Tay and Glenlyon areas of Perthshire, where ash of good timber form can be grown, and also in the Glen Roy, Appin and Glen Nant areas further to the west in Lochaber and Lorne. In the Borders, there are smaller upland 'cleuch' woodlands in the Ettrick and Yarrow catchments.
- **Lowland valleys.** Ash-elm woodlands occur in river valleys cut through younger rocks between the Highland Boundary Fault and the Southern Upland Fault. Many major examples are on Carboniferous limestones, basalts and associated sediments – for example in the Clyde Valley, at Roslin Glen and in the valleys of both the West Lothian and Lanarkshire Rivers Avon. Occasional smaller woodlands of this type occur over the more fertile sandstones and mudstones of Ayrshire and the eastern Borders (Permian at Ayr Gorge, Devonian at Newton St Boswells).
- **Lowland plateaux.** The natural woodland type of lowland plateaux in Scotland with soils of moderate fertility was oak-elm-hazel, with ash only a localised and minor component. Elm remains a significant component of lowland broadleaved plantations on Islay, where it has escaped the effects of Dutch elm disease. It also still occurs in some lowland mixed deciduous woodlands around the inner Moray Firth, in lowland Aberdeenshire and in and around Edinburgh and Dundee.

A very high proportion of ash, elm and hazel woodlands in Scotland are found in relatively small blocks of a few hectares, often with a very high 'edge-to-area ratio'. This is due to their following river valleys and linear features such as coastal cliffs and exposures of base-rich geologies. This physical pattern of distribution creates particular conservation problems for this woodland type, due to the high degree of isolation between the surviving remnants and the large 'edge effect' that they experience due to their linear profile. This can increase the impact of factors such as livestock grazing, fly-tipping and pesticide/herbicide drift coming in from outside.

6.4 Stand dynamics, structure and regeneration

A variety of stand structures are found within ash-, elm- and hazel-dominated woodlands in Scotland (see Plates 11a to 11c). These correspond to the Peterken stand types 1 and 3 (ash-elm and hazel-ash woods) (Peterken 1993). These range from simpler upland ash and hazel woodlands to complex mixed valley woodlands with all three species present. A key difference between these woodlands and the major types described earlier – native pine and upland oak-birch woodland – is that ash and elm frequently regenerate satisfactorily under their own shade. This is because canopy density is often moderate and is also due to the greater shade-tolerance of these species. As a result, ash and elm woodlands can be sustained by dispersed natural regeneration, without requiring episodic disturbance to facilitate regeneration, such as by fire, windthrow or herbivore browsing. There are, however, some exceptions – for example, ash might not have regenerated under a denser oak-elm canopy of the type found in some Scottish lowland mixed deciduous woodlands. Major relevant stand types found are:

- **Hazel stands** – dense hazel scrub, usually with a single hazel (*Corylus avellana*) canopy at 1–3m height. Regeneration is by both seedling and vegetative means. Gap formation is often required for seedling regeneration. Associated tree species include rowan (*Sorbus aucuparia*), aspen (*Populus tremula*), downy birch (*Betula pubescens*) and locally sessile oak (*Quercus petraea*) and holly (*Ilex aquifolium*). These are the typical conditions of Atlantic coastal and some upland hazel woodlands.
- **Ash and ash-hazel stands** – most often found on more upland sites over base-rich geologies. There will normally be a canopy of mature ash (*Fraxinus excelsior*), which can range from 10m to 30m in height depending on exposure and management regime. The stand structure is often open (some examples functioning as wood pastures), with a well-developed ground flora of ferns, herbs and soft grasses. Regeneration occurs by seeding into canopy gaps, which produces a group structure across the woodland. In some cases there will be established patches of hazel in the understorey. Associated tree species include rowan, aspen, silver birch and locally sessile oak and bird cherry (*Prunus padus*).
- **Ash-elm-hazel stands** – found on steep valley-side slopes under both upland and some lowland conditions. The canopy is often structurally complex and may include both ash and wych elm (*Ulmus glabra*), which can range

from 10m to 30m in height. In many cases, the introduced sycamore (*Acer pseudoplatanus*) has now also joined the canopy, often replacing dead elm. An understorey of hazel can also be present, more often in the upland examples. The canopy tends to be denser than in the ash and ash-hazel stand type and regeneration follows the formation of gaps by natural mortality, windthrow and landslips. In some woodlands, oak becomes a significant component, especially on the upper slopes. Associated tree species include rowan, aspen, silver birch, sessile oak, pedunculate oak (*Quercus robur*) and wild cherry (*Prunus avium*).

- **Elm and elm-oak stands** – found on lowland plateau and undulating sites with fertile, heavy clay soils. Few, if any, examples now survive where elm remains dominant over oak, due to the impacts of Dutch elm disease since the 1930s. These woodlands would have had a high-forest canopy of wych elm and pedunculate oak, with a smaller component of ash in some cases. Differential shade-tolerance would favour elm over oak in natural regeneration. Hazel occurred as a localised understorey shrub.

6.5 Botanical interest

The ash, elm and hazel woodlands of Scotland are generally the most diverse in terms of their vascular plants, due to the fertile soil conditions found. The vast majority of such woodlands are covered by the NVC classes W9 (upland mixed ash woodlands) and W8 (lowland ash-oak woodlands) (Rodwell 1991a). In Scotland, the distinction between these two types on botanical grounds is not always clearly defined – both are characterised by dog's mercury with a range of soft herbs and fern species. Ash and hazel woodlands on freely draining western-coastal and upland sites with base-rich geology would almost always be covered by W9. Elm-oak woodlands on imperfectly drained plateau sites in the lowlands of the Central Belt will usually be covered by W8. Valley ash-elm-hazel woodlands in the upland marginal areas such as Perthshire, Angus and Moray can be transitional between these two types. Those in steep-sided narrow valleys at higher elevations tend to W9, whereas those on the lower slopes of broader valleys in the foothills and lowlands tend to W8. Some valley ash woodlands with a considerable proportion of alder in the canopy and a ground vegetation dominated by stinging nettle and meadowsweet are covered by the NVC class W7 (ash-alder woodlands). Western hazel woodlands on less base-rich sites, without ash, are covered by W11, even where oak is absent. These woodlands usually have a grassy ground cover, sometimes with bluebells.

While a number of the vascular plants occurring in these woodlands are quite common, there are several of conservation importance such as the Wilson's filmy fern (*Hymenophyllum wilsonii*), found particularly on the wet rocks along steep gorge walls shaded by ash-elm woodlands. The less acid bark found on ash, elm and hazel supports important communities of mosses, lichens and fungi typical of these woodlands. The Atlantic hazel woodlands of Argyll and the Inner Hebrides are especially valued for these lower plant communities (Coppins and Coppins 2012; Phillips

1994). The hazel gloves fungus (*Hypocreopsis rhododendri*) and the orange-fruited elm lichen (*Caloplaca luteoalba*) are two notable examples. An important requirement of these species is maintenance of stable moisture and light regimes, which may render coppice restoration activity inappropriate.

6.6 WILDLIFE AND BIODIVERSITY

The ash, elm and hazel woodlands of Scotland provide a habitat for many of the same mammal, bird and insect species as upland oak woodlands. However, being less concentrated, there are relatively few 'obligate' species which are uniquely dependent on these particular woodland types.

Hazel woodlands can provide a potential food source for red squirrel in some parts of Scotland, where conifer forests are dominated by the smaller-coned Sitka spruce, as opposed to the Scots pine, particularly in western areas such as Argyll and Lochaber. Pine martens (*Martes martes*) use upland ash woodlands as part of their foraging range in similar areas. Many valley ash woodlands clothe the slopes above streams which are important for aquatic species, including otter (*Lutra lutra*) and water vole (*Arvicola terrestris*). Salmonid fish often spawn on the upper tributaries of rivers lined by upland mixed ash woodlands – especially the Atlantic salmon (*Salmo salar*) and the sea trout (*Salmo trutta*). Woodland provides protection from the sun, avoiding rises in summer water temperature beyond the tolerance of young fish hatchlings, and also supports a source of the insect foods which they require to grow. These insects also provide food for bat species, some of which prefer to hunt along river courses through woodland – including the Daubenton's bat (*Myotis daubentonii*), Natterer's bat (*Myotis nattereri*) and the pipistrelle (*Pipistrellus pipistrellus*).

Woodland grouse species tend not to make particular use of ash-elm-hazel woodland. However, smaller insect-eating bird species, such as pied fly-catcher (*Ficedula hypoleuca*), spotted fly-catcher (*Muscicapa striata*), wood warbler (*Phylloscopus sybilatrix*) and song thrush (*Turdus philomelos*), use these woodlands extensively, as they have open and varied canopy structures, providing a range of habitats for nesting and feeding.

The open structure of many upland ash woodlands makes them particularly valuable for butterflies and moths. Favoured food plants for some butterflies, such as violets (*Viola* spp.), flourish in open clearings within these woodlands. As in the upland oakwoods, the chequered skipper (*Carterocephalus palaemon*) and the pearl-bordered fritillary (*Boloria euphrosyne*) are two significant butterfly species for conservation. The Lochaber area is the main population centre for the chequered skipper within Britain and the upland ash woodlands there make a supporting contribution to the required habitat for this species, alongside oakwoods.

6.7 ELM WOODLANDS IN SCOTLAND

Elm forms a distinct component of the native woodlands of Scotland, but has declined in most areas over recent decades due to Dutch elm disease outbreaks. Elm colonised

Scotland earlier than ash, during the late Boreal phase (H. J. B. Birks 1989). It is believed that the wych elm (*Ulmus glabra*) has been the only elm species native to Scotland since the last Ice Age. Wych elm is distinct from some other elms found in southern England in that it naturally reproduces mainly by seeding rather than by suckering (Rackham 2003). As the Atlantic phase proceeded, elm became a more major component of developing mixed deciduous woodlands on better soils in both upland and lowland areas of Scotland, along with oak, ash and hazel. However, at the end of the Atlantic phase, when Neolithic agricultural impacts were becoming more significant, elm underwent very rapid declines across Britain (Rackham 2003). This was likely to have been caused by a combination of increasing human exploitation, together with earlier outbreaks of the Dutch elm disease or similar pathogens. These effects were probably always more serious in accessible lowland woodland types.

Dutch elm disease is the most catastrophic tree disease for which we have evidence in the British ecological record, and appears to have broken out on several occasions in the past (Rackham 2003). The actual disease-causing agent is an ascomycete fungus (*Ophiostoma* spp.), but this is 'vectored' (carried from one elm tree to another) and introduced to the tree by elm bark beetles (*Scolytus* spp.) (Gibbs et al. 1994). Very large populations of these bark beetles may cause damage alone (as with spruce bark beetle etc.) but, so far as is known, the Dutch elm disease fungus cannot infect a tree without the assistance of the beetle. The beetles are more active during warm, dry summers, when critical 'flying temperatures' are achieved for a sufficient number of days. For this reason, the spread of the disease has usually been more rapid in lowland England than in Scotland. The disease occurs in distinct 'outbreaks' which kill a large proportion of the elms present at that time, followed by quieter periods when it fades into relative obscurity. It is likely that each outbreak follows mutation of the fungal pathogen or introduction of more virulent strains from further afield. There is increasing evidence for outbreaks in prehistory, explaining the prehistoric elm declines, and also more recently. There have been two outbreaks during the past century: (1) during the late 1920s and 1930s and (2) between the mid-1960s and the present. The recent outbreak has been much more severe, almost certainly involving a newly invigorated hybrid pathogen. However, wych elm appears somewhat less susceptible than the English elms (*Ulmus procera* and *U. minor*), in many cases not being killed outright but, instead, reduced to a repeatedly reinfected shrub layer.

Wych elm woodland canopies survive today in Scotland only in those districts beyond the current range of Dutch elm disease. These are mainly the upland mixed ash-elm woodlands of the west Highlands and Inner Hebrides. Until recently, the lowland mixed deciduous woodlands of Aberdeenshire and the inner Moray Firth were also free of the disease, and contained important populations of mature canopy elm. Although the disease has now arrived, these areas present a final chance to see elm as a canopy tree in lowland mainland Scottish woodlands. Most lowland and valley ash-elm woodlands further south have succumbed to Dutch elm disease over the past forty years – for example in the areas around Edinburgh, Perth, Dundee, in the Clyde Valley woodlands and the Borders. In some cases, elm has been extirpated, but in others, it persists as a repeatedly reinfected understorey shrub, along with hazel.

Woodland where elm has died out over recent decades is often colonised by the introduced sycamore, which replaces elm as a shade-tolerant canopy tree on more fertile soils (see Plate 11d).

6.8 HAZEL WOODLANDS IN SCOTLAND

We have seen that hazel formed part of the natural woodlands of Scotland during the early Boreal phase, when it was found in mixture with birch, aspen and juniper in open woodlands of short stature. In those times, it flowered abundantly, leaving a stronger signal in the pollen record (H. J. B. Birks 1989; Tipping 1994) and frequent macro-fossil remains of hazel nuts and shells. This remains the case in exposed areas along the west and north coasts of Scotland and on some of the islands – Skye, Mull and Orkney. Later, during the Atlantic phase, hazel became incorporated within mixed deciduous woodlands of oak, ash and elm throughout much of Scotland below 300m asl. In these situations, hazel functioned as an understorey shrub under a canopy of oak, elm or ash. Where that canopy was dense, as in the lowland elm-oak stands, hazel could no longer flower well and hence it tends to be under-represented in the pollen record. In the more open upland mixed ash woodlands, it will still have flowered to some degree.

Today, hazel is found in four different ecological contexts within Scotland (Peterken 1993; Rodwell 1991a):

- **Northern birch-hazel woodlands** – found in parts of Sutherland, Caithness and Wester Ross which are beyond the climatic tolerance of oak, ash and elm. Aspen and rowan are frequent trees in many of these open woodlands, which are transitional from NVC W11 to W17. The largest examples occur on the west coast around Coigach, Assynt and in the north Sutherland straths. As the hazel is lightly shaded, it can flower and fruit abundantly, regenerating well. Soils are acid brown earths, but more fertile than those occupied by birch-rowan woodland (NVC W17).
- **Atlantic hazel woodlands** – found on more fertile soils along the west coasts of Argyll and Lochaber and on islands of volcanic origin such as Mull, Seil and Skye (Coppins and Coppins 2012). These tend to be denser stands of pure hazel – essentially NVC W9 or W11 woodlands lacking significant oak, ash or elm. As the hazel is generally unshaded it can flower and fruit abundantly, regenerating well.
- **Valley ash-elm-hazel woodlands** – found in both upland and lowland contexts. Here, hazel is operating as the understorey to mixed ash-elm woodlands on steep slopes (NVC W9, more locally W8) which cast a greater degree of shade. Many examples are found on the south-facing slopes of glens running east to west and hence are exposed to additional sunlight coming from the side. This allows hazel to continue to regenerate by a combination of seeding and vegetative means, especially where there are gaps in the ash-elm canopy and only light grazing.

- **Lowland mixed deciduous woodlands**. These tend to be more managed woodlands on plateaux and gentle slopes, where elm has died out and ash was never a major component. Hazel can persist as a patchy understorey, but due to denser shade from the oak canopy it is normally only able to reproduce by vegetative means. In such woods the oak has often been planted and the hazel may also have been introduced for managed coppice or later as pheasant cover.

6.9 HISTORICAL MANAGEMENT – WOOD PASTURE AND COPPICE

By comparison with native pinewoods and upland oak woodlands in Scotland, we have much less written historical evidence for management of ash, elm and hazel woodlands. This is a major contrast with the situation for lowland England, where management of mixed coppices of ash, elm, hazel and maple has been well recorded since medieval times (Rackham 2003).

Upland mixed ash woodlands in Scotland have often been opened to livestock grazing – sometimes as part of deliberately planned wood-pasture systems, but more often as an opportunistic resource around the margins of agricultural settlements. Ash and elm differ from oak in having bark and foliage that is relatively palatable and high in nutrients and therefore suitable as supplementary livestock fodder. This meant that there was a potential value to early farmers in retaining areas of this type of woodland on their holding which could be managed to support livestock production. During the summer months, livestock could be pastured within open woodlands of ash and elm, eating both the grass under the trees and perhaps foliage. This allowed open pastures nearer the farm to be protected from summer grazing, producing hay as winter fodder. This type of careful pasture woodland management ended 150–200 years ago in Scotland, but surviving veteran pollard ash and elm trees (see Plate 11e) can still be found, dating back to the period 1500–1800. Today, many remaining wood pastures in Scotland have become over-grazed, restricting any opportunities for natural tree regeneration. In other parts of Europe, including some remoter parts of Sweden, Finland and Switzerland, traditional types of wood-pasture and 'pollard meadow' management continue (Kirby and Watkins 1998), offering potential analogues for past woodland management in Scotland. These systems do require higher labour inputs than modern upland farming.

There is little doubt that informal coppicing of ash, elm and hazel would have taken place in Scotland, from Neolithic times until the 1800s. This would have made use of these species growing naturally in the surrounding woodlands and might have led to the planting and management of 'hazel beds'. The small-diameter wood produced would have been invaluable for woodfuel, fencing, livestock pens, brush handles and other everyday uses. It would have become apparent fairly early that hazel coppice stools under a dense tree canopy do not regrow reliably and that browsing livestock also seriously reduces any regrowth. Many apparently 'coppiced' hazel stools in upland native woodlands may adopt this form naturally or in response to livestock browsing. By comparison with lowland England, there is less written evidence for more formalised rotational hazel coppicing in medieval Scotland. Some may well have taken place in more accessible woodlands from medieval times onwards, especially concentrated on monastic and royal estates, reflecting southern practice (Smout 1997, 2003; Smout et al. 2005).

6.10 Historical management – timber from high forest

Alongside Scots pine, birch and oak, ash and elm were the next most significant native timber trees in Scotland throughout recorded history. Each of these species has particular timber properties that make it valuable – ash is a tough and hard-wearing material, for example for the production of tool handles and ladders, while elm is especially durable when submerged in water, for example for water and sewerage piping and in dockworks.

While small timbers of ash and elm would have been available from the upland mixed ash woodlands, managed primarily as wood pastures, production of larger-dimension timbers would have required woodlands to be retained and silviculturally managed on a 'high-forest' system. This means that straight stems would need to have been protected from browsing livestock for the first part of the rotation, so that their leading shoot was not browsed off. Valley ash-elm woodlands can be naturally protected from browsing by steep terrain, but the difficult access would always have made it difficult and expensive to extract logs from these to the sawmill.

As in the case of oak, supplies of home-grown hardwood timber had become depleted in Scotland by around 1450 (Mills and Crone 2012; Smout et al. 2005), and this promoted the establishment of plantations, especially on lowland country estates, from the 1500s onwards. Ash and elm were certainly included in some plantations, along with pine, oak and introduced species such as beech, sycamore, larch and silver fir (Anderson 1967). Plantations were created with the objective both of producing valuable timber and of improving the landscape appearance of the private estates. Young plantations were protected from browsing livestock and periodically thinned to produce a final crop of attractive and valuable stems. Although the intensity of management has generally declined, ash plantations with good standing timber (see Plate 12a) can still be found on a number of private estates in different parts of Scotland, including the Borders, Perthshire, Angus and Argyll. Elm plantations in most parts of Scotland have succumbed to Dutch elm disease in recent years, but there are still a few examples in Aberdeenshire, around the inner Moray Firth and on islands such as Islay which the disease has not yet reached.

6.11 Future management of ash – the *Chalara* threat

At present the future of ash in Scotland, as throughout Britain, is threatened by the fungal pathogen *Chalara fraxinea* which causes 'ash dieback'. This is one example of a serious tree disease which has apparently entered this country from abroad over recent years, perhaps assisted by the movement of planting stock for woodland expansion. Once present, the disease spreads locally by wind-borne spores (see Plate 12b). *Chalara* first emerged as a problem for European ash species in Eastern Europe at least twenty years ago. It is possible that hybridisation had occurred between a native European strain of the fungus, to which native trees had resistance, and a translocated Asiatic strain. Infection has spread steadily across Europe since then, probably reaching Britain during the past five to ten years, and first being officially recorded in 2012. At present there are many outbreaks in semi-natural ash woodlands in East Anglia and Kent, while most instances in Scotland are in recently planted woodlands. It is difficult to assess at this stage of the outbreak how serious the impacts will be for the future of ash, but, as with elm, many trees may become infected over the next twenty to thirty years. Researchers are looking at possible ways to produce *Chalara*-resistant ash stocks by selective breeding, but at present there is a moratorium on ash movement and planting. Young planted ash trees that are known to be infected are being removed and destroyed to reduce the rate of spread, but the decision as to what to do with older ash trees is more complex. It is likely that some may be felled early, with others left to 'take their chances'. As a recently emerging tree disease in British woodlands, there is limited published literature to date, but up-to-date information is rapidly becoming available from the Forestry Commission via <www.forestry.gov.uk/chalara>.

CHAPTER SEVEN

Wet woodlands

7.1 Historical development

Both alder and willow woodlands (excepting montane willow scrub – see Chapter 4) have always been restricted to sites with wetter soils. During early post-glacial times (the Boreal phase) these may have been much more restricted in extent than at present. Immature soils were mainly formed from coarse rock fragments of glacial and fluvioglacial origins, which would have formed freely draining soils more suited to pine, birch and hazel woodlands (Fitzpatrick 1980; Gillen 2013). However, localised deposits of finer-textured 'rock flour', compacted into a till layer by periglacial freeze-thaw effects, would have formed poorly drained soils. It is believed that the common shrub willow species (e.g. grey willow (*Salix cinerea*) and eared willow (*Salix aurita*)) would have colonised these sites during the Boreal phase. These are generally light-demanding, wind-propagated pioneer species and cannot persist or naturally regenerate under canopy shade.

By the Atlantic phase, a wider variety of poorly drained sites had developed, offering opportunities for expansion of specially adapted wet woodlands. Rivers were continually depositing alluvium (water-borne sediments) on to their floodplains. As time went on, these deposits were increasingly composed of finer silt and clay materials, rather than the coarse fluvioglacial gravels and sands of the Boreal phase. These finer deposits created larger flat expanses of poorly drained but fertile floodplains along river valleys. Away from the rivers, there was also an increase in the accumulation of basin deposits in concave hollows in the land surface – forming lakes, ponds, fens, swamps and marshes. Around the margins of these, there was again expansion of areas of wet but relatively fertile soils. Where peat (slowly decomposing plant material) built up within such hollows, domed raised bogs formed, fed with moisture mainly by rainfall. Here the peaty soils were certainly wet, but often also rather infertile.

Alder appears to have colonised Scotland relatively late, during the Atlantic phase (H. J. B. Birks 1989; Dickson 1993; Peterken 1993; Tipping 1994). As well as being well adapted to sites with wet soils, it is also a later-successional and shade-tolerant species, capable of colonising existing open-canopy woodlands. This allowed it to take advantage of the poorly drained floodplains and marshy hollows in the landscape, forming the main element of floodplain and sump woodlands. It has an added advantage in dealing with water-logged and infertile sites, in that it can manufacture its own supplies of nitrogen – an important plant nutrient – by means of bacterial nodules on its roots. However, it will not grow well on coarse sand and gravel soils, even where these are consistently wet. During the Atlantic phase, Scotland certainly carried much more extensive areas of floodplain woodland than today, where alder would have dominated along with ash, elm and willow. At the edge of these, where valley slopes began to rise, alder would normally have dropped out of the mixture, leaving valley ash-elm woodland predominant (see Chapter 6). Willow would have remained the main wet woodland species on more disturbed wet sites, such as the braided sand banks along the fluctuating lower channels of the major rivers.

During the 5,000–6,000-year period since human influence became significant, the extent of wet woodland in Scotland has been greatly reduced. While some floodplain woodland was lost directly to early agriculture – especially for creation of productive 'water-meadows' – more has disappeared as a result of later drainage schemes and the confinement of rivers to an artificially narrow channel – known as 'canalisation' – by construction of dykes and bankside walls. Many other wet woodland areas, such as swamps and fens, have been drained for agricultural improvement.

7.2 Current geographical and ecological distribution

Although the total extent of wet woodland in Scotland has been much reduced, it still remains geographically widely distributed throughout the country in many surviving fragments. These occur in most mainland parts of Scotland, although alder is infrequent in Caithness and northern parts of Sutherland. Wet woodlands are found over most geologies of Scotland, wherever suitable soils develop. The recent Native Woodland Survey of Scotland (Forestry Commission Scotland 2014) has identified ~45,000ha of wet woodlands, with some wetter birch and ash woodlands included in Forestry Commission upland birch and upland mixed ashwoods categories.

Many larger native woodland 'complexes' contain a minority component of wet woodland following internal watercourses and around hollows. Some of the best examples are associated with the larger areas of upland oak and birch woodland in Argyll, Perthshire and Galloway. While alder and willow stands most often occur adjacent to, and associated with, valley ash-elm woodland or oak-birch woodland, they can also be found within some native pinewood areas where these reach down to river banks (e.g. at Glen Tanar and Glen Strathfarrar). As a result, alder is perhaps the third most common native broadleaved species within the native pinewoods today, after birch and rowan. The ability of alder to produce its own nitrogen fertiliser in bacterial root-nodules allows it to persist for a time even on very infertile, heathery ground within native pinewoods. However, it only remains a permanent element of the woodland on the more fertile soils along the banks of the Highland lochs and 'burns'. In some cases, alder also extends up wet flushes on to lower valley-side slopes, where it was formerly managed as upland wood pasture. Good examples of such 'slope alder wood pasture' can be seen at Glen Strathfarrar and Glen Finglas.

There are a smaller number of surviving examples of natural floodplain woodland, dominated by alder and willow. These occur where wet woodland still has the opportunity to spread out naturally over a wide, flat floodplain, rather than persisting only as narrower strips of 'riparian alderwood' along the river banks themselves. The best surviving remnants of floodplain woodland are found near the mouths of rivers in the northern Highlands – for example at Urquhart Bay on the west bank of Loch Ness (see Plate 12c), the Mound Alderwoods at Strathfleet in East Sutherland, and the Rivers Spey and Findhorn in Moray. These 'alluvial fan' woodlands provide a glimpse of the floodplain conditions that must once have been more widespread across Scotland, and would have been a very familiar sight for Mesolithic hunter-gatherers making their way up these major rivers to establish early settlements during the Atlantic phase, 5,000–7,500 years ago.

Many of the alder-willow woodlands found in Scotland today occur in isolation from other native woodlands due to their long history of fragmentation by human activity. Many upland rivers have a narrow fringe of riparian alder woodland – often just a single row of mature alder trees along the river bank itself, adjoined by good pasture; similarly with lakes and ponds within open ground, such as those in the designed landscape parks of the lowland estates. Wet woodland composed of more open downy birch and willow can be found on patches of poorly drained ground away from rivers, such as fens, swamps and partially drained raised bogs. Some fairly extensive areas of wet birch woodland occur around the margins of blanket bogs. Willow woodland also develops on rapidly shifting banks of gravel and sand within river courses that have not had the opportunity to develop more mature floodplain woodland by ecological succession. In some cases this willow woodland helps to consolidate the loose shoals, providing an opportunity for more diverse floodplain woodland to form.

7.3 Stand dynamics, structure and regeneration

There are several distinct wet woodland stand types found in Scotland, each finding its own ecological 'niche' within the landscape and distinctive systems for natural regeneration (Forestry Commission 2003; Peterken 1993; Rodwell 1991a). These are:

- **Floodplain and riparian alder-willow woodland.** These are more fully developed floodplain and riparian woodlands (within NVC W6–7) where soil formation proceeds sufficiently to create niches for alder to establish. Most Scottish examples are narrow riparian alder belts (see Plate 12d). Increasing shade under the alder normally confines willow to the wettest areas around the margins of mature alder stands. Alder can regenerate from seed under its own shade and is also readily regenerated by coppice – either by human management or occurring naturally by activity of beavers. Woodland of this type in Europe often contains a component of riverine elm, which may once have occurred in Scotland.
- **Alder carr.** These are 'static' alder woodlands (within W5–7) (see Plate 13a) found either around lochs and ponds, along slow-flowing backwaters or within sumps or hollows. There is generally less willow or birch in these systems as the increasing soil depth gives alder the advantage over time, with the more light-demanding species being shaded out. Alder can grow into an impressive timber

tree with a tall, straight stem. Many alder woodlands of this type, where accessible, have been deliberately coppiced in the past. Hence much natural regeneration in this more stable type of alder woodland is now by vegetative means.

- **Willow woodlands.** With the exception of the montane willow scrub dealt with in Chapter 4, almost all willow woodlands (within NVC W1–3) (see Plate 13b) occur where conditions are unsuitable for other tree species (such as alder and birch) to establish due to periodic disturbance or excessively wet ground. These conditions occur both within river channels and around the margins of ponds/lakes. A variety of willow species are involved, but all are essentially light-demanding, early-successional species. These can only regenerate from seed or by vegetative suckering where the woodland remains open in structure. If soil builds up, trapped by the root systems of the willow trees, there will often be successional development towards an alder woodland.
- **Wet birch woodlands.** These are dominated by downy birch (*Betula pubescens*) (NVC W4) and generally occur on wet, infertile soils. In that sense they are 'wet ground variants' of the acid upland birchwoods dealt with in Chapter 5. They are most often found where the soil is very peaty (organic soils) – either in landscape hollows or around the margins of blanket bogs. Where raised bogs have been partially drained or burnt over, birch woodlands of this type may spread out onto the drying peat surface (see Plate 13c), at least for a period of time. Birch normally regenerates from seed and the structure of the woodland often remains sufficiently open to allow this. Some wet birchwoods are periodically burned off accidentally, triggering fresh bursts of regeneration.
- **Alder-ash woodland.** This is a transitional type (NVC W7), on the way to becoming rich valley ash-elm woodland (NVC W8). It is typical of fertile, periodically water-logged soils of the lower valley slopes, where the landform 'turns up' off the flat floodplain. Ash will normally increase at the expense of alder as one goes further up the slope, but the presence of a geological springline or flush system can sustain alder much further up the valley slopes than might otherwise be expected. Elm and bird cherry occur frequently in some woodlands of this type.

7.4 Botanical interest

The wet woodland communities in Scotland have distinct botanical associations which, although usually composed of relatively common plant species, are of conservation significance due to their small remaining extent within Scotland. Characteristic vascular plant species such as opposite-leaved golden saxifrage (*Chrysosplenium oppositifolium*) and meadowsweet (*Filipendula ulmaria*) occur within this habitat, and there are also some mosses and lichens that are strongly associated with wet woodlands.

Willow woodlands in Scotland correspond to three NVC communities, W1–3 (Rodwell 1991a). In upland areas W3 is the main type – a swampy willow-birch-alder woodland with ground vegetation of sedges (*Carex* spp.) and meadowsweet. In the lowlands, W1 and W2 habitats are found locally. W1 has a herb-rich ground vegetation, whereas W2 is dominated by reeds. Both types can contain some birch.

Wet birch woodlands are covered by the NVC W4 community. In the upland areas these are very often developed over peaty soils, whereas in the lowlands they are found on a wider variety of poorly drained sites, but usually those with infertile soil conditions. The purple moor-grass (*Molinia caerulea*) is almost always a dominant element, but can be accompanied by mosses (*Sphagnum* spp.), rushes (*Juncus* spp.) and various soft herbs.

Alder woodlands in Scotland are mainly covered by the NVC W7 community, particularly in more upland areas. These can contain some ash, willow, hazel and bird cherry. The ground vegetation is normally a lush mixture of stinging nettle (*Urtica dioica*), meadowsweet and tufted hair-grass (*Deschampsia cespitosa*). Narrow strips of alder along river banks are often subject to heavy grazing by livestock on adjacent pastures and may not retain the typical vegetation described by the NVC W7 community. In lowland areas of Scotland there are very localised examples of the swamp (NVC W5) and fen (NVC W6) alder woodland communities. The W5 community is easily recognised by the characteristic dominance of large tussock sedges. The W6 community occurs on flat sites, with a tall-herb vegetation, very often totally dominated by stinging nettle.

7.5 Wildlife and biodiversity

The wet woodlands of Scotland are of particular importance for their protective and nutritional effects on freshwater habitats (examples of 'ecosystem services'). Woodlands along river banks and around the margins of lakes provide shade, which limits rises in water temperature during hot weather, protecting fish stocks from heat stress and oxygen depletion. Wet woodland also acts as a filter, capturing excess nutrient, herbicide and pesticide run-offs from adjoining agricultural land and preventing these pollutants from entering freshwaters, adversely affecting various mammals, fish and invertebrates. Wet woodland acts as a breeding habitat for many insect species that provide a food source for birds, bats and fish that live within the wider freshwater ecosystem (Jeffries and Mills 1990).

Among the mammal species, the otter (*Lutra lutra*) and the water vole (*Arvicola terrestris*) are dependent on freshwater habitats. Until recent years these species had been declining in numbers due to water pollution and destruction of natural riparian vegetation for agriculture, forestry and built development. More recently the otter has recovered significantly in many British rivers. The water vole remains under threat, in particular due to the introduced American mink (*Mustela vison*) which has become a serious predator in many areas. The European beaver (*Castor fiber*) was once a natural component of Scottish wet woodland ecosystems, acting as a significant 'landscape engineer' by virtue of its damming and channelling activities. It became extinct in Scotland over 400 years ago due to a combination of habitat loss and hunting pressure (Yalden 2002) but there have recently been reintroductions. An officially sanctioned trial is taking place at the time of writing in extensive wet woodland at Knapdale, Argyll (see Plate 13d), while a larger number of beavers are now living wild within the River Tay catchment, having reportedly escaped from private collections in the region. A number of bat species prefer to hunt along watercourses (see Chapter 6), and also use the outline of riparian woodlands as an aid to navigation. The most closely associated with freshwater is the Daubenton's bat (*Myotis daubentonii*), also known as the 'water bat'. Wet woodland acts as a breeding ground for insects upon which it relies for food.

Scotland is well known for its valuable salmonid fish populations – the Atlantic salmon (*Salmo salar*) and the brown and sea trout (*Salmo trutta*). These fish rely upon gravelly 'spawning beds' where their eggs are laid and young fish hatch out. Conditions have to be correct in terms of the maintenance of suitable river-bed conditions, water temperatures and oxygen levels to allow the young fish to survive and develop. Floodplain and riparian woodlands support these fish species by filtering out silt which might smother the spawning beds, and by shading the water, thereby limiting summer rises in temperature and maintaining dissolved oxygen levels. As the fish mature, they depend on leaves and insects falling into the water to provide a source of food. Wet woodland along the river banks increases the supply and variety of insect life. The crane-fly species (*Tipula* spp.) are particularly characteristic of these habitats. This also benefits a number of other non-migratory fish species within our rivers and lochs.

A wide variety of waterfowl, including many ducks, are dependent on wet woodland for breeding shelter and food supplies (many ducklings eat insects, before turning to plant foods as they mature). A particular case is the goldeneye (*Bucephala clangula*) which breeds on a few Highland lochs, nesting in trees by the water's edge. Healthy fish populations also support populations of fish-eating ducks such as goosander (*Mergus merganser*) and of the osprey or 'fish eagle' (*Pandion haliaetus*). Amphibians, including frogs, toads and the protected great-crested newt (*Triturus cristatus*), live in streams and pools within wet woodland habitats throughout Scotland.

7.6 Willow woodlands in Scotland

We saw in Chapter 4 that willow species play an important role in the high-altitude montane scrub communities of Scotland, together with dwarf birches and juniper. A variety of scrub willows are found – most commonly downy willow (*Salix lapponum*) and mountain willow (*Salix arbuscula*), forming the NVC W20 community. More locally the woolly willow (*Salix lanata*) is found within this same habitat. However, our attention here focuses on those willows found in wet woodlands at lower altitudes.

Scotland lacks the concentrated areas of lowland 'willow fen' and 'willow carr' habitats found further south in the British Isles – for example the Cambridgeshire Fens, the Norfolk Broads, the Somerset Levels and parts of the Irish Midlands. As a result, it also lacks the tradition of intensively managed willow coppice ('withy' or osier beds) used to produce material for basketry in those areas. Some of the more southern willow species do not feature as significantly in Scotland – crack willow (*Salix fragilis*), white/cricket-bat willow (*Salix alba*) and weeping willow (*Salix x sepulcralis*). However, Scotland does have its own interesting and valuable resource of 'wilder' willow woodlands, distributed across the landscape in a number of different ecological contexts. The main willow species found in these woodlands are the grey willow (*Salix cinerea*), eared willow (*Salix aurita*), bay willow (*Salix pentandra*) and creeping willow (*Salix repens*), with some common osier (*Salix viminalis*) and goat willow (*Salix caprea*). These occur in three NVC communities (W1–3), of which W3 is the most common. Willow also occurs as a secondary component of W4 wet birch and W5 swamp alder woodlands.

Scottish willow woodland occurs in one of three ecological settings:

- **Bog, fens and swamps.** These are areas of wet ground, often peaty, but without significant open water. Most examples in Scotland are known as 'oligotrophic' (meaning nutrient-poor) and some are 'ombrotrophic' (meaning predominantly rain-fed). A minority are more fertile, receiving surface-water inflows bearing mineral nutrient supplies. Especially in lowland Scotland, very many of these sites have been subjected to agricultural drainage attempts over the past 300 years, with varying degrees of success. Naturally, willow woodland tends to be restricted to the better-drained margins of these sites, but it can extend out onto the peatland surface where drainage is artificially increased. Many wet woodlands in these situations also contain birch, being NVC W4 types.
- **Loch and lake margins.** Almost all lochs which do not have steep, rocky shorelines will have patches of willow woodland around their shelving margins. Lochs and lakes vary in the fertility of their waters and lakebed sediments, but willow can occur in most types. Fertile or 'eutrophic' lochs generally have a more muddy lakebed and can support larger areas of wet woodland as a result. Willow will usually extend from just below the high-water mark to just above it, often giving way to NVC W7 alder-birch woodland further up the banks. The willow woodlands in these situations in Scotland are most often NVC W3, locally W1/2.
- **Floodplains and estuaries.** Some of Scotland's rivers have a surviving active floodplain system, where willow woodland develops within the braided river channel. Good examples include the lower River Spey in Moray, the River Conon in Ross-shire, the River Fleet in East Sutherland and the River Endrick where it enters Loch Lomond. Alder tends to take over as the sand and gravel substrate stabilises.

7.7 Historical management – wood pasture and coppice

We saw earlier that a large fraction of the former wet woodland resource in Scotland was cleared to create agricultural land (usually seasonally wet grazing meadows) or as part of river confinement and canalisation schemes. Some of this loss has taken place over the past 300 years, especially during the 'Agricultural Improvements' (1750–1850). However, the remaining alder resource, particularly the better-drained elements of it, has been used over time, both as pasture woodlands and as productive coppice woodlands.

Although young basal shoots may be browsed off, alder is not an especially palatable tree for livestock, and its foliage would not be suitable for seasonal fodder as might ash and elm. Farmers would normally be reluctant to allow their stock to enter very wet alder woodlands where they might become bogged down and at risk of drowning. However, there are a number of sites in the uplands where alder grows on moist springline slopes and riparian river meadows which were used for cattle pasture, at least during the summer. Good examples include the ancient wood pasture at Glen Finglas and areas in Glen Strathfarrar and in parts of the Trossachs, Cowal and Argyll. These sites are relatively fertile and would have supported productive pastures. They are detectable today by the presence of very large veteran alder trees which have the appearance of having been deliberately pollarded above the height to which cattle can reach. If this was not to produce livestock fodder, it might have been to protect livestock from unpalatable foliage or to produce woodfuel or small wood for clogs, tool handles and so on. Very large veteran alder trees occur as an element in some historic lowland oak wood pastures and parklands, notably at Mugdock to the north-west of Glasgow (see Plate 13a).

Some areas of alder woodland were formerly managed fairly intensively as rotational coppices. After oak, hazel and birch, alder may have been the next most significant coppice species in Scotland. However, it is not regarded as a very good species for firewood (burning poorly due to wetness) and rots easily in outdoor applications, by comparison with oak or hazel. The timber rots quickly in the air but (as with elm) is rather durable in water-logged ground. Long, straight coppice poles of alder were useful for 'short-lived' applications demanding light, regular material – especially scaffolding poles, levers, crossbow staves, cheap furniture and so on. In these respects it served in some capacities where conifer timber is often applied today. Alder timber was also used for clog manufacturing – it was light, sufficiently strong and had an attractive red colouration once exposed to air.

By far the most notable use of coppice alder, however, was for gunpowder charcoal (Smout et al. 2005). The physical and chemical properties of the finely ground charcoal produced from alder were particularly suitable for gunpowder. From the 1500s onwards the material was much in demand for this purpose and alder coppice beds were managed close to the main gunpowder works on a regular rotation. The best documented example in Scotland is at Roslin Glen, just to the south of Edinburgh. The peak of this activity was during the Napoleonic Wars (1793–1815), when gunpowder supplies were required in large quantities for both artillery and naval campaigns. Although alder was preferred, a number of coastal mangrove species of the Caribbean, growing in estuarine wet woodland habitats similar to those favoured by alder, were used as gunpowder-charcoal substitutes from the 1600s onwards, when British naval fleets were stationed out in that region.

7.8 Wet woodlands and flood risk mitigation

In addition to their important role in protecting and supporting fish populations in Scottish rivers, wet woodlands are an essential component of the natural system for dealing with potential flood events. Their 'ecosystem services' in this respect are being increasingly valued, as heavy rainfall events appear to be a feature of current changes to the climate of Britain, and are predicted by climatic modelling work to continue into the future.

The main way in which wet woodlands act to control flooding is by 'delaying discharge' within river catchments, releasing it over a longer period of time. This can reduce the peak height of any flood, potentially allowing town defences, such as artificial flood barriers, to remain more effective. This delay and reduction in peak flow is due to the greater 'landscape roughness' of wet woodland as compared to alternative land-cover types such as pasture, arable land and paved surfaces within built developments. The more complex structure of woodland absorbs some of the energy of the floodwater, slowing it down, and also provides opportunities for water to be ponded temporarily within the woodland itself – in pools, backwaters and water-logged soils. Obviously there is a trade-off between retention of wet woodland within the landscape to reduce flood risk and the opportunity for profitable alternative land-use such as agriculture and development. The beneficiaries of wet woodland may be living in a town downstream that will be helped to avoid flood damage, whereas the costs are borne by hill farmers who may have to give up valuable pastures.

It is possible to create new wet woodland by planting as one measure to reduce flood risk. Obviously it takes some time for the woodland to grow to maturity and reach its full effectiveness, but the benefits are potentially significant if the new woodland is placed at well-selected locations in the landscape, taking into account hydrological factors (Nisbet and Thomas 2008). One situation where a greater effect can be achieved is where two rivers meet just above or below a town. If they carry little woodland, any heavy rainfall event in the hills above the town will lead to both rivers rising to a flood peak at very much the same time, with a high risk of over-topping flood barriers and other town defences. However, if new wet woodland is created on one of the catchments, this will cause a time-lag between the peak flows on the two rivers. The 'bare' catchment will peak earlier, whereas the 'wooded' catchment will peak later, with a longer but lower flood profile. This can have a dramatic effect on the peak flood level reached at or below the confluence of the rivers, where the two lower peaks will be felt one after the other, rather than additively at the same time. This can potentially reduce the peak level reached by up to a half. Given the value of economic assets being protected in built-up areas, the costs of creating new wet woodland and compensating landowners for the resulting lost agricultural income may be well justified. It is usually far less expensive to adopt this approach than to increase the height of hard-engineered flood barriers and dykes, and wet woodland has fewer side-impacts on landscape amenity. Much relevant work on this approach has recently been undertaken by Forest Research, with the results available at <www.forestry.gov.uk/research>.

7.9 Wet woodland and fisheries improvement

Creation of new wet woodland, if well planned, is also likely to have significant benefits for the water quality and biodiversity of river systems (Jeffries and Mills 1990; Parrott and MacKenzie 2000). This is of increasing policy importance in the light of obligations under the European Union Water Framework Directive. Erosion and diffuse pollution risks are reduced, water temperatures kept within safe limits and insect life promoted. Many recent wet woodland creation schemes have joint objectives of flood risk mitigation and sport fisheries improvement. Valuable salmonid stocks for sport fishing can be encouraged and protected by well-designed riparian woodland enhancement schemes, such as those pursued on the River Tweed over recent years. There is likely to be a future increase in activity in the field of wet woodland creation in Scotland for the full range of benefits.

CHAPTER EIGHT

Conservation of native woodlands

8.1 History of Scottish native woodland conservation

8.1.1 Woodland conservation awareness prior to 1914

Concerns over supplies of large-dimension timber for naval and other construction became evident from around 1450 onwards, as woodland resources in both England and Scotland were increasingly depleted. The Scottish Parliament recognised this as early as 1503 in an Act which encouraged private landowners to plant trees (Smout et al. 2005). English commentators such as John Evelyn in the 1660s and, later, Horatio Nelson in the 1790s encouraged landowners to plant trees as a patriotic duty. There was also recognition from the sixteenth century that supplies of oak coppice for production of charcoal for iron working were threatened, with the Weald, the Forest of Dean and Cumbria under heavy pressure. Ironmasters opted to switch their attentions to Ireland, then to western Scotland.

However, the first significant evidence of 'modern' attention to the conservation of native woodlands in Scotland came in the late nineteenth century and was largely focused on the native pinewoods and their ability to sustain timber yields (Anderson 1967; Smout et al. 2005). Many pinewoods were, by that time, neglected on Highland estates managed for deer stalking and grouse shooting. Many Scottish-trained foresters had seen service in the Empire territories, such as India, Burma and Canada, where management of forests for 'sustained yield' was then lately emphasised. These insights were brought 'home on leave', raising concerns for the Scottish pinewoods. A number of early excursions of the Royal Scottish Arboricultural Society (later to become the Royal Scottish Forestry Society) visited the major pinewood areas, including Rothiemurchus and Glenmore Forests, discussing future management options for forestry production.

8.1.2 Woodland conservation activity between the two world wars

However, many conservationists would date the beginnings of native woodland conservation to the early twentieth century, when the scientific discipline of ecology was introduced to Britain from the Continent. The British Ecological Society was founded in 1913. Early British woodland ecologists such as A. G. Tansley, A. S. Watt and E. W. Jones were mainly academics based at Oxford and Cambridge, but Scottish woodlands, particularly the native pinewoods, were often studied 'on summer tour'. Early British publications on woodland ecology emphasised the classification of native woodland communities using 'phyto-sociological' approaches, adopted from Europe (Braun-Blanquet 1932; Tansley 1939). This emphasis on recognition and botanical description of native woodland communities remained the main business of woodland ecology in Britain until after the Second World War. Despite designation by the Forestry Commission of individual forest reserve areas in Scotland during the 1930s (e.g. at Coille Phuiteachan, Glen Loy), there was rather limited progress on active conservation of native woodlands until the establishment of the Nature Conservancy in the later 1940s.

8.1.3 Post-war woodland conservation science and planning

An important post-war development for native woodland conservation was the establishment of the Nature Conservancy in 1948 (Warren 2002). This government agency was later renamed the Nature Conservancy Council and subsequently divided into three devolved national bodies in the early 1990s: Natural England, Scottish Natural Heritage and the Countryside Council for Wales. Their early organisational priority was on acquisition and management of National Nature Reserves (NNRs) and the pursuit of biological, ecological and conservation research at these sites and elsewhere. The Nature Conservancy began with a small, highly specialist staff. Several key native woodland sites in Scotland were purchased as NNRs, notably the Beinn Eighe pinewoods and the Taynish oakwoods. Further NNRs were also established within native woodlands under Forestry Commission or private ownership, as at Glenmore, Glen Affric, Glen Tanar and Abernethy (see Table 8.1). From the 1960s, the (by then) Nature Conservancy Council also took on an increased role in protection of habitats outside NNRs, including native woodlands owned by the Forestry Commission and private estates in Scotland. This was achieved by means of the designation of numerous 'Sites of Special Scientific Interest' (SSSIs), within which landowners had to seek consent for 'Potentially Damaging Operations' (PDOs). In some cases this led to tensions between the Nature Conservancy and the commercial forestry sector. As time went on, greater emphasis was placed on encouraging beneficial action through grant-aided management agreements, rather than simply trying to prevent deleterious activity, such as replanting with non-native conifers or excessive grazing by deer and livestock. SSSI provisions were strengthened by the Wildlife and Countryside Act (1981). In recent years an overarching suite of European-level Special Areas of Conservation (SACs) have been designated under the EU Habitats Directive, these frequently being coincident with existing SSSIs. In response to the volume of new site designations, the successor bodies to the Nature Conservancy have inevitably become larger, less scientifically specialist and more administratively complex organisations.

In the early 1970s, the earlier scientific research functions of the Nature Conservancy Council were split off into the Institute of Terrestrial Ecology (ITE), which later merged with the Institutes of Hydrology and Freshwater Biology to form today's

TABLE 8.1 Selected protected areas and species of native woodlands. Source: Scottish Natural Heritage, <www.snh.gov.uk>.

National Nature Reserves	County	Native Woodland Type(s)
Abernethy	Inverness-shire	Native pinewood
Ariundle Oakwood	Inverness-shire	Upland oakwood
Beinn Eighe	Wester Ross	Native pinewood
Clyde Valley Woodlands	Lanarkshire	Lowland mixed deciduous
Craigellachie	Inverness-shire	Upland birchwood
Creag Meagaidh	Inverness-shire	Upland birchwood
Glasdrum Wood	Argyll	Upland mixed ashwood
Glen Affric	Inverness-shire	Native pinewood
Glen Nant	Argyll	Upland oakwood/ Wet woodland
Glen Tanar	Aberdeenshire	Native pinewood
Glenmore	Inverness-shire	Native pinewood
Invereshie and Inshriach	Inverness-shire	Native pinewood/ Montane scrub
Loch Lomond	Dunbarton/ Stirlingshire	Upland oakwood/ Wet woodland
Loch Maree Islands	Wester Ross	Native pinewood
Muir of Dinnet	Aberdeenshire	Upland birchwood
Taynish	Argyll	Upland oakwood

In addition to the above National Nature Reserves (NNRs) there are numerous Sites of Special Scientific Interest (SSSIs) in Scotland that have a significant woodland habitat feature.
Current details of these sites are available from Scottish Natural Heritage (www.snh.gov.uk)

Protected Species	Scientific Name	Protection Category
Bats (all species)	various	European Protected Species
Scottish wildcat	*Felis silvestris*	European Protected Species
Great crested newt	*Triturus cristatus*	European Protected Species
Common otter	*Lutra lutra*	European Protected Species
Natterjack toad	*Bufo calamita*	European Protected Species
Killarney fern	*Trichomanes speciosum*	European Protected Species
Capercaillie	*Tetrao urugallus*	UK/ Scottish legislation (FCS Priority)
Red squirrel	*Sciurus vulgaris*	UK/ Scottish legislation (FCS Priority)
Pearl bordered fritillary	*Boloria euphrosyne*	UK/ Scottish legislation (FCS Priority)
Chequered skipper	*Carterocephalus palaemon*	UK/ Scottish legislation (FCS Priority)
Adder	*Vipera berus*	UK/ Scottish legislation
Badger	*Meles meles*	UK/ Scottish legislation
Bluebell	*Hyacinthoides non-scripta*	UK/ Scottish legislation
Crested tit	*Parus cristatus*	UK/ Scottish legislation
Golden eagle	*Aquila chrysaetos*	UK/ Scottish legislation
Goldeneye	*Bucephala clangula*	UK/ Scottish legislation
Goshawk	*Accipiter gentilis*	UK/ Scottish legislation
Hen harrier	*Circus cyaneus*	UK/ Scottish legislation
Osprey	*Pandion haliaetus*	UK/ Scottish legislation
Pine marten	*Martes martes*	UK/ Scottish legislation
Water vole	*Arvicola terrestris*	UK/ Scottish legislation
White-tailed eagle	*Haliaeetus albicilia*	UK/ Scottish legislation
Woodcock	*Scolopax rusticola*	UK/ Scottish legislation
Crossbills (all species)	*Loxia spp*	UK/ Scottish legislation
Hedgehog	*Erinaceus europaeus*	UK/ Scottish legislation
Mountain hare	*Lepidus timidus*	UK/ Scottish legislation
Juniper	*Juniperus communis*	FCS Priority only
Black grouse	*Tetrao tetrix*	FCS Priority only

The above list should not be taken as exhaustive and is accurate at 2014 only. Current details for all protected species are available from Scottish Natural Heritage (www.snh.gov.uk)

Centre for Ecology and Hydrology (CEH). Arguably, this decision reduced the internal scientific capacity of the NCC (and its successors) and impaired their original purpose.

Further development and improvement of British native woodland description and classification schemes continued between 1960 and 1990 with important work, especially by Oliver Rackham at Cambridge University, George Peterken at the Nature Conservancy Council, Bob Bunce at the Institute of Terrestrial Ecology and John Rodwell at the University of Lancaster. Peterken's classification of stand types (Peterken 1993) and the National Vegetation Classification (NVC) (woodland section) (Rodwell 1991a) are among schemes still in widespread use today.

It was also considered important to develop methods by which authentic 'ancient semi-natural woodlands' might be distinguished from native tree plantations, and thereby afforded special conservation attention. Older plantations of native tree species are sometimes difficult to detect. While historical maps and estate records have been widely employed in developing a provisional Ancient Woodland Inventory (AWI), the concept of 'ancient woodland indicator species' has also proved of considerable value (Peterken 1993) in assessing individual sites. This is based on evidence that certain ground vegetation plant species are only found within woodlands that have not previously been cleared for agriculture. While there is continuing debate about the reliability of this approach, regional lists of these species have now been proposed for different parts of Britain, following George Peterken's original studies in the Lincolnshire limewoods. In the last few years, an ancient woodland vascular plant (AWVP) listing has been proposed for Scotland (Crawford 2009) which can be applied within a range of native woodland types, including native pinewoods. The AWI provides an authoritative (if provisional) basis for both native woodland conservation and ecological restoration planning, and can now conveniently be examined in GIS map format via the SNH website (Walker and Kirby 1989; Whitbread 1990).

It was early recognised that the remaining extent of native woodlands was only a small fraction of their 'potential natural' land cover (McVean and Ratcliffe 1962), and that many surviving fragments were under continued threat from clearance for agriculture, conversion to forestry plantations and decline due to lack of natural regeneration, where browsing pressure was excessive. Having first identified and classified the native woodlands of Scotland, much post-war conservation emphasis has therefore had to be placed on preservation of the surviving remnants from further losses. Active restoration and expansion are more recent priorities.

Clearance of native woodlands for agriculture continued after the Second World War whilst many regarded them as unproductive scrubs. This resulted in significant losses of native woodland area in lowland England, perhaps rather less so in the Scottish uplands. Since that period, progressive introduction of the Forestry Commission 'felling licence' system and the designation by the Nature Conservancy of regional examples of each native woodland type as SSSIs have tended to restrict outright losses of woodland area by land clearance. However, until the mid-1980s (and locally later), ancient semi-natural woodlands were still being converted to plantations of introduced tree species by replanting and under-planting techniques. These are the woodlands that are now being described as 'Plantations on Ancient Woodland Sites' (PAWS), and are being progressively restored toward native woodland composition.

Even where clearance or replanting of native woodland remnants was averted, there was increasing recognition that the lack of natural regeneration would, in the end, lead to woodlands disappearing. Steven and Carlisle (1959) had clearly described the regeneration problem for the pinewoods in their famous book *The Native Pinewoods of Scotland*, and the same problem was evident in the upland oakwoods. In many native woodlands, there had been little seedling regeneration since around 1840, when management for timber declined and red deer and hill sheep became increasingly numerous. While adverse vegetation conditions in some woodlands prevented the establishment of tree seedlings, the main problem remained browsing by red deer on Highland sporting estates and by sheep, particularly on extensive upland hill farms (and elsewhere where livestock were over-wintered within native woodlands). From the 1980s, changes in the economics of upland farming shifted the balance away from the larger hill sheep flocks that had been a feature for two centuries in many Highland districts (Warren 2002), although they continued to be a feature in some parts of the Borders, Perthshire and Stirlingshire. While it was possible over time to reduce sheep grazing in native woodlands by grant-aided stock exclusion programmes (e.g. the Livestock Exclusion Annual Premium, or LEAP), the issues on the Highland deer 'forests' proved more intractable. Some estate owners continued to see native woodlands as essential 'winter shelter' for the high deer populations that they wished to retain for sporting values (see Plate 14). Hence they proved reluctant to apply extensive deer fencing to areas of native woodland other than new plantation schemes. Many ecologists also disliked fencing on the grounds of artificiality, continuing browsing impact on open-land vegetation habitats outside the fence and collision risks to grouse species. They preferred to see significant reductions in red deer numbers by humane culling. As we will see later, this divergence in approaches to securing natural regeneration in upland native woodlands has become one of the more controversial issues in Scottish native woodland conservation, consuming considerable research, operational and financial resources. However, in some native woodlands, considerable progress has recently been made.

8.1.4 The shift from protection to expansion and restoration

The last three decades have seen a diversification of activity in the Scottish native woodland conservation 'movement'. While stand preservation and promotion of natural regeneration continue to be major emphases, a variety of active 'ecological restoration' approaches have been adopted, aimed at promoting the ecological function of native woodlands in Scotland towards their condition before human interference. A growing body of practical experience has been accumulated as to how to attempt this. Chapter 9 will deal with the efforts to create 'new native woodlands' from scratch. However, a variety of approaches have been implemented within existing woodlands (Forestry Commission Scotland 2008, 2012; Peterken and Stevenson 2004; Plantlife 2001; Woodland Trust 2005). These include the selective removal of non-native tree species (especially on ancient woodland or PAWS sites), control of invasive plant species such as *Rhododendron*, and smaller-scale planting of native trees to improve species diversity. As well as lacking natural regeneration, many native woodlands also lack veteran trees and deadwood habitats, due to a history of timber and woodfuel harvesting and forestry management. This is considered to place them in 'unfavourable conservation status' due to the dependence on deadwood of many invertebrate species of conservation importance. While this position could only recover naturally over many decades, various artificial means of accelerating deadwood accumulation have been applied on a localised basis. There are also the beginnings, over recent years, of recognition that it is possible to combine sustainable silviculture for timber production with effective conservation management in Scottish native woodlands – whether of Scots pine, oak, ash, birch or alder. This has the potential to increase the value of these woodlands to their owners by generating some income. Indeed, in many cases, sensitive silvicultural work aimed at producing timber by thinning or coppicing has significant 'knock-on' benefits for conservation (Peterken and Worrell 2001; Thompson 2005; Worrell 1999).

Conservation of native-woodland-dependent plants, birds, mammals and invertebrates has assumed increasing importance over recent years (see Table 8.1), with many key examples being the subject of Species Action Plans (SAPs) under the UK Biodiversity Action Plan (UKBAP). There has also been active experimentation on the restoration of actively managed livestock to native woodlands and, more controversially, on the reintroduction of locally extinct native fauna (e.g. capercaillie, wild boar, beaver, wild cattle). All such avenues are more feasible within a larger, more robust overall native woodland resource.

The recently conducted Native Woodland Survey of Scotland (NWSS) (Forestry Commission Scotland 2014) provides an unprecedented level of spatial detail on the distribution, extent, composition, condition and context of our native woodlands (see Plate 19 and Table 8.2 for summary information and <www.forestry.gov.uk/nwss> for access to more detailed data for analyses). This is particularly important in planning measures to conserve, restore and expand native woodland habitats allocated specific Habitat Action Plans (HAPs) under the terms of the UKBAP.

8.1.5 Recognition of cultural heritage, archaeological and social values

The native woodlands of Scotland also have significant cultural heritage, archaeological and social values (Ritchie and Wordsworth 2010) as one of the least modified and disturbed elements of the country's land cover. This was not always recognised due to a lack of relevant research and more restrictive arrangements for public access to native woodlands on private land. Legislation by the devolved Scottish Government has made woodland legally open to public access on foot, by cycle and on horseback in recent years. There has also been increased activity in archaeological survey within native woodlands in Scotland – both for conventional remains of ancient buildings and monuments and also in respect of 'living archaeological' evidence of traditional forms of woodland management such as coppicing, pollarding and woodland pasture.

TABLE 8.2 Native woodland extent, composition and condition. Source: Native Woodland Survey of Scotland Forestry Commission Scotland (2014).

FC Native Woodland Type	Area (ha)	*% of Total Area*	*% in Satisfactory Condition*	Ancient (ha)	*% Ancient*	Semi-natural (ha)	*% Semi-natural*
Native pinewood	87,599	*28*	*62*	18,396	*21*	19,272	*22*
Upland birchwood	91,235	*29*	*39*	28,283	*31*	80,287	*88*
Upland oakwood	19,474	*6*	*36*	10,126	*52*	17,332	*89*
Lowland mixed deciduous woodland	23,189	*7*	*27*	3,015	*13*	16,464	*71*
Upland mixed ashwood	12,353	*4*	*34*	4,571	*37*	10,994	*89*
Wet woodland	44,742	*14*	*46*	8,501	*19*	36,688	*82*
Scrub types (including montane)	3,782	*1*	*47*	5,033	*15*	3,622	*96*
Other	28,779	*9*				8,346	*29*
TOTAL	**311,153**	***100***	***46***	**77,924**	***25***	**193,005**	***62***
				64,130ha (21%) are both Ancient and Semi-Natural			

In many cases the results of such 'cultural landscape' investigations (H. H. Birks 1989) have become the focus of public interpretation signage and trails (see Plate 15), aimed at raising the tourism profile and recreational use of native woodlands. In addition to ongoing academic research, local communities in rural Scotland have shown increasing interest in native woodlands within their localities as an element of their own social history and as a potential resource for tourism-based business, outdoor recreation, physical exercise and educational initiatives. This reflects a positive change from the position some decades ago when woodlands tended to be regarded as official (if publicly owned) or private-estate preserves. Legislative action to enhance public access to woodlands in Scotland, and to make provision for community land-interests to be recognised and formalised, is beginning to bear some fruit. A small number of rural communities have pursued their interest towards woodland ownership or leasing partnerships, with active timber harvesting (Glass et al. 2013). Key examples include those at Abriachan and Laggan in Inverness-shire and at Birse on Deeside (Aberdeenshire).

8.2 Policy, regulation, grants and ownership

8.2.1 British forestry policy and administration pre-devolution

Modern forestry policy in Britain can essentially be traced back to the critical timber-supply shortages encountered during the submarine blockade of the First World War (Anderson 1967; Fowler 2002; Oosthoek 2013). The foundation of the Forestry Commission in 1919 was a response to this, and the main objective of the new organisation was the establishment of a 'national strategic reserve' of home-grown timber, mainly by creating even-aged plantations of fast-grown introduced conifers. These were planted both on land purchased or leased by the Forestry Commission and, with fiscal incentives, on private estate lands. A secondary objective was the provision of a new source of rural employment, especially for those returning from service in the armed forces. The Forestry Commission has been seen during this period as adopting a 'militaristic approach' to its tasks, emphasising hierarchy, expertise and regimentation (Fowler 2002; Oosthoek 2013). That continued through the Second World War and the subsequent decades.

From the 1960s, it was increasingly argued that timber supply was becoming a less significant strategic requirement with the decline in the use of coal as a fuel (and hence the requirement for mining timber). The Forestry Commission was under growing pressure to justify its investments on purely economic grounds, as assessed by 'discounted revenue analyses'. These encouraged an emphasis on reducing the initial costs of plantation establishment and maintenance, particularly by planting cheaper upland ground and employing more standardised and mechanised site preparation for Sitka spruce crops. Building upon earlier public campaigning in the 1930s, recreational amenity also came to be seen as a key objective of management, raising emphasis on improved forest landscape design.

From the mid-1980s, nature conservation became an article of British forestry policy, in terms of both key wildlife species and, more recently, native woodland habitats. The 'Broadleaves Policy' (Forestry Commission 1985) effectively brought to an end the active replanting of native broadleaved woodlands with conifer species and laid the foundation for enhanced grant assistance to establish new native woodland. The Native Pinewoods Scheme (1989) (Aldhous 1995) provided grant assistance for establishment of new pinewoods within the Caledonian Pinewood Zone (CPZ) in Scotland. In the wake of controversy over rapid commercial afforestation of the 'Flow Country' peatlands in Caithness, changes to forestry tax legislation in the 'Lawson Budget' of 1988 caused a major reduction in the rate of such activity. From the early 1990s onwards, incentives for woodland expansion and management were increasingly in the form of direct grant aid, under successive government schemes; for Scotland these were the Forestry Grant Scheme (FGS), the Woodland Grant Scheme (WGS), the Scottish Forestry Grant Scheme (SFGS) and the Scottish Rural Development Programme – Rural Priorities (SRDP-RP). The UN conference in Rio in 1992 saw increased international emphasis on the conservation and restoration of natural forest habitats, and this was reflected in domestic policies favouring expansion of the native woodland resource by new planting and by restoration of Plantations on Ancient Woodland Sites (PAWS). Grant schemes were increasingly tailored toward achieving these conservation-related policy objectives.

The 1990s saw growing criticism of the Forestry Commission in Scotland on the grounds of its being perceived as a 'remote' landowner and manager. This was despite its GB headquarters having been moved to Edinburgh from London some years earlier, and the widespread public appreciation of its efforts on wildlife conservation and recreational access. The main locus of this criticism can be related back to its earlier 'social objective' of the creation of rural employment, which had been demoted since the 1980s with increased cost controls and mechanised working methods. Many Scottish rural communities surrounded by plantation forest resources developed aspirations to see these managed for local economic benefits, and came to see public-agency ownership and management as an impediment to progress on this. It was felt that if the land was 'wrested away' from the 'centralised hand of the Commission' with its formalised procedures, more could perhaps be achieved. This feeling formed part of the wider move to community land ownership and management (Warren 2002; Glass et al. 2013), starting with the Assynt crofters' buy-out in 1993.

8.2.2 Organisational arrangements for forestry in Scotland

With the advent of the Scottish Parliament in 1999, following a public referendum in 1997, forestry became a 'devolved matter' where most policy decisions are taken at the 'country' (e.g. Scottish) level. The Forestry Commission has been formally retained as a GB-wide body, although Wales established separate arrangements in April 2013 in the form of an integrated environmental agency, Natural Resources Wales. A small number of important aspects of forestry policy and support continue to be dealt with at the GB-wide level, including research, plant health and international forestry issues. Forestry Commission Scotland effectively acts as the Scottish Government's 'forestry department', reporting directly to Ministers. This situation has led to a gradual divergence of forestry policies and support mechanisms between England, Scotland and Wales. Broadly speaking, Scottish Government forestry policy (as expressed in the Scottish Forestry Strategy of 2006) places more emphasis on economic, commercial and rural development aspects than do those of England and Wales, where conservation and recreational amenity have been prioritised, with the National Forest Estate comprising a larger share of the Scottish total.

8.2.3 Conservation legislation and regulation

Forestry Commission Scotland acts as the main government regulatory and grant-aiding body in Scotland relevant to native woodland conservation. Any tree felling above a *de minimis* quarterly timber volume requires a Felling Licence to be issued in advance, which will usually have a condition of effective restocking (by either replanting or natural regeneration) unless there are sound conservation reasons for land reversion to open habitats. In many cases, the Forestry Commission will consult upon proposals for work within native woodlands with 'statutory consultees', including Scottish Natural Heritage, Historic Scotland and local authorities, and also with relevant non-governmental conservation organisations (NGOs), such as the Royal Society for the Protection of Birds (RSPB). While it is possible to apply for a Felling Licence for individual operations in native woodlands (e.g. thinning work), many woodland owners in the public, private and charitable sectors will seek approval on the basis of a Forest Plan, covering an entire land-holding for a ten- to twenty-year period. Preparation of a Forest Plan often requires detailed survey, mapping and consultation for which a 'plan preparation grant' is usually available. Forestry proposals set out in such a plan are expected to conform to the UK Forestry Standard (UKFS), embodying sets of guidelines on key aspects such as soils, freshwater, archaeology and biodiversity. Some owners choose to commit to additional site requirements under the voluntary UK Woodland Assurance Scheme (UKWAS 2011), a domestic form of certification recognised by the Forest Stewardship Council. Adherence to these higher standards can offer timber marketing advantages.

Where native woodlands have been designated as Sites of Special Scientific Interest (SSSIs) and/or Special Areas of Conservation (SACs), many types of work, known as Potentially Damaging Operations (PDOs), will also require prior approval from Scottish Natural Heritage (as the statutory nature conservation organisation). Woodland work that might have an impact on rivers or freshwater bodies may require approval from the Scottish Environmental Protection Agency (SEPA). This would apply particularly where forestry vehicles have to enter or cross watercourses and where there is a risk of river siltation from felling and extraction work. Certain work in woodlands, especially where there is a permanent change of land-use, requires an Environmental Impact Assessment (EIA), which is dealt with by the Forestry Commission as part of their approvals process. This would be unusual in the case of conservation works within existing native woodlands. Some tree-felling work in association with approvals for built development proposals is dealt with by local authorities under the terms of the 'town and country' planning process. Felling of individual trees (or occasionally whole woodlands) subject to specific Tree Protection Orders (TPOs) also requires additional local authority advance approval.

8.2.4 Grant assistance for native woodland conservation

Forestry Commission Scotland also administers the regimes of state grant assistance for both new woodland creation (see Chapter 9) and woodland management work. The relevant grant scheme in force from 2015 to 2020 is expected to be the second round of the Scottish Rural Development Programme (SRDP). This is funded partly by the Scottish Government and partly by the European Union as part of the Common Agricultural Policy (CAP). Grants are available for a wide range of specified management work in native woodlands that is expected to achieve priority objectives related to habitat and species conservation, habitat improvement and the control of invasive introduced species (e.g. *Rhododendron*). Certain types of silvicultural work, such as selective thinning, which produce timber but are still 'cost operations' are also eligible. Grants usually support a majority but not all of the costs incurred. The application process for SRDP grants has been seen as demanding, with the result that not all native woodland owners have participated. Details are available at <www.forestry.gov.uk>.

Scottish Natural Heritage administers some grants potentially relevant to conservation work on designated sites (e.g. SSSIs and SACs) where there is a native woodland component. However, where native woodland is the dominant feature, Forestry Commission Scotland normally takes the lead.

Some charitable NGOs have a remit to assist conservation work in native woodlands. Most restrict this to woodlands under their direct ownership (see immediately below), but there have been situations where they have helped smaller private landowners to plan and undertake conservation work in their own woodlands. Several previous Scottish regional-scale 'native woodland initiatives' have now ceased operations, but Woodland Trust Scotland can and does provide some assistance with handling of applications for relevant state conservation grants, particularly in respect of the restoration of priority PAWS sites.

8.2.5 Implications of changes in woodland ownership patterns

We have seen that changes in Forestry Commission policy since the mid-1980s have been an important influence, promoting native woodland conservation on the National Forest Estate (NFE). While the NFE contains some very important native woodland sites, notably in the Cairngorms, Glen Affric, the Great Glen, Ardnamurchan, Loch Lomond and Galloway, many more are under private ownership. Hence another significant factor in encouraging increased conservation in Scottish native woodlands over the past three decades has been the changing pattern of private land ownership. Whereas native woodland conservation was not a major objective of most traditional private estate and farmland owners, some new owners would place it much higher on their list of management priorities. Three trends in private land ownership are of particular significance (Glass et al. 2013):

- **Charitable ownership.** Since 1980 a number of major upland estates, and many smaller lowland native woodland areas, have been purchased by conservation charities (e.g. Woodland Trust Scotland, RSPB, Scottish Wildlife Trust, John Muir Trust, National Trust for Scotland, Trees for Life). These bodies represent 'communities of interest', often at a distance, with environmental conservation aims. The presence of significant existing native woodland resources on properties is often a principal reason for charitable acquisition. Charitable NGOs are often able to 'top up' state conservation grants with members' donations and to access sources of voluntary labour.
- **Community ownership.** Particularly over the past fifteen to twenty years, a number of larger estates and individual woodland areas have been acquired by local communities, mainly in rural areas. The Scottish Government's 'land reform policy' has encouraged this trend by making available sources of financial assistance for land purchase and by encouraging disposals of state-owned land in some situations. Local communities vary greatly in their objectives for land 'buy-outs'. Typically, achieving a greater degree of local control over the management of, and access to, surrounding land resources is central. Some (especially remoter) communities place considerable emphasis on economic and rural development objectives of management, such as cooperative business ventures and job creation, while many elsewhere emphasise amenity, recreation and habitat conservation. Community land ownership can be associated with increased activity in the field of native woodland conservation, sometimes using voluntary labour inputs. However, dependence on state and charitable sources of financial assistance for such work is typically rather high. Many communities would prefer a 'partnership model', allowing them a say, and an active role, in woodland management without the legal and financial commitments associated with outright purchase and ownership. Several such partnerships have been developed with the Forestry Commission in respect of areas of the National Forest Estate (Forestry Commission Scotland 2005) (e.g. Laggan, Cree Valley, Sunart), but rather fewer with traditional private estates.
- **Small private owners.** Especially in very recent years, there has been an increasing interest in the purchase of smaller areas of woodland in Scotland by private individuals, families or syndicates, some with little or no previous woodland ownership involvement. This follows noticeably earlier trends in southern/central England and Wales. Objectives typically combine private amenity, environmental awareness/interest and subsistence woodfuel production. Mixed mature woodlands in accessible locations and with an existing (or potential) house site are at a premium and command very high prices. Native woodland sites with stringent nature conservation designations are not preferred, as scope for active management tends to be more restricted. Some of this new 'cohort' of smaller private woodland owners are interested in native woodland conservation and management and bring to bear enthusiasm and, often, private funds. With appropriate training and advice this can be seen as a positive development for active native woodland conservation in Scotland.

8.3 Promoting natural regeneration

With legal protection now largely in place against clearance for agriculture, development or forestry replanting, the most significant conservation problem affecting many native woodlands in Scotland is their 'geriatric' age structure and corresponding lack of recent natural regeneration. We saw in the four chapters dealing with the major native woodland types that each has its own natural regeneration system which must be taken into account when planning measures to promote regeneration (Oliver and Larson 1996).

8.3.1 Natural regeneration in native pinewoods

Pine and birch woodlands in the drier parts of eastern Scotland usually regenerate across significant areas at a single point in time, due to events such as fires, windstorms or human exploitation that have long 'return-periods'. These are known as 'stand-replacing events'. These tend to synchronise the age of trees across large sections of a landscape, which will then also reach maturity and senescence at roughly the same time in the future. Good examples can be seen in the Inshriach, Glenfeshie and Glenmore pinewoods of Speyside. In practice, because individual trees vary genetically, they have differing lifespans. Even if, in an extreme case, they were all established in the same single year, they will undergo natural mortality over a period of at least thirty to fifty years, depending on tree species. For example, a stand of Scots pine trees which regenerated after harvesting during the Napoleonic Wars (1793–1815) might be expected to reach the end of their life between 2050 and 2100, but a small proportion might still be alive as veteran individuals in 2250. This natural regeneration strategy carries the risk that if conditions do not become suitable for natural regeneration at any time between, say, 2050 and 2200, the population may not be effectively renewed on that site.

8.3.2 Natural regeneration in native broadleaved woodlands

Other types of Scottish native woodland, such as oak, ash, elm and alder woodlands, normally regenerate by the 'gap-phase mechanism' where the windthrow or natural mortality of one or more mature trees creates the opportunity for a clump of young regeneration to develop. This 'distributed regeneration' strategy results in a wider range of structural classes of trees (seedling, sapling, pole stage, mature and veteran) being present within any area of undisturbed woodland at any given point in time. Factors which prevent successful regeneration, such as browsing impacts, may however prevent young seedlings from 'recruiting' at the bottom of the age-class distribution. Although the older trees may live for several centuries, this will gradually push the woodland towards an artificially elderly age structure. However, unless conditions remain unsuitable for natural regeneration over a very extended period, the woodland will eventually revert to its natural pattern of regeneration and age structure. There is a lower risk of the population dying out due to regeneration failure with this regeneration strategy than is the case in the more even-aged woodland types where regeneration must occur within a narrower window of opportunity.

8.3.3 Factors preventing or restricting natural regeneration

Unfortunately, a significant proportion of native woodlands in Scotland underwent a process of artificial age-synchronisation during the period 1650–1850, which was then followed by a long period when conditions were unsuitable for natural regeneration. This has left many woodlands with an age structure weighted towards mature and, in many cases, over-mature or 'geriatric' individuals. In some situations, this puts woodlands in danger of disappearing over coming decades as old trees die. In the case of the native pinewoods, age-synchronisation was largely due to extensive felling for timber production during the period 1750–1820, particularly during and after the Napoleonic Wars (1793–1815) (Mason et al. 2004). Conditions following these fellings included moderate deer numbers, well-shepherded hill sheep flocks and planned efforts to secure effective regeneration by a combination of temporary stock fencing and replanting. In many of the native pinewoods the most recent natural regeneration stems from 1820 to 1840, represented by trees now in the 'middle years' of their life-cycle. In other cases, fellings during the two world wars created extensive areas of uniform pole-stage pinewood, as at Glenmore and Inshriach. In the case of the lowland oakwoods, some were felled and replanted/regenerated between 1680 and 1860, creating even-aged oak stands today. In most Atlantic and upland oakwoods that were managed as industrial coppices, the last cycle of coppicing took place during the period 1850–1900, when coke took over from charcoal as the main fuel for iron-smelting and chemical tanning agents replaced bark tannin. This sudden end to the coppicing process across large areas imposed an artificially even age structure on oakwoods. However, oak might naturally live for 300–500 years, if left unmanaged. Many former coppice oak woodlands are now dense, even-aged, mid-rotation stands. Birch woodlands often stem from single episodes of natural regeneration onto abandoned open land, for example during the agricultural depression of the 1930s. The native woodlands in Scotland with the most natural age structure today tend to be the ash-elm-hazel woodlands of steep-sided valleys and the wet alder-willow woodlands. Neither underwent the systematic management across large areas that affected pine and oak woodlands, and they thereby avoided artificial age structures.

It was unfortunate that the end of active management for timber and coppice wood in many Scottish native woodlands, during the period 1850–1900, happened to coincide with dramatic increases in the levels of browsing by red deer and grazing by hill sheep. This acted to close off opportunities for successor cohorts of trees to be recruited by natural regeneration. If landowners wanted woodland, they now had to restock it by fencing and replanting, which was a much more expensive process. The previous Highland farming system, with its dependence on seasonal cattle grazing, did not have this deleterious effect. Although cattle might browse young trees at any particular location, they were moved around the landscape by herdsmen to such an extent that they did not seriously restrict long-term woodland regeneration. However, large commercial flocks of the heavier sheep breeds, such as the Cheviot, brought into the Highlands from the 1790s onwards tended to be more static and therefore to have a greater impact on the upland woodlands on the hillsides (Smout 1997, 2000, 2003; Smout et al. 2005). They were also admitted to many formerly enclosed coppice oak woodlands, now no longer required for production. The introduction of these sheep was associated with the process known as the 'Clearances' which removed many people from farmsteads across upland Scotland. The agricultural labour force was therefore no longer sufficient to herd and shepherd livestock carefully, allowing areas of young regenerating woodland to establish, perhaps with some use of temporary fencing.

In many parts of the Scottish uplands it was red deer rather than hill sheep that did most of the damage to the natural regeneration opportunities of native woodlands. From around 1840 onwards, it became fashionable to manage large areas of the landscape for red deer stalking and grouse shooting (Glass et al. 2013). Although red deer are a native species, their numbers were formerly controlled at lower levels by natural predators and by routine hunting for food by local people. The eradication of wolves by the 1750s and the removal of large parts of the human population during the Clearances reduced both pressures and deer numbers began to rise rapidly. This suited the interests of sporting estate owners who wanted to offer their guests reliable quarry. In some cases, artificial feeding and other protective measures were used to allow larger numbers of deer to survive hard winters than would otherwise have been the case. Woodlands became of value mainly as 'winter shelter' for these deer and for their picturesque appearance in the landscape as 'remnants of the Highland wilderness'. In many cases, no effort was made to ensure that they regenerated naturally. Only where timber was still a major enterprise of estate forestry management was woodland regeneration prioritised, this mainly in the eastern Highlands – in the Speyside and Deeside pinewoods especially.

8.4 Protecting regeneration from browsing

Given the significance of herbivory by sheep and deer in limiting natural regeneration, it is not surprising that it has come to be seen as the major conservation issue facing Scottish native woodlands (Forestry Commission Scotland 2014). While the impacts of grazing by sheep have generally declined due to changes in agricultural economics and programmes of grant-aided livestock exclusion, the same cannot be said of deer browsing. Numbers of red deer in the Highlands have increased significantly since the last war, due to declining levels of poaching, growing availability of shelter within plantations and winter feeding. Current estimates of red deer numbers in Scotland exceed 300,000. Their browsing effects on native woodlands have been concentrated in native pinewoods and upland birchwoods. Numbers of roe deer have also increased across all native woodland types, having an important, but less obvious, ecological impact.

There is no historical experience that we can draw upon as to how to secure natural regeneration in native woodlands in the continued presence of such large numbers of deer – it has never happened in the recorded past. Traditional systems of temporary fencing and livestock herding, applied in past centuries, could not cope with this problem. That being the case, two alternative approaches have been used: the use of high-tensile deer fencing to exclude deer during the woodland regeneration phase, and humane deer culling to locally reduce deer numbers to levels that permit natural regeneration without fencing. Each has its pros and cons.

8.4.1 Use of deer fencing to protect regeneration

Deer fencing has been the conventional solution, proposed by those with a 'forestry management' background. It has the distinct advantages of speed, predictability and a reasonable assurance of success in protecting existing natural regeneration (or planted trees) from herbivore browsing. This makes it easier to reconcile with short-term management planning and grant-aid schemes. However, major disadvantages are its cost and logistical challenges on rough terrain. Particularly where applied to small planting schemes, or to natural regeneration areas on rough ground or with an inefficient boundary, it can prove a very expensive solution. Some foresters have resorted to protecting individual trees with plastic tubing tree-shelters. These may be less expensive for smaller schemes, but can have adverse effects on the growth and future stem form of the trees, especially on more exposed sites.

A number of major native woodland conservation projects have used large-scale deer fencing to good effect to protect natural regeneration and areas of planted new native woodland. However, native woodland conservation advocates have brought forward a number of criticisms of deer fencing, over and above cost/logistical issues. At a fundamental level it is seen as an artificial approach not relying upon natural processes, and which ignores the inescapable fact that deer should be a natural part of woodland ecosystems. Although putting up a fence very often results in rapid release of pre-existing natural regeneration (see Figure 8.1), conservationists will argue that this 'doesn't prove anything'. Competitive weeds can prevent fresh natural tree regeneration within fenced exclosures. Only where tree regeneration can occur in balance with natural populations of herbivores can favourable woodland conservation status really be achieved. Fences interrupt the natural patterns of movement of deer across upland landscapes, causing possible welfare problems with lack of food and shelter during the winter season. There are also aesthetic arguments – the appearance of deer fencing and associated access infrastructure is unsightly in the landscape and detracts from the 'wilderness experience'. In some situations this is undoubtedly valid, especially where deer fences cross the sky-line.

Additionally, there are serious issues associated with the collision danger that deer fences can pose to woodland grouse species, particularly the capercaillie, which is a protected species in Scotland (Moss and Picozzi 1994). The bird tends to fly low through the woodland under conditions of poor light (early morning and dusk) and there have been reports of carcasses being found at the foot of deer fences. The occurrence of such collisions may be under-reported as predators often take away the carcasses within a few hours. The problem appears to be most severe where deer fences are erected through existing woodland, as the time between any bird seeing the fence and striking

FIGURE 8.1 *Long-standing exclosure with regeneration, Rannoch. Copyright: Dr Scott McG. Wilson.*

it is reduced by poor visibility. The recorded numbers of capercaillie in Scotland have declined in recent years, during a period when deer fencing has been more widely used, but there is not necessarily a direct link between the two – poor weather and infectious disease are alternative explanations. Various methods of marking deer fences to reduce bird-strikes are now used (see Plate 16), including chestnut palings and plastic mesh.

8.4.2 Use of deer culling to protect regeneration

The preferred approach of the woodland conservation movement is humane deer culling, with the intention of reducing deer populations to a level that allows natural regeneration. This is often estimated at a level of five deer per 100ha (=1km^2), but deer densities across the landscape can vary both spatially and with the seasons of the year. Therefore obtaining an accurate count of deer and then setting an appropriate cull level can be technically difficult, although approaches have been developed in recent years (Mayle 2003; Swanson et al. 2008). However, if it proves possible to reduce deer numbers sufficiently, this approach offers the opportunity to arrive at a more natural, self-sustaining and less expensive solution than those using deer fencing. If it proves difficult to reduce deer numbers sufficiently, it may be necessary to combine this approach with some 'tactical/temporary fencing' to protect regeneration. The main problems with the deer-culling approach are the logistical difficulty of carrying out the cull and the potential impacts on sporting-estate values. Culling has to be well planned, carried out by highly trained stalkers and restricted to permitted periods, to avoid the breeding season on animal-welfare grounds. Severe weather, access issues and a lack of skilled staff can make the culling process slow, difficult and expensive. There have been concerns over animal welfare in specific situations. It is often necessary to reduce deer numbers to a small fraction of the levels traditionally maintained by sporting estates. This has implications for the attractiveness of the property for commercial stalking and hence its future capital asset value. Hence, most successful examples of the culling-based approaches have been on land-holdings where nature conservation and woodland regeneration are the principal management aims. In some districts, neighbouring landowners may feel that intensive deer culling creates a 'population vacuum' into which deer from their property will move, later also to be culled. However, deer do not permanently belong to any particular landowner, rather being available to be shot within season on any property where they are currently residing.

It must be remembered that excessive browsing may not be the only factor preventing natural regeneration, and hence fencing or culling may not alone secure it in sufficient quantity (Mason et al. 2004). Lack of seed production due to an inadequate number, poor health or excessive age of parent 'seed trees' can be an additional problem in some cases, leaving replanting as the only practical option. Dense ground vegetation cover (grass, heather, mosses) can also prevent germination and outcompete young seedlings. Vegetation often becomes dense or 'rank' when livestock or deer browsing is eliminated – for example within a fenced exclosure. A variety of techniques for preparing the seed bed, including vegetation removal and soil scarification, are available (see Figure 8.2), and can be achieved by controlled use of cattle or pigs as part of wider ecological restoration projects.

FIGURE 8.2 *Trial ground preparation to promote natural pinewood regeneration, Mar Lodge Estate. Copyright: Dr Scott McG. Wilson.*

8.5 Control of browsing pressure – field examples

8.5.1 Beinn Eighe National Nature Reserve

As one of the first National Nature Reserves in the Caledonian pinewoods, Beinn Eighe in Wester Ross has served, since 1951, as something of a 'test-bed' for methods of securing native woodland regeneration in the Scottish uplands (Laughton Johnston and Balharry 2001). It has also served, at times, to highlight fundamental differences in philosophy between the ecological and forestry communities as to how to go about this. The reserve is located in a district where higher numbers of red deer have traditionally been maintained for stalking purposes and where some neighbouring estates have wished to continue that tradition. During the 60+ years of management of the Beinn Eighe pinewoods by the Nature Conservancy (later Scottish Natural Heritage), both deer-culling and deer-fencing approaches have been used at times, together with some planting of Scots pine on the lower slopes. The planting option also raised the issue of genetic conservation and local provenancing in this part of Scotland, where the genetics of Scots pine are distinct (Ennos et al. 2000; Forrest 1992; Herbert et al. 1999). Ground preparation has been used to accelerate establishment of young pine where ground vegetation was too competitive. The original regeneration objectives at the time of acquisition of the reserve are now being met, but this has taken longer than was expected. The combination of techniques used are probably more intensive than might be considered in a similar situation today, especially the earlier reliance on fencing, ground preparation and planting. However, effective control of deer browsing and provision of a suitable seed bed for establishment were shown to be essential requirements.

8.5.2 Abernethy Forest, Glenfeshie Estate and Creag Meagaidh NNR

In the case of native woodland regeneration in the uplands, naturalistic approaches centre on the process of reducing deer numbers to a level consistent with natural regeneration, and allowing time for tree seedlings to respond. This 'ecological approach' has been adopted at the Creag Meagaidh National Nature Reserve at Loch Laggan, where intensive control of red deer has allowed upland birch woodland to regenerate onto what were bare hills. Here, ecological restoration being the sole objective of management, the 'no fence' culling approach has been able to be pursued with sufficient consistency to be successful. A similar approach has been applied by the RSPB in the rather different context of their Abernethy Forest reserve on Speyside. Here, mature pinewood is well established, but deer numbers over recent decades had restricted regeneration. Fencing is thought inconsistent with key bird conservation objectives. A persistent programme of deer control has more recently allowed prolific Scots pine regeneration to establish from the upper edges of the forest onto the open hillsides above. There are challenges in maintaining sufficient pressure on deer populations, even where conservation is the primary object of management. Subventions of funds from charitable donations allow Abernethy to forego sporting revenue. The 'no fence' deer-culling approach is also being applied with considerable success in some privately owned native pinewoods, particularly at Glen Feshie in the Cairngorms, where owners now prioritise ecological restoration objectives over deer stalking.

8.5.3 Mar Lodge Estate

The Mar Lodge Estate in the Cairngorm headwaters of the River Dee was acquired by the National Trust for Scotland (NTS) in the mid-1990s. The estate contains significant native pinewood remnants in Glens Derry, Luibeg and Quoich. The land had formerly been managed as a traditional sporting estate with very high red deer numbers. The NTS has sought to combine a sustainable level of deer-stalking activity on the open hill with long-term natural regeneration of the native pinewoods. A management agreement with Scottish Natural Heritage funds significant reduction of deer numbers by culling within the pinewood regeneration zone. A period of some fifteen years had elapsed before there were notable signs of a response by pine seedlings emerging from the protection of surrounding heather, and this response remains variable. There are challenges in maintaining the level of deer control required to secure and extend this regeneration – unlike some other examples, NTS relies heavily on public grant-in-aid. In that situation there is always a danger that patience will run out or funding priorities alter before the point of self-sustaining ecological recovery is achieved. The Mar Lodge situation is also made challenging by a wish to maintain a viable deer-stalking enterprise while reducing red deer numbers. Some foresters have argued that use of 'tactical' fencing to protect areas of regenerating pine would 'take the pressure off' and place less reliance on consistent deer culling. At present some barrier electric fencing is being deployed while exclosure fences are being removed. This, like Beinn Eighe NNR, is a long-term experiment and it may take thirty to fifty years to fully evaluate whether natural Scots pine regeneration is sufficiently extensive and secure.

8.5.4 Ballochbuie and Blackmount native pinewoods

A number of private estates with native pinewood remnants to manage favour traditional forestry deer-fencing systems, with effective marking in areas with capercaillie populations. This can be the most practical approach where the owners' objectives, and the economics of the estate, remain highly dependent on opportunities for deer stalking. The use of deer fencing has previously been adopted to good effect by the Balmoral Estate on Deeside and the Blackmount Estate in the Bridge of Orchy area of North Argyll. Fencing is generally more effective at protecting existing natural regeneration (even if concealed by heather) than in promoting new regeneration. As soon as the exclosure is imposed, the ground vegetation tends to respond quickly to the lack of browsing, and will outcompete tree seedlings unless these are already present and 'ready to go'. In some situations it may be necessary to carry out ground preparation within exclosures, as was tried at Beinn Eighe, to expose a mineral soil surface and provide a window of opportunity for tree seedlings to grow, free of vegetation competition. In Scottish upland conditions, protection by deer fencing can be required for twenty to thirty years, or until regeneration reaches a diameter where it can withstand bark-stripping by deer and will not risk being fatally ring-barked. Very large ring-fenced exclosures can be problematic in terms of the original removal of resident deer and the maintenance of integrity of the fence, especially over rough terrain and after periods of heavy snow. When the fence has outlived its usefulness it will need to be removed, with moderate levels of deer browsing re-admitted to 'respace' what may become an over-dense thicket of regeneration. Ideally, during the lifetime of the fence, deer numbers outside will have been reduced by culling to a level where their landscape-wide impacts on established thicket and pole-stage Scots pine will become survivable.

8.5.5 Glen Nant, Glasdrum, Comrie and Cawdor oakwoods

It is not only in the Caledonian pinewoods that deer fencing may be required to protect native tree regeneration. A number of Scottish oak and birch woodlands are subject to browsing from a combination of resident roe deer and red deer which descend from more upland areas for shelter and browse in times of severe weather. Fencing has been employed around or within oakwoods in several locations including the Glen Nant Caledonian Forest Reserve, Argyll (FCS), the Glasdrum National Nature Reserve, Argyll (SNH), the Comrie oakwoods in Strath Earn (private) and the Cawdor Wood, Nairn (private). In these situations the initial response is often from birch, rowan, ash and any coppiced hazel stools within the exclosure. There can be a longer interval before oak regeneration appears, due to the infrequent seeding ('masting') of oak in Scotland, the level of shade and any rain of defoliating caterpillars from the canopy (Harmer et al. 2010). Where there is a dense, even-aged oak canopy, it may be necessary to wait until the stand structure begins to open up naturally before installation of fenced exclosures is useful. Alternatively, fencing can be used together with preparatory opening of the oak canopy to establish and protect natural regeneration. This type of work is best carried out in response to the initial appearance of young oak seedlings following a 'mast year' rather than on a speculative basis. If there is a long interval between the creation of any gap or exclosure and the supply of acorns from an oak 'mast year', weed competition may have become so well developed that it will prevent the oak seedlings from establishing later. Compared with pine, broadleaved seedlings tend to remain palatable to deer, and vulnerable to browsing damage, for longer. Fencing may need to be maintained for many years to establish a viable successor stand of oak where deer numbers remain very high. Bird-strike by capercaillie is currently a less significant issue within oakwoods.

8.5.6 Keltney Burn and Ettrick and Yarrow cleuchs ashwoods

The main challenge to securing natural regeneration in upland ash-elm-hazel woodlands and wet alder-willow woodlands has traditionally been livestock, rather than deer. These can be excluded with waist-high stock fencing, which is less expensive, rather than shoulder-high deer fencing. Where the underlying geology and soils are sufficiently base-rich to support these types of woodland, pasture is likely to be productive and the farmer may not want to give up any more ground to woodland than is essential. However, steep valley ash-elm woodlands and swampy alder woodlands often occupy sites where livestock can be difficult to manage and can potentially come to harm, especially in poor weather. There may therefore be a mutual benefit to both native woodland manager and farmer in establishing and maintaining stock fencing. This has been realised to good effect in upland hill-farming areas of Highland Perthshire (such as the Keltney Burn) and the Scottish Borders (Ettrick and Yarrow valleys). Nuclei of existing woodland along small upland streams have been mapped out, and agreements reached with neighbouring farmers to protect them by stock fencing under various forestry and agri-environmental grant schemes. There is usually a benefit in negotiating a fence-line away from the edge of the existing native woodland remnant – this can mean the selection of a more efficient fence-line in terms of terrain and the area enclosed per unit length and allows for subsequent expansion by natural regeneration, creating a more robust 'critical mass' of native woodland. As this woodland matures, it may be able to seed out into the surrounding pasture land, making maintenance of stock fencing less essential over time. Future expansion of the woodland may then be able to rely on existing stock fencing around adjoining fields, if an agreement to a permanent change of land-use can be secured.

8.6 Management of non-native tree species

After impacts of browsing on natural regeneration, another significant challenge for native woodlands in Scotland is the influence of introduced plant species. In the case of tree species not native to the site, these have usually been deliberately planted as part of forestry or landscaping schemes. However, there is also an increasing issue with natural regeneration of introduced tree species as they mature biologically and begin to cast seed.

The major challenge posed by introduced tree species is that they are usually more shade-tolerant than site native species and will outcompete them over a period of time. They often regenerate more profusely and as a result will dominate the next canopy. There are essentially two categories of 'problematic' introduced species present in native woodlands in Scotland: beech and sycamore, and non-native conifers.

8.6.1 Long-established introductions – beech and sycamore

First is the long-established introductions of beech and sycamore, dating back up to 400 years. These shade-tolerant hardwoods have often been planted in or near mature native woodlands, and can easily regenerate into them. Beech spreads most easily into freely drained, acidic sites such as upland oakwoods. Sycamore is more often found colonising moister, more fertile sites, for example filling the niche left by dead elm within mixed valley ash woodlands. Veteran beech and sycamore can become valuable habitats for a range of invertebrates and also for bats, and so felling these may become inappropriate. Conservation managers will often tolerate the mature trees, but remove seedlings on a periodic basis (see Plate 17).

8.6.2 Conifer Plantations on Ancient Woodland Sites (PAWS)

The second category of introduced species is the non-native conifers, such as spruce, fir, cypress and hemlock. These date from the 1840s onwards, but predominantly from the period after 1920. Western hemlock is particularly shade-tolerant and can regenerate into a wide variety of native woodland types, whereas Sitka spruce requires rather more light. These species should not be planted in or near native woodlands in the future. Where these species are already colonising, they are generally best removed.

An important context requiring management of introduced tree species are the so-called PAWS sites (Plantations on Ancient Woodland Sites) (Harmer and Thompson 2013; Thompson et al. 2003; Woodland Trust 2005; Wilson 2012). These are sites where ancient semi-natural woodland of native species was either felled and replanted with non-native species or under-planted to achieve a similar end result. Although there are some older examples, the term 'PAWS' is generally restricted to those sites where the replanting has taken place since around 1920. These can often be identified from a combination of map evidence and indicator plant species. Many such sites are now being restored to native species composition by removal of the non-native conifer species. This can be done by a single intervention, clearfelling all of the conifers at one time, or by a process of gradual restoration over time, using 'continuous-cover forestry' (CCF) techniques (Harmer and Thompson 2013; Wilson 2012). The latter approach is slower, but causes less ecological and landscape disturbance. Priority is given to restoring those sites where features of the former native woodland survive but are under threat from the heavy shade cast by the introduced conifers. Such original features can include surviving native trees (often drawn-up by lack of light) and ancient woodland ground vegetation. Where patches of ancient woodland features survive within a conifer plantation, a process of 'halo thinning' can be applied, to release them from shade without felling the entire stand (see Figure 8.3). This allows most of the conifers to grow on to economic maturity, realising their financial value for the landowner. Some conifers pose more threat to native woodland features than others – young stands of shade-casting species such as spruce and hemlock are generally worst, while older mixed stands of fir, pine and larch have a much lower ecological impact. Where original native woodland was completely felled, managers may well have to replant or rely on natural regeneration to establish a new stand of native tree species (see Figure 8.4).

8.7 MANAGEMENT OF INVASIVE PLANT SPECIES

In addition to tree species, there are a range of other plants that can become a problem within Scottish native woodlands. While a few are natives growing to excess in the

FIGURE 8.3 *Release of surviving oak in a PAWS plantation, Yorkshire. Copyright: Dr Scott McG. Wilson.*

FIGURE 8.4 *PAWS restoration work in upland oakwoods, Loch Sunart. Copyright: Dr Scott McG. Wilson.*

wrong place, such as bracken (*Pteridium aquilinum*) in some oak and birch woods, most are species that have been introduced to Scotland in the past for garden or landscaping purposes. A number of these tend to be restricted to the banks of streams and rivers running through woodlands, such as giant hogweed (*Heracleum mantegazzianum*), Japanese knotweed (*Reynoutria japonica*) and Himalayan balsam (*Impatiens glandulifera*). These weedy species have the capacity to spread very rapidly if left unmanaged, so it is always best to intervene as soon as possible. If they are allowed to spread they can shade out more sensitive native plants and contribute to other forms of ecological damage (e.g. bankside erosion). The Scottish Wildlife and Natural Environment (WANE) Act (2011) makes it an offence to allow certain invasive plant species to grow into the wild.

Of greater significance in most Scottish woodlands are a range of mainly evergreen shrubs introduced over the past 200 years for landscape gardening and game-bird cover. The best known is *Rhododendron* (mainly the purple-flowered *Rhododendron ponticum*), but others include cherry laurel (*Prunus laurocerasus*), snowberry (*Symphoricarpus albus*) and the New Zealand broadleaf (*Griselinia littoralis*). These species tend to be much more shade-tolerant than native tree species and 'fill up' the shrub layer within woodlands, crowding out native shrubs and shading out ground plants. The ground under these species can become covered in a dense litter layer which is chemically hostile to seedlings of native tree and plant species. In the case of the Atlantic oakwoods, *Rhododendron* has become the most common shrub after the native holly and hazel, and in some cases it has grown to great size over the past 100–150 years, joining oak in the canopy layer. A variety of techniques are used to control *Rhododendron* (Edwards 2006). Where there is good access to the site, heavy machinery can be used to physically destroy the bushes, followed up with controlled application of herbicide to the young regrowth which almost always arises. Harvested *Rhododendron* biomass can be chipped and taken away for use as woodfuel. Many native woodlands, however, have poor physical access, preventing the use of machinery. In some situations bushes can be felled with chainsaws or hand tools and, again, the regrowth treated with herbicide (see Plate 25). Felled material is usually burned or chipped on site. On very steep slopes and ravine-sides, where access is only possible with ropes, it is more efficient to kill the *Rhododendron* by injecting a systemic herbicide into the stem, allowing the plant to rot away over time where it stands. Recently an alternative manual control method known as 'lever and mulch' has been attempted, where the bush is physically levered apart and the stump hammered to reduce the risk of regrowth from buds. Brash material is then piled up over the stumps as a mulch, excluding the light and suppressing regrowth from surviving buds.

An added imperative to tackle the challenge of *Rhododendron* in Scottish native oak woodlands is the threat of an introduced disease called 'sudden oak death'. This is caused by a fungus-like pathogen (*Phytophthora ramorum*) that is closely related to the potato and tomato blights. Shrubs such as *Rhododendron* are the primary host, but the disease can potentially go on to infect certain trees such as larch, oak and beech, and also common heathland plants such as blaeberry (*Vaccinium myrtillus*).

Unfortunately this disease has begun to affect some of Scotland's famous west-coast *Rhododendron* woodland gardens. While it can probably be controlled to an extent within the managed environment of woodland gardens, if it spreads into native woodland and heathland habitats nearby, it may become impractical to control in future. The impact of this disease on larch crops in south-western Scotland has recently become very serious. This is one example of the recent trend of serious tree disease outbreaks in Scotland that will be addressed for the future in Chapter 11. A similar fungal infection (*Phytophthora austrocedrae*) now affects native juniper throughout Scotland.

8.8 RESTORATION OF NATIVE WOODLANDS – FIELD EXAMPLES

8.8.1 Sunart Oakwoods

One area in Scotland where the effects of PAWS restoration work can be most clearly seen to date is in the Atlantic oakwoods along the northern side of Loch Sunart on the Ardnamurchan peninsula, between Strontian and Salen/Acharacle (Forestry Commission Scotland 2008). The majority of these sites are owned and managed by Forestry Commission Scotland, but some remain in private hands and the Ariundle Oakwood is managed jointly with Scottish Natural Heritage as a National Nature Reserve. During the decades following the Second World War, these Atlantic oakwoods were extensively replanted and under-planted with introduced conifers, particularly the Sitka spruce. The oak woodlands were regarded as unproductive, as they had been neglected since the ending of industrial coppice working prior to 1900 – some had been partly felled and some heavily over-grazed by sheep in the intervening decades. At the time of replanting, some areas of the original oak woodlands were felled, some were chemically treated by stem injection to kill the oaks standing, and some open areas of oak woodland were simply under-planted with conifers. These were the standard forestry improvement methods of that time. The resulting plantations are now coming up to their normal economic felling age and the decision has been taken to restore large areas to native woodland during the next rotation. That process is now well under way (see Figure 8.4).

Due to the economics and logistics of harvesting conifer timber in such a remote area, much of the removal of the planted trees has to be achieved by 'clearfell and naturally regenerate' methods of PAWS restoration, perhaps not ideal in the sense that it can cause a sudden change in the ecological conditions (light and moisture) experienced by rare mosses and lichens. It also causes a sudden change in the visual appearance of the forest landscape which can attract adverse public reaction. However, it does have the advantage of restricting use of heavy machinery to a single intervention. Before this is carried out, the woodlands are surveyed in some detail to locate, identify and map features that have survived from original native woodland. These include native trees, living, but often severely 'drawn-up' by the shade of the conifers, native woodland ground vegetation (with some ancient woodland indicator species) and associated animal species which may be legally protected (e.g. bats, nesting birds of prey). When the conifers are harvested, these surviving features will be protected as far as possible, both for their own value and for their importance in speeding up the subsequent process of ecological restoration through recolonisation. Generally, there is a fairly rapid initial regeneration response to the conifer removal, with a dense mass of birch and rowan seedlings coming up to begin with. Patches of surviving natural ground vegetation also expand once conifer shade is relieved. However, it may take many years for re-expansion of later-successional tree species like oak, elm and alder from seed sources within adjoining woodland stands. If this proves too slow, enrichment planting may have to be considered at a later date.

With long-term restoration work of this kind, initially causing ecological and visual disruption to landscapes, it is important to provide local people and tourist visitors with good information to enable them to interpret what is happening, why, and what the long-term benefits are intended to be. Artists' impressions and computer-generated landscape visualisations can both play an important role in allowing people to see what the restored woodland landscape might look like in the future.

8.9 Control of invasive plant species – field examples

8.9.1 Ardtornish, Rahoy and Doire Donn oakwoods

The Ardnamurchan and Morvern peninsulas, together with the adjacent Ardgour area, also provide some of the best examples of *Rhododendron ponticum* management within Atlantic oak woodland habitats in Scotland (Forestry Commission Scotland 2008). The species was introduced to this part of Scotland in the nineteenth century as an attractive landscape gardening shrub and has since spread into the surrounding woodlands, becoming an invasive pest. The same does not apply to many rare 'species *Rhododendrons*' found within the famous 'west coast gardens' of Scotland – these are much less likely to spread out of their garden environment. *Rhododendron ponticum* is ideally suited to the mild, wet, frost-free climate and is able to grow well even on very infertile peaty soils. Botanically, it should be thought of as a giant version of the ericoid sub-shrubs – heather, blaeberry and so on. Being highly shade-tolerant, it is capable of shading out native tree regeneration, native woodland vegetation and rare mosses and lichens. Once established, its litter also has a chemical effect on the soil, known as 'allelopathy', that restricts the growth of native plants. Similar issues are faced by woodland managers in Cumbria, Wales (especially Snowdonia), Ireland, Cornwall and Brittany, where *Rhododendron* was originally introduced during Victorian times.

Work has been under way for some time by Ardtornish Estate, the Scottish Wildlife Trust (Rahoy and former Doire Donn reserves), the Forestry Commission and Scottish Natural Heritage to remove *Rhododendron ponticum* from oak woodlands in this area. The main method employed has been felling of the *Rhododendron ponticum* by excavator-mounted flails and motor-manual chainsaws, with subsequent burning of the felled material and follow-up herbicide treatment of stump and seedling regrowth. That conventional approach has been followed successfully in the very heavily *Rhododendron ponticum* affected woodland adjacent to Ardtornish Castle and in some of the private woodlands along the north side of Loch Sunart, within the recent European-funded Sunart Oakwoods Initiative. This method has allowed large areas to be treated by a single intervention, but does have a fairly noticeable effect on the site until alternative vegetation responds to the removal of *Rhododendron* shading, covering the bare ground and burnt brash material. *Rhododendron* brash can be removed from the site and used as very satisfactory woodfuel in the form of either logs or woodchips. The Scottish Wildlife Trust has also been applying the less intensive 'lever and mulch' method of *Rhododendron* control on its local reserves. Workers lever down the stems of the plant, breaking them off from the stump. The stump is then hammered to destroy potential sprouting buds. Brash is not burned or removed, but piled on top of the cut stumps, excluding light and suppressing any potential regrowth. No herbicides are used on these sites, but follow-up hand removal of seedling regrowth is necessary in some cases. This method is more labour-intensive, realistically requiring the availability of a volunteer workforce, but seems to be rather effective when applied consistently to smaller areas of *Rhododendron*. It has much less visual and ecological impact than conventional approaches using heavy machinery and herbicides, and is more easily reconciled with organic and low-impact land-management ethics. Stem injection with glyphosate herbicide (trade name 'Roundup') remains a suitable method for control of *Rhododendron* on very sensitive and steep, roped-access sites (Edwards 2006).

8.10 TREE PLANTING IN EXISTING NATIVE WOODLANDS

Chapter 9 will deal in detail with the establishment of new native woodland habitat onto open land, including by planting. Where there is an existing native woodland seed source, it is preferable to rely on natural regeneration wherever deer control is adequate. For example, recent proposals for tree planting to accelerate recolonisation of the Ryvoan Pass from Abernethy have proved controversial on the grounds that natural regeneration processes could achieve the same effect, with sufficient time. Natural regeneration costs are typically lower than for planting, and natural seedlings tend to establish better within existing woodland than do transplants. This may be due to their being ecologically better adapted to the site conditions, as 'the tree grows best in the land of its sires' (Tolkien 1955). The root system of a natural seedling is more robust, as it has not been disturbed by the act of transplantation. There is some evidence that transplants are richer in foliar nutrients, having been artificially fertilised within the nursery, which makes them attractive to herbivores. Also, emergent tree disease risks make it less desirable to introduce potentially infected seedlings from outside native woodland environments.

8.10.1 Tree planting to augment natural regeneration

Having said this, there are circumstances where planting of native trees into native woodlands can be justified on conservation grounds. The main benefit is in terms of species reintroduction where it is believed that species were removed in the past by human management or, perhaps, tree diseases. Many pine and oak woodlands in Scotland are thought to have included species such as holly, hazel, elm, aspen, juniper and bird cherry that have been removed over past centuries. These might well take centuries to recolonise naturally by seed, if indeed that ever happened. Planting can speed this process up, helping to recover associated lost biodiversity (Ogilvy et al. 2006). Where there is the opportunity to extend native woodland onto adjoining open land, planting can sometimes be the appropriate option where rapid progress is a priority. Care must be taken to make sure conditions are suitable for the planted trees to succeed. In particular, there is little point in planting seedlings of a light-demanding or medium-tolerant tree species into the understorey of a closed woodland (Harmer et al. 2010). This mistake has sometimes been made in oakwoods managed for conservation over the past forty years, where under-planted oak, ash, hazel and so on in tree-shelters have failed for lack of light. It is worthwhile considering why no natural tree regeneration is present already before deciding to plant. Similar factors may make it unlikely that any planted trees will thrive – excessive shade, weed competition, deer browsing, soil drought, insect pests and so on. It is often recommended to make clearings within a woodland and then replant these – however, especially on fertile sites, weeds frequently over-top and swamp planted trees. Planting within woodlands is most successful under a partially opened canopy, and planting can certainly be effective on adjoining open agricultural land with suitable weed control in place.

8.10.2 Tree planting and genetic conservation

A very important consideration when planting trees within or near existing ancient semi-natural woodland is genetic conservation (Ennos et al. 2000). In many cases the trees already present within the woodland will have undergone a long-term process of adaptation to the conditions of a particular site – climate, soils, endemic pests and diseases. Plants sourced from a nursery may be from a different environment and may perform less well. If they do grow to maturity, their genetic contribution to future natural regeneration within the woodland may tend to 'dilute' the level of local ecological adaptation – this is known by geneticists as 'outbreeding depression'. Where biodiversity conservation and habitat restoration are the main objectives, plants should be raised in the nursery from seed collected within the same woodland. If that is impractical, seed may be collected from another woodland in the same part of the country on a similar site (Forestry Commission Scotland 2006b; Herbert et al. 1999; Hubert and Cundall 2006). For example, Scots pine for planting in a west Highland pinewood should not come from the east of Scotland, as it may be poorly adapted to climate and soils. Seeds should be collected from a sufficient number of trees (at least twenty to thirty) to preserve genetic diversity and avoid 'inbreeding depression'. The potential effects of climate change must now also be taken into account when selecting seed sources for tree planting (Ray 2008).

8.11 Planting in existing woodlands – field examples

8.11.1 Planting of aspen into the Glen Affric and Glen Moriston pinewoods

One main reason for planting trees within existing native woodlands is to restore natural species diversity. Aspen (*Populus tremula*) would naturally have formed part of the native pinewood ecosystem, but has often been depleted as a consequence of human activities – forest management, tree felling and excessive deer browsing. Two charitable organisations – Trees for Life and the Highland Aspen Group – have been involved with work to reintroduce aspen to existing pinewoods, albeit on a small scale. Trees for Life has focused on the pinewoods of Glen Moriston, Glen Affric and Guisachan/Cougie, whereas the Highland Aspen Group has mainly worked on Speyside and Deeside. The work involves collecting aspen root cuttings and, when possible, seed from mature aspen trees growing within these areas in order to ensure genetic adaptation. Plants are then raised in nurseries and made available for enrichment planting within the pinewood areas. This not only enhances tree species diversity but also ensures that a range of aspen-dependent insects, fungi and mosses have a continuity of suitable habitat. These projects have also provided an incentive for research into the population genetics of aspen in Scotland and viable systems for its nursery propagation. Similar work in the future may concentrate on restoring other species that were once minor components of the native pinewood ecosystem, such as holly and bird cherry. Although the total number of trees planted is small in relation to the overall areas of pinewoods managed, this work may have significant benefits for forest biodiversity. However, we must bear in mind that our knowledge of past natural occurrence and distribution of native broadleaves with pinewoods is still incomplete.

8.11.2 Planting of oaks within the Hamilton and Dalkeith deer parks

Another key reason for planting trees within existing native woodlands is to regenerate populations where natural regeneration is considered inadequate. Oak is considered a difficult native tree species in Scotland for which to secure natural regeneration. In the context of historical lowland parks, levels of grazing by cattle and deer are often too high for oak regeneration to establish, and there is an existing competitive grass sward. As the presence of livestock is part of the historical management system, overall exclusion to favour regeneration is unlikely to be a desirable option. Tree planting, with protection within small fenced exclosures, may always have formed part of the management of these areas, at least since the Middle Ages. At present, the managers of the Cadzow Oaks (Hamilton High Parks) in the Clyde Valley are using these techniques to ensure that there are future generations of widely spaced oaks to join those present on the site, which are 400–500 years old (see Figure 8.5). At the same time, the land can continue to be used as a productive cattle pasture. Acorns are collected from individual mature oaks and raised in the nursery in batches that can be planted near the parent tree but beyond the shade of its canopy. This helps to ensure that the genetic heritage of these veteran trees is preserved for the future, although

FIGURE 8.5 *Halo oak planting in medieval park, Cadzow, Lanarkshire. Copyright: Dr Scott McG. Wilson.*

there is no certainty that old oak trees at such sites are ultimately of local origin. The Dalkeith oakwood near Edinburgh faces similar conservation challenges. It is hoped that natural regeneration of oak can be secured by careful use of cattle grazing to restrict growth of the grass sward, with periodic exclusion of cattle from patches of ground to protect oak seedlings as they arise. If that proves insufficient to regenerate the woodland, there may be a role for small-scale planting here.

8.12 CONSERVATION SILVICULTURAL TECHNIQUES

There are a variety of silvicultural management techniques that can contribute to conservation within Scottish native woodlands. It would be fair to say that a significant proportion of our native woodlands have not seen very active silviculture in recent decades, as the majority of forestry attention has been on the conifer plantations. Many native woodlands which are designated conservation sites are now retained on a 'non-intervention' basis. This may be the most appropriate approach where ecological processes, including natural regeneration, are robust and active, and where the objective of management is conservation. However, there is also a good case to be made for active silviculture, especially in some larger native pine, oak and ash woodlands where management objectives are more diverse. There is no reason why this should compromise conservation values, while it offers the chance to produce some timber, woodfuel and economic income.

Although there are other possibilities of local relevance, we focus here on four major types of silvicultural intervention in native woodlands.

8.12.1 Silviculture to promote natural regeneration

We have seen that very many native woodlands in Scotland have an artificial structure as a result of historical management and a lack of natural regeneration. While browsing is one of the major causes of lack of regeneration, another is excessive shading by canopy trees. This can potentially be addressed by thinning to generate open conditions more suitable for natural regeneration. For each tree species, there is a maximum stand density or 'threshold basal area' below which regeneration can be expected to begin, as long as the canopy trees are producing sufficient seed. This threshold will be lower for a light-demanding species such as pine or birch (see Plate 18) than for medium-tolerant species such as ash and elm (Harmer et al. 2010). Oak requires fairly open conditions. Care must be taken not to thin the stand too heavily or weed competition may prevail. It may be best to wait for a year in which plenty of seed is produced by the canopy trees before carrying out any thinning – some species, such as oak, produce seed only infrequently (every five to ten years in Scotland). If seed or seedlings are already present, they will have a much better chance to overtake emerging weeds. An important decision is whether thinning to promote natural regeneration is actually justified. Thinning in most cases 'brings forward' regeneration to an earlier part of the stand life-cycle (Oliver and Larson 1996) (see Figure 8.6); in woodlands with a diverse canopy structure, it may be better to wait for a stand to open up by natural processes. However, where there is a dense canopy of tall, even-aged trees, there is a danger that many may fail over a short period. If so, it can be sensible to

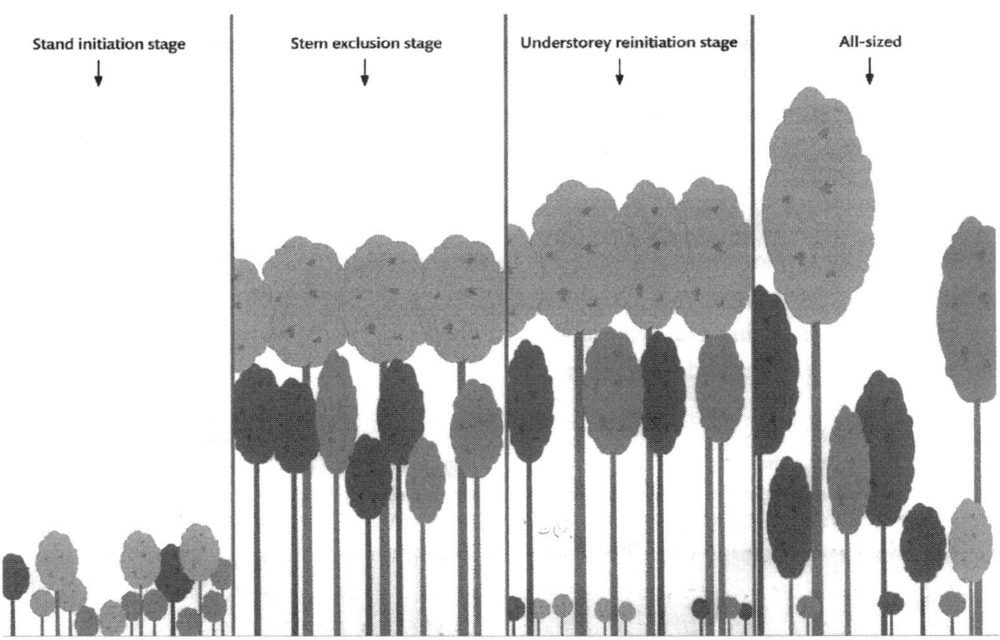

FIGURE 8.6 *Diagrammatic representation of stand development. Originally used in R. Harmer et al. (2010),* Managing Native Broadleaved Woodland, *Edinburgh: The Stationery Office; reproduced with kind permission from the Forestry Commission. Crown copyright.*

bring on some regeneration in advance of that happening, especially where scope for natural colonisation outside the wood is limited.

8.12.2 Silviculture to restore a historical management practice

Conservation managers sometimes intervene in native woodlands to restore a historical management practice such as coppicing, pollarding or wood pasture (see below). This can be motivated by historical interest, a wish to provide a focus for public interpretation or a desire to meet the ecological requirements of conservation priority species. There is very often an experimental element to projects of this kind, as there is very little recent practical experience of these management systems. When considering re-coppicing or pollarding of native trees after a long interval (often more than 100 years), is is important to consider how they will respond. It often makes sense to try the intervention out on a small scale, perhaps on a few trees in an out-of-the-way corner of the woodland, in case there are adverse effects. Trees that have not been coppiced or pollarded for many decades may not sprout very well after recutting, and in some cases they can die back. There can also be problems in securing sufficient regrowth after cutting where there are higher numbers of deer present than when the woodland was previously managed as coppice. Temporary fencing of recently cut coppice coupes will be an essential precaution. In addition, rare species, such as lichens and mosses, may suffer if woodland is suddenly opened up by coppicing or pollarding (Harmer et al. 2010), creating a lighter, drier microclimate. It can be easier to secure project objectives by creating new areas of coppice or pollards outside the boundaries of a valued ancient woodland habitat.

8.12.3 Silviculture to benefit conservation priority species

Due to our long history of management of woodlands for wood pasture and coppice, we have relatively few plant and insect species that favour dense, dark primary woodland of the type found in parts of Europe and North America. Most tend to favour mixtures of woodland, scrub and open land, with plenty of 'edge habitat'. This is true of many plants, insects (such as butterflies) and birds associated with woodland. Conservation managers often carry out work to introduce more structural diversity into neglected native woodland, by thinning, coppicing and cutting back encroaching woodland vegetation from the edges of streams, ponds, rides and paths. This creates a more open feel to the woodland, with habitat niches for many species. Some insect, bird and bat species depend on deadwood habitats provided by standing dead trees and living ancient or veteran trees that have significant areas of rotten wood. Normally, these features would take decades or even centuries to develop within any native woodland that begins with an even-aged early- to mid-rotation stand structure. We have seen that this applies to many of our native pinewoods and Atlantic (former coppice) oak woodlands, where the current stands date from before 1900. Some experiments have been carried out on 'accelerated' standing deadwood formation, using arboricultural techniques to reduce the crowns of mature trees artificially, creating cut-faces where rot fungi are likely to take hold more quickly. Fallen deadwood accumulation can be accelerated by leaving a proportion of timber from any thinnings lying within the wood.

8.12.4 Silviculture to improve potential for small-scale timber production

Native woodlands in Scotland have not been the major focus for timber production over the past 100 years, with the exception of a small number of the larger native pinewoods. Although there is a need for some areas to be retained as non-intervention reserves, in order to observe natural succession and structural development, there is no reason why many sites should not produce some pine and hardwood timber. In most cases, if the timber harvesting is done sensitively, there should be no significant negative impacts on the nature conservation values of the woodland. Timber produced from such woodlands can be processed locally, contributing to sustainable rural development and increasing the economic value of native woodlands to the local community, particularly in remoter areas (Peterken and Worrell 2001; Worrell 1999). In existing native woodlands, the main measures likely to be taken for timber include periodic thinnings to concentrate final crop timber production on a smaller number of straighter, higher-value stems (Thompson 2005). Thinnings now have potential economic value as woodfuel in most parts of rural Scotland. Final harvesting would almost always be carried out on a selective basis, so that no area of the woodland is actually cleared and there is always a steady supply of mature stems coming forward for harvesting on a 'constant offtake' basis (Willis et al. 2008). Natural regeneration will normally be the preferred method of restocking in ancient woodlands, perhaps with some enrichment planting with local provenances to diversify the species mix. In newer native woodland, improved seed sources can be planted for timber production where that is the main objective of management (see Chapter 9).

8.13 CONSERVATION SILVICULTURE – FIELD EXAMPLES

8.13.1 Morangie Forest – silviculture for biodiversity species

Capercaillie populations thrive best in Caledonian pine forest with a range of age classes, including patches of younger, regenerating trees for shelter of their young (Moss and Picozzi 1994). There are large areas of even-aged plantation Scots pine woodland across the Caledonian Pinewood Zone that could potentially provide suitable capercaillie habitat but have not reached the required stage of structural development. If these stands are left until ready to be felled for timber, according to the normal economic forestry rotation, it might be another thirty to forty years before areas of young regeneration arise. Some forest managers are taking action to bring forward natural regeneration by thinning and felling pine stands in advance of the normal rotation age. This improves the structural diversity of the forest and improves habitat for capercaillie and other priority species. There may be some loss in market value of the pine timber harvested at a smaller diameter, but this can be compensated for by funding for biodiversity conservation-related management. This approach has

FIGURE 8.7 *Restructuring for biodiversity in pine plantation, Morangie. Copyright: Dr Scott McG. Wilson.*

been adopted within the Forestry Commission's Morangie Forest in Easter Ross. This forest was planted during the period 1940–70 onto open moorland, but lies within the Caledonian Pinewood Zone. A healthy population of capercaillie still exists in this area, together with several other conservation priority species. Some mid-rotation stands of Scots pine have been thinned to stimulate natural regeneration under a shelterwood system. This is a simple form of 'two-storey' continuous-cover forestry management, as some of the mature trees are retained until a replacement crop has regenerated from below. Other areas are being group-felled, creating temporary openings in the forest which are also favourable for capercaillie and other species. The groups are then either naturally regenerated or replanted with pines (see Figure 8.7).

8.13.2 Abernethy Forest – silviculture to increase deadwood habitats

Some of Scotland's native woodlands are judged to have 'unfavourable conservation status', mainly because they have a lower component of deadwood than natural forests. Both standing deadwood – dead 'snags' and areas of rot within living veteran trees – and fallen deadwood should be present (Harmer et al. 2010; Mason et al. 2004). Surveys of woodland to systematically assess amounts of deadwood present usually record only a fraction of what is found in natural forests and much of this material is of small diameter, less valuable for many species. This is due to a history of trees being harvested for timber before natural mortality and removal of deadwood for use as woodfuel and to reduce the risks of damaging insect outbreaks – known as 'forest hygiene'. Even where such forestry management has ended, as on many nature reserves and designated sites, it would take several decades or even centuries for the amount of deadwood to build up to favourable levels. Many species of conservation importance, including hole-nesting birds, insects and fungi, depend on there being an adequate supply of deadwood. Some of these 'deadwood species' are associated with a particular tree species – oak and aspen, for example, have a number of 'obligate' deadwood insects dependent upon them. At the RSPB Abernethy Forest reserve, as on many nature reserves and designated sites, deadwood is now allowed to accumulate naturally. The process of fallen deadwood accumulation is also being accelerated at Abernethy by felling some mature trees in advance of natural mortality and leaving them to decay on the forest floor. Standing deadwood is being promoted by killing some trees using a variety of specified arboricultural methods including ring-barking, high-stumping and branch-stripping.

8.13.3 Silviculture of Scots pine and silver birch for timber production

Both Scots pine and silver birch within natural forests are used for timber production in Scandinavia. There is increasing interest in using these species productively in Scotland, albeit on a smaller scale. Forestry Commission Scotland and Highland Birchwoods have been active in recent years in promoting the opportunities to manage native pinewoods and upland birchwoods for quality timber (Macdonald et al. 2008; Mason et al. 2004; Worrell 1999). This has been taken forward by a combination of research work, promotional and training events and demonstration of silviculture and end-uses. A major obstacle here has always been the poorer stem form of Scottish native material compared with Scandinavian, and the resulting lack of established markets for final crop logs. A major step forward in this regard would be more regular thinning of a proportion of the stands within native woodlands to produce a better final crop. Potential markets for home-grown Scots pine include construction, for timber framing and cladding, particularly for rural buildings within the Highland region. Silver birch can be used for flooring, furniture-making and, for the straightest logs, veneering for plywood manufacture. Some of these applications, such as birch plywood, would require significant capital investment in processing equipment, which is unlikely to be forthcoming until a suitable reserve of quality timber is available from the Scottish forests. This is the so-called 'chicken and egg' problem within alternative timber market development. In all of these areas, we have much to learn from our Scandinavian neighbours on the northern edge of Europe, who have longer experience in productive uses of native timbers. Establishing sustainable markets for Scottish home-grown pine and birch would be valuable in encouraging and resourcing the establishment and management of additional stands.

8.13.4 Sunart Oakwoods – regeneration silviculture of oak

The majority of the Atlantic oak woodlands of Argyll and Lochaber have essentially been unmanaged since the ending of industrial coppicing activity prior to 1900. As a result, many are effectively over-stocked with oak timber, and could now support a sustainable harvest that would also improve opportunities for natural regeneration within these woodlands. The slow-grown oak timber produced should be in demand for local processing – for example for furniture-making and green-oak building projects – and this would help to support local employment and businesses. However, as many of these oak woodlands are conservation-designated (SSSIs and SACs), getting official approval for any tree-felling work is complicated. There is particular concern over potential for disturbance of nesting birds and changes to the light and moisture regimes for sensitive lichen and moss species. Similar considerations apply to the potential for re-coppicing Atlantic hazel stands within the same area. A development project has been undertaken, as part of the Sunart Oakwoods Initiative, to recommend and trial sustainable thinning, timber-harvesting and extraction regimes for application in these woodlands (Forestry Commission Scotland 2008). Leading woodland ecologists Rick Worrell and George Peterken were involved (Peterken and Worrell 2001). A number of different regimes were suggested, mainly involving thinning and selective harvesting of oak (see Figure 8.8) and its subsequent management using 'continuous-cover forestry' (CCF) techniques (Thompson 2005; Willis et al. 2008). The Forestry Commission West Argyll and Lochaber Districts have recently set up a scheme for small-scale local processing and marketing of oak harvested within their own oak woodlands, ensuring that it is made available to local small-scale 'artisan' users. It is expected that sustainable timber production from the Atlantic oakwoods will increase over the coming decades.

8.14 Conservation grazing and wood pasture

Recent years have seen increasing interest and a number of new project initiatives in the field of wood-pasture restoration and conservation grazing within Scottish native

FIGURE 8.8 *Selective harvesting trial in upland oakwood, Castramont. Copyright: Dr Scott McG. Wilson.*

woodlands (Wilson 2013a). There have been two main reasons for this: (1) improved understanding from historical and archaeological studies of the wood-pasture management systems formerly used in Scotland (Quelch 2000–1; Smout et al. 2005; Stiven and Holl 2004) and (2) experience from other parts of Britain and Europe of the conservation benefits that well-managed woodland grazing can deliver. As a result of this there have been three key categories of initiatives in this field.

8.14.1 Grazing projects prioritising improvement of habitat condition

These tend to be situations, most commonly on publicly owned or charity-owned woodland nature reserves, where the manager is selecting woodland grazing as a tool for conservation management. More recently there have been grant-in-aid schemes that allow some private woodland owners to engage in similar work. There are usually a set of objectives or 'indicators of favourable conservation status', against which the impacts of woodland grazing can be assessed. The grazing animals are therefore seen as a 'means to an ecological end'. However, there is not usually an intention to radically alter the ecosystem, rather to restore it to a more favourable condition. The inspiration for this approach actually came from outside the woodland sector with the concept of 'flying sheep flocks', used to manage semi-natural calcareous grasslands in England. The plant diversity of these grasslands is often dependent on seasonal grazing, but this had tended to die away with agricultural intensification since the last war. Without a full-time shepherding workforce available, it became difficult to manage sheep flocks to achieve the desired grazing regimes on a permanent basis. Reductions in the number of rabbits during the myxomatosis outbreak of the 1950s was also a factor in reduced grazing levels. The idea of the 'flying flock' was to retain a flock of sheep that could be transported to nature reserves and conservation sites for shorter periods of time to deliver regulated grazing inputs. In the woodland context it has been more common to use cattle (Wilson 2013a) and pigs, rather than sheep. The main conservation aim is usually to disturb the ground cover (mosses, mor humus) and to control competitive weed species in order to promote natural tree regeneration.

Pigs can be used effectively to prepare a seed bed for tree regeneration (see Figure 8.9), especially in oak woodlands. They are essentially simulating the natural action of the extinct wild boar. Numbers of pigs have to be carefully controlled at a level well below that which would be normal for an agricultural enterprise, or there will be deleterious impacts on ground vegetation. The length of time they are held in the woodland must also be regulated – if it is too long, the pigs can cause compaction of the soil, resulting in impeded drainage, and they can also artificially increase the soil fertility by manuring, stimulating weed competition.

Cattle are usually the species of choice for controlling weedy vegetation. Their browsing action and trampling will reduce the density of heather, bracken, bramble and nettle, for example, giving tree seedlings a better chance of 'getting away'. Cattle should be selected carefully – hardy breeds such as Highland, Luing and shorthorn-crosses are better as they can survive outdoors throughout the seasons and have

FIGURE 8.9 *Trial of wild boar in a birchwood enclosure, Glen Moriston. Copyright: Dr Scott McG. Wilson.*

a lower food requirement and greater resistance to pests and tick-borne diseases. Nonetheless, animal welfare regulations require the cattle to be visited regularly and to receive supplementary feeding and veterinary attention whenever necessary. Where well planned and implemented, woodland grazing can effectively promote regeneration and species diversity in native woodland habitats.

8.14.2 Grazing projects emphasising livestock production

A second category of woodland grazing project places more emphasis on the animals themselves, rather than the woodland habitat condition. In these situations it is however essential that management of the livestock remains consistent with woodland conservation objectives set for the site.

A number of woodland grazing projects form part of conventional agricultural enterprises, in terms of permanent range or seasonal shelter with additional feeding. The main objective of the land manager is to make a profit from raising and selling stock, and therefore there can be an incentive toward over-stocking. For many years such systems very often resulted in evident over-grazing within native woodlands, with consequent prevention of natural regeneration and decline in the conservation status of the sites. More recently, there have been attempts to combine the needs of agricultural businesses with the 'conservation grazing' approach described above. In part, this resulted from a recognition that continued agricultural land-use, especially in the uplands, is often better for native woodland conservation than land abandonment. This can be achieved if there is careful planning of the seasonal stocking regimes and monitoring of the impacts that livestock are having on the vegetation across the site. There is often a need for more intensive management of stock, through herding, shepherding and temporary fencing, than has been the case over recent decades. This may have implications for labour availability and farm business planning. Especially with cattle and pigs, care must be taken to avoid severe localised habitat impacts, such as poaching, soil compaction and excessive dunging.

8.14.3 Grazing projects emphasising natural processes

The last decade has seen a number of projects where livestock, especially cattle and horses, are introduced to native woodlands on a less intensively managed basis. While there may be some production of meat for sale, the main objective is to observe how the woodland ecosystem develops over time in the presence of large herbivores. Tourism may also be a spin-off benefit of projects of this kind. Some such projects have been described as 're-wilding', reflecting the landowners' ambition to restore their land to a former, self-regulating natural condition. The original inspiration for work of this kind were the theories put forward by Frans Vera (2000) (see Chapter 3) with regard to the natural role of large herbivores in the prehistoric woodlands of Europe. Breeds of cattle and pigs approximating as closely as possible to the extinct wild ox (aurochs) or to wild boar are often employed. A well-known project of this kind is the Oostvaardersplassen reserve in Holland, originally established by Vera himself. Many projects of this kind in Britain have been on a much smaller scale – for example in the English lowlands at Epping Forest, the New Forest and Savernake Forest (and accidentally with wild boar in the Forest of Dean). These are mostly areas that have had an unusual continuity of pasture woodland management until relatively recently, in the case of the New Forest until the present time. Over the last few years, there has been increasing interest in undertaking similar projects at a landscape scale in the uplands. Extensive grazing by Highland cattle has been trialled by the Forestry Commission in the heavily modified native pinewoods of Glen Garry and is also now being implemented in the upland oak and birch woods around Loch Katrine. Similar work is being pursued in the Cumbrian valley of Ennerdale. These projects combine the functions of ecological research/demonstration, visitor attraction and the promotion of more diverse species composition and stand structures in native woodlands. Some complications have arisen in respect of public safety and animal welfare regulation in the British context. The closest approach to the Oostvaardersplassen model is perhaps the recent trial reintroduction of wild boar and elk within the private Alladale pinewoods.

8.15 Woodland grazing and pasture – field examples

8.15.1 Glen Garry cattle-grazing project

In the last few years, Forestry Commission Scotland has become involved in the use of controlled cattle grazing within forests as a tool in securing natural regeneration.

The main mechanism by which this is achieved is the formation of a suitable seed bed by physical disturbance of the soil surface and control of competing rank vegetation by trampling and browsing. A cattle-grazing trial has been undertaken in the Glen Garry native pinewoods (see also Chapter 4). These woodlands had been extensively replanted with Sitka spruce and lodgepole pine after the Second World War which are now being progressively removed to allow for natural regeneration of Scots pine, birch and other native trees. There are seed trees remaining on site, but there is a major risk that competitive weeds such as bracken will swamp the site rapidly after spruce clearfells, preventing later native tree regeneration. Cattle grazing can potentially prevent this, while not being at such a high level as to browse off the tree regeneration. Highland cattle have been deployed within parts of the regeneration area at Glen Garry, which has been divided up into areas where different cattle-stocking regimes (numbers of cattle, length of exposure, etc.) can be tried and the results monitored. The results at this stage look promising, and this technique may have applications in other similar situations. The RSPB has also used cattle for small-scale trials at Abernethy. The Glen Garry trials also highlighted some of the issues that have to be considered with woodland grazing, including livestock welfare and inspection, supplementary feeding in winter and management of livestock interactions with the visiting public/dogs.

8.15.2 Loch Katrine Highland cattle-fold project

Forestry Commission Scotland has recently taken over management of the native woodlands surrounding Loch Katrine in the Trossachs from the water authorities. There are now plans to regenerate and expand these woodlands for the purposes of water-supply catchment protection, biodiversity enhancement and carbon sequestration. These woodlands form part of a larger native woodland creation and conservation initiative within the Loch Lomond and Trossachs National Park called the Great Trossachs Forest. This is funded by BP and the Forestry Commission, but also includes the Woodland Trust Scotland land-holding at Glen Finglas and the RSPB land-holding at Inversnaid on the eastern banks of Loch Lomond. As part of its work to conserve and restore historic oak-birch-hazel pasture woodland around Loch Katrine, the Forestry Commission is creating a herd (known as a 'fold') of Highland cattle. These will be managed directly by the Forestry Commission and will be used to carry out targeted grazing within the Loch Katrine woodlands. The grazing should help to control bracken, allowing more effective natural regeneration of the oak woodlands. The Highland cattle-fold project also represents the trial restoration of a historical form of agriculture in this area, well known from Sir Walter Scott's books, and later films, based on the story of the cattle drover Rob Roy MacGregor, active ~1700–20. Interpretation of these historical associations and the modern role of the Highland cattle-fold will form part of the 'tourist experience' for visitors to Loch Katrine, alongside the opportunity to sail on the loch and view the woodlands from the vintage steamer *Sir Walter Scott*. If the cattle achieve their ecological objectives, the Forestry Commission may well adopt the same approach elsewhere.

8.15.3 Conservation grazing in farm woodlands – Argyll and Lochaber

There is also potential for conservation grazing in smaller private woodlands, especially on upland livestock farms. Where this has clear and measurable conservation objectives, it is eligible for agri-environmental grant support. Within the West Highland Woodland Grazing Project, a number of private woodland owners in Argyll and Lochaber have established smaller-scale woodland grazing projects, mostly using cattle, but in some cases also sheep. Conservation grazing has proven to have considerable benefits to native woodland regeneration, by controlling rank competing vegetation while offering the farmer the opportunity for winter shelter for his/her livestock. However, combining ecologically sensitive woodland grazing with the management of a commercial livestock enterprise is not always easy, and it might be difficult to sustain in the absence of agri-environmental grants. In order to ensure that grazing regimes remain sustainable it is essential to start out with a set of measurable objectives – for example, minimum number of tree seedlings per hectare after three years, maximum proportion of tree seedlings showing browsing damage and so on – set out in an agreed Conservation Grazing Management Plan. The Forestry Commission and Scottish Natural Heritage have developed a computer-based Woodland Grazing Toolkit to inform plan preparation. There should be regular monitoring and a willingness to modify, and if necessary reduce, stocking levels if these objectives are not being achieved. Historical systems of wood-pasture management relied on intensive herding of cattle and shepherding of sheep to avoid excessive grazing pressure in favoured areas. This required a labour force of herdsmen or shepherds, who stayed out with their charges even in severe weather. That kind of commitment is very difficult to secure in the modern era, when more extensive systems of livestock husbandry are usual. Volunteer input may therefore be needed.

8.15.4 Restoration of the Glen Finglas ancient wood pasture

The ancient wood-pasture section at Glen Finglas in the Trossachs is probably the best surviving example of original upland pasture woodland in Scotland. The woodlands consist of veteran birch, hazel, alder and oak which appear to have been subject in the past to some form of pollard treatment or browsing which had the same physiological outcome. It was discovered within a land-holding acquired by the Woodland Trust for an extensive new native woodland planting project. Historical research showed that the area had formed part of a royal hunting forest during the late medieval period, and that there had been deliberate regulation over a long period to protect remnant woodland cover from livestock. More recently, fairly heavy commercial sheep grazing had been the norm, and there was a lack of natural tree regeneration as a result. The Woodland Trust decided to exclude this area from its native woodland planting scheme and manage the wood-pasture area using livestock to secure its continuity through natural regeneration. This forms part of the wider Great Trossachs Forest project under the Scottish Forest Alliance initiative. At present, conservation grazing using Luing cattle is being permitted within the wood pasture to prevent it from filling up with bracken and other rank vegetation. It is hoped that this will allow widely spaced regeneration of native tree species to come up over time without the need for planting. Some fencing is being used to protect areas of regeneration from deer browsing, as deer tend to enter the area from neighbouring sporting estates. There may also be a case for future restoration of pollarding activity. Glen Finglas provides a valuable 'test-bed' to study the effects of modern livestock grazing within areas of native woodland that have previously been managed as wood pastures and which retain historical elements. The lessons learned may be adopted elsewhere in private woodlands where the owners do not have the resources available to carry out their own research and development.

8.16 Reintroduction of extinct animal species

Over the period since the end of the last Ice Age, a number of bird and mammal species have become extinct from Scotland's native woodlands. This has occurred through a combination of natural climatic and ecological changes during the early part of the Holocene, loss of habitat through human activities and hunting/trapping pressure. The balance of these factors varies between species and, to an extent, geographically. There is now growing interest in reintroducing at least some of these species as part of efforts to expand and restore large-scale natural forest ecosystems to Scotland. These species are best considered in four groups, reflecting the state of progress.

8.16.1 Birds

The most successful species reintroductions to date have been of bird species. The capercaillie (*Tetrao urogallus*) (a large woodland grouse) became extinct (or nearly so) in Scotland before 1800, but was then reintroduced from Sweden in the 1830s (Moss and Picozzi 1994). The original extinction was due to climatic change and hunting pressure and the main motivation for the reintroduction was for game birds on private estates. Despite remaining legal quarry for the next 150 years, capercaillie continued to expand in both range and number across Scotland. However, since around 1970, numbers have fallen from around 20,000 birds to 1,000–2,000. The reasons are not entirely clear, as shooting has been banned since 2001, but a combination of climate change, deer fences and disease is likely. Active conservation is being pursued and it is hoped numbers are once again rising. The osprey (*Pandion haliaetus*) is a migratory fish-eating bird of prey that uses forest lochs in Scotland as summer breeding and feeding range. It had become extinct by 1900 due to persecution, but began nesting again in the 1950s by Loch Garten (within Abernethy Forest). Since that time it has spread to many other locations, notably the Scottish Wildlife Trust reserve at Loch of the Lowes, by Dunkeld. Continued protection is required to prevent nest disturbance and the theft of eggs. In recent decades two other birds of prey that make subsidiary use of Scottish native woodland have been successfully reintroduced – the red kite (*Milvus milvus*) from Sweden, Germany and England since 1989, and the white-tailed (or sea) eagle (*Haliaetus albicilla*) from Norway since 1976.

8.16.2 *Smaller mammals (including beaver)*

The pine marten (*Martes martes*) is a native woodland mustelid species typical of native woodlands in Scotland, primarily the pinewoods. It had been dramatically reduced by game-keeping pressure until the early- to mid-1900s, but with legal wildlife protection it has been steadily re-extending its range, perhaps with some human assistance. It can now be found in many northern, and some southern, parts of the country in a variety of types of native woodland and conifer plantation. A number of 'feeding stations' have been established by tourist businesses where pine martens are drawn in by the offer of rich food (peanut butter, jam, etc.) at dusk, allowing visitors a close-up view of what is otherwise a very elusive animal. The otter (*Lutra lutra*) has also recovered in recent years on many rivers flowing through native woodland in Scotland, largely due to removal of hunting pressure and improvement in the water quality following the prohibition of DDT and related pesticides. It is hoped that the water vole (*Arvicola terrestris*) will continue to recover with more effective control of the introduced American mink (*Mustela vison*), its main predator, and restoration of bankside vegetation, including wet woodland habitats.

The red squirrel (*Sciurus vulgaris*) is native in Scotland and remains common in most of the native pinewoods and some extensive conifer plantations, with around 120,000 animals present (Forestry Commission Scotland 2012). It also persists in some remoter oak woodland areas in the north and west Highlands. During the past half-century it has been progressively displaced from deciduous woodlands in much of southern and eastern Scotland by the American grey squirrel (*Sciurus carolinensis*), introduced to Britain prior to 1900. Grey squirrel have been spreading out from centres of introduction in Glasgow, Edinburgh, Dundee and Aberdeen, and are also now migrating into Scotland from the Carlisle area. This last route of introduction is also associated with the squirrelpox virus, carried by greys but lethal to reds. A small number of red squirrel translocation projects have been undertaken to introduce the species to areas of suitable but unpopulated habitat, isolated from grey squirrel populations. Within stronghold areas of native pine and planted conifers, there are tactical restrictions on the planting of young oak, beech and hazel which may tend to favour the grey squirrel, along with humane culling of greys in some localities.

Over the past decade there has been great interest in the potential for reintroduction of the European beaver (*Castor fiber*) to Scotland. This species is believed to have become extinct during the sixteenth century due to hunting pressure for both its fur and the pharmaceutical substance *castoreum*, secreted by beavers from a scent gland. In later centuries, Scottish beaver trappers (particularly from Orkney) devoted their attentions to the North American beavers of Canada, famously working in the service of the Hudson's Bay and North West Companies. Over the past century, beavers have been successfully reintroduced to a number of areas of mainland Europe from which they had earlier been hunted out – parts of Norway, France and Poland, for example. However, reintroduction of beaver in Scotland has proved controversial, mainly because of the potential effects on infrastructure, woodland and farmland near rivers. Beavers fell trees for food (mainly bark and foliage), form dams using wood and earth, modify hydrological regimes and can burrow into river banks. In recent years, small captive populations of beaver have been established in Scotland on private land – for example, Aigas Estate in the Highlands and Bamff Estate in Perthshire. These are confined by electric fencing, but have been monitored by the landowners to assess their ecological impacts. During 2009, an official trial reintroduction began in the Forestry Commission Knapdale Forest in Argyll (see below). Here the beavers are not fenced in, but are confined to some degree by sea-water inlets, which they appear reluctant to cross. They are also radio-tracked. The aim of this five-year project is to make a detailed study of their potential impacts on the ecology of the area, before any formal decisions are taken on their wider reintroduction to Scotland after 2015.

In the last few years it has become apparent that a feral population of 150–200 beavers has become established on the River Tay and tributaries in Perthshire and Angus, reportedly deriving from private collections in the region. How these are managed into the future will also be influenced by the anticipated outcomes of the official trial at Knapdale.

8.16.3 Large ungulates and wild boar

Apart from the red deer (*Cervus elaphus*) and roe deer (*Capreolus capreolus*) which survive to this day, there are a number of ungulates (hoofed herbivores) that may have been present in Scotland during the Boreal phase, after the end of the last Ice Age, but are now extinct. There is limited fossil evidence and a considerable degree of scientific debate as to which were present (Yalden 2002). The species involved include the biologically extinct wild ox or aurochs (*Bos primigenius*), the wild horse or tarpan (*Equus przewalksi gmelini*) and the elk (*Alces alces*). These species became extinct in prehistory due to a combination of habitat loss and hunting pressure. The wild boar (*Sus scrofa*) was recorded in Scotland as recently as medieval times (AD 1200–1300). Especially since the publication of Frans Vera's theories on the role of browsing animals in prehistoric woodland ecology, there has been interest in trial reintroductions of wild boar, Heck cattle (similar to aurochs, produced by back-crossing) and possibly Konik horses (similar to tarpan) to a variety of habitats in Britain, including native woodland, wetlands and semi-natural heathland. There are a number of locations in Scotland where wild boar have been introduced within fenced enclosures, and the Alladale Estate recently trialled a small number of Swedish elk. Projects using cattle for woodland grazing in Scotland generally still use the native breeds (e.g. Highland and Luing) as opposed to Heck cattle. Konik horses have been trialled on the Loch of Strathbeg RSPB reserve in Buchan. In order for such projects to represent realistic demonstrations of the restoration of fully functioning wildland habitats, large tracts of land would need to be involved and controversial decisions taken as to how to deal with animal welfare issues. At present, British legislation forbids mixing of carnivores with their prey within enclosures.

8.16.4 *Carnivores*

The largest carnivores surviving in Scotland today are the red fox (*Vulpes vulpes*) and the wild cat (*Felis sylvestris*). While the fox has remained common, the wild cat has become very rare and localised, largely confined to some of the more remote native pinewood areas in the Highlands. It was extensively persecuted by game keepers between 1800 and 1900 and has not proved able to recover effectively, following release of this pressure, in the way that pine marten has over the past 50–100 years. During the period since the last Ice Age, three other large carnivores have been present in Scotland: the lynx (*Lynx lynx*), the wolf (*Canis lupus*) and the brown bear (*Ursus arctos*) (Yalden 2002). The brown bear appears to have become extinct during prehistory and the lynx perhaps as recently as the post-Roman/early medieval period. Again a combination of habitat loss and hunting/persecution by livestock herders was most likely responsible. Occasional reports of brown bears in Britain at later dates are likely to refer to captive animals brought into the country from Europe for circuses and travelling fairs. Wolves persisted in Scotland until the last were killed during the period 1650 to 1750 in the northern Highlands (Smout et al. 2005), but they had been rare since the later medieval period, due to hunting and persecution by farmers. There is periodic speculation about the possibility of reintroducing lynx and wolf to Scotland – lynx has been reintroduced to parts of Germany, and wolves to Sweden and the Yellowstone National Park in the USA. Realistically, wolves could only be introduced to Scotland within a fenced enclosure. There were initial ideas for this at the Alladale Estate, but zoos legislation in Britain essentially precluded their implementation. Lynx is potentially a more realistic candidate for a reintroduction to an extensive wildland area such as the Cairngorms National Park, as it could operate at a very low density and might have minimal human contact. The main prey would be rabbits and young deer. A scheme for compensating occasional losses of pets and immature livestock would however be required.

8.17 Reintroduction of extinct animals – field examples

8.17.1 *European beaver – Bamff and Aigas Estates*

Over the last ten years, two private estates in Scotland have carried out small-scale trials of the introduction of European beaver. These were the Bamff Estate, near Alyth in Perthshire, and the Aigas Estate, near Beauly in Inverness-shire. Both of these projects were inspired by earlier beaver reintroductions that the owners had seen in other parts of Europe, particularly in Norway. Apart from personal interest, the main objectives were to promote the idea of beaver reintroduction on a wider scale in Scotland, to improve and create wetland habitats on these estates and to provide a focus for eco-tourism businesses. The Aigas Estate has operated a successful private field-studies centre for a number of years. As these were not official projects to reintroduce the beaver to the wild in Scotland, the animals have had to be confined within fenced enclosures and managed under the same legislation as would normally apply to zoos. Beavers were sourced from live capture of surplus individuals from locations in Norway, and subjected to quarantine on import to the UK. Small groups of a few animals were introduced in each case. In both cases the initial introductions were to small lochs and lakes within the estates, but with opportunity for the beavers also to use stream banks. Despite some early mortality, the beaver have established successfully, building small dams and lodges and beginning to rear their young. Their effectiveness as wetland engineers is becoming obvious, with modification of water levels and some felling of small birch, alder and aspen for dam building. The projects have attracted scientific interest and monitoring.

8.17.2 Trial reintroduction of beaver – Knapdale Forest, Argyll

This official beaver reintroduction trial, which began in earnest in 2009, is being conducted by the Scottish Wildlife Trust and the Royal Zoological Society, on land owned by Forestry Commission Scotland at Knapdale Forest in Argyll. The project follows an extensive exercise in public consultation over several years by Scottish Natural Heritage (SNH), who were its original sponsors. Although there was majority support for the concept, the Scottish Government decided that it was not appropriate for SNH to conduct any trial themselves. However, intensive scientific monitoring of the trial is being coordinated by SNH over the period 2009–14. In this project, four family groups of quarantined and radio-tagged beaver, sourced from Scandinavia, were introduced to freshwater lochs within a large area of native woodlands and conifer plantations. The animals have begun to establish themselves well and breed over the past five years. They are not fenced in at this site, but their movements are restricted to a degree by sea-water inlets which they tend to avoid. The trial area is generally remote and inaccessible and has little internal infrastructure (roads etc.). The objective of this trial was to provide evidence of the likely impacts of any future wide-scale reintroduction of beaver to Scottish forests, at the same time as creating an eco-tourism attraction within this historic 'Dalriada' area of West Argyll. At the time of writing, there is a programme of public information signage, interpretation and ranger-guided walks for interested visitors. No decisions have been reached as yet as to whether beaver will be retained after 2015.

8.17.3 Wild boar – Glen Moriston

In lowland England, wild boar have effectively been reintroduced to the wild through a series of escapes and deliberate releases from game farms over the past two decades. There are now established feral populations within the Forest of Dean and in a range of woodlands across Hampshire, Surrey, Sussex and Kent. The ecological role of wild boar in natural regeneration of oak woodland is well known from the Continent. The position for native pinewoods is much less clear. Boar are present in plantation pine forests in parts of Poland, northern Germany and so on, but are not a major feature of Scandinavian boreal forests. There is limited evidence that they were ever a major ecological agent in the native pinewoods of Scotland (Lambert 1998) before they became extinct in the Middle Ages. Recently, a number of projects have trialled wild boar, fenced within native woodlands, as a tool to secure natural regeneration through their capacity to disturb rank vegetation, improving the seed bed and the chances of seedling establishment. Production of organic meat for sale can be a significant by-product. To be effective, such projects must involve careful regulation of wild boar numbers and residence time to avoid unacceptable impacts on soil fertility and ground vegetation. Most recently, wild boar have been deployed by Trees for Life at their recently purchased Dundreggan Estate, in Glen Moriston, to reduce the dominance of bracken and promote natural regeneration of native pinewood and upland birchwood habitats.

8.17.4 Wildlife reintroduction in Caledonian pinewoods – Alladale Estate

The Highland Wildlife Park at Kincraig (an outpost of the Edinburgh Zoo) has operated for some years with various species that were once native to Scotland, such as wolves and lynx, in small enclosures. However, the project proposed at Alladale Estate in Sutherland was the most ambitious to date in terms of wildlife reintroduction in Scotland, inspired by South African game parks. The original conception had been to create a very large electric-fenced enclosure at or beyond the scale of a single estate and over time to introduce a mix of species including herbivores (elk, wild boar, European bison, etc.) and carnivores (lynx, wolf). This would have formed part of an ambitious habitat restoration project within the remnant native pinewoods on the estate. Reintroduction of these species without a fence would require government approval, which was unlikely to be forthcoming. However, with a fence, the project legally became a zoo, and enclosure of carnivores with their potential prey was prohibited. There was also some opposition under the terms of Scotland's countryside access legislation to the erection of an electric-fenced enclosure which might discourage public access to a large tract of open land. A recent pilot project saw wild boar and a small number of elk introduced to a smaller-scale electric-fenced enclosure within native pinewoods. The impacts of these species on pinewood regeneration and competing ground vegetation were monitored as part of the trial. Currently work at Alladale emphasises conventional pinewood restoration approaches with localised use of cattle.

Many of the field examples of native woodland conservation management referred to in this chapter are located within major native woodlands that are suitable for self-guided visiting. For relevant details, see Chapter 12.

CHAPTER NINE

Expansion of native woodlands

9.1 History of native woodland creation

Tree planting in Scotland with the express intention of creating new native woodland habitat is essentially a phenomenon of the last thirty years. However, much more significant areas of native species plantations have been created over the past 350 years, with objectives of landscape enhancement and timber production – the main tree species used have been Scots pine and oak, with smaller amounts of ash, elm, cherry and birch. Plantation forestry began on the major private estates from around 1680 onwards, tending to be concentrated in certain parts of the country – Perthshire, Aberdeenshire, the Borders, Argyll – where there was a mixture of woodland and farmland. Often native trees were planted together with introduced species – beech, sycamore, lime, larch, spruce and fir – forming mixed 'policy woodlands' (see Chapter 10). A period of intensified plantation establishment occurred during, and immediately after, the Napoleonic Wars (1793–1815), in response to shortages of timber for naval construction (Anderson 1967). Some areas of oak woodland were also planted to extend areas available for charcoal and tanbark coppice. However, by the time these private estate plantations matured and were ready for harvest, iron had come into use for shipbuilding, coke for iron working and chemicals for tanning, and markets for timber had declined. Greater supplies of timber from overseas were also becoming available. From 1919 onwards, the Forestry Commission also began to create plantations (Anderson 1967; Oosthoek 2013) – in Scotland there was fairly limited use of the native hardwoods, but significant areas of Scots pine woodland were planted to produce timber for railway sleepers, pit-props and other uses. These earlier plantings of native tree species began the process of recovery of overall woodland cover in Scotland from a low point of 5–9%, and now form a resource of semi-mature native woodlands that can be managed to become more natural.

9.2 Rationales – biodiversity and ecosystems

Between 1900 and the 1990s, woodland expansion by the Forestry Commission and by private estates concentrated on upland plantations of introduced conifers. These have increased the overall woodland cover of Scotland from ~6% in 1900 to ~18% today (Smout et al. 2005), and are now providing a valuable resource of conifer timber for industrial processing. However, from the mid-1990s, attention has switched to the creation of new areas of native species woodland as part of a process of ecological restoration (van Andel and Aronson 2012). There have been several arguments put forward for doing this, which will be considered in this chapter, but the most important centre around the historic loss of natural woodland cover in Scotland and the implications that this has had for forest biodiversity. Research and observation in overseas forest ecosystems has raised awareness of the dangers of forest fragmentation through human exploitation and land clearance, and the effects that this may have on the levels of biodiversity that forests can support. In particular, the 'island biogeography' theory (MacArthur and Wilson 1967) argues that if forest is divided up into small patches, the diversity of plants and animals surviving within each retained patch is related to its own size, and will almost always be much lower than in more extensive intact forests of the same ecological type. Small patches are often at risk of disappearing, because of their exposure to external 'edge effects', in turn endangering the key biodiversity species that depend upon them. This has made ecologists in Scotland realise that our native woodlands have become fragmented by human activity over many thousands of years, and that this is likely to have contributed to a decline in animal and plant biodiversity supported by them. The process of ecological restoration offers one way to actively reverse this decline.

A variety of targets have been suggested for the scale of woodland restoration, with the current Scottish Forestry Strategy proposing an increase of total forest cover in Scotland toward 25% by 2050, with perhaps half of the overall increase comprising native species woodland. A major difference between new native woodland creation and earlier establishment of native tree plantations is the intention to restore a more complete, functioning natural woodland ecosystem, preferably using natural processes as far as possible. It is hoped that by doing this, the 'biodiversity carrying capacity' of these new native woodlands will be greater – they should have a more diverse tree species composition, canopy structure and ground vegetation, which should, in turn, provide ecological niches for a greater diversity of mammals, birds, insects, lichens and so on (Forestry Commission Scotland 2008; Humphrey et al. 2003; Rodwell and Patterson 1994). There is also a preference to avoid intensive woodland establishment operations such as ploughing, drainage and artificial fertiliser applications that are often believed to cause undesirable environmental impacts and to compromise the philosophy of ecological restoration. These ambitions have not always proven easy to achieve in practice, given the complexities of the woodland creation process in a high labour-cost environment. Much of the upland moorland and grassland being used for new native woodland creation is inherently exposed, wet and infertile, having been used for many centuries for livestock grazing. In addition, lower-impact methods of tree establishment recently attempted lack an established track record elsewhere, so the work in Scotland has been partly experimental. Lessons have been learned and recent schemes have been much better planned as a result. The longest-established new native woodlands (now twenty-five to thirty years old) are starting to recruit increased biodiversity as species colonise these new habitats, and this is likely to gain momentum over the coming decades. In some cases deliberate future reintroduction of animals and plants may be considered, if the new woodlands remain too isolated for natural colonisation to occur.

A major aspect of woodland habitat restoration where understanding has developed is that of landscape-scale processes. These emphasise the need for native woodlands to be organised within a landscape so that they are functionally inter-connected (Fowler and Stiven 2003; Peterken et al. 1995; Watts et al. 2005). Some species that live in native woodland patches can cross areas of open farmland, plantation forestry or built-up areas to 'reach the next patch'. This is true of most birds and some mammals. However, some 'specialist' species have such a strong dependence on a native woodland environment that they cannot do this, or have such slow rates of dispersal that it would not happen within a reasonable period of time. Some species require larger areas of native woodland habitat (or woodland/open-land mosaics) in order to find sufficient food or to successfully complete their breeding cycle. Where small populations of any species persist within isolated fragments of woodland, there is a danger that they will suffer adverse genetic effects from possible inbreeding and accidental 'genetic drift' over the generations. Once the total woodland cover of any landscape falls below around 30%, the proportion of woodland located in physically isolated patches tends to increase markedly. There is therefore a potential advantage in positioning new native woodland into landscapes so that it joins up with existing woodlands to form a 'forest habitat network' (FHN) (Fowler and Stiven 2003; Peterken et al. 1995; Watts et al. 2005), through which woodland-dependent species can move. This should make the best 'ecological use' of a usually limited land area and financial budget for woodland creation activity. Active research is being undertaken to evaluate the biodiversity benefits achieved by improving woodland connectivity at the landscape scale. Natural woodland habitat linkages tend to survive along river valleys, where clearance of woodland for agriculture has been less extensive and there are good mechanisms for seed to be transported (e.g. by floating). When creating new native woodlands, it is better not to rely on very narrow 'habitat corridors' such as hedgerows, but to make more robust connections with existing areas of woodland in the landscape. There is also still a role for the creation of large new focal patches of native woodland habitat, known as 'nodes'.

9.3 RATIONALES – FRESHWATER AND SOIL PROTECTION

While creating additional habitat for biodiversity is the long-term aim of most new native woodland creation, there are other benefits that can arise in the short to medium term. Some of the more important of these fall into the field that was traditionally known as 'protection forestry' and more recently as 'natural capital and ecosystem services' (Kareiva et al. 2011) – sequestration of atmospheric carbon, prevention of soil erosion from hill-slopes and associated siltation of river waters, reduction of flood risks to agricultural land and built-up areas, and conservation of freshwater habitats and fish stocks from pollution. Creation of well-planned new native woodlands in the headwaters and along the floodplains of rivers can make a significant contribution to addressing these protection requirements.

9.3.1 *Soil and freshwater protection*

By comparison with many overseas territories with steep slopes, Scotland has a limited problem with erosion of soils from the land surface. This is due to the generally well-established vegetation cover on upland moorland and grassland slopes. Only where this vegetation cover is breached by agricultural cultivation, forestry management or landslips is there a significant risk of downslope soil movement. In some areas, where tilled agricultural land or forestry clearfell activity comes down to the banks of rivers, there is a localised problem of siltation during heavy rainfall events, and this also carries the risk of fertiliser and pesticides entering watercourses. These risks are normally greatly reduced by the maintenance of a 'riparian buffer zone' of bankside vegetation which acts as a filter, preventing run-off from reaching the river or loch (Forestry Commission 2011). While herbaceous wetland vegetation – tall herb, meadowsweet, rushes and so on – can perform this function to a degree, native woodland ecosystems are more effective. Creation of wet woodland by planting along river banks can make a major contribution to the freshwater quality of rivers and lakes in agricultural landscapes (Parrott and MacKenzie 2000).

There has been discussion for many years as to whether creating conifer plantations close to the banks of streams is ecologically damaging. Certainly, during the early and middle years of the life-cycle of conifer stands, when shading is intense, the bankside ground vegetation can be suppressed. This leaves a bare soil surface that is prone to erosion by heavy rainfall events, risking siltation of salmon and trout spawning beds. On narrow streams, the trees on both sides of the river can shade its whole width, reducing the biological productivity of aquatic vegetation and associated invertebrates that provide a food source for fish. Extensive conifer afforestation in upland catchments had become associated with declines in freshwater quality and salmonid fish populations in some parts of Scotland through acidification processes. For these reasons, the Forestry Commission's Forest and Water Guidelines (2011) no longer advise planting conifers close to the banks of any stream. Fewer restrictions apply to plantings of native hardwoods as their shade is less dense and the impacts on ground vegetation less severe. However, in some overseas territories where shade-tolerant conifer forests are naturally occurring, coniferous cover does come right down to the banks of forest rivers and does not appear to restrict salmonid fish populations. Indeed, the forested rivers of the Pacific Northwest, many fringed by mature Sitka spruce forests, hold some of the world's most productive rod-caught salmon fisheries. The difference may be that these rivers tend to be broader and that the mature conifer forests regenerate naturally in a more structurally diverse way, without extensive stretches of the streams being subject to heavy shade from even-aged thicket growth (Wilson 2011a). It also may be that freshwater invertebrates in catchments where conifers are naturally dominant are better adapted to decomposing their litter.

Creation of new native woodlands of the wet woodland type has become increasingly common as a feature of river catchment management projects in Scotland (Parrott and MacKenzie 2000). These are aimed at consolidating river banks, preventing erosion and resulting siltation of salmon spawning beds. Many such projects have

FIGURE 9.1 *Restoration of riparian native woodland, Aberdeenshire. Copyright: Dr Scott McG. Wilson.*

taken place on the headwater streams of the major salmon rivers such as the Tweed, the Tay and the Dee, with the objective of securing more productive salmon spawning and an enhanced commercial fishery. Such improvements normally have spin-off benefits for other aspects of freshwater biodiversity – non-sport fish stocks, invertebrates, waterfowl, bats and so on. Where conifer stands adjacent to rivers are harvested (or cut back as part of ecological restoration), areas of new native riparian woodland can be created in their place. Where agricultural land comes down to the river bank, most commonly pasture land, it is possible to create a buffer zone of new native woodland along the river, protected from browsing by a stock fence (see Figure 9.1). This not only creates woodland habitat and prevents bank erosion and siltation, it also reduces the risk of mineral fertilisers and pesticides entering the watercourse and may avoid hazards to livestock posed by boggy ground.

9.3.2 Flood risk mitigation

In recent years, Scotland has seen a number of exceptional rainfall events which have caused flash-flooding of agricultural land and built-up areas. These often arise from a rainstorm in the hills, with a resulting pulse of water moving rapidly downstream. Where headwater streams converge, often near a settlement, these peak flows can be combined, causing significant damage to buildings and infrastructure. In most cases, the upper catchments involved have long been deforested – experience from overseas shows that such 'denuded' catchments usually 'respond' much more quickly to heavy rainfall events than do naturally forested catchments. There is a good argument that creating more native woodland habitat in the upper catchments could help to slow down floodwaters. This works in a number of ways – in the main, the roots of trees such as alder and willow trap silt and other debris, forming a network of finer channels and pools that can store water within the catchment for a period of time, reducing the peak flow on a particular stream. The presence of woodland on the floodplain also increases 'roughness' – some of the energy of the water is absorbed in pushing against the stems of the trees themselves and the associated ground vegetation, reducing the speed of water flow downstream of the woodland. Woodland usually offers greater protection from scouring and other forms of soil erosion – this reduces the burden of silt carried by the river and damage to adjoining fields, and so on. Where two streams come together at a confluence, there can be a considerable benefit in measures upstream of that point that will help to 'stagger' the time of arrival of flood peaks. This can significantly reduce the peak water level achieved and, in some cases, avoid the risk of over-topping flood defences protecting built developments and farmland further downstream (Nisbet and Thomas 2008). That, in turn, offers the opportunity for cost savings. If there is only a limited amount of resources available for riparian woodland creation, it may make sense to concentrate the effort on one of the streams where there is the greatest potential to delay floodwater in the catchment. That will usually be the stream which has a wide, flat floodplain rather than a steep-sided valley. By doing this, there will be a maximum effect on the timing of the flood peak on that river, while the other remains unaltered. This will spread out the flood peak experienced downstream, perhaps making it longer and smoother or bimodal (double-peaked), but reducing the maximum heights attained. Recent research conducted on river catchments above Pickering in Yorkshire (Nisbet and Thomas 2008) suggests the effectiveness of this approach, where woodland creation is well planned and carefully located. There are several locations in Scotland where a similar approach might prove valuable in reducing risks and costs associated with periodic flood events, for example above the towns of Huntly, Fochabers and Elgin.

9.4 Rationales – timber, woodfuel and carbon storage

Another major set of reasons for creating new native woodlands relate to the woody biomass that they produce and the end-uses to which this can be put. These are potentially important in terms of both the rural economy and the wider imperative to avoid and mitigate climate change.

9.4.1 Sustainable timber production

While the annual rate of wood formation in native woodlands is typically only 2–6m^3/ha, compared with 10–18m^3/ha in productive conifer plantations, the wood from native hardwoods in particular can be valuable for specific higher-value end-uses. These include green oak for cruck-frame construction, Scots pine for post and beam construction and a variety of the native hardwood species for furniture-making and craft wood-working (Fife 1994; Martynoga 2011). In recent decades the harvest of native timber in Scotland has tended to be small and, with the exception of Scots pine, has been drawn from older woodlands that have undergone a long period of neglect. This has meant that the timber is often of poor form for productive uses and is difficult and expensive to extract. Conservation designations applying within these woodlands can also complicate the options for timber harvesting. However, in new native woodlands planned and managed with future timber production in mind, there is no reason why Scotland should not be able to grow and use Scots pine and native hardwood timbers of high quality, as in mainland Europe. This means that the appropriate decisions need to be taken from the outset in terms of species and provenance choice, initial stocking density, establishment method, cleaning, thinning and pruning. Those aspects will be dealt with in more detail later in this chapter. Production of high-quality native timber, and its subsequent processing using flexible sawmill equipment, form a potentially important element of sustainable rural development along the lines found in many European countries. New native woodlands aimed at timber production (also known as 'woodlots') can be on privately owned farms or small-holdings (Forestry Commission Scotland 2006a) or within community-owned woodlands. Harvesting is normally carried out by a process of continual thinning to remove stems that have reached economic maturity under forms of 'continuous-cover forestry' (CCF). Farmers may use harvesting and forwarding equipment that they have for other purposes, while small private owners and community woodland groups may hire equipment from 'machinery-rings'. The development of efficient, durable and relatively affordable portable sawmills (Wood-Mizer, Lucas, Peterson) in recent years has also allowed timber to be processed on-site or nearby for local uses such as construction of affordable housing. This retains the economic value of the timber within local communities and avoids the need to transport timber over long distances, consuming fossil fuels. Valuable native hardwood trees can also be grown on farms for timber and woodfuel in combination with livestock husbandry or food crops. Such 'agroforestry' systems have been used extensively in parts of southern Europe, but are less familiar in Scotland. Trees are established at wide spacing to retain forage or crop production (see Figure 9.2) and, where livestock are present in the early years, require more robust protection. Widely spaced trees grown for quality timber may need to be pruned to produce a good stem form.

9.4.2 Woodfuel production

With recent rises in fossil fuel prices, and concerns over 'greenhouse gas' emissions, there has been increasing interest in alternative sources of renewable energy. The use of biomass fuels, including woodfuel, is an important element in that equation. While there has always been a steady demand in the rural parts of Scotland for logs for burning on open fires and in stoves, there is now potential for considerable expansion of the 'energy wood' market, including wood-chips and pellets for automated boilers. These can be installed in domestic premises, community facilities (schools, care homes, hospitals, swimming pools, etc.) and smaller commercial and industrial buildings. With increasing demand for woodfuel, consideration has to be given to where it will be

Figure 9.2 *Demonstration of silvopastoral agroforestry, Glensaugh. Copyright: Dr Scott McG. Wilson.*

sourced, preferably without the need for long-distance transport. Ideally, it is better to avoid burning logs that could find higher-value end-uses as sawn timber or in particle-board and paper manufacture. Some material can be obtained from the by-products of timber production – 'lop and top' from the forest, sawmill residues and so on – and similarly with woody material 'arising' from arboricultural operations in parks and gardens, which would otherwise be composted. There has also been an increase in thinning activity in some existing woodlands that had been neglected. At least to begin with, this is likely to improve the condition of those woodlands by admitting more light, promoting more natural regeneration and improving the opportunity for the better-quality stems to produce a valuable final crop. This applies in both conifer plantations and existing native woodlands. Obviously if abstraction of woodfuel were taken too far, it could represent over-cutting of these woodlands. To avoid that, there is a current emphasis being placed on creating new areas of woodland with the specific objective of producing woodfuel for the future. To bring these supplies on-stream earlier, so-called 'short-rotation' management systems are likely to be applied. Some native tree species such as willow and aspen might be suitable for management under 'short-rotation coppice' systems with a three- to seven-year cutting cycle, whereas others such as hazel and birch might be operated under 'short-rotation forestry' systems with a seven- to twenty-five-year cutting cycle, perhaps needing to be replanted at the end of that time. These intensively managed fuel woodlots are likely to make a major contribution to wood energy supplies in the short to medium term, but even more conventional new native woodlands, created mainly for biodiversity, landscape and timber production, can produce valuable supplies of woodfuel for sustainable harvest in the longer term.

Species such as hazel, birch and alder, which are relatively fast-grown and will coppice easily, are likely to prove the most suitable for that form of management, as in the past. The Forestry Commission has produced a number of recent guidance notes on short-rotation forestry and woodfuel production relevant to Scotland.

9.4.3 Carbon sequestration

Wood accumulated in trees represents a store of carbon, which is fixed from the carbon dioxide (CO_2) content of the atmosphere by the process of photosynthesis. This helps to regulate the CO_2 concentration in the atmosphere which is rising as a result of emissions from the burning of fossil fuels, causing 'global warming' (Read et al. 2009). However, when wood is burned, or rots away, the carbon is released back into the atmosphere. Reductions in forest area in the tropics are therefore a major contributor to climate change. End-uses such as construction timber and furniture-making can lock up the carbon for long periods, whereas those such as paper-making and woodfuel result in its earlier re-release. The ability of forests to act as a 'carbon sink' therefore depends on their extent, type, rate of carbon accumulation (growth rate) and the time period for which the carbon is locked up (carbon life-cycle). New native woodlands tend to have a slower rate of accumulation than productive conifer plantations, but also to lock up carbon for longer due to the ways their timber is used. Timber left in the forest, for example as veteran trees and deadwood within non-intervention native woodland reserves, can lock up the carbon for many centuries until the timber decays and also contributes to soil carbon accumulation. Hardwood timber in buildings and furniture can lock up carbon for at least several decades, centuries in some cases. Creation of woodland intended to lock up atmospheric carbon should probably aim for a mix of fast-grown conifers, which will have an early impact over the first twenty to fifty years, and slower-grown native hardwoods, which will represent a longer-term store of carbon over decades and centuries. In the case of woodfuel, it is also necessary to consider the resulting reduction in fossil fuel combustion. Although the carbon locked up in the woodfuel is re-released when it is burned, this means that an equivalent amount of fossil fuel may not need to be used, avoiding the release of its carbon content. There is therefore a net reduction in the carbon otherwise being added to the atmosphere. New native woodlands established as long-term, low-intervention stores of carbon are likely to be able to meet other objectives such as biodiversity conservation and landscape enhancement.

9.5 RATIONALES – AGRICULTURAL SHELTER AND FIELD SPORT

Many private landowners will consider creating new native woodlands as part of improvement schemes on their farms and estates. Major benefits that can be obtained include improved shelter for crops and livestock and improved cover for game species such as pheasant and woodcock. These have direct economic implications in terms of revenue from agricultural and sporting enterprises and increases in capital value of the land.

9.5.1 Game for field sports

Game birds such as pheasant and woodcock require a proportion of woodland on the estate to provide shelter for roosting, feeding and, in some cases, nesting. Experience has developed over the years in designing such 'game coverts' to have the maximum benefit (Hart 1993). The aim is to create woodland that will 'hold game' by providing protection from cold winds and form effective 'game drives' by being suitably positioned on the landform – for example on a rising slope. There has been a tendency to use introduced 'game cover' shrubs such as laurel and snowberry, which help to create the necessary wind shelter rapidly. However, these can become invasive if used in or near native woodland. It is possible to produce good game cover, especially on lowland sites, using native hardwoods, although these may take rather longer to reach maturity. Evergreen species such as holly and yew can be included in order to maintain winter shelter. Some upland estate owners also create new native woodland with the intention of providing winter shelter for red deer, with deer numbers then having to be managed at levels consistent with natural regeneration.

9.5.2 Agricultural shelter

New native woodland can increase the agricultural productivity of upland and coastal farmlands by providing improved shelter (Palmer et al. 1997). Traditional shelterbelts and wind-breaks form a barrier to the wind, behind which livestock or arable crops can be protected. Reduced wind-chill will allow livestock to feed more productively and to gain more weight within a given time. Many were created as part of the Agricultural Improvements, between 1750 and 1850. Introduced species such as beech, sycamore and lime, together with evergreen conifers, were most commonly used, but there is no reason why native trees such as oak, ash and elm cannot serve the same function, perhaps with an understorey of hazel or holly. Recently, research and development work has been undertaken by the James Hutton Institute and the Scottish Agricultural College to support the creation of new pasture woodlands in the Scottish uplands, where livestock might be sheltered within the woodland itself (Wilson 2013a). Such 'silvo-pastoral' systems worked well in the past where there was mature wood pasture already in existence (e.g. at Glen Finglas, Cadzow, Dalkeith – see Chapter 5). Creating pasture woodland 'from scratch' poses some extra challenges – particularly the need to protect the young woodland from deer and to exclude livestock until it becomes well established. Some approaches centre on creating a regular layout of widely spaced hardwood trees (e.g. oak, ash) which can be protected by tree-shelters and managed for valuable timber, while livestock graze at fairly high stocking levels on an improved grass sward between the trees. Other schemes have attempted to create areas of denser but less formally planned new native woodland, to which livestock can later be re-admitted at lower stocking levels. The aim here is to create the more naturalistic type of pasture woodland generally found on historical sites in the Scottish uplands. At a later stage, traditional forms of wood-pasture management, such as coppicing and pollarding, might be reinstated to produce winter fodder for the animals and also some woodfuel.

9.6 Rationales – landscape amenity and tourism

The final major reason for creating new native woodland is to enhance the landscape and improve its potential as a setting for eco-tourism activities.

The Scottish landscape (especially in upland areas) is fairly unique in Europe in not being dominated by forests. As we have seen, this has resulted from a very long process of change with both natural and human components. While many people admire the classic open landscapes of the Scottish Highlands, together with their isolated Caledonian pinewoods, others prefer the more intimate, partly wooded landscapes of Perthshire and Argyll, for example. Hence it is difficult to reach any consensus as to whether increasing woodland cover in the Scottish countryside would result in it being viewed as more or less attractive, and even more difficult to predict what the effects on overall tourist activity might be. Increases in forest cover during the past century have mainly been by coniferous afforestation, which, in more recent phases, tended to create more uniform, less varied landscapes. There was also an increase in the perceived artificiality of the landscape, with straight-edged forestry plantations. As conifer plantations mature, and become structurally diverse, they are viewed as more attractive by the visiting public (Grant and Worrell 2012), as at Drumlanrig, Dunkeld and Glentress (see Chapter 10). The creation of well-planned new native woodland tends to be rather more gradual than coniferous plantation afforestation and makes less striking changes to the landscape. It is therefore likely that increases from the current generally low levels of native woodland cover would increase landscape diversity and, for some time at least, result in perceived enhancement of landscape amenity, if well placed in the landscape. However, a cogent alternative view is that Scotland's open upland landscape is the primary tourist advantage (with most European countries more heavily wooded) and that establishing more woodland of any type in that landscape will decrease unique wildland value.

Some eco-tourist activities depend simply on a visually attractive rural landscape in itself – for example cross-country walking and skiing, pony trekking and landscape photography. These can be served by a variety of forest types, including well-planned coniferous plantations. Increases in woodland cover tend to increase the 'eco-tourism carrying capacity' as compared with an open landscape – more visitors can be accommodated before their mutual experience is degraded by congestion and a loss of the feeling of 'wildness'. Other activities have a more direct dependence on native woodland cover – for example, wildlife safaris, wildlife photography, bird watching, amateur botany and field visits to reintroduction projects (beaver, osprey, etc.). For these it seems certain that increasing the cover of native woodland, and its degree of landscape inter-connection, would enhance economic potential. Many of the existing native woodlands are small, isolated remnants on rather inaccessible sites for which the main objective of management is, rightly, nature conservation. Only larger, more robust native woodland 'nodes', such as the pinewoods of Deeside, Speyside and

Glen Affric and the oakwoods of Galloway, Argyll and Ardnamurchan, play a major eco-tourism role. If creating new areas of native woodland served to link up some existing smaller patches, creating new landscape-scale 'nodes', these would be likely to increase tourist carrying capacity. There would also be greater scope for the type of woodland-related activities that form the basis of tourist enterprises – mammal reintroduction projects, building of timber lodges, adventure facilities and so on. However, as with timber production, these benefits are only likely to become manifest over many decades. This can make it difficult to persuade private estates to fund native woodland creation themselves, and systems of governmental grant-in-aid may still remain important in promoting activity of this kind.

9.7 IDENTIFYING LAND AND FINANCIAL RESOURCES

We have seen that there are a wide range of potential benefits to be derived from creating new native woodland in Scotland. The Scottish Forestry Strategy of 2006 set ambitious new targets for the expansion of the native woodland resource over the coming decades. The main challenges to achieving these targets are constraints on the availability of suitable land and on the financial resources to undertake the woodland creation work.

9.7.1 Land resources

As Scotland has little true 'waste' or abandoned land, most new native woodland will have to be created on land that is currently being used for something else. This means that there must be a willingness on the part of the owner to change the land-use toward native woodland (Sing et al. 2013). In many, but not all, cases this may mean losing a source of income from that land, at least in the short to medium term. The main categories of land potentially available for conversion to native woodland are as follows:

- **Semi-natural uplands/unimproved grasslands.** This is by far the most extensive type in Scotland, including moor and heath and upland acid grassland. This is often also the cheapest type of land to acquire per hectare, especially where hill-farming enterprises are winding down, but also carries additional challenges and costs for woodland creation (poor soils, water-logging, exposure, difficult access). This type of land is only suitable for upland woodland types – pine, birch and oak. In most cases the land is currently in use for either field sports (grouse, red deer) or extensive livestock rearing (sheep, cattle). Renewable energy generation is also becoming a significant land-use in some areas and can be difficult to reconcile with woodland expansion of most kinds. In many situations there is also a competing nature conservation interest in open habitats that are regarded as being of high value themselves (Sing et al. 2013). Where land is covered by a depth of peat exceeding 50cm, the carbon storage value of the peat is such that woodland creation is now considered inappropriate. Archaeological values may also be high.

- **Improved grasslands/arable land.** These are usually the most valuable types of land, both ecologically for native woodland creation (oak, ash, elm, hazel, alder, willow) and also in terms of financial value for productive agricultural and built development uses. Such 'better land' can be found in lowland and upland marginal areas of eastern, central and southern Scotland, but most private owners remain very reluctant to release it for long-term afforestation. The open-market costs for this type of land tend to put it beyond reach for new native woodland creation, but it will be essential for lowland woodland types. Some wet woodland is created on riparian strips running through such land-cover types. Much attention for woodland expansion in Scotland focuses on land of intermediate quality, such as 'semi-improved' permanent pasture in the upland margins, conventionally used for beef cattle. This has come to be known as the 'squeezed middle', where objectives of woodland expansion and security of food production compete strongly.
- **Brown-field/ex-industrial land.** Significant amounts of this type of land exist, particularly within central Scotland, as a legacy of the long history of industrial, mineral extraction and waste-disposal activities. Native woodland creation can help to ameliorate ex-industrial sites and make them more attractive for other forms of future land-use – mainly residential and commercial property development. These sites are usually close to existing population centres, for which new woodland can provide enhanced recreational and physical exercise opportunities. However, physical conditions on these sites often make for challenges in creating woodlands – shallow soils, poor drainage, residual pollution, vandalism, fire risks and so on. Careful choice of species and establishment methods is essential to secure any successful outcome to tree planting.
- **Plantation forestry.** Some of the areas planted with introduced conifers during the past century are potentially suitable for conversion to native woodland, mainly in the context of PAWS restoration (see Chapter 8). This can be achieved either by a 'clearfell and restock' approach or by gradual silvicultural conversion, using CCF approaches.

9.7.2 Financial resources (including grant support)

Creating new native woodland costs money, although the amount varies a great deal, depending on the type and source of the land and the methods chosen to establish any woodland.

The major costs involved for any new native woodland scheme (Hart 1993) are normally (1) land acquisition/alternative income foregone, (2) woodland planning and design, (3) site preparation, protection, planting stock and establishment, and (4) weeding and stand tending. In some cases these costs may all have to be met up front in cash – for example where a new private or charitable owner purchases planting land and lets one or more contracts for woodland planning, design, establishment and maintenance. In other cases, many costs may be able to be covered 'in kind', for example where a farmer or private estate owner uses surplus land and can carry out fencing, ground preparation, planting and maintenance work using existing farm equipment. In that case, cash costs may be restricted to fencing materials and nursery plants, perhaps with a small amount for professional planning and design advice if the owner is not sufficiently expert. Some categories of owner may use voluntary labour for tree planting – many major conservation charities use volunteer work parties/ summer camps. Lower-intensity methods such as natural colonisation can significantly reduce costs compared to planting, although fencing remains a major cost.

At present a proportion of new native woodland planting in Scotland is being carried out by the Forestry Commission using public funds, in areas near to the major urban centres. Some of the funds being used are derived from the sale of other public forests – mainly conifer plantations in remoter upland areas – known as 'repositioning'. The objective is to create new woodlands that provide opportunities for biodiversity, public amenity and carbon capture, whilst also producing some timber and woodfuel supplies. The Forestry Commission can make use of its existing internal sources of expertise in forest planning, establishment and maintenance and may not always need to pay external forestry contractors for this. As a large programme of work is involved, there may be economies of scale in the sourcing of fencing materials, planting stock and so on, although other costs (e.g. for supervisory time) may be rather higher in a public service organisation.

In the case of new native woodland creation, any financial return to a private owner from timber and woodfuel sales, improved livestock shelter, eco-tourism opportunities and so on is usually delayed by at least fifteen to twenty years, while the woodland becomes established. Hence most private owners will only establish native woodlands on their land if there is significant assistance with the initial establishment costs from grant-in-aid. A few very wealthy private landowners and major charitable bodies may create new native woodland without claiming grant, from philanthropic motives. The nature and generosity of forestry grant schemes has changed regularly over the past twenty to thirty years, and that seems likely to continue. The current scheme is the Scottish Rural Development Programme (Rural Priorities) and is seen by many landowners as being more complex than some earlier schemes. This complexity largely stems from increased requirements to comply with European Union regulations. Few grant schemes cover the cost of land acquisition, but most cover a significant proportion of the costs an existing landowner will incur to establish a woodland and maintain it for the first ten years' growth. Where the land is currently used for agricultural production, there was also a Farm Woodland Premium (FWP) to replace lost annual income over the first ten to fifteen years. Farmers need to consider what effects woodland establishment on their land might have for their eligibility for other agricultural grant schemes, such as the Single Farm Payment (SFP). For up-to-date information on available grants see <www.forestry.gov.uk>.

9.8 The policy and regulatory framework

We saw in Chapter 8 that Forestry Commission Scotland is responsible for forestry policy, regulation and grant assistance in Scotland. This includes the creation of new native woodland habitats. The current Scottish Forestry Strategy encourages expansion of national woodland cover as a whole (currently 17–18%) towards 25% by the year 2050. This requires a tree-planting rate of some 10,000ha per annum, in excess of that achieved in some recent years. It is intended that new woodland created in the coming years will be roughly 60% commercial conifers and 40% new native woodland, whereas the latter has predominated in recent years. While some woodland expansion may occur on the National Forest Estate, most will take place on private land. In the case of native woodland expansion, where future income from timber production is likely to be limited, most owners will only proceed with grant assistance, the availability of which will regulate the amount of woodland actually created. Larger-scale new native woodland creation projects also trigger Environmental Impact Assessment (EIA) as they represent a significant change of land-use at catchment scale.

The recent Scottish Government Woodland Expansion Advisory Group (WEAG) reported in 2012. A major strand in that group's work was to examine ways in which woodland creation could be combined with continuing use of land areas for agricultural production, sporting deer range and conservation of designated open land habitats in upland areas. This consideration resulted from continuing concerns among farmers, estate managers and nature conservationists that woodland expansion represented a potential threat to other land-management priorities. While some such concerns are less acute for native woodland creation than in the case of coniferous plantation afforestation, the competition with farming and 'food security' remains. Unfortunately, Scotland lacks a recent historical tradition of integrated farm forestry or agroforestry that might offer a potential way forward here, as it does, for example, in parts of both Scandinavia and the Mediterranean region. Successful trial-scale adoption suggests that there is potential for future development in agroforestry.

Another potential emerging source of income from land on which new native woodland is established is so-called 'Payment for Ecosystem Services' (PES). Ecosystem services are typically non-market benefits that accrue to parties other than the landowner who bears the costs of their provision – for example carbon sequestration, flood risk mitigation, fisheries improvement and catchment-scale soil conservation (Kareiva et al. 2011). It has been proposed that those who agree to establish suitable woodland habitats on their land should be eligible to receive payments from private-sector beneficiaries (e.g. residential developers, house insurers and business owners), in addition to state grant support on behalf of society as a whole. While some voluntary mechanisms have been set up in respect of carbon sequestration and freshwater improvement, the level of such benefits is generally disappointing to date. It is unlikely that this will change in the foreseeable future without the adoption of mandatory levies on the 'polluter pays' principle – which would effectively be a form of 'green taxation'. A minor proportion of philanthropic owners may self-fund service provision.

9.9 Positioning new native woodland in the landscape

There are usually insufficient land and financial resources available to create new native woodland habitat everywhere that might be desirable. There are competing calls on the land area of Scotland for agricultural production, plantation forestry, renewable energy and built development, and there are competing demands on public finances, especially in the current climate. Many decisions about where new native woodland is created are partly accidental – for example, a private owner may plant part of his/her estate for amenity, or a hill farmer may retire, making his/her land available for purchase by a conservation body. However, official decisions also have an influence through the planning system and the design of locationally targeted grants to promote woodland creation. In these respects it is beneficial to have logical frameworks to guide decision-making. Areas can be prioritised for native woodland creation at the regional or local catchment scales based on a combination of spatial and land-suitability criteria.

9.9.1 Spatial configuration criteria

These cover the considerations affecting where creation of new native woodland would yield the greatest value in terms of the key objectives of the process – in practice, mainly biodiversity enhancement and freshwater catchment protection, with visual landscape amenity considerations acting as a constraint in some situations. This process helps to identify those parcels of land where woodland creation would have the maximum benefit per hectare, before considering existing alternative land-uses or economics.

Many recent approaches to this problem are based on the concepts of 'island biogeography theory', discussed earlier. In recent years the concept of 'forest habitat networks' (FHNs) has come to the fore, developed by the woodland ecologist George Peterken and others (Fowler and Stiven 2003; Peterken et al. 1995; Watts et al. 2005). The concept is to create networks of native woodland habitat at the landscape scale that can support populations of woodland-dependent animal and plant species and provide opportunities for them to migrate across the landscape, perhaps in response to a changing climate. Networks are composed of 'nodes' (large patches of native woodland habitat) and 'linkages' (either continuous, such as shelterbelts, or intermittent, such as a chain of small woodlands acting as 'stepping stones'). The land surface between native woodland habitat networks is assessed in terms of its 'permeability' to typical woodland biodiversity species. Some artificial land-cover types, such as intensive arable agriculture or built development, act as an effective barrier to woodland species moving between habitat networks, whereas established gardens, semi-natural heathland or scrub will usually be more permeable. Narrow linear features such as hedgerows can serve as weak linkages or 'habitat corridors' between networks, but not all woodland-dependent species can use these effectively due to 'edge effects'. Existing areas of plantation conifer forestry are somewhat controversial in this respect. Some ecologists argue that they can be included within woodland habitat networks, especially once they have matured and become structurally diverse. Others argue that only ancient semi-natural woodland should be included in existing habitat networks. For most, less specialist, woodland biodiversity species, plantation forestry is probably more permeable than most open land-cover types. Creation of new native woodland can sometimes be aimed at creating a new 'node' but more often at completing or reinforcing a habitat 'linkage' – for example along a valley corridor. It is better to create linkages that are fairly broad and robust, rather than a web of very fine shelterbelts and hedgerows that may be vulnerable to disruption and are less ecologically effective.

9.9.2 Land suitability at the landscape scale

When planning new native woodland creation, it is essential to assess the suitability of the land available, both to decide whether woodland creation is a viable option and, if it is, to decide on the correct species to use and site preparation methods required. Land suitability assessment (Towers et al. 2004) is often considered at three spatial scales: (1) the landscape scale, (2) the forest or catchment scale and (3) the stand or site scale. At the larger two scales the key decisions that have to be taken are (1) is the land suitable for native woodland creation and (2) what type (or mosaic of types) of native woodland is likely to be the most appropriate.

Over the past century a variety of systems of land suitability or 'capability' assessment have been developed, for application in different situations. These are sometimes called 'land classification schemes'. There are basically two types: (1) those schemes that classify land capability or potential based on direct assessment of abiotic variables (altitude, aspect, slope, climate, geology and soils) and (2) those schemes that rely to a greater extent on the existing semi-natural vegetation cover to give an indication as to the types of native woodland that would be most suitable. In some cases, existing vegetation cover can be surveyed by remote-sensing techniques – from either aircraft or satellites – making this process quicker and cheaper than where detailed ground soil survey is required. Where there has been site disturbance in the past (e.g. plantation forestry, agricultural cultivation, industrial development), the first type of classification scheme, although potentially costlier, is usually more reliable than the second.

For use in Scotland, the main land classification scheme using direct climate and soil information is the Forestry Commission's Ecological Site Classification (ESC) (Pyatt et al. 2001). This has been developed since the early 1990s, building on an older system for Scotland produced by Professor Mark Anderson at the University of Edinburgh and published in his famous book *The Selection of Tree Species* (1961), which acted as the 'Scottish foresters' bible' for many years. The ESC also adopts site classification principles from British Columbia in Canada, which has a very similar climate to Scotland and from where many of our introduced coniferous tree species derive. For application at all scales, the ESC takes information about climate from UK Meteorological Office maps which can be used within a computer Geographical Information System (GIS). While there are good maps of soils for certain parts of the country (mainly within existing public forests), most of the country is only covered by small-scale national soil mapping which is not suitable for detailed site-scale forestry assessments. It can however be analysed to give a reasonable indication of conditions at the larger landscape and catchment scales. The ESC provides predictions of potential suitability for each National Vegetation Classification (NVC) woodland community.

To get round the problems created by the lack of detailed existing soil mapping, another tool has been developed by the James Hutton (formerly Macaulay) Institute in Aberdeen called the Native Woodland Model (NWM) (Towers et al. 2004). This uses similar information about climate and soils to that used within the ESC, when applied at the landscape scale. However, it also makes use of information about the existing vegetation cover on the site where this is naturally occurring (e.g. heathland, moorland, unimproved grassland). This information was collected by interpreted remote-sensing techniques for the Land Cover of Scotland (LCS) survey in 1988. The vegetation information acts as a 'surrogate indicator' of underlying soil conditions, providing greater detail than would national soil mapping resources for many localities. The NWM makes predictions of potential suitability for each NVC native woodland type and for mosaics of these.

9.10 Planning new native woodland at the site scale

Coming down to the scale of the individual site where new native woodland creation is planned, the Forestry Commission Ecological Site Classification (ESC) provides a valuable framework for planning and decision-making. There are, however, other similar approaches to achieve the same ends. The main decisions that need to be taken are (1) which NVC native woodland communities (see Chapter 2) should be the targets for ecological restoration on the site (Rodwell and Patterson 1994), (2) how should the ground be prepared for woodland creation and (3) which native tree species should be planted or naturally regenerated from the outset, depending on objectives.

The 'site scale' can vary from a small patch of ground on a farm or along a stream up to a large field or plantation forestry 'felling coupe' covering several hectares. In the case of larger planting schemes it may be necessary to divide the area up, reflecting major changes in topography, soils and existing vegetation, with different target NVC communities. There is also a need to build a proportion of open space into schemes, which can be up to 15–20% in some cases (see section that follows on scheme design).

The first step in site-scale planning is to create an accurate 'backdrop map' of the scheme area on a suitable scale of Ordnance Survey map (1:10,000). This is required for public consultation and grant application processes. Key features and 'constraints', such as rivers, ponds, archaeological remains and existing protected habitats, should be drawn onto the map to define the woodland planting area. Often this is now carried out in computer GIS mapping systems (Heywood et al. 2011) (see Plate 20).

The input information required for the Ecological Site Classification covers climate, geology (sometimes termed 'lithology') and soils. Climate data from the Meteorological Office is already contained within the computerised ESC Decision-Support System (ESC-DSS) which is available from the Forestry Commission website. The only other information required is a six-figure map reference for the site which can be taken up from the Ordnance Survey maps. Geological information is available from the British Geological Survey 'ten-mile' maps, held by many public libraries. Care should be taken if the site is large and has significant changes in aspect or topography which might reflect geological boundaries or give rise to important variation in climatic exposure. For example, an upland site on both sides of a steep-sided ridge or valley, running east to west, may have a different climate (and resulting vegetation and soils) on either side.

Collection of the required information about soils may prove rather more demanding. If you are lucky, there may be a good map of soil types at 1:10,000 scale or better, which can be used within the ESC-DSS to refine estimates of soil moisture regime (SMR) and soil nutrient regime (SNR) (see Chapter 2). This is more often the case within existing forested areas, particularly those owned by the Forestry Commission. However, for most areas, the best soil mapping available is the small-scale Soil Survey of Scotland maps, which are not really suitable for use as a site-planning tool. In these cases, it is necessary to collect soil information from fresh field-survey work. This will involve digging one or more soil pits to a depth of up to one metre and describing the layers in the soil profile. These will allow the soil to be visually assigned to one of the standard types (Kennedy 2002) – which can then be used within the ESC-DSS to refine estimates of SMR and SNR. Where soil varies across a site it is essential to map out the main soil types and dig at least one soil pit to describe each. This will be of importance to determine the NVC woodland types to be created and their configuration.

When surveying any planting site before woodland creation it is also useful to collect information about existing vegetation on the land, especially where this is semi-natural – for example scrub, moorland, heathland, unimproved grassland (Rodwell 1991b). Major changes in the type of vegetation may be due to changes in soil moisture or fertility levels – this will help the process of soil mapping and site analysis. Some vegetation may resemble that found in the field layer of individual NVC woodland communities (Rodwell 1991a), giving a clue as to the most appropriate woodland types to create on that site (Rodwell and Patterson 1994). The presence of ancient woodland indicator plants (Crawford 2009) (e.g. bluebell) may mark areas where native woodland was formerly present. Where detailed quadrat information is collected about ground vegetation, including common species present and their abundance, this can be used by the ESC-DSS to produce more refined assessments of soil nutrient regimes.

Once all of the information described above has been collected and analysed within the ESC-DSS or by an equivalent method, it should become clearer which NVC woodland communities should be targeted for restoration on each part of the site (see Plate 20). If there is doubt, it is safer to select a less demanding woodland type (e.g. upland oak-birch) but to include minor proportions of more demanding species (e.g. alder, elm, hazel). This reduces the risk of large-scale failure when planting woodland. Additional tree and shrub species can often be added later by 'enrichment planting'. If only very small areas of the site appear suitable for any given native woodland type, it may not be worth trying to establish it from the outset, unless it is of particular value (e.g. wet woodland).

9.11 ACCOUNTING FOR CLIMATE CHANGE, PESTS AND DISEASES

9.11.1 Climatic change

Recent years have seen increasing concern about the possibility of changes in climate as a result of the build-up in the atmosphere of carbon dioxide, deriving from burning fossil fuels. Given that new native woodlands created in Scotland today are being expected to live for many decades or centuries, it is important to take into account the potential impacts of climate change that may happen during that period. At present, we only have scientifically based predictions for the next fifty to eighty years – less than the lifetime of most native tree species. Predictive climate models remain subject to a considerable degree of uncertainty and can only be used as a guide to likely trends. For Scotland, central predictions suggest a somewhat milder climate overall, with less winter snow and frost on average (Ray 2008). Eastern areas may become drier in summer, but western areas may become even wetter than today. Storm and flood events may become more frequent and severe than at present, but this is particularly uncertain. Disturbance of the Gulf Stream could lead to markedly different trends. Changes in climate may encourage greater incidence of damaging pests and diseases. Some of the ways foresters and ecologists can take climate change into account are as follows:

- **Risk identification and evaluation.** Within the regional climatic predictions, not all potential sites for native woodland creation will carry the same risk levels. For example, a site with a shallow sandy soil in the east of Scotland may have an extra risk of drought damage to growing trees in future, while one on the floodplain of a river on the west coast may have an extra risk of flood-induced soil erosion. It is important to assess these risks carefully before choosing species/woodland types. Where it appears that conditions are only marginally suitable for any particular tree species or woodland type today, and may become less suitable in future, it will be more sensible to choose a less demanding species or woodland type that is more resilient. It is best to avoid creating woodlands that will operate under climatic stress, as these may become more susceptible to damage from pest and disease outbreaks.
- **Adaptation actions.** When planning a new native woodland creation project, it is possible to make decisions that will reduce the risks posed by climate change. Usually, increasing the species and genetic-level diversity of tree plantings will reduce risk by offering more options for the future, depending on how the climate changes. There can be merit in selecting at least a proportion of tree species and seed provenances (Hubert and Cundall 2006; Hubert and Cottrell 2007) that come from areas with a climate today resembling that predicted for the planting area in the future – for example, choosing some oak of English or French provenances, in addition to local Scottish material. However, care must be taken not to jump too far ahead – material planted must be reasonably adapted to the site conditions of today or it will not establish properly. Some of these decisions inevitably take us in a direction away from the traditional native

woodland communities of Scotland – for example, should species like beech, sycamore and lime, suited to warmer climates, now be accepted for planting? Some existing woodland communities, such as native pinewood, may become restricted to smaller areas of the Scottish landscape where climates remain optimal. Where existing ancient woodland sites have been designated for conservation of particular native woodland communities, there is often a regulatory requirement not to plant non-native tree species or provenances on adjoining sites, where this could compromise their genetic integrity (Forestry Commission Scotland 2006b). However, where timber production is an important objective of woodland creation, it may well be appropriate to use novel species mixtures in order to reduce risks of species failure and take opportunities to include more productive – but more warmth-demanding – tree species for the future.

9.11.2 Emerging pest and disease risks

The last decade has seen an increase in the reported incidence of novel pests and diseases affecting trees in Britain. Notable examples include the fungal pathogens *Chalara fraxinea* affecting ash, *Dothistroma septosporum* affecting pines (Brown and Webber 2008), *Phytophthora ramorum* affecting larch, oak and beech, and *Phytophthora austrocedrae* affecting juniper, as well as the insect pests oak processionary moth and Asian longhorn beetle affecting oak. Tree pests and diseases as such are not a new phenomenon and have caused significant damage in the past, as with Dutch elm disease in the 1930s and again in the 1960s and 1970s. However, there does appear to be a combination of factors at present that is giving rise to added concern. One key factor is the increased long-distance transportation of living plants which are capable of transmitting new pests and diseases from one territory to another. In some cases, wood products and packaging materials can also be a 'vector' of infection, especially if bark has not been removed. Once introduced to a new territory, pathogenic organisms can affect host populations lacking natural resistance. As northern temperate forest regions of North America, Europe and Asia share common tree genera (see Chapter 1) there are often susceptible hosts present. For example, *Chalara* is believed to be a natural pathogen of ash (*Fraxinus* spp.) in eastern Asia, where native tree populations are resistant. However, when European ash populations are exposed, they are badly affected. A warmer climate may make it more likely that introduced pests and disease organisms can establish and spread (Green and Ray 2009).

Establishing new native woodland is in itself an activity that carries the risk of introducing tree pests and diseases through the movement of infected seed or plants which may have been raised at some distance away, even abroad. There is also a risk that planted trees may be susceptible to a pest or disease that is already present or is introduced at a later stage. Some sensible precautions can be applied to mitigate, but not eliminate, these risks:

1. **Diversity** – using a wider range of tree species and provenances to reduce the risk of an entire planting scheme being affected by any given pest or disease.

However, only those species and provenances that are well adapted to the site should be used – poorly performing or stressed growing stock may be more vulnerable and might act as a focus for subsequent infection. We have seen that some native woodland types in Scotland (notably native pinewood) naturally consist of only a few native tree species, and options for diversification may be limited in purely native woodland schemes.

2. **Sourcing** – when using transplanted nursery stock, taking prudent measures to reduce the risk of it being infected when deployed. Purchase only from a recognised source – nursery or plant breeder – who is able to supply the appropriate official documentation. Prefer planting material that has been sourced and raised within the United Kingdom, rather than propagated abroad. If possible, order planting stock well in advance so that there is not a 'last-minute rush' to 'source it from wherever possible', often implying overseas supply. Ensure that the planting stock is healthy when delivered to the site and reject any material that shows poor vigour or suspicious signs. Consider opportunities to use natural colonisation to expand native woodland or to use plants raised from seed collected more locally. Do not use any tree species that is known to be particularly susceptible to a disease likely to be already present in the locality, and consider the risk from new diseases moving into the area. In 2014 there was a moratorium on the planting of ash for this reason.
3. **Biosecurity** – taking reasonable measures to reduce the risk of pests and diseases being brought onto the site during and after the woodland establishment phase. Require your forestry and planting contractors to disinfect vehicles, clothing, footwear and tools. Avoid the bulk movement of soil onto the site as part of woodland creation or landscaping, as this carries a much higher risk of transmitting some infections. Where this is unavoidable, for example on landfill reclamation sites, ensure that topsoil has been proficiently sourced and treated. Properly treated compost associated with containerised nursery plants should not present the same risks. The risks of subsequent introduction of infection by casual visitors are likely to be fairly limited, and biosecurity measures more difficult to enforce. Little can be done to protect against airborne fungal pathogens.
4. **Vigilance** – continuing to inspect your planting scheme regularly after establishment to detect, at an early stage, any signs of pests or diseases emerging on site. Remove and destroy any ailing stock, and consider replacement with a different species. Seek advice from experts on the identification of any symptoms that appear suspicious or unfamiliar. Report any notifiable diseases to the authorities.

9.12 TAKING ADVANTAGE OF NATURAL COLONISATION

One of the best ways to create new native woodland is to take advantage of natural colonisation onto open land from an adjoining native woodland. This normally has the advantage of being significantly cheaper than creating woodland by tree planting and often ensures that the genetic stock used is inherently suited to the site climate and soils as they are at present. Once naturally regenerated trees are established, they tend to be less susceptible to failure as a result of herbivore browsing, pests and climatic conditions, as they often develop a more robust root system than nursery transplants. The stocking density achieved can be higher than in planted schemes, which offers a greater choice of stems to select from for a final timber crop and normally produces cleaner, straighter stems by competition. The main disadvantages of natural colonisation are that woodland creation can be slower than by planting and that the manager has a lower degree of control – the species which colonise naturally may not be those desired and there may be an uneven 'patchy' stocking distribution across a site. If relying purely on natural colonisation, there is no opportunity to introduce new species or provenances to reduce risks from climate change or to take advantage of superior-form stock produced from tree improvement programmes.

In order to make a success of woodland expansion by natural colonisation, the following considerations must be taken into account (Harmer 1999; Thompson 2004):

1. **Why is there no natural colonisation at present?** The usual reasons will be a lack of seed, unsuitable ground/seed-bed conditions and browsing off of seedlings by deer/livestock. There is normally little that can be done about a lack of seed other than to wait for the adjoining woodland to mature to seed-producing age or for 'mast' years. However, the ground conditions and browsing pressure can usually be modified.
2. **What site preparation and protection work is required?** In Scottish conditions many natural colonisation schemes will require effective deer fencing for at least ten years and very often for twenty to thirty years in the more exposed uplands where growth will be slower. This carries a significant cost – the major cost associated with this form of woodland expansion, as there are no planting works. Rabbits may also need to be controlled. In some cases, ground preparation in the form of herbicide control of weeds and mechanical scarification may be required if there is a dense cover of ground vegetation, moss or litter. The minimum necessary disturbance should be used but it should be borne in mind that weed competition may become more serious soon after any fence is erected.
3. **Targets, monitoring and follow-up work.** Most woodland creation by natural colonisation is carried out under forestry grant schemes which require measurable results after a given period, or the grant may later have to be repaid. This is usually after ten years, which may be too early under the ecological conditions of upland Scotland. This has become a serious problem for some woodland owners over recent years. If the required natural regeneration does not appear within the first half of the agreed period (e.g. after five years), ground conditions and protection should be considered once again, but it may be necessary to carry out some follow-up tree planting to increase the stocking density to required levels, known as 'reinforcement'. Very often, the earlier natural regeneration is mainly of 'pioneer' tree species such as birch, rowan and alder. Species such as oak and ash might not appear for thirty years, especially if the seed sources are distant.

If it is desirable (or required by grant schemes) for these to appear earlier, there may be a need for enrichment planting.

9.13 Selecting tree species for establishment

When the decision has been taken to create new native woodland by planting rather than natural colonisation, the forester or ecologist has to choose which tree species should be included. We have seen that systematic site description and classification, using a technique such as the Forestry Commission Ecological Site Classification (ESC) (Pyatt et al. 2001), can inform this process. The ESC can produce suggestions (not decisions) as to which NVC native woodland community should be targeted for eventual restoration on the site, and which individual native tree species will grow best in native plantations. The latter may be of particular interest if timber or woodfuel production is a key objective of the planting scheme.

9.13.1 Using the National Vegetation Classification as a guide

Some of the NVC native woodland communities (Rodwell 1991a), such as native pinewood (W18) or upland acid oak-birch woodland (W17), contain two or three principal tree and shrub species, whereas some of the more complex mixed ashwood types (W8 and 9) could eventually comprise six or eight. It is not always necessary or sensible to try to include within the initial planting mix all of those species that might eventually be desirable. Some species (usually the more light-demanding 'pioneer' species) can establish well on an open site, whereas others are more likely to succeed if introduced to the scheme later, once woodland conditions mature. Many woodland planting schemes will include species like birch, rowan and alder which tend to grow well on open sites and may colonise naturally. Where Scots pine is an intended part of the new native woodland, it should also be included from the outset, although in natural 'boreal' forests, Scots pine might also colonise later once birch has established. There is an ecological case for delaying planting of species like oak, cherry and elm, which favour more sheltered woodland conditions, until these pioneer species have established. However, economic considerations, especially when forestry grant schemes are involved, tend to favour a single planting operation at the outset, with all desired species being included from that stage. This can result in a higher rate of failure of the more demanding species such as oak.

It is generally better to avoid using standardised or generic 'mixed deciduous' planting mixtures of the type favoured for some small-scale farm woodland creation projects. Not all species included in these may be suited to any given site and the components of the mixture may not be compatible with each other. The 'target NVC woodland community' approach to planting scheme design (Rodwell and Patterson 1994), although it can be seen as rather rigid, does provide some ecological logic behind the selection of species and should reduce the risk of large-scale failure of schemes due to mismatching of the selected species to the site conditions.

9.13.2 Selecting native tree species for timber production

Where hardwood timber or industrial woodfuel production is a major priority there can be some departure from the 'target NVC' approach as there is a desire to devote a greater proportion of the growing space to selected species (e.g. oak, cherry, silver birch) that will produce the required wood products. There is often an operational logic to concentrating these productive species in a given part of the scheme with favourable access for tending and timber extraction. However, in order to emphasise ecological restoration of native woodland rather than creation of a hardwood plantation, sufficient age, structural and species diversity must be retained in the scheme, taken as a whole. In productive schemes there is often a greater attention given to adaptation to climate change in the sense of selecting species that may be better suited to anticipated future site conditions than would be the current target NVC community, based on existing local examples. Where the woodland creation site adjoins any existing ancient semi-natural woodland, it may not be appropriate to include non-native tree species such as beech, sycamore or walnut within any new plantings.

9.14 Seed source selection

J. R. R. Tolkien's saying, 'the tree grows best in the land of its sires', reflects the fact that natural tree populations become genetically adapted to the conditions under which they are growing by the process of natural selection, acting over many generations. This results in what is called 'adaptive genetic variation' between native tree populations in different areas. There is also 'neutral genetic variation', which usually reflects the history of colonisation after the last Ice Age, but which does not convey any advantage in relation to current site conditions (Ennos et al. 2000). It is important to conserve natural genetic diversity, as a component of overall biodiversity, and this needs to be taken into consideration when selecting seed sources for native tree planting schemes. The approach depends on the planting context (Forestry Commission Scotland 2006b):

9.14.1 Planting within or close to ancient semi-natural woodlands

When creating new native woodland within or near to existing ancient semi-natural woodland, genetic conservation must become the major factor influencing the choice of seed sources. Natural regeneration should be used wherever possible. If planting, use of 'local' seed sources ensures that genetic diversity is conserved and trees produced should be well adapted to current environmental conditions. The question 'how local is local?' is often asked by foresters. At present, Scotland has been divided into 'Native Seed Zones' (Herbert et al. 1999), and it is desirable to source seed from within the same seed zone as the intended planting site wherever possible (see Figure 9.3). There is no demonstrated genetic conservation advantage to using seed from an adjacent woodland or very localised source. When choosing a seed source, it is best to collect seed from woodlands that are believed to be ancient semi-natural (local origin) rather than long-established plantations (local provenance, but unknown origin). Where woods were planted in the past, the seed or plants used may not have been locally sourced, defeating the genetic objectives of using local sources at the present time. This criterion may become very difficult to meet in the case of tree species such as oak that have been widely planted over many centuries. It is also desirable to select seed sources that are growing well on similar soils to the planting site and should be well adapted. Obtaining the correct seed, locally sourced, may take some time, especially where individual seed collections are required, and must be planned well in advance. Generally plants should be ordered from tree nurseries at least two to three years before planting work is scheduled, but this may be difficult to reconcile with the timing requirements of certain forestry grant schemes.

9.14.2 Plantings isolated from ancient semi-natural woodlands

Where new native woodlands are being created at a distance from existing ancient woodlands, and particularly where timber production is a key objective, use of non-local seed sources may become appropriate. There are two potential advantages to using a wider range of material. First, it allows the forester to select material that may offer a better chance of adaptation to predicted future climatic conditions – so-called 'predictive provenancing' (Hubert and Cottrell 2007). For example, oak from France or southern England may offer advantages in this respect. Second, it allows the forester to take advantage of the results of scientific tree-breeding programmes, such as that coordinated by the Future Trees Trust, which aim to produce genetic stock of native trees that will grow more quickly and produce straighter, more valuable timber stems. These programmes generally use material selected from a wider Region of Provenance (RoP), rather than individual Native Seed Zones (NSZs). Whichever seed source is used, it must be ecologically suitable for current conditions or it will not thrive. If attempting to take account of predicted climate change it is usually best to use a mixture of sources from the local area and from more distant regions that are believed to match predicted future climates – this is called 'portfolio provenancing'. This reduces the risk of all of the planted stock failing during the rotation – either at the outset due to current conditions or in the future after climatic change. Again, plants from selected or improved provenances need to be ordered well in advance of the intended planting date to secure adequate supplies.

9.15 DESIGN OF NATIVE WOODLAND PLANTING SCHEMES

Creation of new native woodland by planting gives the forester or ecologist the opportunity to plan out the scheme in response to information collected about the site and the future objectives of the woodland. Three main factors should be considered:

1. **Site suitability.** Physical features of the site, such as slope, aspect, soils and drainage, should determine the layout of the scheme in terms of the native woodland types to be created and the distribution of open space. There is little

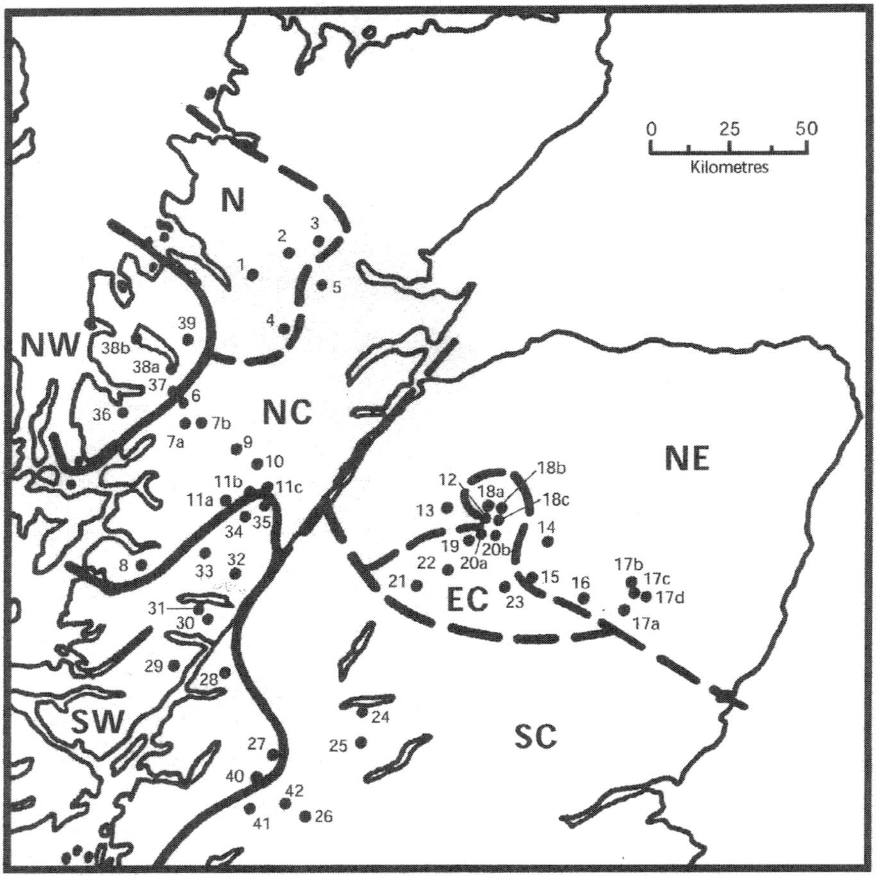

Note: a. The list of woodlands is not exhaustive.
b. Several woodlands contain more than one sampling point.

North (N)
1. Rhiddorroch
2. Glen Einig
3. Strath Oykell
4. Strath Vaich

North West (NW)
EXCLUSION ZONE
36. Shieldaig
37. Coulin – Loch Clair
38a. Loch Maree
38b. Loch Maree Island
39. Coir A'Ghamhna

South Central (SC)
24. Rannoch
25. Meggernie
26. Glen Falloch
41. Glen Orchy (south)
42. Coille Coire Chuilc

North Central (NC)
5. Amat
6. Coulin – Easan Dorcha
7a. Achnashellach – Golden Valley
7b. Achnashellach – Glen Carron
8. Barisdale
9. Glen Strathfarrar
10. Glen Cannich
11a. Glen Affric – west
11b. Glen Affric – central
11c. Glen Affric – east

East Central (EC)
18a. Abernethy – Loch Garten
18b. Abernethy – Fairy Tree
18c. Abernethy – Cuchanlupe
19. Rothiemurchus
20a. Glenmore – Loch Morlich
20b. Glenmore – Lodge
21. Glen Tromie
22. Glen Feshie
23. Glen Derry

North East (NE)
12. Abernethy – Torehill
13. Dalnahaitnach
14. Glen Avon
15. Glen Quoich
16. Ballochbuie
17a. Glen Tanar – Fir Hillock
17b. Glen Tanar – Tanar
17c. Glen Tanar – Gairney
17d. Glen Tanar – Allachy

South West (SW)
EXCLUSION ZONE
27. Black Mount
28. Glen Nevis
29. Ardgour
30. Glen Loy
31. Glen Mallie
32. Glengarry
33. Glen Loyne
34. Cougie
35. Guisachan
40. Glen Orchy (north)

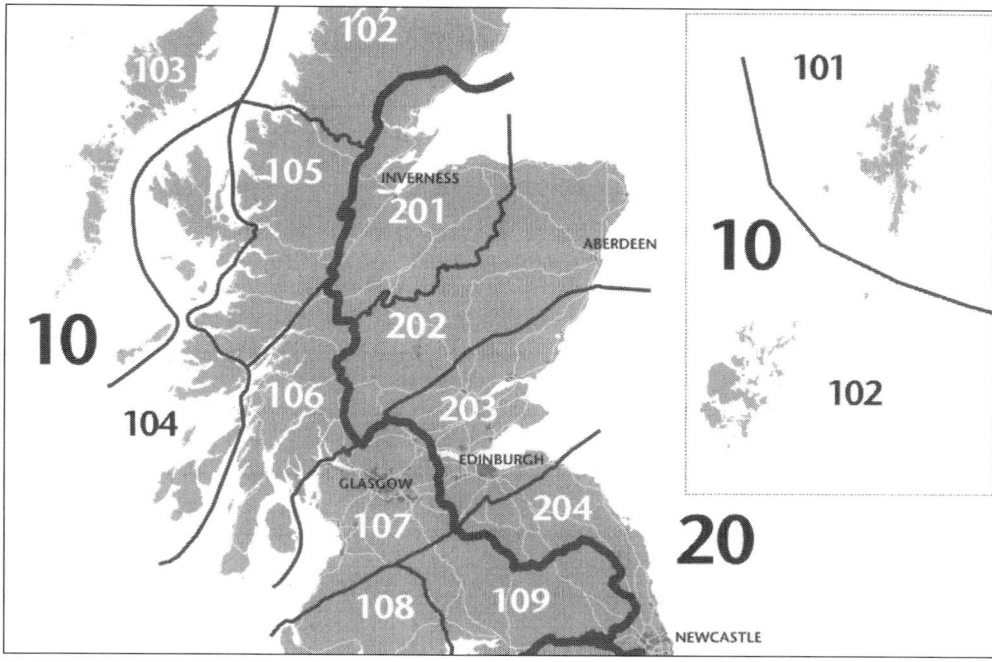

Figure 9.3 *Native seed zonation in Scotland for Caledonian pine (opposite) and all other native tree and shrub species (above). Left-hand map originally used in Forestry Commission (2003),* The Management of Semi-Natural Woodlands, 7: Native Pinewoods, *Forestry Commission Practice Guides, Edinburgh: Forestry Commission. Right-hand map adapted from Figure 1 in R. Herbert et al. (1999),* Using Local Stock for Planting Native Trees and Shrubs, *Forestry Commission Practice Note 8, Edinburgh: Forestry Commission. Both reproduced with kind permission from the Forestry Commission. © Crown copyright and database right (2014). All rights reserved. Ordnance Survey Licence number 100021242.*

point in creating an idealised scheme on paper or in a GIS or computer-aided design (CAD) system that flies in the face of realities on the ground. It is often best to adopt a relatively simple design at the outset that can be refined as the woodland develops – for example, creating very small patches of particular NVC woodland types to match very small-scale soil variations may not be worth pursuing at the outset.

2. **Constraints.** These are factors, in addition to physical features of the site, that need to be taken account of in scheme design (Forestry Commission 2011; UKWAS 2011). A major example is visual landscape amenity, particularly where the scheme is on a prominent site in the locality or will result in major changes to views from a popular walking route. Woodland creation represents a fairly sudden change to landscape appearance and may cause public concern and reaction. During public consultation, it is essential to convey accurately what is proposed and how it will develop visually over time, as trees grow. Computer-aided landscape design and artists' impressions can assist with this (see Plate 21). It is often possible to resolve problems with visual aspects of

scheme design by minor modifications. Another key constraint can be areas of existing habitats that have been designated for conservation significance, such as heathland or wetland. These areas may need to be excluded from planting proposals and a 'buffer zone' imposed around them to avoid adverse impacts from shading, ground preparation and so on. In some cases, large areas are designated for priority species such as golden eagle and this may affect the scope for native woodland planting over a wider area. Freshwater habitats such as rivers and ponds should generally be buffered also, other than where wet woodland habitat is deliberately being created within a given scheme. Scheduled ancient monuments and other archaeological remains should certainly not be planted over/through or disturbed during woodland establishment operations. For both of these constraints, detailed advance survey work is often required. In the case of large planting schemes an Environmental Impact Assessment (EIA) may be required to identify key constraints and satisfy European Union environmental regulations.

3. **Access and maintenance.** Where the objective is purely to create new native woodland habitat for biodiversity, future access to the site may not be essential, although it is always useful for subsequent monitoring and maintenance works. However, where the option of future timber or woodfuel production is involved, planned access for thinning and extraction is vital. If only part of the area is to be planted at higher stocking densities for future timber production, those areas should be located with access in mind, to shorten the length of access tracks that are required and to reduce the potential impacts on 'quieter' areas of the woodland created. Sometimes nuclei of denser planting can be located along access tracks. Steep slopes and water-logged ground should generally be avoided for timber production as extraction will prove problematic, and the routing of access tracks should steer well clear of freshwater and open-ground conservation habitats wherever possible.

9.16 Establishment and maintenance

With an agreed woodland design and planting plan in place, establishing the new native woodland essentially comprises four phases (Hart 1993).

9.16.1 Ground preparation

In almost all cases, some work to prepare a suitable planting surface will be required. The main aims are (1) to create a well-drained and rootable planting position for each tree, (2) to control weed competition for long enough to allow the young nursery transplants to establish securely and (3) to provide sufficient plant nutrients for the seedlings. In the past, foresters tended to rely on ploughing and broadcast mineral fertiliser application to prepare upland planting sites, but this is now regarded as undesirably intensive, with possible adverse environmental impacts. However, it is essential to do sufficient work to achieve satisfactory establishment.

FIGURE 9.4 *Mounding on an upland planting site.*
Copyright: Dr Scott McG. Wilson.

While 'flat' or 'notch' planting into a soil surface is sometimes sufficient, in most cases it is necessary to create a raised, well-drained planting position either by spade-work, in smaller planting schemes, or by excavator mounding over larger areas (see Figure 9.4). Excavator mounding may be inappropriate when restoring native woodland on PAWS sites that retain former woodland soil conditions. Trees should be planted with a spot application of phosphorus and potassium (P&K), unless the soil has recently been improved for agriculture, but nitrogen (N) should not be needed other than on very infertile sites where woodland will be marginal. When using containerised 'plug plants' it is unwise to depend only on the small amount of fertiliser provided within the plug – this will run out after a few months, leaving the young plant short of nutrients and prone to 'going back' in height. Weed competition varies dramatically between planting sites and may become much worse once the scheme has been fenced out. Application of a general herbicide such as glyphosate in a one-metre circle around each tree is frequently required, and may need to be repeated later, using a conical tree guard, on more fertile sites. Bracken may have to be controlled by mechanical methods, if the specific herbicide Asulam/Azulox is no longer available for use.

9.16.2 Protection of the growing stock

In some areas it may still be possible to 'get away' without protecting young trees from browsing, but this is rarely the case in Scotland. Where livestock are present, stock fencing is usually the best course, and this may need to be supplemented with rabbit netting in the lower part. Where there is a dense grassy sward that will grow out within a stock fence, vole attack should be expected, and each tree then needs to be fitted with a spiral vole guard. Some wood-pasture situations with cattle grazing may merit individual wooden stockades around widely spaced trees, but this is an expensive option. Away from the agricultural situation, the main problem will be red and roe deer. In smaller schemes, use of individual tube tree-shelters may be an option, but these can become expensive, give the scheme an artificial appearance, and may have adverse effects on later stem form and timber potential. Installation of two-metre deer fencing is the standard approach on larger schemes, with suitable marking in areas where capercaillie are thought to be present. Water-gates may be needed where streams are crossed. Fence-lines should be chosen with practicality of installation and snow maintenance in mind, alongside visual amenity. It may prove much cheaper in the long run to use somewhat more fencing material, rather than select a 'shortest possible' fence-line running over inaccessible or rough terrain. Access gates through deer fences are essential to permit safe access for maintenance.

9.16.3 Planting practice

We have already discussed the seed-sourcing issue, and the need to order plants well in advance. The main planting seasons in Scotland are September to November ('back-end' planting) and February to April (spring planting), the latter being more common today. Later planting, into the early summer season, is sometimes driven by poor early spring weather but carries a heightened risk of drought damage to plants during May/June. There is a key choice between traditional bare-root and containerised planting stock (see Figure 9.5). Either can produce satisfactory establishment results if used properly. Containerised plants are more expensive but may represent a safer option if there are likely to be delays on the planting site – bare-root plants will then need to be 'heeled in'. It is generally better to avoid plants being delivered too far in advance of planting and lingering on site – they will almost always suffer some degrade. An exception is where the nursery and the planting site are both operating a cold-storage system. Poor or damaged plants should not be accepted, and plants should not be roughly handled after site delivery. Stocking density is an essential consideration and varies somewhat with species. Where timber production is the major objective of the scheme, minimum planting densities of 3,000 stems per hectare are required under the Scottish grant schemes for Caledonian Scots pine and 3,100 for oak. Higher densities of up to 5,000 stems per hectare for hardwoods are desirable in terms of later stem form, but carry significant additional costs for planting stock – this is one argument in favour of the natural regeneration approach. Sometimes it may be advisable to establish nuclei of higher-density plantings for timber in accessible parts of larger planting schemes. For conservation and biodiversity plantings lower stocking densities of ~1,600 stems per hectare are acceptable for grant but will produce trees of more heavily branched form. Stocking density may vary considerably in larger conservation plantings on rough hill ground.

FIGURE 9.5 *Growing bare-root native trees in a commercial nursery. Copyright: Dr Scott McG. Wilson.*

9.16.4 Young-growth tending

Early stand tending, in the first ten to fifteen years, is aimed at ensuring that the target initial stocking density and mix of species is achieved and that trees are free to develop. The main operations are (1) supplementary weed control (if required), (2) cleaning to remove competing naturally regenerated trees and shrubs and any failed or malformed planted saplings, and (3) beating up (supplementary planting) to fill gaps in the established plantation and ensure the required stocking density for grant is attained. The critical ages for official grant-scheme stocking assessments are usually five and ten years. Not all schemes will require all operations, but regular inspection and self-assessment is always required. Schemes where ecological restoration and biodiversity are the main aims may not receive such intensive cleaning and beating up, as a greater emphasis is placed on natural development and a greater variation in stocking density is usually acceptable. Schemes where timber or wood-fuel production is the major aim may merit extra operations such as respacing and formative pruning to favour a final crop selection. These can begin from five to seven years in a fast-growing crop of ash or birch on fertile land, but may not be of much relevance to slower-grown upland plantings on poor soils. If formative pruning to remove side branches is carried out, the trees that have been selected for this need to be marked for retention at later thinnings. Selective thinning begins when trees begin to compete with each other undesirably – that can be at anything between ten and thirty years of age, depending on the site, tree species and resulting growth rate. More light-demanding species, such as ash and birch, require earlier and heavier thinnings in most cases, whereas oak and elm can wait longer.

FIGURE 9.6 *Establishing native woodland on a challenging upland site. Copyright: Dr Scott McG. Wilson.*

9.17 MANAGEMENT FOR BIODIVERSITY

The oldest of the new native woodlands created in Scotland are now reaching their 'twenty-year mark' when decisions have to be taken about their future management. Many of these woodlands were created primarily for purposes of ecological restoration and biodiversity enhancement. Initial stocking was often low, at 1,100–1,200 stems per hectare, and ground preparation was sometimes inadequate, particularly on the upland sites. Many such schemes have received limited early stand tending, and quite a number are only partially stocked with trees at present, as a result of variable establishment from the outset (see Figure 9.6). There are lessons to be learned from these experiences, and future rounds of new native woodlands may be established using more intensive forestry methods.

There are three alternative options available to managers of existing native woodland schemes: (1) non-intervention, (2) remedial action/improvement by management or (3) replacement. Some schemes have established soundly and are already fairly well stocked (see Figure 9.7). Enrichment planting with additional tree species may be appropriate in those cases where this is needed to achieve the composition of the original target NVC community. A majority of partially stocked schemes are likely to be left to develop ecologically over a longer period of time under forms of non-intervention or limited-intervention management. They may always fall short of what would traditionally have been regarded as fully stocked established woodland, but have started to achieve some of their aims in terms of landscape diversification and biodiversity enhancement – particularly for birds and invertebrates that use native woodland mosaics at the sapling/scrub stages. Further gradual infilling of gaps in new native

FIGURE 9.7 *Productive new native woodland scheme, Clashindarroch. Copyright: Dr Scott McG. Wilson.*

woodlands by natural regeneration can be expected, initially from mature seed trees in the locality, but later from seed produced by the planted trees within the schemes themselves. From that point of view, it may be worthwhile to maintain/renew deer control by culling and/or fencing, as this will aid the process of natural regeneration.

Schemes where establishment has been less successful and which are poorly stocked may not develop into satisfactory new native woodland on any reasonable timescale. Here, a fresh look must be taken at the original decision to create new native woodland. Where sites are too exposed, infertile and poorly drained it may be necessary to 'learn lessons' and abandon the attempt. In certain locations, especially in upland areas, there are now increased constraints on woodland creation due to the recognition of open-land habitats as of conservation significance. In those situations also, the attempt to create new native woodland may be re-evaluated. In some situations the ambition to create new native woodland may have been appropriate, but the methods selected to achieve this have not been a success, with few trees established. Here it may be more effective to start again, with more thorough site preparation, vegetation control and protection measures. Elsewhere, remedial management action may be the best way forward, intervening in the schemes by improved protection, supplementary ground preparation and infill planting in weakly stocked areas. This can be an expensive approach and will often have to be carried out at the owner's expense if the original establishment has failed to meet grant assessment criteria. In future new native woodlands, where the ground is sufficiently accessible and potentially productive, it will usually be appropriate to build in more of an emphasis on timber (or at least woodfuel) production, in order to address current policy and economic priorities for woodland expansion. While there are some remoter locations where native woodland creation 'purely for biodiversity' is the right way forward, these may no longer be seen as a high priority for allocation of public grant-in-aid.

9.18 Management for timber production

Very few of the new native woodlands created in Scotland over the past two decades have been designed with timber production as their major objective. However, a reasonable proportion of schemes, especially on better land sites in eastern Scotland, do have some potential in this regard if their future management is suitable. There is no reason why management of this kind should reduce the potential values of the woodland for other benefits such as biodiversity, landscape amenity and tourist recreation. In many cases management may enhance potential by improving structure and access.

The key priorities when creating and managing future new native woodlands for timber and woodfuel production (Evans 1984; Forestry Commission Scotland 2006a; Worrell 1999) are:

- **Access and extraction.** Timber production will be restricted to new native woodlands on more accessible lowland and midslope planting sites. Suitable provisions must be made to access the site for maintenance, management and final extraction of timber. This need not mean a permanent network of surfaced roads and tracks – a variety of lightweight equipment exists for extraction of timber to woodland boundaries (e.g. horse-logging, quad-bike forwarding, log-chutes) (see Plate 22). From there it can be forwarded using farm/road vehicles.
- **Selection of target species.** Usually only a selection of tree species planted within new native woodland schemes will be valuable for timber and woodfuel. The main native tree species with timber interest are Scots pine, oak and silver birch, with alder, cherry and elm perhaps managed for timber on a more localised basis. Ash was also favoured until the onset of the recent *Chalara* outbreak. The introduced hardwood species sycamore and beech, although not planted in recent native woodland schemes, are also long-standing productive timber trees in Scotland and can be included as a minor proportion in some new native woodlands. Only species that grow well on a site should be managed for timber – any investment will be wasted if trees do not thrive.
- **Allocation of growing space.** While it is not appropriate to reduce diversity in native woodland schemes by complete exclusion of minor species, management for timber will usually involve allocating a greater proportion of the growing space to 'target' species through the process of selective thinning. Early thinning may favour a target species as such, but later interventions will look to allocate growing space to groups of potential 'final crop trees' whose stem form appears to be promising. Any trees which compete with these, or interfere with their crowns, should be removed during successive thinning operations. Traditionally such trees would have been 'marked' by the forester before the thinning, but more often nowadays these operations are combined. Harvested material from

thinnings may find a good market as woodfuel. The sets of final crop trees will inevitably reduce as time goes on – some may die naturally, blow over, suffer grey squirrel damage or have to be felled to relieve competition. The original selection should contain many spares. The intensity and timing of thinnings, as in existing woodlands (see Chapter 8), will depend on the target species and the productivity of the site. More fast-grown woodlands will generally require more frequent and heavier thinning operations, as will species that demand a lot of light to grow to their maximum potential. These include ash and birch, for example. Slower-grown, more shade-tolerant species such as oak, elm and beech may be thinned later and more lightly. Sycamore is generally considered intermediate in this regard.

- **Stem improvement.** Timber value is almost always highest for straight-stemmed hardwood trees without side branches within the first six metres or so of timber (known as the 'butt log'). In an ideal world, such good straight stems will develop naturally, by the action of 'self pruning' (natural shedding of side branches) and 'mutual cleaning' (suppression of side branches by shading from neighbouring trees). These can then be favoured by selective thinning alone. However, this does not always occur in practice. A poor choice of provenance may give rise to trees that are not well adapted to the site or have a genetic tendency to poor stem form, forking or heavy side branching. These risks are generally reduced with the use of stock from well-planned local or regional tree-breeding work, such as the British and Irish Hardwood Improvement Programme (BIHIP) (now Future Trees Trust). However, even with well-chosen planting stock, inadequate initial stocking density (<2,500 stems per hectare) will often produce heavily branched stems. Inadequate stocking can result from not planting enough trees to start with, or from too many dying out in the early years of the plantation. Use of natural colonisation can have the advantage of higher initial stocking density (in extreme cases more than 100,000 stems per hectare). Where there are inadequate good stems from which to make an initial selection of potential final crop trees, it is possible to carry out 'formative pruning' to improve the prospects of the 'best of the rest'. Formative pruning (at five to ten years) normally aims to remove side shoots that may compete with the leading shoot, producing a forked or multiple-leader stem. Later pruning tends to focus more on removing smaller side branches or 'epicormic shoots' that will create knots in the stem timber. Pruning can be an expensive operation and requires a fair degree of skill. It is only worth applying to stems that have some potential to be taken through to a final crop of quality hardwood timber (not usually to woodfuel).
- **Harvesting.** In most cases, final felling of hardwood timber from new native woodlands in Scotland is at least fifty years away. The shorter-rotation species such as silver birch may be harvested at thirty to forty years of age, while ash, pine, cherry and sycamore on productive sites would often be ready for harvest at seventy to eighty years. Oak and beech would typically be harvested at 100 to 120 years, and older on poorer, less productive sites. In most situations mature timber will be harvested by selective felling of individual stems or small groups

as they reach a marketable size, known as 'target diameter felling'. This allows the woodland to be managed under a 'continuous-cover forestry' (CCF) system (see Chapter 10), relying on natural regeneration to produce a follow-on crop for the future. Extraction of timber should be planned to minimise impacts on the surrounding native woodland habitat, using sensitive, lighter-weight equipment. Timber can be sold standing or felled – many buyers prefer the timber to be presented felled so that major defects such as 'shake' in oak are more easily assessed. In a few situations, where light-demanding species such as Scots pine and silver birch are harvested for timber, the uniform shelterwood system may be applied. Most of the mature trees on a larger area are felled, leaving only a small number of 'seed trees' of good form. Once the new even-aged crop establishes by natural regeneration from those trees, they too can finally be felled.

Effective management of native woodlands for timber requires a skilled forestry workforce at all technical levels. As there has been a long period of time during which hardwood timber production was not seen as a priority, these skills have tended to fall away. It can now be difficult and expensive to source the necessary workforce to carry out high-quality management. This must be tackled through improved training of forestry personnel at the Scottish universities and colleges and on modern apprenticeship schemes.

9.19 Management for woodfuel production

Most of the native hardwood species are capable of producing valuable woodfuel in the form of logs, wood-chip and wood pellets. In the case of Scots pine, while some logs are burned, attention focuses on production of industrial wood-chip and pellets. The majority of Scottish woodfuel is currently used in small domestic manual stoves in the form of logs. Some is also used by the whisky and fish-/game-smoking industries, in the form of wood-chip or sawdust, where it acts as both a fuel and a flavouring agent. In recent years, with growing concerns over fossil fuel consumption, energy security and climate change, attention has turned to the potential for larger-scale use of woodfuel as a component of mainstream energy supply. Large-scale mechanically fed boilers installed in power-generation and industrial plants, municipal buildings, large rural private premises and district heating schemes tend to use wood-chip. Small-scale mechanically fed boilers installed in urban private homes use wood pellets for convenience. A large amount of information on woodfuel options and practicalities is available from the Forestry Commission at <www.forestry.gov.uk>.

These trends have caused increased interest in the creation of new woodlands with woodfuel supply as a major objective of management. While a proportion of the supply, mainly of logs for domestic consumption, will come from early thinnings in woodlands managed mainly for timber production, there is also a case for the use of dedicated short-rotation systems comparable to traditional management of industrial oak coppice to produce charcoal (see Chapter 5). These systems will mainly supply industrial woodfuel in the form of wood-chip and pellets. A wider variety of species are likely to be involved – faster-growing options such as birch, aspen, alder and willow may be most suitable. Some non-native species may also be considered. Two systems are possible: short-rotation coppice (SRC), with a three- to seven-year rotation, and short-rotation forestry (SRF), with a seven- to twenty-five-year rotation. SRC is essentially a semi-agricultural cropping regime in which woodland conditions do not develop. In the case of SRF, there is more of a transition towards woodland conditions, and stand regeneration can be achieved by coppice regrowth, natural seedling regeneration or replanting. Both systems have the potential to use planting stock that has been selectively improved for greater volume yield/calorific value with stem form suitable for highly automated harvesting and processing equipment.

A major challenge in new native woodland created primarily for woodfuel production is reconciling that priority with other objectives, such as biodiversity and landscape amenity. This is more difficult than in the case of traditional hardwood forestry for timber, and tends to be more of an issue with very short rotation systems. Coppice management of a more traditional type is known to benefit some aspects of biodiversity – certain plant species that require more light, butterflies and so on – but this may not be so under more intensive automated woodfuel production systems. It is probably best to include areas or 'coupes' for woodfuel production under SRC or (preferably) SRF systems within large complexes of new native woodland, where they will increase the structural diversity of the habitat overall. Traditionally, coppice woodlands were divided into the same number of felling 'coupes' or compartments as the number of years in the rotation, with some standard trees retained to maturity for production of larger timbers. Hence all ages were represented at one time within a given woodland. It may be more difficult to achieve the desired efficiency of woodfuel production, with low labour inputs, under such complex systems of growing and harvesting the material. However, compromise will be required to produce woodfuel from diverse woodlands that also provide biodiversity and landscape benefits. In particular, a proportion of growing stock in a woodland should be retained to maturity and natural mortality for biodiversity and deadwood values.

9.20 WOODLAND EXPANSION PROJECTS – FIELD EXAMPLES

There are three main classes of native woodland creation in Scotland:

1. **Large-scale catchment schemes.** There are several large-scale and quite successful new native woodland habitat creation schemes occupying whole upland catchments or similar. These have mainly been pursued by the voluntary conservation bodies and, latterly, the Forestry Commission. The main examples are Carrifran (Borders), Cashel Farm, Loch Katrine and Glen Finglas (Loch Lomond and the Trossachs). Scheme objectives centre on habitat restoration and biodiversity enhancement.
2. **Medium-scale estate/farm schemes.** These are deer-fenced planting or natural regeneration schemes, often carried out by private estates, under forestry grant schemes, adding to existing native woodlands on their property. Success with

such schemes has been variable. The Scottish Forest Alliance has also undertaken plantings of this type and some are now being undertaken by the Forestry Commission. Many have involved native pinewood, upland oak-birch woodland and montane scrub habitats on poorer land. Objectives include biodiversity, sporting shelter, recreational amenity and carbon sequestration.

3. **Smaller-scale farm and riparian woodland schemes.** These have been pursued by private farm owners, tenants and crofters. In some cases these are isolated blocks of new woodland, but in recent years there has been increased emphasis on reinforcement of forest habitat networks, especially by creation of riparian woodland along river valleys. Objectives include biodiversity enhancement, livestock shelter, fisheries improvement and landscape amenity. Often the availability of forestry and agri-environmental grants are the critical factor in promoting activity, but well-planned schemes yield additional benefits such as soil conservation, woodfuel production and game or livestock shelter.

Details of more prominent woodland creation projects from the past twenty years in Scotland that can be conveniently visited are given in Chapter 12.

CHAPTER TEN

Relationships with plantation forests

10.1 History of plantation forestry in Scotland

When the term 'plantation forestry' is used with reference to Scotland, it often conjures up unappealing images of dense, dark, uniform stands of Sitka spruce on a remote hillside with artificial, straight edges. However, this is only part of the story, typifying commercial plantations created during the years 1960–1990 (Foot 2010). Scotland has a much longer history of tree planting, over the past 300–400 years, which has created attractive mixed forests of both native and introduced species (Anderson 1967; Fowler 2002). Indeed, along with England, France and Germany, Scotland has among the longest experience of creating plantation forests. There is many times as much plantation forestry in Scotland as there is ancient semi-natural woodland (MacKenzie 1999; Forestry Commission Scotland 2014), and hence plantation forestry has an important interface with many native woodlands.

10.1.1 The 'Planting Dukes' and early 'policy plantings'

Throughout the long period from 1600 to 1920, plantations were established on the major private estates in Scotland. Several important landowners, such as the 'Planting Dukes' of Atholl, Argyll and Buccleuch, the Marquis of Montrose and the Earls of Seaforth and Breadalbane, were particularly associated with tree planting. Their reasons for creating plantations varied – some were primarily interested in producing timber for sale as an estate commercial venture, but they were perhaps in the minority. Many landowners had their eye mainly on sport, with forests as shelter for deer, pheasants and so on. Most created plantations as part of what they called 'estate improvements'. This meant making your landed estate more visually attractive and well managed – more like a fashionable English country estate and less of a 'Highland wilderness'. This applied especially after the Jacobite uprisings of 1715 and 1745, when there was a political campaign to 'tame' the Highlands and reduce the chances of any future disturbances.

Most earlier plantation forests were created in areas such as Argyll, Perthshire, Angus, Moray and the Borders, located around the margins of the remoter upland districts. Some were planted on open grazing land that was of limited value for agriculture, being too steep, exposed or infertile for the production of crops or quality livestock. Many were replanted on the sites of former native Scots pine and oak woodlands that had been over-exploited for timber and by excessive grazing pressure. In the early years, native Scots pine and oak were the tree species commonly used, but these were soon joined by beech from southern England and by sycamore, lime, Norway spruce, silver fir and larch introduced from mainland Europe. These species added visual interest (e.g. the yellow foliage of larch in winter, formal plantations and avenues of fine beech trees) and also produced potentially valuable timber if they were well managed. Many landowners drew inspiration from European forests and estates seen during their 'Grand Tours' to France and Italy – an early aristocratic form of today's student 'gap year'. When they got home to their estates, they might engage a forester to create similar woodlands, using planting stock imported from England, France or Belgium. Some of these early plantations were pure timber stands of a single species such as larch or beech, but often they were attractive mixed stands or 'groves' of several species, known as 'policy woodlands', particularly in landscaped areas close to the 'big houses'. Common mixtures of favoured tree species, especially beech, Scots pine, European larch and Norway spruce, became known as 'gentlemen's mixtures' for these reasons. This type of mixed forestry contributed to the development of many modern 'continuous-cover forestry' techniques.

10.1.2 Mature hardwood plantations

We saw at the start of Chapter 9 that there is an established record of creating plantations of native tree species in Scotland from around 1600 onwards, primarily of Scots pine and oak, with some examples using ash, elm and birch. These served both to produce timber and to improve landscapes.

One of the most significant impacts of these earlier phases of plantation forestry in Scotland was the introduction of beech and sycamore, and, to a lesser extent, lime. These are shade-tolerant hardwood tree species native to southern England and Continental Europe. We saw in Chapters 1 and 2 that Scotland's native woodlands generally lacked shade-tolerant tree species, with the exception of wych elm, alder and holly. Although beech and sycamore were often planted in separate woodlands, they proved capable of natural regeneration under the shade of our native tree species, and have been colonising existing Scottish native woodlands over the past 300–400 years. Colonisation by these species has become a challenge for many Scottish native woodlands, alongside later introductions such as *Rhododendron ponticum*, Sitka spruce (*Picea sitchensis*) and western hemlock (*Tsuga heterophylla*). The earlier conifer introductions from Europe, such as European larch (*Larix decidua*) and Norway spruce (*Picea abies*), have not proved a significant problem from this point of view.

Sycamore and beech, when grown well away from ancient semi-natural woodlands, can be attractive, productive and valuable timber trees, either in single species plantations or in mixture with conifers under 'continuous-cover forestry' systems. As we will discuss later, there is a strong possibility that beech and sycamore (and possibly lime) will become more important woodland species in Scotland over the coming decades. Their ability to regenerate well within existing woodlands will inevitably lead to their spreading, and a changing climate may favour them over some of our native tree species. The current resources of beech, sycamore and lime in Scotland vary significantly. Although there are some plantations of pure sycamore, established for timber, most sycamore is found in mixed woodlands. Beech, on the other hand, was widely planted in single-species stands, avenues and shelterbelts (see Plate 23a) (Wilson 2006, 2010). Many were created between 1680 and 1920, mainly for landscape amenity on private estates, with future timber production as a secondary objective. Beech was particularly favoured for shelterbelts in lowland agricultural districts, as it is tolerant of wind exposure. Although some of the better examples of Scottish beech woodland were felled for emergency timber supplies during and after the two world wars, some survive in areas such as the Borders, Angus and Moray. Lime has always been primarily a species of avenues, parks and other formal landscape plantings within Scotland.

While fewer new beech and sycamore plantations have been created for timber production over the past fifty years, they could well have an increasing role in the future. Sycamore is most likely to be managed in the context of new mixed woodlands of broadleaved tree species, established for timber and woodfuel production. It produces a valuable timber for decorative joinery (flooring, doors, kitchen worktops) and is also likely to be quite suitable for management under short-rotation forestry systems to produce quality woodfuel. Beech is perhaps more likely to form part of mixed forestry managed under continuous-cover silvicultural systems, where its shade-tolerance makes it easy to combine with productive conifers. Some beech might be retained until eighty to 120 years old for quality timber production, with most managed as an understorey (nursing quality conifer stems), then cut out after thirty to forty years for woodfuel supply.

10.1.3 The 'plant hunters' and diverse conifer plantations (1840 to 1960)

Two major changes took place in the type of forestry plantations being created in Scotland from the 1840s onwards (Anderson 1967). Firstly, there was an increased emphasis on timber production as opposed to landscape amenity – this applied particularly from around 1890 onwards, when it became clear that another European war was possible, and that maritime supplies of timber from overseas might once again be under threat of blockade. Serious timber-supply problems had developed during the earlier Napoleonic Wars in a similar situation. Although shipping was now constructed mainly from iron and steel, timber was still required for a variety of strategic industrial uses, notably for pit-props. Secondly, a wider variety of introduced conifers became available from the Pacific Northwest and from the Far East. This was as a result of the famous 'plant hunting' expeditions to these territories that were promoted by major private estates in Scotland from the 1830s – Atholl, Murthly, Scone and so on – who vied to have the latest introduced tree species in gardens and tree collections. The most prominent of these plant hunters were David Douglas and Archibald Menzies, who concentrated their efforts in the Pacific Northwest of North America – California, Oregon, Washington and British Columbia. A range of highly productive conifer species were introduced – Sitka spruce, Douglas fir (*Pseudotsuga menziesii*), grand fir (*Abies grandis*), noble fir (*Abies procera*), western hemlock and western red cedar (*Thuja plicata*) were those widely adopted for timber production in Scotland, alongside the Japanese larch (*Larix kaempferi*) from the Far East. Many of these were tested in arboreta and forest garden trial plots (see Plate 23b), before being widely planted out (Macdonald et al. 1957; Wilson 2007, 2011a). Some other conifer species, such as Pacific silver fir (*Abies amabilis*) and Japanese red cedar (*Cryptomeria japonica*) showed promise but were less widely used.

Private estates (and also the newly created Forestry Commission from 1919 onwards) used these various conifer species, together with Scots pine, Norway spruce, European larch and European silver fir (*Abies alba*), to create productive forestry plantations. A few were planted as intimate mixtures, with a view to future management using traditional Continental-style selection forestry systems ('continuous-cover forestry'). However, most were designed to be operated on the even-aged, regular, 'clearfell and replant' system, where a whole stand would be felled and replanted at an optimum economic 'rotation age' for that species (e.g. sixty years for spruce, eighty to ninety years for larch and Douglas fir and so forth). The planning of these forests was guided by an overall approach called 'species-site matching', which was effectively an early form of the Ecological Site Classification system, described in Chapter 9 for the creation of new native woodlands. Soil and vegetation were observed, allowing planting sites to be divided into areas that would be best suited to each of the tree species available for use. The intention was very much to 'match the species to the site', rather than 'alter the site to suit the species'. These methods were later formalised in Professor Mark Anderson's famous book *The Selection of Tree Species* (1961). Where there was a lot of small-scale variation across planting areas, this led to diverse forests with a range of tree species being grown in relatively small stands. Not only did this offer better prospects of success for each individual stand of trees, it also made for attractive diversity in the structure and appearance of plantations created by these methods, especially as those have continued to mature over the decades since (see Plate 24). These diverse forests are now more suitable for conversion to 'continuous-cover forestry', relying on natural regeneration, as they have a range of tree species present with differing shade-tolerance. Many such forests have also become popular for recreation and tourism activities, including rambling, mountain-biking and canopy adventure.

10.1.4 Uniform upland conifer plantations (1960 to 1990)

A major change to Scottish plantation forestry came during the 1960s. The categories of land becoming available for planting tended to be more exposed, poorly drained and infertile. Much of the better planting land had either already been afforested since the establishment of the Forestry Commission in 1919, or was reserved for productive agriculture. This move of plantation forestry 'further up the hill' was assisted by the increased post-war availability of heavy machinery for cultivation and drainage operations and of mineral fertilisers to improve site productivity. The emphasis was now placed on preparing sites to meet the needs of favoured tree species, rather than on matching species to the sites. As a result, the processes of detailed 'site matching', and the resulting varied species composition found in earlier plantation forests, were no longer pursued. The favoured species in most situations was the Sitka spruce. Among the conifer species introduced from the Pacific Northwest by the 'plant hunters', Sitka spruce had shown an excellent combination of reliable initial establishment, rapid growth and production of a sought-after timber with a high strength-to-weight ratio. This made it particularly suitable for applications such as aircraft-framing and building construction. A particular advantage was the ability of Sitka spruce to thrive on exposed upland peaty sites in Scotland that would have been unsuitable for more traditional species such as Scots pine and oak. It was also more resistant to deer browsing than most alternative species.

For roughly thirty years, between 1960 and the mid to late 1980s, plantation forestry in Scotland emphasised intensive site preparation – linear plough cultivation and broadcast application of mineral fertilisers – followed by planting of pure Sitka spruce at regular spacing. On particularly poor, peaty soils, the Sitka spruce was sometimes planted in 'nursing' mixtures with the lodgepole pine (*Pinus contorta*). Although not a particularly valuable timber tree in itself, lodgepole pine has an ability to improve aeration of water-logged peaty soils, thereby helping the Sitka spruce to establish well. The design of plantations was simplified, with large, even-aged stands of pure spruce with straight boundaries. Some of these uniform plantations were thinned to produce a superior final crop of sawlogs, but in locations that were exposed to strong winds, thinning was avoided to reduce the risk of instability. This meant that the final crop consisted of a larger number of small, spindly stems (so-called 'small roundwood') suitable mainly for the manufacture of particle-board and pulp. The material produced – both sawlogs and small roundwood – has supported the development of a major industrial wood-processing industry in Scotland that did not exist previously, creating valuable employment as a result.

Despite this timber productivity, from the 1980s onwards there was increasing public opposition to the so-called 'blanket afforestation' of parts of upland Scotland (Foot 2010). The uniformity and regularity of more recent plantations, coupled with their lack of species diversity, tended to attract more criticism than the earlier, pre-war examples. There was increasing pressure for an improvement in visual design standards through the application of the methods of landscape architecture (Grant and Worrell 2012). Environmental impacts of plantation afforestation on natural habitats, freshwater quality and archaeological features was a subject of growing concern. These issues were addressed by the production of the 'Forestry Guidelines', most recently within the UK Forestry Standard (Forestry Commission 2011). Some examples of plantation afforestation, for example in the Flow Country peatlands of Caithness, were particularly derided, especially where activity was seen to be driven by tax avoidance under tax regulations that were reformed in 1988. There had been growing interest in the conservation and restoration of Scotland's native woodland resources from the mid-1970s onwards, and the Forestry Commission's 1985 'Broadleaves Policy' gave this a formal basis in policy and regulation.

10.2 Management of plantation forests in Scotland

10.2.1 Regular forestry – the 'clearfell and replant' system

Until recently almost all Scottish plantation forests were managed using the German-inspired 'clearfell and replant' system. This is what is known as 'regular' or 'even-aged' forestry (Hart 1993). Adoption of this approach was driven in the first instance by the fact that plantation forests were created over a short period of time – often whole landscape-scale units, such as former hill farms, were planted up within a five-year period. This represents only a small fraction of the normal economic management rotation (forty to seventy years), let alone the natural lifespan (400 to 500 years), of many conifer species used. Hence, although the earlier plantation forests sometimes contained quite a degree of conifer species diversity, their age range and structural diversity remained very limited. There was no quick and easy way to introduce greater structural diversity to forests, as we will discuss below.

The regular forestry system was developed in Germany during the eighteenth century. Some see it as a rather 'militaristic' or artificial management approach. However, it has a number of apparent advantages for commercial timber production. Firstly, there are the perceived benefits of simplicity and predictability. Fairly predictable amounts of timber per hectare, of a uniform size, are produced, matched to the requirements of a target market – sawmilling, pulp-and-paper and so on. This can be difficult to achieve in more complex forests that comprise a range of species and age/size classes in mixture. Secondly, there is the perceived efficiency of operation. Regular forestry allows forest management work for any given 'compartment' to be concentrated during short 'interventions', which may well increase the efficiency, especially of mechanised operations. In some better-managed stands there may be several thinnings during each rotation, but the majority of forestry activity is concentrated during the period at final harvest and restocking (either by replanting or by natural regeneration). Under some circumstances, this may also reduce environmental impacts, for example the number of years when machinery disturbs nesting birds, or the amount of soil compaction by heavy machinery – the 'brash-mat' from concentrated final felling operations can mitigate this.

The disadvantages of the regular system of forestry can be divided into economic, aesthetic and ecological issues. It is potentially quite an expensive system if replanting and uneconomic early thinnings are required, but this can be offset if natural regeneration is employed. There is also a tendency for plantations to have an unattractive monotonous or 'blanket' appearance where trees of the same species and age are grown in regular rows in plantation blocks with straight edges. This can be improved as the plantation matures by deliberate measures to increase species, age and structural diversity (see below). The main ecological issues are departure from the regeneration dynamics of natural forest ecosystems and the need for periodic intensive disturbance and stand replacement. This can affect not only the forest itself, but also soil, freshwater and biodiversity. However, it should not be forgotten that some natural types of coniferous forest – particularly the pine forests of the northern boreal zone – operate this way naturally (see Chapter 1). Large fires or insect outbreaks may destroy stands over very extensive areas, with subsequent natural regeneration. By contrast, this is not the natural pattern in the more diverse conifer forests of the Pacific Northwest, from which Sitka spruce, Douglas fir, western hemlock, western red cedar, grand fir and noble fir derive. There, it is more usual to find a much wider range of age and size classes present in any area of forest.

10.2.2 Regular forestry – diversifying the species mix and age structure

Given some of the recognised drawbacks of the early generations of regular, even-aged conifer plantations in Scotland, opportunities presented by harvesting and restocking to diversify these forests have been exploited. A large part of the plantation forest resource created between 1940 and 1960 is now in its second rotation, whilst some earlier forests are now into their third and subsequent rotations. Diversification can usefully be approached at either the 'between stand' level or the 'within stand' level, or indeed both.

Diversity 'between' stands can be increased by ensuring that adjoining stands are felled at an interval of several years, and in some cases restocked with different species. This increases the range of both species and age classes of trees within a forest as a whole, while continuing to manage each stand on a regular, even-aged basis. This process is known as 'forest restructuring' (Hart 1995) but does not actually affect stand structure, which remains regular. There are however a number of challenges to achieving this in practice. On many plantation forestry sites in Scotland, diversifying tree species can be made difficult by infertile, poorly drained soils and climatic exposure – most of the alternative conifer and hardwood tree species are more difficult to establish than Sitka spruce on such sites under open conditions, and deer-browsing pressure can be an additional problem. There is also a belief that timber of many alternative species can be more difficult to sell into local markets than Sitka spruce, which is more familiar (Wilson 2011a). In order to improve the age diversity of plantations that were created at a single point in time, it is necessary to delay felling in some parts of the forest beyond the optimum rotation age, or alternatively to fell some parts before the optimum. Early felling can reduce timber value and delayed felling can increase the risk of windthrow damage on some exposed sites. Ideally neighbouring felling 'coupes' should be separated by at least seven years, but this is often impractical in first-rotation upland plantations that are very uniform. Where the original forest was planted in large unbroken areas of the same age, it can be difficult to divide these up into smaller felling coupes due to a risk of progressive windthrow. This is because of the lack of 'internal windfirm edges'. Where roads or tracks divide up a plantation, the edge trees become more firmly rooted, resisting windthrow. Sometimes it is necessary to fell the whole of the larger area but divide it up into smaller sub-compartments when it is replanted, creating additional windfirm edges for future rotations. Restructuring also allows for the removal of artificially straight edges and for the liberation of areas within the forest for open space, native woodland and riparian habitats.

Diversity 'within' plantation stands can sometimes be achieved by a combination of targeted silvicultural interventions including thinning and enrichment planting. This is effectively a process of 'transformation' or 'conversion' to the 'continuous-cover forestry' forms of management discussed below. Sometimes this is done as part of the process of PAWS restoration (see Chapter 8), with the aim of converting the stand to predominantly native tree species over time, without the need for clearfelling (Wilson 2012). In other situations the aim is to diversify the range of conifer species used – for example to introduce Douglas fir to a stand of pure larch or Sitka spruce. This approach has clear advantages over the type of 'forest restructuring' described above – most notably the avoidance of clearfelling, which can have high visual landscape impacts, and the maintenance of a more sheltered 'forest microclimate', which will aid the establishment and growth of more sensitive alternative tree species. These two approaches can be used together within a single large plantation forest. However, British foresters generally have less recent experience of managing stands in these more intricate ways. There can be difficulties sourcing the relevant skills or machinery, and operating costs can be higher.

10.2.3 Irregular forestry – managing plantations with mixed species or ages

A smaller proportion of Scotland's plantation forests are managed in a very different way from the regular, even-aged, 'clearfell and replant' system described above. These approaches are known by foresters as 'alternative' or 'irregular' silvicultural systems, but more popularly as 'continuous-cover forestry', or CCF for short (Hart 1995; Matthews 1989; Wilson 2013b). All of these systems have in common avoidance of the need for clearfelling large areas of the forest at any one time (see Figure 10.1). Therefore at any given point in time there should be 'trees on the ground' across the whole forest area, helping to maintain a sheltered forest microclimate, protect soils and avoid adverse visual landscape impacts. Many such systems rely significantly on natural regeneration, and have more than one age class of tree present within each stand in the forest. This last feature is what gives rise to the term 'irregular' or 'uneven-aged' forestry.

In fact, there is one alternative silvicultural system, uniform shelterwood, which retains a regular, even-aged structure. This is usually applied in stands of species like Scots pine (Mason et al. 2004), larch and oak that do not regenerate well under their own canopy shade. When the stand nears the optimum harvesting age on economic grounds, most of the trees are felled, leaving only a sparse cover of widely spaced 'seed trees' (20–30% are left standing). The 'seed rain' from those trees provides a replacement stand of trees by natural regeneration, with a dense thicket of young seedlings coming up at one time, under conditions of near full lighting. When these are sufficiently well established, the remaining canopy trees are felled, completing the stand replacement process. Although there is never a time with no trees on the ground, because the new stand is young, even-aged and looks very much like a plantation, this is not true irregular silviculture. This type of forestry is sometimes called a 'two-storey structure' and is most often applied to stands of a single tree species.

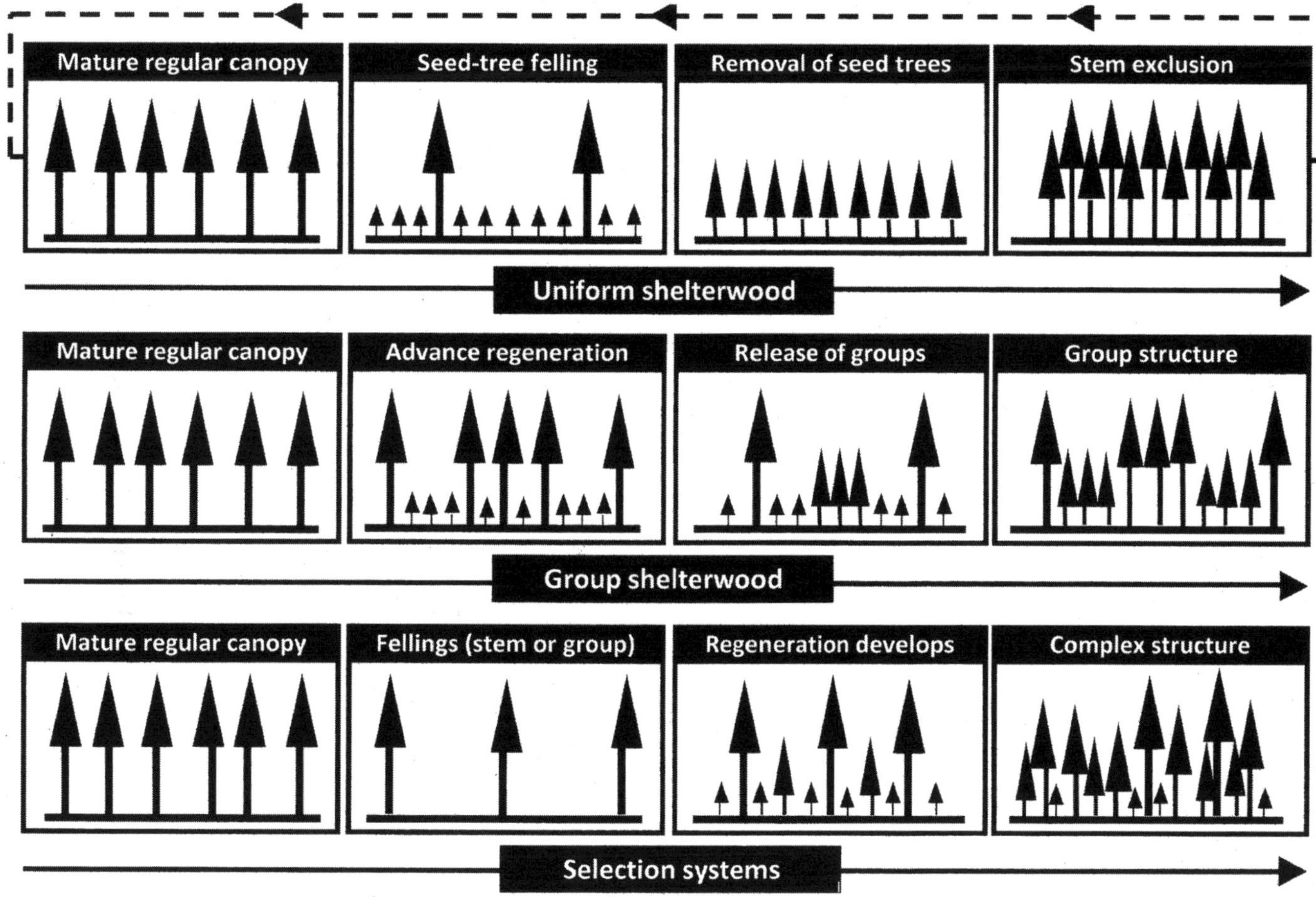

FIGURE 10.1 *Schematic representation of silvicultural transformation systems in plantation forests. After Hart (1993) and Matthews (1989). Copyright: Dr Scott McG. Wilson.*

The true 'irregular' silvicultural systems involve felling either individual trees within the forest as they mature (single tree selection) or small groups (group selection). This then provides a 'gap phase' within which natural regeneration can establish or, more rarely, trees can be planted. A variant of the group selection approach is the group (or irregular) shelterwood system, where some seed trees are left in the canopy above natural regeneration at the group scale. The difference between these 'group' systems and the 'patch' clearfelling system is the size of any gaps created. As a very rough guide, if the gap is bigger than two 'tree heights' across, you are dealing with a patch clearfell system; smaller than that, it is a group system. Many mature forests managed using irregular systems have at least three age classes of tree present – a 'three-storey structure' – which will usually be mature canopy, pole/sapling stage and small seedlings. Very often, there is a wider range of tree species present, sometimes with differing levels of shade-tolerance. The actual size of gaps created by group fellings to promote natural regeneration largely depends on the shade-tolerance of the tree species the forester is seeking for the next crop. Single tree selection systems can only be applied reliably with species that are very shade-tolerant (e.g. beech, western hemlock, western red cedar, grand fir). This is particularly so in a northern country like Scotland where the angle of sunlight for much of the year is shallow and the sun will not shine down into the top of small gaps. With trees of moderate shade-tolerance (e.g. ash, Sitka spruce, Douglas fir), it is better to operate at the group scale, creating somewhat larger canopy gaps. Foresters using the irregular silvicultural systems tend to carry out planned felling and regeneration operations across the forest, ideally every year or at least every three to five years. Trees can be selected for harvest either by 'looking up' – when they reach a 'target diameter' for the sawmill or when they start to compete with their neighbours – or, alternatively, by 'looking down' – when it is necessary to remove some canopy cover to 'release' natural regeneration below. A common approach combines 'target diameter felling' at, say, 60cm stem diameter with release of groups of regeneration. The aim is to allow the best stems to grow on to maturity for harvest. Over time, the plantation forest takes on a more and more natural appearance, without obvious stands of trees of the same size and age and with an intimate mix of tree species.

Because of the greater complexity of irregular forestry systems, they tend to be applied to 'valued' areas of the plantation forestry estate which are most productive, have a higher landscape significance and enjoy expert and consistent management. They are less often applied in the remoter and less productive plantations of the Scottish uplands. There are a number of well-established private estates and a few older Forestry Commission forests where managers have accumulated experience of these methods (Hart 1995; Wilson 2013b). There is still an ongoing discussion among foresters as to whether alternative silvicultural systems are cheaper or more expensive than regular 'clearfell and replant' forestry. Economics differ, in that regular forestry concentrates income and costs at the time of felling and replanting, whereas CCF spreads both out more evenly. CCF also produces a wider range of harvested tree size, but this may include a number of large, high-quality stems that attract a premium price. To apply irregular silviculture, it is best to favour that system from early in the life of any plantation, either by planting a range of tree species, perhaps 'staggered' by a number of years, or by early selective thinning. However, this has rarely been done. In most cases Scottish foresters have to 'transform' or 'convert' regular stands to irregular forestry at a mature stage. This can be difficult in exposed stands of light-demanding or medium-tolerant tree species, where opening gaps increases the risk of windthrow. Once CCF achieves a 'steady state', beyond the early transformation phase, it is probably more efficient than regular plantation forestry, but we have very few examples in Scotland as yet that have developed to that stage. Costs can, however, appear significantly higher for CCF during the transformation phase itself, which can last for several decades, depending on tree species used. Successful CCF requires a consistent, but moderate, input of highly skilled management, whereas regular forestry has peaks of very high labour/machinery input demand.

As this book is primarily about Scotland's native woodlands, readers may well ask why they are being told so much about managing forestry plantations of introduced conifers. Beyond personal interest, the main reason is that the irregular or CCF forestry systems offer a good way for the 'twain to meet'. In many situations native woodland habitats (newly created or ancient semi-natural) physically adjoin plantation forests, and, over time, these are likely to merge to a degree. In some situations this is probably a good thing ecologically, but perhaps not always. Mature plantations of native tree species such as Scots pine, oak, ash or silver birch can be 'naturalised' using CCF approaches, becoming more like ancient semi-natural woodlands and more supportive of woodland biodiversity (see below). Many plantations established on ancient woodland sites (PAWS) contain fragments of native woodland habitat, such as veteran trees and ground vegetation (ancient woodland indicator plants). CCF forestry techniques can be used to protect and expand these remnants without the whole conifer stand having to be felled (Harmer and Thompson 2013; Wilson 2012). This retains financial value in the conifer crop and limits visual and ecological impacts. In some situations, CCF management of a plantation allows native species to seed into the understorey from a neighbouring semi-natural woodland, helping to naturalise the plantation over time. However, natural regeneration 'in the other direction' can certainly become a problem (e.g. where *Rhododendron*, western hemlock or Sitka spruce colonises an adjoining ancient semi-natural woodland).

10.2.4 Native species plantations – management for naturalisation

A special case of plantation management is where the plantation is itself of tree species that are 'site native'. This applies mainly to older plantations of oak and ash throughout Scotland, and to plantations of Scots pine within the Caledonian Pinewood Zone. Here, there is an opportunity to use the existing plantation as an ecological 'short-cut' to a more mature native woodland – often a lot cheaper and more reliable than planting a new native woodland on bare land. Here, we are dealing with plantations originally created for timber production, dating from the 1950s or earlier, long before the recent phase of new native woodland creation. Most will have a rather uniform age structure, many will be denser than a natural woodland of the same age and there will often be a lack of native 'non-timber' tree and shrub species. There is usually a benefit to promoting the development of a wider range of age classes and increased natural regeneration, employing sensitive silvicultural techniques. This will often increase the 'biodiversity hosting capacity' of the plantation by creating a range of habitat niches suited to species normally found in ancient woods (Harmer et al. 2010; Mason et al. 2004). However, it is vital to avoid sudden or invasive management that may disturb habitats and species that are already becoming established within the plantation – there is usually no hurry.

Many old Scots pine, oak and mixed hardwood plantations date from 1750–1850, when there was a period of enthusiasm for plantation forestry, stimulated partly by naval timber demands. However, by the time these plantations had matured, demand had reduced due to the use of iron and steel for shipbuilding. Similar considerations apply to oak originally planted for charcoal coppice and tanbark (Anderson 1967). In these cases, it can be quite difficult to distinguish plantations from semi-natural woodlands. A range of indicative features can be used to detect plantations, such as evidence of 'ridge and furrow' from earlier phases of agricultural cultivation, straight lines of planted trees, lack of ancient woodland indicator species (Crawford 2009) and remains of buildings. However, if the plantation was created on an ancient woodland site in the distant past, it may be impossible to be certain of its status today. Many foresters feel instinctively that they should thin or group-fell in old pine and oak plantations to secure a 'pulse' of natural regeneration. Sometimes, groups of trees are felled and a fenced exclosure created, where deer or sheep numbers are currently preventing natural regeneration. However, pine and oak plantations are often too young to have reached the understorey re-initiation stage (Oliver and Larson 1996) and over-eager thinning or felling work may adversely affect lichen and moss species, sensitive to light and drought. On fertile sites, weed growth under canopy gaps may be too strong for tree seedlings to compete, especially if there is a lack of seed from canopy trees. Gentle thinning, combined with controlled grazing to restrict competing weed growth, may offer a better option. In special cases, non-intervention management may be more appropriate. Enrichment planting with 'missing' tree or shrub species can be useful in native plantations.

In younger native plantations, especially of Scots pine, there can be a case for more active silvicultural management to accelerate the process of structural development and stand naturalisation. Species such as birch, aspen and holly might be planted into the woodland understorey to diversify it. Sometimes gaps are created by early felling to encourage biodiversity, such as capercaillie, and to introduce an irregular structure from an earlier stage of the rotation, but there is little prospect of pine regeneration before the stand is about seventy years old. If the Scots pine that was originally planted was not of a local provenance, there is a much weaker case for attempting naturalisation work – it may be better to clearfell and replant the stand.

10.3 Linking native woodlands and plantations

There are a range of situations where links between plantation forests and native woodlands can be deliberately developed, creating more extensive areas of habitat suitable for biodiversity and providing opportunities for future timber and woodfuel production. These include approaches where the two types of woodland 'meet at the edges' but do not physically merge, together with those where mixed woodland forms gradually over time.

10.3.1 Plantation forests within forest habitat networks

We saw in Chapter 9 that, when dealing with creation of new native woodlands, forest habitat networks (FHNs) are an important planning tool (Peterken et al. 1995; Fowler and Stiven 2003). They provide a logical basis for targeting invariably limited financial and land budgets for new native woodland creation, to maximise benefits for landscape and biodiversity. While many projects ideally seek to link up existing areas of ancient semi-natural woodland to create native woodland habitat networks, plantation forests should not be ignored. Although there certainly are some plants and animals (known as 'ancient woodland specialists') that require ancient woodland to survive, a greater range of species (known as 'woodland generalists') can make use of a variety of types of woodland. Some animal species will use plantations simply as a reasonably 'safe route' between their preferred native woodland patches, while others will make full use of plantations as breeding habitat and foraging territory. Ancient woodland plant species will colonise adjoining plantation forests at rates varying from a few months to a few centuries, depending on the ecological conditions within the plantation and the strategies of individual plant species (Grime and Pierce 2012). Ecological acceptability and value to woodland biodiversity species improve considerably as the plantation structure matures, becoming more open and structurally diverse. Inclusion of a well-planned proportion of native trees (and other hardwood species) can also be of great assistance in improving habitat quality, even if that proportion remains fairly minor at first. Application of 'continuous-cover forestry' systems in plantation forests helps to sustain woodland conditions and resulting 'permeability' to biodiversity, and should also allow the retention of a proportion of older trees. Development of a deadwood resource within forestry plantations is usually the slowest aspect of naturalisation, and insects and fungi that depend upon deadwood will be among the later species to colonise. It must be borne in mind that some plants and insects have such a strong 'obligate' dependence on particular native tree species (whether dead or alive) that they may never colonise a coniferous forestry plantation.

When planning woodland habitat networks that include elements of plantation forestry, it is important to consider how 'ecologically permeable' the inter-connection between the components is. Normally, it is better to have a long 'contact interface' between the two types of woodland, rather than sharp 'point contacts' – for example where a narrow corridor of newly planted native woodland meets a plantation edge at right angles. There may also be a need to 'blur the edges' by creating a more gradual 'contact zone' or 'ecotone' between the two woodland types. This will assist species in moving from the native woodland habitat into the plantation by reducing the effects of 'ecological contrast'. This applies particularly where the forestry plantation is uniformly dense and dark (e.g. young even-aged spruce) and is much less important in older mixed conifer plantations with a more open structure, managed using CCF systems. Care needs to be taken where there are invasive species within the conifer plantation, such as western hemlock and *Rhododendron*, that might colonise nearby native woodlands.

10.3.2 Restoration of Plantations on Ancient Woodland Sites (PAWS)

We discussed the restoration of plantations on ancient woodland sites (or PAWS for short) in Chapter 8 on the conservation management of existing woodlands. This can be of particular value to biodiversity where the plantations form part of potential woodland habitat networks otherwise consisting of native woodlands (ancient and newly planted). This is quite often the case where a complex of native woodlands follows the slopes of a river valley. Some parts may have been replanted with conifers since the last war, while other parts survive as native woodland. It is possible to convert any area of conifer plantation to native woodland given sufficient time and resources. However, PAWS sites are of particular significance in that they often retain features of the pre-existing ancient semi-natural woodland (Harmer and Thompson 2013; Thompson et al. 2003; Wilson 2012; Woodland Trust 2005) such as deadwood and woodland specialist plants and invertebrates. These can act as a focus for more rapid ecological recovery following de-coniferisation of the site, and will often prevent the need for later artificial reintroduction of key species, which can be very expensive. If there are limited resources available for PAWS restoration work, these should be concentrated on those situations where an area of PAWS might be acting as an ecological 'bottleneck' within a woodland habitat network. As discussed above, this is most likely to happen where the plantation is relatively young, is uniform in terms of tree species and structure, and casts a heavy shade on the ground vegetation. Older mixed and CCF woodlands on PAWS sites are usually more permeable to movement of biodiversity and will have more limited effects on surviving ancient woodland features. They are therefore a lower priority for restoration and can be attractive landscape features in their own right, potentially valuable for timber production.

When restoring PAWS sites as part of forest habitat networks, as elsewhere, it is important to minimise unnecessary ecological disturbance. This should help to avoid a situation where the restoration process itself diminishes the ecological value of the PAWS site, for example through extensive clearfelling operations. Many PAWS restoration projects now use continuous-cover silvicultural approaches, where the conifer canopy is gradually opened to protect surviving ancient woodland features and to promote natural regeneration of native tree species. Where the conifer crop is short of normal economic harvesting age, preliminary measures are possible, such as a 'halo-thinning' around submerged veteran trees and above surviving 'hotspots' of ancient woodland ground vegetation. When carrying out thinning or group felling to promote natural regeneration of native tree species, it is essential to consider where the seed will come from. Newly planted native woodland on an adjoining site will not produce much seed during its first twenty to thirty years, whereas mature conifers, beech, sycamore and *Rhododendron* in other parts of the same plantation may be producing large amounts of shade-tolerant seed. This can lead to the gaps created filling up quickly with non-native species rather than the desired natives, and unwelcome colonisation outward into adjoining native woodland habitats. However, where there is mature native woodland adjoining, this approach can work well. Normally it is best to plan PAWS 'restoration silviculture' to progressively reduce the difference between adjoining types of woodland. Where the native woodland component is already mature, this can rely on natural regeneration, but where any native woodland remains young, enrichment planting within the plantations may be more reliable. PAWS restoration work is best started near the interface between conifer plantation and more mature native woodland habitats, working gradually inwards to the centre of areas dominated by pure, heavy-shade conifers.

10.3.3 Introducing a native element to plantations by enrichment planting

In some situations, complete conversion of conifer plantations to native species woodland may not be consistent with the owners' objectives or may not be feasible within a reasonable time period. However, it is still possible to introduce a native species element within such plantations by means of enrichment planting. This approach is appropriate where the woodland owner wishes to combine timber production with landscape amenity and biodiversity 'enhancement'. In some cases, the native tree species may be introduced purely to benefit amenity and biodiversity, for example along the edges of watercourses, but equally they can make a contribution to future quality timber or woodfuel production if they are suitably managed.

Enrichment can be achieved by restocking whole stands or compartments to native species (either by natural colonisation or by replanting) or by inter-planting them as a component within the existing conifer crop. There is usually an advantage in 'clumping' together new native species elements within plantation forests as this makes them easier to manage and creates more robust areas of native woodland habitat. However, this may have the disadvantage of requiring patch clearfell operations. If areas of native species woodland are being introduced to a large conifer plantation, some attempt should be made to create 'internal habitat networks' by connecting these patches with corridors of native species woodland, for example along watercourses (Humphrey et al. 1998). Compared with ecologically isolated patches of native woodland habitat, this will be likely to support a larger and more diverse complement of biodiversity.

An important consideration when planting native trees into existing conifer plantations or mixed woodland is relative shade-tolerance (Harmer et al. 2010). There is usually a mature canopy in place, casting significant shade. This may prevent planted seedlings or saplings of light-demanding or medium-tolerant native tree species from thriving. As was explained in Chapter 2, few tree species native to Scotland are fully shade-tolerant, with the exceptions of wych elm and holly. Beech and sycamore do offer more reliable prospects for use in mixture with conifers, but are not considered native. Generally, the more light-demanding the species that you wish to introduce, the larger any gaps that are created in the conifer plantation will need to be. Species like pine, birch, aspen, willow and rowan will require large canopy gaps to be created, amounting to small clearfells, but will often colonise these by natural regeneration. Very heavy thinning can sometimes achieve a similar result. Species like oak, ash, alder and cherry can be planted into smaller gaps, but there must still be sufficient top-light to encourage strong growth. Slope aspect needs to be accounted for – if the site is on a steep north-facing slope, it may be necessary to make canopy gaps larger in order to achieve the same effect, due to the low angle of the sun. If native trees are being planted into conifer woodland without opening canopy gaps, preparatory thinning will almost always be needed. The intensity of this thinning will similarly be determined by the height of the surrounding conifers, shade-tolerance of the tree species to be inter-planted and slope aspect. There is no point in inter-planting native trees into dense plantations without preparatory thinning – most will inevitably fail due to excessive shading. Beech and sycamore are a different story, and can be under-planted in intimate mixture with conifers, once these begin to open out. When creating gaps or thinning conifers on fertile sites, weeds may grow up rapidly from a seed-bank in the soil, and can pose a severe competitive challenge to young trees. Herbicide treatment may be needed to 'get trees away'. In many cases fencing or tree-shelters will be required to protect palatable hardwood seedlings from browsing by resident deer.

10.3.4 Creation of new mixed species plantations

We have seen that, in recent decades, most new woodlands created in Scotland have followed one of two alternative models: conifer plantations (usually of introduced species, occasionally of Scots pine) or new native woodlands (aiming to restore one or more of the National Vegetation Classification (NVC) native woodland communities). However, there is a longer tradition, dating back as far as the seventeenth century, of creating mixed or 'policy' woodlands, which combine native and introduced species, hardwoods and conifers within the same stands. In some cases, particularly from 1840 to 1960, these amounted to arboreta or 'forest gardens', trying out new species for forestry under Scottish conditions. Although some mixed woodlands have continued to be created for landscape amenity within public parks or private grounds, rather few of these have been managed for timber production in recent years.

There is a good argument at the present time – and associated grant support available – for the creation of a new generation of mixed species woodlands. A variety of factors encourage this, including (1) the predicted effects of climate change and pest and disease outbreaks on tree species, (2) increased demand for quality coniferous and hardwood timber and for woodfuel, (3) growing enthusiasm for adoption of continuous-cover/selection silviculture and (4) the attractiveness of mixed woodlands for landscape amenity and recreation, especially close to major population centres. In general, mixed woodlands offer a good way to address several objectives on the same land area, while producing resilient woodlands.

When creating any mixed plantation from scratch, it is very important to consider how it will develop over time, what the main objectives are and how the woodland will be managed into the future. There is generally little point in creating a woodland composed of stands containing random 'planting mixtures' of tree species, even if these are all ecologically suitable for the site. Some essential factors to be taken into account are:

- **Species** – select a group of species, native and introduced, which are suited to the site, will meet the objectives of woodland creation (timber, woodfuel, amenity, biodiversity) and will grow well together in mixed stands. Anderson (1961) made some initial suggestions for valid 'future species groups'. There is usually little advantage in having more than about six species under management within any forest area. If species are of varying shade-tolerance, the manager needs to think about how these will interact over time, and whether all will persist to maturity.
- **Structure** – in some situations it may be appropriate to have all the species used growing in an 'intimate mixture', but more often it may be better to have some element of concentration or 'clumping' of species, especially if they are to be managed for timber or woodfuel. This will make it easier to apply suitable management to stands of perhaps one, two or three species and to gain access for thinning and harvesting.
- **Management** – some forms of mixed plantation can be operated successfully with periodic management interventions (e.g. harvesting), whereas others will require constant 'fine-tuning' (e.g. pruning, thinning) to improve the average quality of the stems and the balance between different tree species. If the intention is to work light-demanding species such as pine, larch, birch and ash in mixtures, action may be required to 'favour' them over shade-tolerant competitors. There is only any point in creating complex and demanding mixed woodlands if the required level of skilled future management can be provided on an ongoing basis.

Creation of mixed plantations including non-native species on ancient woodland sites is more controversial, as the preference has been to model any new woodland there on the NVC classification (Rodwell and Patterson 1994). However, climate change and pest and disease outbreaks are forcing woodland managers to consider the potential role of non-native species to replace native species that are no longer viable for use on a given site. At present the most common situation is the use of sycamore in place of ash or elm in mixed deciduous plantations. However, it might become necessary to consider alternative conifer species (e.g. Macedonian pine, Serbian spruce) in place of native Scots pine if *Dothistroma* impacts become more serious.

10.4 IMPACTS OF CLIMATE CHANGE, PESTS AND DISEASES

We saw in Chapter 9 that it is important to consider predicted climate change, pests and diseases (Ray 2008) when planning the creation of new native woodland. These factors also have significant implications for plantation forestry in Scotland and for its interactions with native woodlands. There is already evidence that some introduced tree species that are currently used for plantation forestry (e.g. Sitka spruce) can suffer drought damage in drier summers when grown on freely draining soils in the east

(Green and Ray 2009). Other conifer species, such as larch and lodgepole pine, have suffered damaging outbreaks of pests and diseases that may be spreading more easily due to increasing climatic warmth. These developments have led foresters to think actively about changing, or at least diversifying, the range of plantation tree species that are grown, in an attempt to mitigate climate, pest and disease risks (Wilson 2007, 2011a). This is one of the main arguments in favour of mixed forestry. This may include selection of more native species for productive use, especially where these are suitable for production of woodfuel, or of alternative conifers (e.g. Douglas fir, larch, western red cedar) that can produce timber suitable for use in exterior construction. Substitution of home-grown wood products for fossil fuels or high embodied-energy construction materials (e.g. concrete, steel) is part of the contribution that forestry can make to the fight against climate change, alongside carbon sequestration (Read et al. 2009).

In some parts of Scotland, climate change may allow use of more demanding plantation species that are currently thought too sensitive to frost damage. This could certainly open up wider opportunities for the production of quality hardwood timber, using native species like cherry that were traditionally only able to be grown for timber on more sheltered lowland sites, in high demand for agricultural production. However, there are also a range of non-native hardwood species, such as beech, sycamore, field maple, wild service and walnut, that might be considered. These have traditionally been used for valuable hardwood timber production further south in Great Britain, but to a lesser extent in Scotland. In the case of beech, which is native in southern England but under threat from increasing drought there, wider cultivation in Scotland could potentially offer a refuge for beech woodland and its associated biodiversity (Wilson 2006). Sycamore could also be grown for timber in a more organised way in Scotland, while field maple, wild service and walnut may be grown on a smaller scale on very favourable sites, where they can produce high-value timber. Planting such species in ancient woodland remains controversial.

When creating these new mixed species plantations (sometimes known as 'future forests'), a key approach to dealing with environmental risks is to build in 'resilience' for the plantation itself to respond dynamically to change as it occurs. It may not always be possible, for economic and social reasons, for foresters to 'micro-manage' forests to help them survive emerging challenges – they may need to 'adaptively self-manage'. Artificial forests and woodlands that require intensive management may not prove viable in the longer term. Therefore those planning new plantation forests should try to make them resilient, whatever the current objectives of management might be. The key approaches to ensuring environmental adaptability and resilience in new plantation forests are similar to those discussed for new native woodlands in Chapter 9 – ecological site matching, diversity of provenance and species, forest hygiene precautions, structural diversity and so on. In the mixed species plantation forestry context there is generally greater flexibility in the choice of tree species and silviculture.

CHAPTER ELEVEN

Native woodlands – a view to the future

11.1 Conservation of native woodlands

Much has been achieved over the past sixty years in terms of protecting and consolidating the ancient semi-natural woodlands of Scotland. Critical threats from unlicensed felling, replanting with non-native tree species and conversion to other land-uses have been greatly reduced. However, more insidious threats from excessive deer browsing, invasive plant species, new pests and diseases and climatic change remain active and will require continuing attention throughout the new century. The Native Woodland Survey of Scotland (Forestry Commission Scotland 2014) indicates that under half the resource is currently in a 'satisfactory' ecological condition, with excessive browsing the major adverse factor elsewhere. It must remain our objective to secure more robust natural tree regeneration within native woodland habitats, at a frequency and distribution consistent with the ecology of the specific woodland types – regeneration need not be present in every native woodland at any given time. This would preferably be achieved without the need for repeated intervention in the form of fencing, deer culling, scarification and so on, but given the multiple land-use contexts within which native woodlands operate in Scotland, these may be required.

Until recent years, ancient semi-natural woodlands in Scotland have been reserved mainly as 'low-intervention' areas, often ecologically isolated from one another, and very often without significant tangible economic outputs (despite their much longer-term history of productive management). This conservation model was undoubtedly appropriate to the critical ecological condition in which these woodlands were 'rediscovered' during the period 1930–1980, but it is not optimal for the longer term. While there will certainly be valuable ancient semi-natural woodlands where the low-intervention model remains appropriate, it is too often regarded as the automatic choice for conservation. This results in a complex body of conservation 'rules and regulations' affecting designated sites in particular, which consume significant resources of finance, time and enthusiasm. Many native woodland habitats are likely to have a more secure future if they can be treated in a more pragmatic way, as productive elements of a working rural landscape. The old saying 'the wood that pays is the wood that stays' may become essential wisdom in an environment of reducing resources in public, voluntary and research sectors. It should be possible to combine functional ecological conservation of Scottish native woodlands with sensitive forms of timber and woodfuel production, game and livestock rearing, tourist enterprise, renewable energy generation and dispersed residential development. The larger extent of Scottish native woodlands compared to those of England and Wales creates more realistic options in this regard, and we still have much to learn from practical land-use experience in Norway, Finland, Sweden and some parts of North America.

A key priority for the future of native woodlands in Scotland is overcoming their inherited ecological isolation and fragmentation. This is likely to become even more of an adaptive 'Achilles' heel' given climatic change and land-use pressures. The development of the 'forest habitat network' concept over the past thirty years, while perhaps somewhat over-analysed and over-formalised at times, is one of the major advances of the British native woodland conservation movement since its inception. There are undoubtedly situations where some isolation may remain a good thing – for example in the face of the spread of invasive introduced plant species or novel pests and diseases (e.g. grey squirrel, *Chalara*). For these reasons we should always proceed with proper caution. However, in the majority of cases, the guiding principle should be that increased functional connectivity will make for more secure woodland habitats and greater opportunities for species (including woodland-dependent biodiversity) to 'shift their stances' in response to future environmental drivers such as climatic change.

11.2 Expansion of native woodlands

Creation of new native woodlands in Scotland as a deliberate act of ecological restoration is really only a feature of the last thirty years, although we have observed that older plantations of native tree species such as Scots pine and oak, originally created for timber production and landscape amenity, can offer a valuable 'short-cut' to more mature native woodland habitats in some cases. It would be fair to say that some recent experience in the creation of native species woodland has been rather mixed. While there have been some very successful and valuable schemes, a significant proportion of newly created native woodlands in the uplands have failed to thrive or have only become established with low and variable stocking densities. Especially in the case of some schemes on more exposed and infertile sites, there remains doubt as to whether these can form long-term additions to native woodland cover in Scotland. While the continuing high levels of deer browsing in many parts of Scotland have been a factor where tree protection in place was ineffective or withdrawn too early, other important causes have related to the suite of methods selected for initial establishment. Given conservation concerns surrounding the intensity and environmental impacts of conventional forestry establishment techniques applied to conifer plantations, it was perhaps inevitable that the 'native woodland movement' would react against these factors by favouring very low-impact methods. However, on reflection, this was perhaps taken to an extreme, to the detriment of the progress and credibility of the new native woodland creation effort itself. This applies especially to work on upland sites that have not carried woodland cover for centuries or even millennia. Given ever-increasing demands to demonstrate value for public money in grant-aided forestry programmes, a different balance between environmental impact and certainty of outcome may have to be struck in the future.

A key consideration in future new native woodland creation is likely to be a greater emphasis on timber and woodfuel production. Very many of the woodland habitat creation schemes pursued over the past thirty years have focused mainly on biodiversity and landscape objectives, and have not been designed to produce timber or fuel. The selection of establishment sites (remote, poor physical access, exposed, unproductive soils) has tended to militate against productivity, as have the rather low initial stocking densities (both intended and achieved) and the lack of attention to improved provenance selection. It seems unlikely that this mode of new native woodland creation will continue to attract public funding on the same scale of operation that it has over the past twenty years. Attention may properly focus on the creation of smaller areas of new native woodland using more intensive and reliable techniques (selection of better sites, more intensive site preparation, higher planting density, choice of selected and improved provenances, better stand tending). This will inevitably be more costly in terms of £/hectare for woodland initially established, but should produce a much more reliable and robust outcome in terms of woodland area going forward to maturity. Future production of timber and woodfuel will improve the economic equation of these schemes but, if well planned, should not have any significant detrimental impact on their ability to simultaneously address biodiversity, landscape amenity and recreational objectives of management. There should be greater adoption of 'higher-quality' schemes by landowners as a valued estate resource, rather than something mainly undertaken for grant. Species composition and spatial positioning of such new productive woodlands in the landscape should certainly be guided by the principles of effective site classification and adoption of the 'forest habitat network' approach as an overall framework. However, persuasion of landowners to invest, based on sound forestry advice and methods, will remain the main determinant of where new opportunities can be realised.

11.3 Coping with climate change, pests and diseases

Predicted climatic change, pests and diseases are inevitably going to be major forces affecting the planning of native woodland conservation, expansion and management throughout the new century. There are essentially two major challenges: developing solutions that address the predicted pressures themselves, while maintaining sufficient flexibility in natural systems to deal with the very high levels of uncertainty in these predictions. The best approach to this double challenge must lie in a three-pronged strategy:

1. **Predicting and reducing risks** – continued environmental research, observation and monitoring will hopefully improve the resolution of our predictions and enable better targeting of response measures. It will also be essential to maintain vigilance for emerging pests and diseases that may have inter-connections with a changing climate and try to intervene early to limit their potentially damaging effects. The 'resilience' of newly created native woodlands can be effectively improved by ensuring adequate inbuilt diversity in terms of both species and

provenance choice. Species and provenance selections made must suit environmental conditions of the present, whilst holding out the prospect of continued suitability under reasonably predictable conditions – for example greater summer droughts. There are greater intrinsic difficulties in buffering existing ancient semi-natural woodlands against *in situ* environmental change, especially for those ecological types, such as native pinewood and montane juniper scrub, that may already be close to their tolerance thresholds. At present, artificial species diversification there might still be considered inappropriate, but the need to consider 'species augmentation' (e.g. with Macedonian pine or Eurasian spruce species in native pinewoods) may arise. Actions to limit avoidable ecological stresses on woodland ecosystems, such as excessive deer browsing and invasive plant species, will become of increased importance.

2. **Enabling natural adaptive responses** – however hard we may try, planned resilience measures may not be sufficient to deal with arising climatic changes or pest and disease challenges. For this reason we must aim to give native woodland ecosystems the best possible chance of spontaneous adaptation through natural selection, ecological succession and spatial migration. Diversity at the species and genetic levels will play an essential role here, but equally important will be landscape-scale connectivity and available opportunities for 'habitat migration' by colonisation of neighbouring land. In the case of ancient semi-natural woodlands, ecological buffer zones should ideally be maintained around them to ensure that they have the opportunity to expand and migrate over time. Improved inter-connection through establishment of new native woodlands in strategic locations within woodland habitat networks will also assist. Application of available resources for woodland habitat restoration should balance the need to create large new 'nodes', with a sufficient scale to be robust, with the need to strengthen existing habitat networks through 'filling in the missing links'.
3. **Recognising and realising opportunities** – native woodlands have the potential to contribute significantly to climate change mitigation through *in situ* carbon sequestration, production of woodfuel (which substitutes for fossil fuels in energy provision) and production of quality timber (which substitutes for higher embodied-energy materials such as concrete and steel in construction). Realising these opportunities should not be fundamentally incompatible with biodiversity conservation, landscape amenity and recreational objectives, but will require us to 'raise our game' in terms of silviculture in mature native woodlands and the planning, establishment and management of new native woodlands. These opportunities hold out the prospect of 'leveraging' greater financial and organisational resources for native woodland expansion.

11.4 Placing an economic value on native woodlands

The last 150 years have been unusual in that native woodlands in Scotland have not been making a significant direct economic contribution. Indeed, over the past thirty years they have come to be seen primarily as something upon which money (public, private and charitable) needs to be continually expended. For many private landowners their conservation can become an ongoing financial commitment which is only partially offset by public grant-in-aid. For their future to become more secure as the new century proceeds, they need to once again make more of a contribution to the rural economy, without compromising their conservation status, biodiversity or landscape and recreational values. This will be more easily achieved in parts of the country with larger, more robust resources. Economics are likely to improve with the rising cost of fossil fuels for transport of timber from overseas and the increasing search for more local sources of renewable energy. Some of the types of economic use that are likely to be practical include:

- **Timber** – production of quality hardwood and Scots pine timber for sawn applications: post and beam construction, timber framing, external cladding, furniture-making, boat-building and so on. This will require at least some stands of native trees to be established or regenerated at sufficient stocking densities, using selected/improved planting stock, and subsequently managed to produce a final crop of quality timber. Processing and end-uses should be local (or, failing that, regional) wherever possible. Inclusion of a component of introduced species (e.g. beech, sycamore, spruce, Douglas fir, red cedar) may be worth considering away from the priority ancient woodland conservation sites.
- **Woodfuel** – the coppicing system and modern equivalents such as short-rotation forestry have the potential to produce valuable woodfuel for industrial chip and pellet manufacture, supplementing the existing domestic firewood market in Scotland. The scale and planning of such production needs to be sensitive and appropriate to its setting – there will inevitably be greater constraints in ancient semi-natural woodlands than in new productive woodlots of native tree species established on agricultural land. The native coppice species such as alder, birch, aspen and willow, together with longer-standing introductions like sycamore and beech, will provide sufficient opportunities for the foreseeable future without extensive recourse to faster-grown exotic hardwoods.
- **Game, food and eco-tourism** – native woodlands can act as supporting habitats for a range of plant, animal and bird species with potential either as sources of food (e.g. mushrooms, berries, game birds, rabbits), as quarry for field sports (pheasant, woodcock, deer) or as a basis for eco-tourism (e.g. pine marten, red squirrel, capercaillie, birds of prey). Scotland has a shorter and weaker record of exploiting these opportunities than comparable Scandinavian, Continental European and North American regions, and this needs to be addressed in the effort to broaden the economic contribution of woodland to our rural economy.
- **Built development** – there has been a certain amount of traditional building in some native woodland areas in Scotland (e.g. the native pinewoods of Strathspey and Deeside) but this is on a smaller scale than in Scandinavia and elsewhere. An increase in sensitive, dispersed residential development, preferably using timber construction systems, should be able to be accommodated within more extensive

pine, birch and oak woodland complexes. The current 'forest crofts' and 'hutting' initiatives and recent architectural innovations show clear promise.

11.5 Native woodland research and development

Despite all that we have learned over the past century, there remains a surprising amount that we don't know about the ecology of our native woodlands, past, present and future – and that means that an active programme of relevant research will continue to be required. Some of the key aspects where further research work is necessary are:

- **The past** – research into how the Scottish native woodland cover has responded to environmental and climatic change in the past and how human populations have made use of the resource over time. Of particular importance is the development of woodland cover in British upland areas in the later phases of previous interglacial periods and how it responded to the rapid changes in climate and onset of human influence after the end of the most recent Ice Age. This places emphasis on the methods of archaeology and palynology rather than historical research. We still need answers to the important questions posed by Frans Vera about the role of open space, shade-tolerance and large herbivores in native woodland systems prior to major human influence, tailored to the more upland conditions of Scotland. Genetic studies into the adaptive development and variation within and between native tree populations will continue to be essential to inform future conservation.
- **The present** – the recently completed Native Woodland Survey of Scotland (NWSS) (Nelson 2010; Forestry Commission Scotland 2014) provides an unprecedented amount and precision of information as to the current status, composition and condition of our native woodlands. We will now need to develop informative but cost-effective means of monitoring changes within the native woodland resource as time goes on. This is essential to detect the possible effects of climate change and novel pests and diseases at an early stage, allowing us to plan and implement effective mitigation. It is likely that remote-sensing technologies – whether operated from satellites or aircraft – will be very important in this regard, allowing prioritisation of the rather limited field survey and monitoring that available human and financial resources will now support. Where new native woodlands have been created, we need to try to build in more effective and consistent mechanisms for recording, at the outset, the methods adopted and species included and then monitoring scheme development. Similar considerations apply to restoration work (e.g. on PAWS sites).
- **The future** – climate change inevitably looms large in any consideration of research into the future of native woodlands. This includes continued modelling work on the likely nature, severity and timing of changes and also prediction of their likely impacts on native woodland ecosystem content and distribution. Where there will be specific adverse effects on particular native woodland types,

tree species, provenances or biodiversity attributes, the sooner we know about these the better. That will allow us to adopt the best response strategies in terms of risk avoidance, mitigation and adaptation, for example to drought or pest/ disease impacts. We also need to continue to develop our knowledge of effective ways of using the timber and woodfuel resource that is potentially available from native woodlands, so that their contributions to sustainable rural development and climate-change mitigation (via energy and construction material substitution) can be maximised. Of particular value will be approaches that can make use of the generally small-dimension and poor-form timber material that is currently available from most native woodlands, prior to implementation of strategies for selective improvement of native tree species and adoption of new, more effective silvicultural techniques.

11.6 Governance and native woodlands

The future conservation, expansion and development of native woodlands in Scotland will inevitably be affected by changes in land ownership patterns, public policies and sources of funding. These are each difficult to predict.

We have seen in earlier chapters how the Forestry Commission, which owns one third of the woodlands in Scotland, has changed from a 'single-objective' agency, based on the coniferous afforestation programme, to a 'multi-objective' agency with significant additional remits for conservation management, environmental regulation and grant aid to the private sector. It is currently a key player in determining what happens to native woodland in Scotland and appears likely to remain so due to political and public support. Recent decades have seen some very considerable progress in conservation management of that part of the native woodland resource that is secured within the National Forest Estate. As it approaches its centenary in 2019, the Forestry Commission may need to increase emphasis on technical support for those in the charitable and private forestry sectors who have to take on more of the workload of native woodland conservation and expansion. There are already moves in that direction. Many in the Scottish forestry sector have been critical of the complexity of forestry regulation and grant-in-aid schemes that are operated in Scotland. These are often seen to deter woodland creation/management activity or present artificial financial and logistical barriers to small private owners and agents. Although the Forestry Commission and other branches of Scottish Government, such as Scottish Natural Heritage, administer these regulations and grants at the 'country level', much unwelcome complexity arises from their inter-connection with European Union mechanisms. It is those mechanisms that may need to be redesigned to ensure continued local relevance and freedom of action.

The private land-owning sector in Scottish forestry is likely to have an increasing role in future native woodland activity. The two long-standing components of the private woodland sector – the traditional estates and the investment forestry companies – are being added to at present by a growing interest in small-scale private woodland ownership. While perhaps not yet as prominent as in southern England or Wales, new semi-recreational woodland ownership is a growing force, often with a commitment to nature conservation, native woodland and amenity-sensitive silviculture. With growing demand for woodfuel and improved timber prices, investment in private woodland ownership is seen as increasingly attractive, and the potential for use of native species is recognised by some private buyers. Some farmers, traditionally sceptical of involvement in forestry work, are beginning to see native woodland on their land as a potential agroforestry resource that can be integrated with crop and livestock production. At present, much private-sector involvement with native woodland activity in Scotland remains very sensitive to the levels and administration of public grants. There would be great benefit if a more autonomous approach could be fostered, such that owners made decisions on intrinsic merits of woodlands in the longer term – economic income, increased sporting value, recreation amenity and so on. This is more characteristic of the English situation.

The last two decades have seen the growth of woodland ownership in Scotland by charitable conservation bodies (e.g. Woodland Trust, RSPB, Trees for Life, National Trust for Scotland, Borders Forest Trust). These bodies often prioritise native woodland expansion and conservation and are, in some cases, able to access considerable additional sources of finance from their membership ('communities of interest'). This is particularly valuable in a period of severe public-spending constraint. However, it would be desirable to see a wider range of native woodland management models pursued on the charitably owned forest estate, including options for more active economic silvicultural management of woodlands as an aid to rural development. Advocacy bodies such as Reforesting Scotland and the Community Woodland Association have played an important role over recent years in highlighting the rural development and social potential of native woodland.

Recently, a number of 'communities of locality', both rural and urban, have acquired ownership of or, at least, management influence over woodlands in Scotland. This seems very likely to be a growing influence on the native woodland scene, although it may well prove vulnerable to any reduction in public financial assistance for capital land acquisition and recurring management costs. While there are many and varied rationales for community woodland initiatives, those in rural Scotland tend to place greater emphasis on local employment, financial income and rural development potential. By contrast with southern England, there is a lesser emphasis on purely recreational, biodiversity conservation and landscape amenity benefits, although those may be more significant to ex-industrial and urban communities in central Scotland. The Central Scotland Forest and Woodland In and Around Towns (WIAT) initiatives represent notable successes since 1990 in providing access to woodland in these districts. Economic factors and fiscal disciplines are very likely to require many community-owned native woodlands in Scotland to 'pay their own way' to a greater extent, and that may involve some reconciliation with established conservation-based regulatory regimes and requirements.

There is almost certainly a considerable benefit from having a wide spectrum of land ownership interests involved with native woodland management in Scotland, bringing to bear a range of views, expertise, objectives and resources (not least financial). This pattern is less likely to prove vulnerable to volatility in public policy and grant regimes. A careful balance needs to be struck between appropriate regulation of habitat management for conservation and leaving open sufficient flexibility and options for those wishing to actively manage native woodland for profit or other tangible benefits. While some sites of particular conservation sensitivity might need to be managed on a non-intervention basis, this does make these sites inherently dependent on public and charitable sources of finance and increases the proportion of sectoral time and effort that has to be devoted to grant application/compliance and charitable fundraising. In as many situations as possible, the guiding principle should be 'the native woodland that pays is the native woodland that stays' – whilst recognising that payment can come in many forms, such as enhanced capital value, better livestock shelter, home woodfuel production or a better pheasant drive.

11.7 DEVOLUTION AND THE REFERENDA – A FOOTNOTE

At the time of writing, Scotland is preparing for the historic eventuality of the independence referendum of 18 September 2014. By the time of publication, the result will already be known, and may have important consequences for the management of natural resources, including woodland.

On balance, the last fifteen years of the 'devolved settlement' have certainly been beneficial for forestry and conservation in Scotland. These topics have a much greater importance for Scotland than for the UK as a whole and hence have received greater attention in the Scottish Parliament than they had at Westminster (at least until the last few years). While native woodlands in England and Wales are generally viewed in terms of conservation and amenity, those in Scotland are also expected to fulfil a wider range of more economic functions. In addition, the appropriate scale of management for native woodlands in Scotland, especially in the Highlands, is more extensive than in lowland England. Reflecting this, the Scottish Government has, since devolution in 1999, been able to develop distinctive, locally tailored policies for the management of native woodlands by the Forestry Commission on the National Forest Estate. Their ability to do so in respect of grant-in-aid to private and charitable woodland managers has been more significantly constrained by EU regulations. Both trends may well persist, even if Scotland were to opt for independence.

Of much greater significance, particularly in respect of private-sector forestry, might be the outcome of the proposed UK 'in/out' referendum on the EU in 2017. Currently, essentially one half of the rural grant-support budget for Scotland comes from the EU as 'match funding', although it can be argued that this is ultimately a return of money paid into the EU by Britain. Hence the fundamental financial position outside the EU might be similar. However, membership of the EU imposes significant constraints on how rural support funding is delivered, through the operation of the Common Agricultural Policy (CAP) and so-called 'state aids' regulations. Hence the national Rural Development Plans and Programmes implemented by the Scottish Government cannot be optimised for Scottish conditions, instead representing a compromise with priorities and needs of other EU countries. It is argued by some that even if rural aid budgets were reduced outside the EU, the flexibility of mechanisms and 'freedom to spend' might be greater. Certain habitat and species conservation regulations might also be eased, thereby creating greater opportunity for pragmatic woodland management.

For those with any involvement in the Scottish forestry sector dating back before devolution in 1999, there are some perceived negative effects. Those might become more pronounced in the event of independence and specific attention would need to be devoted to mitigating them. The most significant is fragmentation of the valuable body of accumulated expertise in formerly GB-wide public agencies, such as the Forestry Commission and the Nature Conservancy, and resulting loss of 'forestry critical mass'. The reduction in opportunities for career professionals to gain experience working on woodlands in different parts of Britain, and a tendency for development of previously unnecessary 'inter-country' processes for policy formulation and research commissioning, can be seen to be negative trends, given the strength of the British forestry profession developed 'on the back' of the former colonial service and the twentieth-century home afforestation drive.

While an independent Scotland would certainly be able to manage its forest resources (including native woodlands) as well as does Norway, Denmark, Holland, Ireland or New Zealand, there would inevitably be a period during which autonomous capacity in key areas was reconstructed. Interesting and challenging times either way!

CHAPTER TWELVE

Visiting native woodlands

12.1 General advice for woodland visits

Many Scottish native woodlands are on land owned by Forestry Commission Scotland, Scottish Natural Heritage, Woodland Trust Scotland, RSPB Scotland, National Trust for Scotland and other public and charitable bodies, usually with unrestricted pedestrian access. Occasionally, localised restrictions may apply for forestry or conservation reasons, but diversion routes will usually be indicated. For many native woodlands on private land, current Scottish countryside access legislation permits responsible access on foot, cycle or horseback for non-commercial purposes. There are restrictions on public access to a small number of native woodlands closer to private residences, under the 'curtilage' rules. This situation differs from that in England and Wales, where it is common for private woodlands to be legally closed to public access. When visiting, care should be taken to avoid interfering with farming, forestry or field sports activities being undertaken in or near native woodlands. Time should be taken to assess the conditions before entering any woodland site, especially on private land, to ensure a safe and trouble-free visit. Where active field sports are taking place in or near a wood, visits should be postponed. Deer and other wildlife should not be approached or disturbed, nor fences damaged by climbing over. Vehicles should not be taken off the public road without landowners' permission. When parking, for example near the entrance to a track, do not block the road or owners' access. Dogs must be kept on a lead wherever necessary to protect wildlife and livestock from disturbance. This applies particularly where ground-nesting birds may be present or where livestock have young. Walkers going out onto the open hill above the woods, off main hill paths, should check with estate staff, especially during the deer-stalking season. The Scottish Outdoor Access Code is available at <www.snh.gov.uk>.

Ensure that you take all sensible steps to protect your own health and safety. Avoid any area where mechanised forestry operations are in progress, obeying relevant signage. Care should be taken where livestock are grazing in fields, especially when a dog is present. It is very often possible to find an alternative route to avoid this. Some native woodlands are in relatively remote locations with 'long walks in'. Some are on very steep, rough, rocky or boggy ground. The weather can change quickly, leading to risks of dehydration on hot summer days and exposure in cold or wet weather. Before setting out, plan your route and decide how long your walk should take, turning back at the latest half-way through that time. The return leg may take longer if it is uphill or if you get tired. Take suitable footwear, outdoor clothing, map, energy food, first-aid kit, torch and a hot drink. A compass can be useful. GPS and a mobile phone are also helpful, if used responsibly. If you are an inexperienced lone walker, it is wise to leave your plans with someone. Ticks are present in native woodlands between April and October and can carry Lyme disease and other infections. Make sure you familiarise yourself with advice on tick bite avoidance and treatment.

Current tree disease outbreaks affecting ash, pines, juniper and larch have raised concerns that visitors to the countryside might inadvertently transfer pathogens from one woodland to another. The chances of this are relatively small for recreational visitors as opposed to forestry workers. Nonetheless it makes sense to clean mud, dead leaves and so on off your clothing and footwear before leaving any woodland site. Disinfectant can be used to clean the soles of footwear if any area is known to have a higher risk. Do not carry any wood, leaves or cuttings from one woodland site to another. Advice on biosecurity measures is available from the Forestry Commission.

12.2 Native pinewoods, aspen and juniper

12.2.1 The Strathspey pinewoods

This area contains several major pinewoods with good visitor access:

Abernethy Forest (owner: RSPB). Best access is from the RSPB Loch Garten Osprey Centre at NH 978184. There is an attractive network of easy/moderate way-marked trails from there. A longer walk, on rough hill paths, over the Ryvoan Pass departs from Forest Lodge at NJ 020161. Abernethy Forest, covering 4,500 hectares of undulating ground, is managed for biodiversity conservation, with emphasis on pinewood mammals, birds and invertebrates. Deer have been controlled by culling over a number of years and natural tree regeneration is now promising.

Glenmore Forest Park/Ryvoan Pass (owner: FCS). Convenient access is from the FCS Glenmore Visitor Centre (with charged car parking) at NH 978098. A network of easy/moderate way-marked trails set out from there. There are further FCS car parks along the road up towards the Cairngorm Ski Centre. The long walk, on hill paths, over the Ryvoan Pass to Abernethy departs from the FCS Visitor Centre, and includes the spectacular green waters of Lochan Uaine. The Glenmore pinewoods are managed for a combination of timber production, nature conservation and public recreation. There are some ancient native pinewood stands within the Queen's Forest and in Ryvoan Pass, but some of the wider Glenmore Forest area has only been cleared of introduced conifer species over the past twenty years and regenerating Scots pine is still young. Some areas retain a regular plantation structure.

Rothiemurchus Forest (owner: private). There are several potential access points – the Rothiemurchus Estate Visitor Centre at Loch an Eilein (charged parking) at

NH 897084 has toilets and so on, but the forest can also be approached from the north at either Coylumbridge (NH 915107) or Loch Morlich (NH 957098), the former with free road-side parking, the latter with charged FCS parking nearby. There is an extensive network of attractive easy/moderate way-marked woodland trails within Rothiemurchus Forest, as well as the start of demanding hill tracks to the south towards the Lairig Ghru and Glen Einich. Rothiemurchus Forest has a long history of active native pinewood management for timber production, and has areas of pine woodland at a range of life-stages. Nature conservation and public recreation are also key objectives of the current management regime within the Forest.

Glen Feshie (owner: private). There is vehicle access up Glen Feshie on either side as far as the public road end, with simple FCS car parks at either NH 842009 (on the west side) or NN 851985 (on the east side). The long 'there and back again' walk up Glen Feshie is rewarded by views of the atmospheric native pinewoods on either side for about six kilometres, containing pine trees up to 320 years old. This was the backdrop of Landseer's famous painting *The Monarch of the Glen*. The woodlands were formerly expected mainly to support red deer for stalking, but recent changes in management regime have promoted much increased natural seedling regeneration. It is best to stick to the major paths running along the bottom of the glen on either side, as the wooded slopes are steep and rough. Due to collapse of the former bridge at Carnachuin, the Feshie cannot now be crossed above the new footbridge above Achleum, and the choice of banks must be made there. The path on the eastern side is more demanding, with the Allt Garbhlach side-stream having to be waded.

12.2.2 The Deeside pinewoods

Mar Lodge (owner: NTS). Vehicles should be left at the NTS car parks (charged, but free to NTS members) at either the Linn of Dee (for Glen Derry/Glen Luibeg) (NO 063898) or the Linn of Quoich (for Glen Quoich) (NO 116909). Both glens have good 'there and back again' trail walks offering stunning landscape views and access to the mature native pinewoods and younger pine plantations. Walkers in Glen Derry should turn back at the end of the woods (NO 040960), but it is possible to do a loop walk within Glen Quoich of around ten miles. Shorter, easier walks in the lower reaches of the glens give access to some of the best pinewoods. The Mar Lodge pinewoods were formerly heavily browsed by red deer, retained for sport stalking, but current management by the NTS aims to reduce deer numbers over a number of years and to promote Scots pine regeneration with limited use of deer fencing.

Glen Tanar (owner: private). For visitors to the main Glen Tanar pinewoods, vehicles should be left at the charged car park at NO 480965. There is also a smaller car park further up the road at NO 474957. There is an easy five-mile loop walk on forestry tracks through the best of the Glen Tanar pinewoods, going out on one side of the river and back on the other and using Victorian stone bridges. Slightly more strenuous 'there and back again' extensions can be made up to Half Way Hut in the valley of the Water of Tanar or to the end of the woods in the valley of the Water of Allachy (each of which adds another three to four miles to the round trip). The Glen Tanar pinewoods are among the most attractive native pinewood remnants in Scotland, the oldest part being within a National Nature Reserve. Management is for timber (outside this reserve), nature conservation and public recreation. There has been some experimental burning to enhance capercaillie habitat.

12.2.3 The Beauly catchment pinewoods

Glen Affric Caledonian Forest Reserve (owner: FCS). The main native pinewoods are on the slopes of Carn Fiaclach and along the southern banks of Loch Beinn a Mheadhoin. Parking at the Dog Falls car park (NH 283283) allows for a range of interesting shorter trail walks through the best of the pinewoods, ranging from easy to demanding. There are similar trails starting from the car park at the western end of the loch (NH 200233), but the pinewoods are somewhat more disturbed there. A longer trail walk along the southern shore of the loch lets you see most of the pinewoods, but is rather strenuous due to distance unless a lift back is arranged. Glen Affric is one of the most impressive pinewood glens, although it has lost some areas of ancient woodland to hydro-electric operations and forestry replanting since its classic motor-touring 'heyday' in the 1930s and 1950s. Non-native plantations have been steadily removed and the pinewood habitat is recovering strongly, assisted by the recent Trees for Life habitat restoration projects.

12.2.4 The Wester Ross and East Sutherland pinewoods

Beinn Eighe (Coille na Glas-leitire) (owner: SNH). Vehicles should be parked at the car park at the foot of the woodland (NH 002650), from which there is an underpass to the start of the way-marked woodland and mountain trails. The woodland trail is a little steep in places but offers a safe and atmospheric opportunity to get the feel of native pinewoods on a steep slope. The Beinn Eighe pinewoods were purchased by the Nature Conservancy in the early 1950s to establish one of the earliest National Nature Reserves, which is now managed by Scottish Natural Heritage. These woodlands have been the focus of pioneering research on regeneration methods that have been applied in several other pinewoods. There is a small seasonal SNH Visitor Centre at Anancaun and an excellent book explains the history of the reserve and the scientific record of its development (Laughton Johnston and Balharry 2001). The FCS car park at Slattadale, further to the west (NG 888720), gives good views across the loch to the native pinewoods on the Loch Maree Islands and of the remote Letterewe oakwoods.

12.2.5 The Great Glen pinewoods

Glen Loy (Coille Phuiteachan) (owner: FCS). This interesting pinewood has effectively been managed as a forest reserve by the Forestry Commission since the 1930s and is currently being expanded by restoration of areas formerly replanted with introduced conifers. Vehicles can be left by the minor public road at NN 096846, where there is signage for the reserve. There is a network of narrow paths throughout the woodland, but some parts are steep and rough and the paths can become very overgrown with bracken during the summer months. The lower parts of the woodland have a variety of species, including oak, birch and hazel, with Scots pine prevailing higher up – this gives a good opportunity to observe transitions between native woodland types. There is also an interesting archaeological history to this site.

12.2.6 The Highland Perthshire pinewoods

Black Wood of Rannoch (owner: FCS). The Black Wood, although fairly remote, is one of the most ecologically important and visually attractive of the native pinewoods, and has been studied since the 1940s. This long-term monitoring has demonstrated the benefits of maintaining a deer population that is in balance with the need for woodland regeneration. It is a fairly easy pinewood to visit, being located along the minor road on the southern bank of Loch Rannoch, and possessing a good network of well-maintained paths and tracks. While there is an FCS car park and way-marked trails at Carie, it is better to drive further west, parking considerately and entering the wood near Blackwood Cottage (NN 560564). A looping path takes you up through the best of the ancient pinewoods, past one of the oldest deer-fenced exclosures (which shows the impact of having no deer) and back down to the roadside near Dall. Areas above the pinewood to the south were planted with introduced conifers (spruce, lodgepole pine) in the 1960s and 1970s – these are now being felled to allow for expansion of the pinewood.

12.2.7 The south-western pinewoods

Glen Falloch (owner: private). This, the most southerly native pinewood remnant, can be viewed easily from the A82 road, the West Highland railway line or the West Highland Way walking route, just south of Crianlarich (NN 359227). There are a number of clumps of mature Scots pine, surrounded by 'halos' of natural birch and pine regeneration where deer fencing has been in place for a number of years.

Coille Coire Chuilc (owner: private). This is an attractive and fairly compact native pinewood, just to the east of Tyndrum. Vehicles should be parked in the public car park at Dalrigh (NN 343291), from where a walk on a well-made track can be followed up to the pinewood to the south-west (a three-mile round trip). Although the track passes through the eastern edges of the pinewood and gives good views over the remaining part, most of the pine is on the far side of the Allt Gleann Auchreoch burn and it is not readily accessible. Fencing (now removed) was used to promote natural pine regeneration from the mid-1970s onwards, one of the earlier examples of such work on private estates.

12.2.8 Juniper woodlands

There are a number of impressive populations of juniper which are worth visiting, but where Scots pine is not a significant component.

Tynron Juniper Wood (owner: private). This is probably Scotland's best-known juniper woodland, near Penpont in Dumfriesshire. It was at one time a National Nature Reserve. It can be viewed easily from a lay-by on the A702 at NX 829929. Both the low-growing and the fastigiate forms of juniper are found together. With a recent reduction in grazing pressure, other tree species have rapidly colonised this site, making the juniper less obvious from the road than was formerly the case.

Sketewan/Balnaguard Glen (owner: SWT/private). There are good populations of both the low-growing and fastigiate forms of juniper throughout the silver birch woodlands leading up Balnaguard Glen, near Grandtully in Perthshire. Vehicles can be left by the B898 at Balnaguard (NN 947518), with a stiff walk for a mile or so up the track through the woodlands. Parts of the glen are operated as a nature reserve by the Scottish Wildlife Trust, while the Sketewan birchwoods are private.

Strathavon and Glenlivet (owners: private). Some of the most accessible upland juniper woodlands are in the Tomintoul area of the eastern Cairngorms. The best sites are along the eastern side of Strathavon immediately to the south of Tomintoul village – park at the walkers' car park at NJ 165177 and walk southwards along the track for a mile or so through birch woodlands with abundant juniper in the understorey. The Bochel woods along the River Livet above Tamnavoulin also carry good populations of juniper – a minor public road between the forest car parks at Tombae and Allanreid provides excellent access. There are also good montane juniper stands along the A939 (Cockbridge to Tomintoul) road between Tomintoul and the Lecht ski centre, with convenient parking at Well of Lecht (NJ 235153).

12.3 Oak and birch woodlands

12.3.1 Atlantic oakwoods – Argyll, Lochaber and Wester Ross

Taynish NNR (owner: SNH). This is one of the most impressive, accessible and well-interpreted of the major Atlantic oakwood sites, located on the Taynish peninsula, to the west of Lochgilphead. Vehicles can be left at the small reserve car park at NR 737852. Way-marked nature trails wind through extensive areas of formerly coppiced oak woodland and lead down to the coast in places. There are excellent views over Knapdale and interpretation of archaeological remains found within the reserve.

Dalavich, Inverinan and Glen Nant (owner: FCS). These attractive sites, easily accessible from the minor public road from Ford to Taynuilt, are good examples of the restoration of Atlantic oak woodlands, some previously replanted with introduced conifers. There is a nature trail through the Dalavich oakwoods, accessible from the road at NM 969139. Further north are the Inverinan and Glen Nant sites, accessible with parking at NM 998176 and NN 019273. Access is along paths and forest roads through the oak, hazel and alder woodlands.

Loch Sunart oakwoods (owner: FCS/SNH/private). The Atlantic oakwood complexes on the Ardnamurchan and Morvern peninsulas are the most extensive remnants of this type of woodland in Scotland. There are a variety of sites, some easily accessible from the public road and others with much longer walks in. Many visitors start with the Ariundle Oakwood NNR (owned and managed by SNH), with parking/access at NM 826636, by Strontian. The oakwoods along the A861 road, on the northern shore of Loch Sunart out to Glenborrodale, are also accessible. Sections of these woodlands are in the process of PAWS restoration from past replanting with introduced conifers, and there is interpretation at several Forestry Commission car parks along the public road.

12.3.2 Upland oakwoods – Stirlingshire and Perthshire

Loch Lomond oakwoods (owner: FCS/RSPB). There are extensive areas of upland oak woodland around Loch Lomond. These were mostly managed intensively for charcoal and tanbark between 1650 and 1850, and a number have interesting archaeological remains from that era. For the visitor, the most accessible woods are those on the eastern bank of Loch Lomond. Along the minor public road from Balmaha to Rowardennan, a number of Forestry Commission car parks give easy access to the old oakwoods on trails and paths – the best spots are at Cashel (NS 398938), Sallachy/Ross Wood (NS 380958), Rowardennan (NS 360986) and Ptarmigan (north on the West Highland Way). Some of these woodlands had introduced conifers planted within them during the 1950s, which are currently being progressively removed to restore their native species composition. It is also possible to drive down to the lochside and park at Inversnaid (by the minor public road running west from Aberfoyle). The West Highland Way to the north of Inversnaid leads through the RSPB reserve to Pollochro and onwards to Doune and Ardleish. These are among the most intact of the Loch Lomond woodlands, with mainly native tree cover and stunning bluebell carpets in late spring/early summer, but some sections of the path are rocky and strenuous. Feral goats can often be seen here.

The Trossachs oakwoods (owner: FCS). These are acid upland oakwoods with a similar history of industrial coppice management to those of Loch Lomond and Argyll. The easiest woods to visit are near the Forestry Commission Visitor Centre at David Marshall Lodge, by Aberfoyle (NN 524014), which have good interpretation and a network of easy, way-marked footpaths. There are also attractive oakwoods at the eastern end of Loch Katrine and along its northern bank for some way. Vehicles can be left at the Forestry Commission car park at NN 505069, or at the Loch Katrine pier car park (NN 496072), which is charged. A sail on the loch on the steamer *Sir*

Walter Scott gives good views of the woodlands on the southern bank, otherwise only accessible by a strenuous walk over rough terrain. Highland cattle have been introduced here recently.

12.3.3 Upland oakwoods – Dumfries & Galloway and the Borders

Wood of Cree (owner: RSPB). Vehicles can be left at the free RSPB car park at NX 381709, on the minor public road running on the east bank of the River Cree, north of Minnigaff. There is interpretation signage there also. The woodland is primarily a very acid former oak coppice, but there are also areas of birch and hazel within the complex. There is a very good network of way-marked trails for the less experienced woodland walker, but some are quite steep and slippery in places.

Glentrool woodlands (owner: FCS). These are the most famous of the Galloway oak woodlands and are easily accessible. Vehicles can be left at either of the Forestry Commission car parks (NX 397792 and NX 415804). There are three woodlands: Caldons (at the south-western end of the loch), Buchans (on the north side of the loch) and Glenhead (at the eastern end of the loch). All are acid, sessile-dominated upland oakwoods, thought to be largely natural in origin. The latter two woods are on the Southern Upland Way, with Caldons Wood being only a few minutes' walk off this to the south.

Castramont Wood (owner: SWT). This is a very attractive oak woodland nature reserve a few miles north of Gatehouse-of-Fleet, formerly part of the private estates of the Murray-Usher family. Oak is dominant, but most may have been replanted during the period 1880–1940. This wood has seen some recent small-scale harvesting of oak to diversify its structure. There are some impressive old pollard or 'bundle-planted' beech and veteran Scots pine. There is a good network of footpaths throughout the woodland, which is well known for its birdlife, particularly the spotted fly-catcher and the wood warbler. Vehicles can be left in a small car park at the foot of the wood (NX 589602).

Woodhall Dean (owner: SWT). This is one of few surviving natural oakwoods at the eastern end of the Southern Uplands. It is located just south of the village of Spott in East Lothian. The woodlands were acquired by the Scottish Wildlife Trust in the 1980s and are managed for nature conservation. There is an enjoyable path-walk up the Dean, which is clothed on either side with upland acid oak woodland. Vehicles must be left at the public roadside at NT 685734, but there is very limited space there, often fully occupied on popular summer walking days.

12.3.4 Acid oakwoods of north-eastern Scotland

Spinningdale/Ledmore Oakwood (owner: WTS). This famous acid oak woodland is on steep slopes on the northern side of the Dornoch Firth and is the most northerly oak woodland on the east coast of Scotland. It is now part of the Woodland Trust land-holding in the area, together with the Migdale pinewoods to the north. The wood is believed to have a coppice history and is made up of a high density of short-stature oak trees of roughly even age, which may well have been planted 150–200 years ago. There is birch and juniper in upper parts of the woodland. The ground vegetation is of heather and bilberry. The woodland itself is really too steep for walking, but can be viewed with care from the A949 public road at the foot of the slope (NH 665890).

Quarry Oakwood, Elgin (owner: FCS/Moray Council). This highly accessible acid oak woodland is along the north side of the busy main A96 road, just to the west of Elgin. This wood is one of the few examples in Scotland of the NVC W16 acid lowland type, with vegetation of heather and bilberry. The oak is of small stature and twisted form, and is thought to have arisen following a fire during the early 1800s. It is hard to rule out the possibility that this wood was replanted at that time. Safe vehicle parking is available at NJ 198634, with a pleasant woodland walk of about a mile, through mixed beech woods, to Quarry Oakwood itself. Access direct from the A96 is dangerous and not to be advised.

Craigendarroch, Ballater (owner: private). This Site of Special Scientific Interest is one of the highest-elevation oakwoods in Scotland, reaching up to ~350m. Above this, it shades into Scots pine and birch woodland on the rocky summit of the craig. It has a history of coppice management for tanbark and spoke-wood, but there is a likelihood that some of the oak was replanted during the period 1700–1900. The vegetation is of a very acidic type. The woodland has a network of amenity footpaths and can be accessed from the back edge of Ballater town at NO 364961. This site is steep in parts and considered unsuitable for wheelchair access.

12.3.5 Birch and aspen woodlands

Newtyle Hill, Dunkeld (owner: private). This is one of the most impressive silver birch woodlands in Scotland, with tall, straight trees of excellent timber form. The birch woodland itself is on a steep slope at NO 046418. It is best to leave vehicles in Dunkeld town centre and walk out along the minor public road to the east, turning left up the estate track to Haughend, which passes an old coppice oak woodland (probably replanted) on the left. Take the left fork, passing the farm, and then turn right onto the track up to the radio mast. The birch woodlands are on both sides of this and show the potential of silver birch as a timber tree on the right Scottish sites. Seeds have been collected from these trees to establish many new birch woodlands throughout Scotland in recent years, and birch from this site is a major contributor to current tree-breeding research to produce better silver birch for future use in Scotland.

Assynt (Loch Roe and Ardbhair) (owner: private). These are some of the best coastal birch-hazel-aspen woodlands of the far north-west. A drive around the B869 from Lochinver to Kylesku allows many of these woodlands to be seen from the public road. It is worth taking a short detour to the left, down the side-road to Achmelvich. This leads to some more accessible woodlands, including the fine stands of aspen at Loch Dubh (a short walk off the road to the left). There are also good views of coastal woodlands on steep gorge slopes at Pollachapuill, Nedd and Ardbhair on the north coast of the Assynt peninsula. Views up the wooded gorge from the bridge at NC 147316, east of Nedd, are fine.

Morrone Birkwood NNR, Braemar (owner: private; manager: SNH). These are some of the most attractive and accessible high-elevation birch-juniper-aspen woodlands in Scotland, reaching 600m asl. The reserve has good access on well-made footpaths. Vehicles can be left at Auchendryne, by Braemar (NO 143911), or along the minor public road leading up to the Linn of Dee (e.g. at NO 119898), from both of which footpaths set out. You will see good stands of montane birch, aspen and juniper, together with deer-fenced exclosures to promote natural regeneration. The climate can be harsh at this site at any time of year. There are plans for conservation grazing work at this site from 2014.

Muir of Dinnet, Deeside (owner: private; manager: SNH). These extensive upland birch woodlands have developed on dry heathland around the Loch of Kinord during the past seventy years. Vehicles should be left at the SNH Burn o'Vat Visitor Centre (NO 429997), where there is interpretation signage and the start of a range of way-marked trails through the birch woodlands. There is an attractive stand of aspen on the north side of the Loch of Kinord at NO 445998, the best on Deeside.

Craigellachie NNR, Speyside (owner: private; manager: SNH). This is a prominent upland birchwood National Nature Reserve on the steep east-facing slopes opposite Aviemore. The woodland has a particularly good network of way-marked footpaths and interpretation signage allowing for safe exploration, giving a real close-up feel of the upland birchwood type. Vehicles should be left in Aviemore town centre, from where a way-marked underpass, adjacent to the youth hostel, leads under the main A9 road directly into the woodlands themselves (NH 892120).

Insh Marshes (owner: RSPB). This is a large area of floodplain marsh along both sides of the River Spey between Kingussie and Kincraig, managed by the RSPB as a nature reserve. Especially along the eastern edge of the reserve, there are interesting areas of willow carr, grading into dry acid birch and impressive aspen woodlands. There are various potential viewing and access points along the B970 public road. The car park at Torcroy (NN 776998) has way-marked trails and there are fine stands of mature aspen nearby at Tromie Mills and Invertromie (NN 783998).

Strathnaver (owner: private). There are numerous attractive stands of aspen strung out along Strathnaver from the bridge at Dalvina Lodge down to Bettyhill at the coast. Some can be seen from the B873 public road along the western side of the glen and from the A836 at the northern end. Others are more inaccessible on private farmland.

Falls of Shin (owner: FCS/private). There are impressive stands of aspen on steep slopes along either side of the River Shin within the Achany Glen between Lairg and Invershin. It is best to leave vehicles at the privately run Falls of Shin Visitor Centre on the B864, midway along the western side of the glen. Many of the best aspen stands are visible from the B864 road, across the southern end of the glen.

12.3.6 Wood pastures and veteran oaks

Glen Finglas (owner: WTS). The best-known upland wood-pasture site in Scotland is at Glen Finglas in the Trossachs. This site formed part of a royal hunting forest of the Scottish kings during the late medieval period. The wood pasture consists of a mixture of veteran pollard oak, birch, hazel, rowan and alder and was rediscovered as part of the planning for a major new native woodland project in recent years. This led to it being conserved 'on its own merits' rather than being included within the planting scheme. Vehicles must be left in a small car park at the foot of the glen (NN 531073), leaving a straightforward trail-hike of about three miles (each way) to the ancient wood-pasture sites in the two main upper glens of Finglas and Meann. The best examples of the ancient wood pasture can be viewed on slopes from NN 510110 in Glen Finglas. By contrast, there are large areas of new native woodland plantings establishing well, currently in the absence of all grazing, on the left-hand side of the neighbouring Glen Meann.

Dalkeith Park (owner: private). This is the most accessible of the major lowland deer parks of Scotland. There is a significant area of ancient oak parkland on a raised plateau between the valleys of the Rivers North and South Esk, just above their confluence (centred at NT 339687). These oaks are believed to be 400–500 years old, and some may be even older. Efforts are now under way to promote oak regeneration around the old trees, to secure the future of the parkland. Vehicles should be left at the entrance to Dalkeith Country Park (NT 334677), leaving an easy walk of about a mile through the parkland itself. Cattle are present at times within the woodland area as part of a conservation grazing project, and these should be avoided by visitors, especially when accompanied by dogs. Other woodland at Dalkeith includes fine beech.

Cadzow Oaks, Hamilton (owner: private/local authority). This is a fascinating area of veteran parkland oaks within what is called Hamilton High Parks, in the River Avon valley above its confluence with the Clyde at Hamilton. Many of the trees are believed to be at least 500 years old. Efforts are under way to secure the future of the parkland (which is currently used at times for cattle grazing) by planting locally sourced oak around the old trees. For visitors, the site should be approached from the South Lanarkshire Council's Chatelherault Visitor Centre. From there, a way-marked trail gives good views of the ancient oaks from the eastern edge of the site, albeit through a wire fence.

Lochwood Castle Oakwood (owner: private). This small and atmospheric site is no longer an active wood pasture but consists of impressive veteran oaks (probably at least 400 years old) which formed part of a historic parkland around Lochwood Castle in Dumfriesshire (a few miles south of Moffat/Beattock). The oak woodland is easily accessible, standing on both sides of a minor public road at NY 084971.

Cumloden Deer Park/Knockman Wood/Garlies Castle (owner: FCS/private). This is an interesting site just north of Newton Stewart which contains the remnants of the historic deer park of Cumloden. The major part of the deer park, containing numerous veteran oaks, is now within the Forestry Commission's Knockman Wood holding. Vehicles should be left at the FC car park at NX 408673. There is then an interpreted loop walk of some three miles, leading up to the oak woodland area. In summer this can become rather overgrown with bracken and tall grass. To the north-east of this site (a detour from the FC walk) is the privately owned Garlies Wood around the ruined Garlies Castle. This is a collection of very old veteran oaks, somewhat similar to those described for Lochwood Castle. There is also veteran oak along the Penkiln Burn and around Cumloden itself. Cattle may be found in these fields and care must be taken, particularly by walkers with dogs.

12.3.7 Lowland oak woodlands

Cawdor Wood (owner: private). This is one of the largest lowland oak woodlands in Scotland. Vehicles can be left by the minor public road running along the western edge of the woodland, with entry to the woodland on foot over the bridge at NH 840491. There are a range of pleasant walks through the woodland which are well maintained by the estate for forestry access. There is a large area of oak woodland with a high-forest structure, not having been coppiced (both sessile and pedunculate oaks are present). The vegetation is dominated by woodrush, for which this woodland is well known. It seems likely that at least some of the oak has been planted in the past, as this wood has been managed for timber over many centuries. There is a strip of richer ash-elm woodland along the gorge at the western edge of the woodland. There are also a range of planted trees, including Scots pine, larch and some of the most impressive veteran beech in Scotland.

12.3.8 Lowland mixed deciduous woodlands

In Scotland, these sites are transitional between lowland oak-dominated woodland (NVC W10) and valley ash-elm woods (NVC W8/9). Generally oak predominates on the upper slopes and river terraces, with ash-elm on the steep colluvial slopes leading down to the river itself.

Clyde Valley Woodlands, Lanark (owner: private/SWT/SNH/local authority). These woodlands have recently been the focus of coordinated conservation work. There are various valley ash-oak woodlands in this area, some of which are difficult to access due to steep slopes and multiple private ownerships. The easier woods to explore are Cleghorn Glen to the north-east of Lanark (park and walk from NS 886452) and Falls of Clyde/Corra Linn (park and walk from New Lanark World Heritage Site). Views can be taken of the Avondale woods from the old railway bridge south of Millheugh (NS 754503) and of the Nethan Gorge from the Nethanfoot to Craignethan Castle path (NS 816464).

Roslin Glen, Midlothian (owner: private/local authority). Parts of this valley woodland complex contain considerable amounts of oak, although much is valley ash-elm woodland. Vehicles are best parked at the main public car park (NT 273628). A network of footpaths lead along the valley northwards towards the ruins of Mavisbank House.

12.4 ASH, HAZEL AND ELM WOODLANDS

12.4.1 Ash woodlands

Due to the current *Chalara* disease threat to ash populations, it has been decided not to specifically recommend visits to key ash woodland sites.

12.4.2 Atlantic and inland hazel woodlands

Ballachuan Hazel Wood, Isle of Seil (owner: SWT). This is probably the most famous of the pure Atlantic coastal hazel woodlands, located over a small outcrop of base-rich Dalradian hornblende-epidiorite at the south-east corner of the Isle of Seil. There is a short walk over rough farmland from the end of the B8003 public road at NM 754143. This site is particularly valued for the diversity of its hazel-dependent lichens and fungi.

Henderland Bank, Borders (owner: private). This is a small area of upland hazel scrub in the Scottish Borders – remnants of what was once a more extensive woodland type in this area. The Henderland Bank site is on a steep south-facing slope in the upper Yarrow Valley by St Mary's Loch, and is easily visible from the minor public road above Cappercleuch (NT 237231).

Torboll Woods, East Sutherland, and Dunbeath Water, Caithness (owners: private). Hazel is a major component of the scrub woodlands in several East Sutherland and Caithness straths. The most extensive and accessible examples are at Torboll, on the southern side of Loch Fleet (accessible along a minor public road, leaving the main A9 at NH 767978), and along the north side of the Dunbeath Water above Dunbeath (accessible along a good way-marked footpath from the car park off the A9 at ND 159300). These woodlands comprise an attractive and diverse mixture of birch, hazel, alder, aspen and bird cherry.

12.4.3 Lowland elm woodlands

While most lowland elm woodland has been destroyed by Dutch elm disease since the 1970s, a small number of localities remain where it can be seen. Some of these are now under active threat from the disease:

Aberdeenshire Lowlands (owner: NTS/local authority/private). There are a range of sites in lowland parts of Aberdeenshire where wych elm populations survive, some being mature plantations. This is one of the few parts of the country where Dutch elm disease has not yet eliminated the species as a canopy tree. The country park at Haddo House (by Ellon) contains a considerable amount of elm within the designed landscape to the south of the house (e.g. at NJ 872344).

Bridgend Woods, Isle of Islay (owner: private). The policy woodlands surrounding Islay House on Islay are one of the few remaining disease-free locations in Scotland at which living elm of suitable size and form for timber can be found. Most of the elm here will have been planted in Victorian/Edwardian times, and some has been harvested in recent years, but these woods deserve a visit to see the potential of elm. There is surviving elm in the River Sorn valley running east of the A846, and also in woodlands further west at Eallabus.

Ayr Gorge, Failford (owner: SWT). The valley woodlands along the River Ayr contain a considerable proportion of elm, together with oak. These woodlands are developed on rather fertile, soft red sedimentary beds of Permian and Triassic ages. The best place to view these woodlands is from the Scottish Wildlife Trust nature reserve at Failford (enter at NS 458261), within which a good footpath runs for a couple of miles downriver. Cars should be parked safely within Failford village.

12.5 ALDER AND WILLOW WET WOODLANDS

12.5.1 Floodplain alder-willow woodlands

Lower Spey woodlands (owner: FCS/private). This is one of the largest and most natural areas of floodplain woodland surviving within the British Isles. A variety of stand types are present, including willow woodland on more unstable areas of the braided shingle and large stands of both valley and fen alderwoods where the substrate has become more stable. The woodlands run for several miles between the road and railway bridges at Boat o'Brig (NJ 320518) down to the coast (NJ 347650). Some parts are virtually inaccessible on foot, but it is possible to walk along the western bank of the river for much of the way between Orton and Fochabers. The Forestry Commission car park and viewpoint at Earth Pillars, Ordiquish (NJ 336562), south of Fochabers, offers good landscape views upstream. Perhaps the best location for a vantage point is the old railway viaduct footpath near Garmouth (NJ 347642).

Mound Alderwood, Strathfleet (owner: private). Although essentially created by the construction of an artificial barrage across the estuary of the River Fleet shortly after the Napoleonic Wars, this is one of Scotland's largest and most ecologically intact floodplain alderwoods. This site is rather trackless and inaccessible from the point of view of safe walking, but there are excellent overview points from the A839 road running along the northern edge and the minor public road at the southern side (NH 761986). To the east, there is a viewpoint on the barrage on the A9 (NH 775983). It is safer to stop and park at the latter.

Urquhart Bay woods, Loch Ness (owner: WTS). This is a very good example of a swamp woodland on the floodplain of the River Enrick where it enters Loch Ness at Drumnadrochit. Alder dominates in the wet centre of the woodland, with a rich fringe of ash-elm-cherry woodland on the drier margins. There are good overviews of the woodland from the main A82 road, both north and south of the town. Parts of the woodland are too boggy for walking but there are signed access trails from the area behind the church/cemetery (NH 516296).

12.5.2 Riparian alderwoods

River Farrar and River Beauly (owners: private). These are fine examples of 'narrow' upland riparian alder woodlands of Scotland, running down the River Farrar from Culligran to its confluence with the River Beauly at Struy Bridge and then continuing down the latter past Erchless Castle to the Crask of Aigas. There are excellent views of the alder woodlands on the River Beauly meanders from either the A831 along the northern side or the minor public road on the southern side. The best stands are at roughly NH 430400. Turning up the minor road from Struy Bridge along lower Glen Strathfarrar gives close-up views of the riparian alderwoods on the River Farrar as far as Culligran Wood.

Ettrick Valley, Borders (owner: FCS/BFT/private). Small patches of riparian alder woodland survive along the River Ettrick from Selkirk up to the Ettrick Village area. Some floodplain areas had been replanted with conifers and others subjected to heavy livestock grazing. Recently, the Borders Forest Trust has undertaken work, jointly with the Forestry Commission and private landowners, to restore wet woodland by fencing and removal of planted conifers. One of the best places to see this is along the foot of FC plantations at Gatecleuch and Gamescleuch, from car parking and view-points along the B709 (e.g. NT 281150).

River Dee, Aberdeenshire (owners: private). The River Dee has a number of stretches of riparian woodland of the classic 'alder-bird cherry' type, despite having a river-bed substrate of coarse fluvioglacial gravels and sands. There are interesting alder wood-lands along the river above the bridge at Dinnet, easiest to see from the bridge itself (NO 462982) and the South Deeside Road (B976) running westwards for a couple of miles. Similarly, the stretch downstream from Bridge of Ess, past Waterside and Birse to the Quithel, has important examples of alderwoods with bird cherry, ash, hazel and birch. The best spots to see these woodlands are from the South Deeside Road (B976), at NO 505973, NO 525980 and NO 575975 (the last a short walk off the road).

12.5.3 Slope and sump alderwoods

Cally Woods, Gatehouse-of-Fleet (owner: FCS). Although perhaps of planted origin, this small sump alderwood, containing impressively tall and straight alder trees, illustrates the potential of alder for timber production in Scotland. It is best to park at the Forestry Commission visitor car park at NX 606561 and take a short walk over good paths to the alder stand at NX 607558, which is within the alluvial fan formed by the confluence of two small streams amidst these plantation woodlands.

Mugdock Wood (owner: local authority). Drier slopes support oak woodland, although birch, alder and ash can be locally frequent or dominant. Poorly drained level areas and flushed slopes dominated by ancient multi-stemmed alders are major features of these woodlands, one of the best examples in Central Scotland. If coming by car, park in Mugdock Country Park South Lodge car park (NS 554768) and walk down on path and boardwalk, or park at NS 539770 and walk along the West Highland Way by the Allander Water through the woodland.

12.5.4 Wet birch-willow woodlands

Flanders Moss, Port of Menteith (owner: FCS/SNH/private). Flanders Moss is one of the largest lowland bog systems in Scotland, on the upper reaches of the River Forth. During the post-war decades some areas of Flanders Moss were artificially drained and planted with conifers, most of which are currently being removed, prior to blocking of drainage ditches as a wetland habitat restoration project. Some parts of the Moss have, however, carried extensive wet birch-willow woodland as a natural component. The official access and interpretation points are to the west off the B822, south of the village of Thornhill.

12.5.5 Lochside alder-willow woodland

Knapdale Forest, Argyll (owner: FCS). This is an extensive complex of native woodland on rough and remote terrain surrounding a number of small lochs south of the Crinan Canal. Large parts of the terrain were planted up by the Forestry Commission with conifer crops after the Second World War, but these are being progressively removed in favour of native woodland restoration. Although quite a lot of the surviving native woodland is of the acid oakwood type, similar to that at nearby Taynish, there are several types of alder-willow woodland present around the margins of the various lochs. There are a network of paths and tracks through the Forestry Commission woodlands. This area is of additional interest in that it is the site of the current official beaver reintroduction trial by the Scottish Wildlife Trust and the Royal

Zoological Society of Scotland. Vehicles can be parked and access taken on foot from Barnluasgan (NR 790910, NR 784907), where there is mapping and interpretation, with a new beaver-viewing platform at Loch Coille-Bharr. The status of the beaver trial after 2014 is undecided.

12.6 NATIVE WOODLAND CONSERVATION PROJECTS

Many of the potential woodland visit sites referred to above have ongoing conservation work of various types in progress. However, the following additional sites are of interest for specific ongoing conservation projects:

12.6.1 Native pinewood conservation sites

Dundreggan Estate, Glen Moriston (owner: Trees for Life). This estate is on the north side of the main A887 road, several miles west of Invermoriston in the Great Glen. There are extensive upland birchwoods with some remnant Scots pine above Dundreggan Lodge and a little further west before the road crosses the River Moriston at Torgyle. The enclosures stocked with wild boar are within these woods, which tend to be thick with bracken in summer. Trees for Life has recently acquired this estate and is developing plans for future woodland regeneration and expansion. There is now a car park and interpretation at the site.

Glen Garry (owner: FCS). For walkers, vehicles should be left at the FCS car parks at either White Bridge (NH 283013) or Mandally (NH 282004) at the eastern end of these woodlands. One of the best silver birch woodlands in Scotland is located close to White Bridge car park. There are a network of FCS roads and footpaths stretching westwards through the pinewoods as far west as Glen Kingie. Most walkers will turn back at or before Laddie Wood or Greenfield Farm. The Glen Garry pinewoods have a chequered history, with significant modification by clearfellings, fires and replanting with introduced conifers. The visitor today encounters a mosaic of ancient pinewood stands, conifer plantations and significant areas of felled conifer plantations currently regenerating to native pinewood. An experimental woodland grazing project, using Highland cattle, is being undertaken in parts of these woods. For motor tourists, fine views of the woodlands can be taken from the minor public road along the north side of the glen as far west as the Kingie hydro-electric power station – this may give a more complete picture of these woods than a short walk in from the eastern end only.

12.6.2 Broadleaved woodland conservation sites

Glasdrum National Nature Reserve (owner: SNH). This attractive nature reserve is on the northern side of Glen Creran in the Appin area, north of Connel. It combines oak-birch woodland with ash-hazel on more fertile soils over Dalradian limestone outcrops. There are some bracken glades which are excellent for butterflies. From the new road bridge on the A828 Oban to Fort William road, head along the northern bank of Loch Creran and keep going up the glen. There is a free car park for the reserve on the left signed up a sloping entry road (NN 013467). There is a good network of way-marked nature trails within the woodland, although some are quite steep. This is a site best appreciated in fine weather – as with Taynish, it becomes a bit more difficult when wet.

12.7 New native woodland creation projects

12.7.1 Large-scale catchment schemes

Cashel Farm, Loch Lomond (owner: RSFS Forest Trust Company). This was the earliest large new native woodland created in Scotland, as part of the Millennium Forest for Scotland (MFS) project, marking the year 2000. A former sheep farm on the eastern slopes of Loch Lomond was planted with a range of native woodland types – mainly oak-birch woodland at the slope foot and pine-birch on the higher slopes, with smaller amounts of various other native trees in places. There was some existing native oak-birch and alder woodland along the lochside. Conventional site preparation methods were employed and, as a result, establishment has been satisfactory, with the exception of the upper edges, where pine-juniper scrub is now being developed for black grouse. In contrast with other projects of this kind, the RSFS Forest Trust Company wanted to demonstrate the potential of new woodland for timber production as well as for biodiversity and landscape enhancement. The scheme is likely to be managed into the future for multiple objectives, within the context of the Loch Lomond and Trossachs National Park. Some of the more productive stands on the lower slopes may be suitable for a first thinning within the next decade, moving towards eventual timber crops. A visitor interpretation facility has been created in the old farm steading and there are a good range of way-marked trails and walks, some quite steep. A variety of educational activities are pursued at this site. The private car park for the site can be reached from the minor Balmaha to Rowardennan road at NS 399940.

Carrifran Valley, Moffat (owner: BFT). This large native woodland creation scheme in Dumfriesshire began with the objective of ecological restoration of an upland valley largely denuded of woodland by heavy grazing over centuries. The project was developed in the 1990s by the Wildwood Group, a local community group that helped to form the Borders Forest Trust. Purchase by public subscription was completed on Millennium Day with nearly a thousand people having become Founders or Stewards. A phased planting programme established ~300ha of native woodland at up to 500m asl, funded by forestry grants and a charitable trust, with about a fifth of the planting done by volunteers. Ground preparation has been of the 'low-impact ecological' type, but perimeter fencing and roe deer culling has been required, after sheep and goats were removed. Sourcing local-provenance planting stock was problematic, given the low woodland cover in the locality. Genetic advice informed use of small fragments of surviving woodland as seed sources. Seed collection was by volunteers but propagation mainly by commercial nurseries. The main woodland types established have been upland oak-birch and upland mixed ashwood, with some wet birchwood and localised alder-willow along burns. Recently, experimental planting (without grant aid) has been extended onto the plateau at up to 750m asl, using juniper and various willows forming part of natural montane scrub. The main planting shows continued, though slow, growth. Recently the Borders Forest Trust has acquired areas of adjoining land with potential to form the core of an even larger area of upland habitat restoration within the boundaries of the historic Ettrick Forest. Visitors to Carrifran should park in the small parking area beside the A708 road at NT 159115. There is an easy circular trail near the mouth of the valley, while an old farm track leads up the lower part of the valley through areas of new planting. The more adventurous can venture up steeper slopes on either side of the valley.

12.7.2 Medium-scale schemes

Crannach, Deeside (owner: RSPB). This was one of the earliest, pioneering new native pinewood schemes, after the introduction of the Native Pinewood Grant in the 1980s. The land was then owned by a private partnership of native woodland enthusiasts. Recently, the RSPB has bought this site. Pine and birch have been established within a deer fence on acid hill ground on the eastern face of Crannach Hill near Ballater (elevation 300–500m asl). Establishment to date has been promising. Access can be taken up a hill track that leaves the A93 northwards just to the east of Milton of Tullich (NO 389976). The main aims of the scheme have been to promote woodland restoration and increase woodland biodiversity, linking with older woodlands nearby.

Darrochwids, Huntly (owner: FCS). This scheme, creating mainly upland oak-birch woodland with some ash, pine, juniper and other species, has been pursued under the Scottish Forest Alliance project. This is a partnership between Forestry Commission Scotland, Woodland Trust, the RSPB and the BP oil company as sponsor. Areas of new native woodland have been created with the objectives of biodiversity enhancement, experimental carbon sequestration and some timber. The Darrochwids scheme used a number of unplanted upland pasture sites adjoining the mature FCS plantations at Clashindarroch Forest. The scheme was planned out using the FC Ecological Site Classification approach, and was established into grasslands with fairly light site preparation. Initially, there was an ambition to rely purely on deer culling for protection, but fencing has had to be added to some parts of the scheme due to continued deer pressure. Some areas have been established at a higher initial stocking density to serve as trials of timber production, but this will also require stand tending and thinning. The most attractive and accessible area to visit is the Coynachie Valley plantings – follow the minor public road leaving the A97 westward at Bridgend. This road runs up the Coynachie Valley to the FC parking area at Coynachie itself (NJ 490344). Vehicles can be left there and the new plantings explored on either side of the road for about a mile, leading up to the FC forest entrance at Drumfergue. There are also plantings at Merdrum and Blackmiddens to the south of the Clashindarroch Forest.

12.8 Plantation forests of specific interest

12.8.1 Diverse conifer plantations, including continuous-cover examples

Craigvinean Forest and the Hermitage, Dunkeld (owner: FCS/NTS). This major forest area lies on the western side of the main A9, just north of Dunkeld. Formerly part of the Atholl Estates, it has been managed as productive conifer plantations over three centuries. Since the last war, the forest has been managed mainly by the Forestry Commission and includes one of Britain's tallest Douglas fir trees (at 60–65m) on the southern bank of the River Braan – which can be accessed via the 'Hermitage', managed by the National Trust for Scotland and containing a fine stand of mature Douglas fir. In recent years the FC has been implementing transformation to 'continuous-cover forestry' across the lower slopes, involving a number of species (Douglas fir, Norway spruce, grand fir, larch). The main starting point for forest walks, including the Hermitage, is off the A9 at NO 013422.

Glentress Forest, Peebles (owner: FCS). This site, best known as one of Scotland's leading forest mountain-biking venues, includes the largest of the 'continuous-cover forestry' trials initiated by Professor Mark Anderson in the 1950s. It is managed by FCS, in consultation with Forest Research and the University of Edinburgh. An area of even-aged spruce plantation is being converted to CCF management (group selection system) over a period of around ninety years. There is impressively large Douglas fir, along with a number of other conifer and hardwood species. A network of attractive forest trails lead through the stands, but watch out for those mountain-bikers! Access the Forest Drive off the A72 at NT 284396.

Bowhill Estate, Selkirk (owner: private). This property forms part of the Buccleuch Estates forestry holdings in Scotland. There is an unusually long record of careful management using 'continuous-cover forestry' techniques. There are fine mixed conifer and hardwood stands managed on the selection system – particularly the area known as The Cants, south-east of Bowhill House. Vehicles can be parked in the Bowhill Estate car park (with a modest charge) at NT 425278, although it is also possible to walk into The Cants from NT 434277.

12.8.2 Beech plantations

Darnaway Forest, Forres (owner: private). These are probably the finest stands of beech in Scotland, established in the mid-1800s but very slow-grown. Access is easy on foot (about half a mile) from Conicavel yard eastward over estate forestry tracks. There are two parts to this registered seed stand, at NJ 002532 and NJ 004525.

Burn Estate, Edzell (owner: private). These are impressive stands of mature plantation beech at several locations around the former Burn Estate, north of Edzell. There is a good stand at NO 598725, a short walk in along an estate track to the east of the minor public road, just south of the caravan site, and others along the banks of the River North Esk, immediately below the B966 bridge at NO 601709 – these last being accessible from footpaths running along both sides of the bridge.

Pass of Killiecrankie, Perthshire (owner: private/NTS). This is one of the best examples in Scotland of beech woodland that has developed partly by natural regeneration. Vehicles should be parked in the car park at Garry Bridge (NN 913610) at the southern end of the gorge, from where there is a short path walk down to the narrow bridge across the chasm which gives spectacular views of the woodlands along the River Garry. The Tenandry oakwood is nearby and is a good example of the conservation issue of beech colonising semi-natural woodlands.

12.8.3 Naturalisation of plantation stands – Scots pine

The majority of examples to date of naturalisation of plantations of native tree species have been pursued in the long-established Scots pine plantations of north-east Scotland.

Glenmore Forest (owner: FCS). The Forestry Commission has used the Queen's Forest area, north of Loch Morlich, as a major trial area for the naturalisation and natural regeneration of Scots pine plantations since the 1930s. There are a variety of thinning trials of various ages, showing how stands develop under different thinning regimes. The interested visitor should obtain information in advance from Forest Research on the latest progress and location of these trials, as they are marked but not visually interpreted on the ground. It is best to park in the FC car park at Loch Morlich (NH 958097) (charged) or at the Badaguish Outdoor Centre (NH 957114) (with permission in advance), from where the trials are a short walk through the plantation pinewoods.

Culbin Forest, Nairn (owner: FCS). The Culbin Forest (and similarly Roseisle Forest further east) was established by the Forestry Commission in the 1920s on shifting coastal sand dunes, with the aim of consolidating these and producing timber. The main crops established were Scots pine and Corsican pine. Although very slow-grown due to the infertile soils, the pine is now maturing and trials of conversion to group shelterwood and selection systems are being pursued, mainly to avoid the high costs associated with replanting following clearfell. Some of the results of this work can be seen in the area west of the main Cloddymoss car park at Culbin, along the forest roads near NH 973602.

Morangie Forest, by Tain (owner: FCS). This is a large twentieth-century Forestry Commission conifer plantation in the hills south-west of Tain. Much is of Scots pine, due to the poor moorland soils, but there are other conifer species in parts. The best areas to see silvicultural work for the benefit of biodiversity species and group shelterwood trials are along the southern edge of the forest (around

NH 664742 and NH 750780). There is an easy access point with free car parking, information boards, maps and way-marked walks by East Lamington, and access on foot at Stittenham.

Principal internet sources for woodland visiting information

Forestry Commission Scotland: <www.forestry.gov.uk/Scotland>
Scottish Natural Heritage: <www.snh.gov.uk>
Woodland Trust: <www.woodlandtrust.org.uk>
National Trust for Scotland: <www.nts.org.uk>
RSPB: <www.rspb.org.uk>
Scottish Wildlife Trust: <www.scottishwildlifetrust.org.uk>
Trees for Life: <www.treesforlife.org.uk>
Borders Forest Trust: <www.bordersforesttrust.org>

Bibliography

Aldhous, J. R. (1995), *Our Pinewood Heritage*, Edinburgh: Forestry Commission, RSPB and Scottish Natural Heritage.

Anderson, M. L. (1961), *The Selection of Tree Species*, Edinburgh: Oliver & Boyd.

Anderson, M. L. (1967), *A History of Scottish Forestry*, 2 vols, London and Edinburgh: Thomas Nelson and Sons.

Andersson, F. (ed.) (2005), *Ecosystems of the World 6: Coniferous Forests*, Amsterdam: Elsevier.

Bain, C. (1987), *Native Pinewoods of Scotland: A Review 1957–1987*, Edinburgh: RSPB.

Bain, C. (2013), *The Ancient Pinewoods of Scotland: A Traveller's Guide*, Dingwall: Sandstone Press.

Birks, H. H. (ed.) (1989), *The Cultural Landscape, Past, Present and Future*, Cambridge: Cambridge University Press.

Birks, H. J. B. (1989), 'Holocene isochrone maps and patterns of tree-spreading in the British Isles', *Journal of Biogeography* 16: 503–40.

Bradley, S. (2014), *Palaeoclimatology, Reconstructing Climates of the Quaternary*, 3rd edn, Oxford: Academic Press.

Braun-Blanquet, J. (1932), *Plant Sociology*, New York: McGraw-Hill.

Broadmeadow, M. and D. Ray (2005), *Climate Change and British Woodland*, Forestry Commission Information Note 69, Edinburgh: Forestry Commission.

Brown, A. and J. Webber (2008), *Red band needle blight of conifers in Britain*, Forestry Commission Research Note 2, Edinburgh: Forestry Commission.

Bunce, R. G. H. and J. N. R. Jeffers (eds) (1977), *Native Pinewoods of Scotland*, Cambridge: Institute of Terrestrial Ecology.

Byrd Davis, M. (ed.) (1996), *Eastern Old-Growth Forests: Prospects for Rediscovery and Recovery*, Washington, DC: Island Press.

Cairngorms National Park Authority (2008), *The Forests of the Cairngorms: Cairngorms National Park Forest and Woodland Framework*, Grantown-on-Spey: Cairngorms National Park Authority.

Chambers, F. M. (ed.) (1993), *Climate Change and Human Impact on the Landscape*, London: Chapman & Hall.

Chinery, M. (2012), *Insects of Britain and Western Europe*, London: A. & C. Black Publishers Ltd.

Coppins, S. and B. Coppins (2012), *Atlantic Hazel: Scotland's Special Woodlands*, Kilmartin: Atlantic Hazel Action Group.

Cosgrove, P. and A. Amphlett (2002), *The Biodiversity and Management of Aspen Woodlands*, Grantown-on-Spey: Cairngorms Biodiversity Action Plan.

Crawford, C. L. (2009), 'Ancient woodland indicator plants in Scotland', *Scottish Forestry* 63 (1): 6–19.

Crone, A. and C. M. Mills (2002), 'Seeing the wood and the trees: dendrochronological studies in Scotland', *Antiquity* 76 (293): 788–94.

Cross, J. R. (2012), *Ireland's Woodland Heritage*, Dublin: Department of Arts, Heritage and the Gaelteacht.

Department of the Environment (1994), *Biodiversity: The UK Action Plan*, London: HMSO.
Dickson, J. H. (1993), 'Scottish woodlands: their ancient past and precarious future', *Botanical Journal of Scotland* 46: 155–65.
Edwards, C. (2006), *Managing and Controlling Invasive Rhododendron*, Forestry Commission Practice Guide 17, Edinburgh: Forestry Commission.
Edwards, K. J. and I. B. M. Ralston (eds) (2003), *Scotland: Environment, Archaeology and History, 8000 BC–AD 1000*, Edinburgh: Edinburgh University Press.
Ehlers, J., P. L. Gibbard and P. D. Hughes (2011), *Quaternary Glaciations – Extent and Chronology: A Closer Look*, Developments in Quaternary Science, Amsterdam: Elsevier.
Ennos, R., R. Worrell, P. Arkle and D. Malcolm (2000), *Genetic Variation and Conservation of British Native Trees and Shrubs: Current Knowledge and Policy Implications*, Forestry Commission Technical Paper 31, Edinburgh: Forestry Commission.
Evans, J. (1984), *Silviculture of Broadleaved Woodlands*, Forestry Commission Bulletin 62, London: HMSO.
Fenton, James H. C. (2008), 'A postulated natural origin for the open landscape of upland Scotland', *Plant Ecology and Diversity* 1 (1): 115–27.
Fife, H. (1994), *Warriors and Guardians: Native Highland Trees*, Glendaruel: Argyll Publishing.
Fitzpatrick, E. A. (1980), *Soils: Their Formation, Classification and Distribution*, Harlow: Longman.
Fletcher, J. (2011), *Gardens of Earthly Delight: The History of Deer Parks*, Oxford: Windgather Press.
Foot, D. (2010), *Woods and People: Putting Forests on the Map*, Stroud: The History Press.
Forestry Commission (1985), *Guidelines for the Management of Broadleaved Woodland*, London:. Forestry Commission.
Forestry Commission (1994 and 1998), *Caledonian Pinewood Inventory*, Edinburgh: Forestry Commission.
Forestry Commission (2003), *The Management of Semi-Natural Woodlands*, Forestry Commission Practice Guides, Edinburgh: Forestry Commission.
Forestry Commission (2011), *The UK Forestry Standard*, Edinburgh: Forestry Commission.
Forestry Commission Scotland (2005), *Community Partnerships on the National Forest Estate*, Edinburgh: Forestry Commission Scotland.
Forestry Commission Scotland (2006a), *The Creation of Small Woodlands on Farms*, Edinburgh: Forestry Commission Scotland.
Forestry Commission Scotland (2006b), *Seed Sources for Planting Native Trees and Shrubs in Scotland*, Edinburgh: Forestry Commission Scotland.
Forestry Commission Scotland (2008), *Action for Scotland's Native Woods*, Edinburgh: Forestry Commission Scotland.
Forestry Commission Scotland (2012), *Variety is the Spice of Life: Action for Nature on Scotland's National Forest Estate*, Edinburgh: Forestry Commission Scotland.
Forestry Commission Scotland (2014), *Scotland's Native Woodlands: Results from the Native Woodland Survey of Scotland*, Edinburgh: Forestry Commission Scotland.
Forrest, G. I. (1992), 'Relationship of some European Scots pine populations to native Scottish woodlands based on monoterpene analysis', *Forestry* 55: 19–37.
Fowler, J. (2002), *Landscapes and Lives: The Scottish Forest Through the Ages*, Edinburgh: Canongate.
Fowler, J. and R. Stiven (2003), *Habitat Networks for Wildlife and People: The Creation of Sustainable Forest Habitats*, Edinburgh: Forestry Commission and Scottish Natural Heritage.
Fraser Darling, F. (1947), *Natural History in the Highlands and Islands*, London: Collins.
Fraser Darling, F. (1955), *West Highland Survey: An Essay in Human Ecology*, Oxford: Oxford University Press.

Fraser Darling, F. and J. Morton Boyd (1969), *The Highlands and Islands*, rev. edn, London: Oliver & Boyd.

Gibbs, J., C. Brasier and J. Webber (1994), *Dutch Elm Disease in Britain*, Forestry Commission Research Information Note 252, Farnham: Forest Research.

Gilbert, D., D. Horsfield and D. B. A. Thompson (eds) (1997), *The Ecology and Restoration of Montane and Sub-Alpine Scrub Habitats in Scotland*, SNH Review No. 83, Edinburgh: Scottish Natural Heritage.

Gilbert, J. M. (1979), *Hunting and Hunting Reserves in Mediaeval Scotland*, Edinburgh: John Donald.

Gillen, C. (2013), *Geology and Landscapes of Scotland*, 2nd edn, Edinburgh: Dunedin.

Glass, J., M. F. Price, C. Warren and A. Scott (2013), *Lairds, Land and Sustainability: Scottish Perspectives on Upland Management*, Edinburgh: Edinburgh University Press.

Grant, A. and R. Worrell (2012), *Achieving Diversity in Scotland's Forest Landscapes*, Forestry Commission Practice Guide 103, Edinburgh: Forestry Commission Scotland.

Green, S. and D. Ray (2009), *Potential Impacts of Drought and Disease on Forestry in Scotland*, Forestry Commission Research Note 4, Edinburgh: Forestry Commission.

Grime, J. P. and S. Pierce (2012), *The Evolutionary Strategies that Shape Ecosystems*, Chichester: Wiley-Blackwell.

Harmer, R. (1999), *Using Natural Colonisation to Create or Expand New Woodlands*, Forestry Commission Information Note 23, Edinburgh: Forestry Commission.

Harmer, R., G. Kerr and R. Thompson (2010), *Managing Native Broadleaved Woodland*, Edinburgh: The Stationery Office.

Harmer, R. and R. Thompson (2013), *Choosing Stand Management Methods for Restoration of Plantations on Ancient Woodland Sites*, Forestry Commission Practice Guide 21, Edinburgh: Forestry Commission.

Hart, C. (1993), *Practical Forestry for the Agent and Surveyor*, 3rd edn, Stroud: Alan Sutton.

Hart, C. (1995), *Alternative Silvicultural Systems to Clear Cutting in Britain: A Review*, Forestry Commission Bulletin 115, London: HMSO.

Herbert, R., S. Samuel and G. Patterson (1999), *Using Local Stock for Planting Native Trees and Shrubs*, Forestry Commission Practice Note 8, Edinburgh: Forestry Commission.

Heywood, I., S. Cornelius and S. Carver (2011), *An Introduction to Geographical Information Systems*, Harlow: Pearson/Prentice-Hall.

Hubert, J. and J. Cottrell (2007), *The Role of Forest Genetic Resources in Helping British Forests Respond to the Effects of Climate Change*, Forestry Commission Information Note 86, Edinburgh: Forestry Commission.

Hubert, J. and E. Cundall (2006), *Choosing Provenance in Broadleaved Trees*, Forestry Commission Information Note 82, Edinburgh: Forestry Commission.

Humphrey, J., K. Holl and A. Broome (1998), *Birch in Spruce Plantations: Management for Biodiversity*, Forestry Commission Technical Paper 26, Edinburgh: Forestry Commission.

Humphrey, J., A. Newton, J. Latham, H. Gray, K. Kirby, E. Poulsom and C. Quine (2003), *The Restoration of Wooded Landscapes*, Proceedings of a Conference in Edinburgh, September 2000, Edinburgh: Forestry Commission.

Jeffries, M. and D. Mills (1990), *Freshwater Ecology: Principles and Applications*, Chichester: Wiley-Blackwell.

Kareiva, P., H. Tallis, T. H. Ricketts, G. C. Daily and S. Polasky (eds) (2011), *Natural Capital: Theory and Practice of Mapping Ecosystem Services*, Oxford: Oxford University Press.

Kennedy, F. (2002), *The Identification of Soils for Forest Management*, Field Guide, Edinburgh: Forestry Commission.

Kimmins, J. P. (1997), *Forest Ecology: A Foundation for Sustainable Management*, 2nd edn, Upper Saddle River, NJ: Prentice Hall.

Kirby, K. J. (2004), 'A model of a British forest-landscape driven by large herbivore activity', *Forestry* 77: 406–20.

Kirby, K. J. and C. Watkins (eds) (1998), *The Ecological History of European Forests*, Wallingford: CABI.

Lambert, R. A. (ed.) (1998), *Species History in Scotland*, Edinburgh: Edinburgh University Press.

Laughton Johnston, J. and D. Balharry (2001), *Beinn Eighe – The Mountain Above the Wood*, Edinburgh: Birlinn.

Lindsay, J. M. (1975), 'Charcoal iron smelting and its fuel supply: the example of Lorn furnace, Argyllshire, 1753–1876', *Journal of Historical Geography* 1 (3): 283–98.

Lindsay, J. M. (1977), 'The iron industry in the Highlands: charcoal blast furnaces', *Scottish Historical Review* 56 (1): 49–63.

Linnard, W. (2000), *Welsh Woods and Forests: A History*, Llandysul: Gomer Press.

MacArthur, R. H. and E. O. Wilson (1967), *The Theory of Island Biogeography*, Princeton, NJ: Princeton University Press.

Macdonald, E., G. Cooper, I. Davies and B. Freke (2008), 'Scots pine timber: current utilisation and future market prospects in Scotland', *Scottish Forestry* 62 (4): 12–21.

Macdonald, J., R. F. Wood, M. V. Edwards and J. R. Aldhous (1957), *Exotic Forest Trees in Great Britain*, Forestry Commission Bulletin 30, London: HMSO.

McGowan, P. and C. Dingwall (2011), *Conserving Trees and Woodlands in Scotland's Designed Landscapes*, Forestry Commission Practice Guide 102, Edinburgh: Forestry Commission Scotland.

MacKenzie, N. A. (1999), *The Native Woodland Resource of Scotland: A Review 1993–1998*, Forestry Commission Technical Paper 30, Edinburgh: Forestry Commission.

MacKenzie, N. A. and R. F. Callander (1995), *The Native Woodland Resource in the Scottish Highlands*, Forestry Commission Technical Paper 12, Edinburgh: Forestry Commission.

McVean, D. N. and P. R. Ratcliffe (1962), *The Plant Communities of the Scottish Highlands*, Nature Conservancy Monograph No. 1, London: HMSO.

Mai, D. H. (1989), 'Development and regional differentiation of the European vegetation during the Tertiary', *Plant Systematics and Evolution* 162: 79–81.

Martynoga, F. (2011), *A Handbook of Scotland's Trees*, Reforesting Scotland: Edinburgh and Glasgow: Saraband.

Mason, W. L., A. Hampson and C. Edwards (2004), *Managing the Pinewoods of Scotland*, Edinburgh: Forestry Commission.

Matthews, J. D. (1989), *Silvicultural Systems*, Oxford: Clarendon Press.

Mayle, B. M. (2003), *Managing Deer in the Countryside*, Forestry Commission Practice Note 6, Edinburgh: Forestry Commission.

Miles, H. and B. Jackman (1991), *The Great Wood of Caledon*, Lanark: Colin Baxter Photography Ltd.

Miles, J. (1985), 'The pedogenic effects of different species and vegetation types and implications of succession', *Journal of Soil Science* 36: 571–84.

Mills, C. M. and A. Crone (2012), 'Dendrochronological evidence for Scotland's native timber resources over the last 1000 years', *Scottish Forestry* 66 (1): 18–33.

Mitchell, F. J. G. (2005), 'How open were European primeval forests? Hypothesis testing using palaeoecological data', *Journal of Ecology* 93: 168–77.

Moss, R. and N. Picozzi (1994), *Management of Forests for Capercaillie in Scotland*, Forestry Commission Bulletin 113, London: HMSO.

Nelson, D. G. (2010), 'The Native Woodland Survey of Scotland', *Scottish Forestry* 64 (3): 14–17.

Nisbet, T. R. and H. Thomas (2008), *Restoring Floodplain Woodland for Flood Alleviation*, Project SLD2316 Final Report, London: DEFRA.

O'Connor, T. and J. G. Evans (2005), *Environmental Archaeology: Principles and Methods*, Stroud: Sutton Publishing Ltd.

Ogilvy, T. K., C. J. Legg and J. W. Humphrey (2006), 'Diversifying native pinewoods using artificial regeneration', *Forestry* 79 (3): 309–17.

Oliver, C. D. and B. C. Larson (1996), *Forest Stand Dynamics*, New York: McGraw-Hill Inc.

Oosthoek, K. J. (2013), *Conquering the Highlands: A History of the Afforestation of the Scottish Uplands*, Canberra: Australian National University E-press.

Orians, G. H. and J. Schoen (eds) (2013), *North Pacific Temperate Rainforests: Ecology and Conservation*, Seattle: Washington University Press.

Ovington, J. D. (ed.) (1983), *Ecosystems of the World 10: Temperate Broad-leaved Evergreen Forests*, Amsterdam: Elsevier.

Palmer, H., B. Gardiner, M. Hislop, A. Sibbald and A. Duncan (1997), *Trees for Shelter*, Forestry Commission Technical Paper 21, Edinburgh: Forestry Commission.

Parrott, J. and N. MacKenzie (2000), *Restoring and Managing Riparian Woodlands*, Aberfeldy: Scottish Native Woods.

Parrott, J. and N. MacKenzie (eds) (2009), *Aspen in Scotland: Biodiversity and Management*, Boat of Garten: Highland Aspen Group.

Pearsall, W. H. (1971), *Mountains and Moorlands*, London: Collins.

Peterken, G. F. (1993), *Woodland Conservation and Management*, 2nd edn, London: Chapman & Hall.

Peterken, G. F. (1996), *Natural Woodland: Ecology and Conservation in Northern Temperate Regions*, Cambridge: Cambridge University Press.

Peterken, G. F., D. Baldock and A. Hampson (1995), *A Forest Habitat Network for Scotland*, Research, Survey and Monitoring Report 44, Edinburgh: Scottish Natural Heritage.

Peterken, G. F. and A. Stevenson (2004), *A New Dawn for Native Woodland Restoration on the Forestry Commission Estate in Scotland*, Edinburgh: Forestry Commission Scotland.

Peterken, G. F. and R. Worrell (2001), *Conservation of the Sunart Oak Woodland SAC and the Potential for Rural Development*, Report to Scottish Natural Heritage on behalf of the Caledonian Partnership, Edinburgh: Scottish Natural Heritage.

Phillips, R. (1994), *Grasses, Ferns, Mosses and Lichens of Great Britain and Ireland*, London: Macmillan.

Piggott, C. D. and J. P. Huntley (1978), 'Factors controlling the distribution of *Tilia cordata* at the northern limit of its geographical range. I. Distribution in north-west England', *New Phytologist* 81: 429–41.

Plantlife (2001), *Flowers of the Forest: Managing Scottish Woodlands for Wild Plant Biodiversity*, London: Plantlife.

Pritchett, W. L. and R. F. Fisher (2000), *Properties and Management of Forest Soils*, 3rd edn, New York: Wiley-Blackwell.

Pyatt, D. G., D. Ray and J. Fletcher (2001), *An Ecological Site Classification for Forestry in Great Britain*, Forestry Commission Bulletin 124, Edinburgh: Forestry Commission.

Quelch, P. R. (2000–1), 'Upland pasture woodlands in Scotland', *Scottish Forestry* 54: 209–14 and 55: 85–91.

Rackham, O. (1990), *Trees and Woodlands in the British Landscape*, rev. edn, London: Dent.

Rackham, O. (2003), *Ancient Woodland: Its History, Vegetation and Uses in England*, new edn, Dalbeattie: Castlepoint Press.

Ray, D. (2008), *Impacts of Climate Change on Forestry in Scotland: A Synopsis of Spatial Modelling Research*, Forestry Commission Research Note 101, Edinburgh: Forestry Commission Scotland.

Read, D. J., P. H. Freer-Smith, J. I. L. Morison, N. Hanley, C. C. West and P. Snowdon (eds) (2009), *Combating Climate Change – A Role for UK Forests*, Edinburgh: The Stationery Office.

Ritchie, G. and A. Ritchie (1991), *Scotland: Archaeology and Early History*, Edinburgh: Edinburgh University Press.

Ritchie, M. and J. Wordsworth (2010), *Identifying the Historic Environment in Scotland's Forests and Woodlands*, Forestry Commission Practice Guide 101, Edinburgh: Forestry Commission Scotland.

Roberts, A. J., C. Russell, G. J. Walker and K. J. Kirby (1992), 'Regional variation in the origin, extent and composition of Scottish woodland', *Botanical Journal of Scotland* 46: 167–89.

Rodwell, J. S. (ed.) (1991a), *British Plant Communities, Volume 1: Woodlands and Scrub*, Cambridge: Cambridge University Press.

Rodwell, J. S. (ed.) (1991b), *British Plant Communities, Volume 2: Mires and Heaths*, Cambridge: Cambridge University Press.

Rodwell, J. S. and G. S. Patterson (1994), *Creating New Native Woodlands*, Forestry Commission Bulletin 112, Edinburgh: Forestry Commission.

Rohrig, E. and B. Ulrich (eds) (1991), *Ecosystems of the World 7: Temperate Deciduous Forests*, Amsterdam: Elsevier.

Sansum, P. (2005), 'Argyll oakwoods: use and ecological change, 1000–2000 AD – a palynological-historical investigation', *Botanical Journal of Scotland* 57 (1): 83–97.

Shaw, H. and R. Tipping (2006), 'Recent pine woodland dynamics in east Glen Affric, northern Scotland, from highly resolved palaeoecological analyses', *Forestry* 79 (3): 331–40.

Simmons, I. G. (2000), *An Environmental History of Great Britain from 10,000 Years Ago to the Present*, Edinburgh: Edinburgh University Press.

Sing, L., W. Towers and J. Ellis (2013), 'Woodland expansion in Scotland: an assessment of the opportunities and constraints using GIS', *Scottish Forestry* 67 (4): 18–25.

Smout, T. C. (1993), *Scotland since Prehistory: Natural Change and Human Impact*, Aberdeen: Scottish Cultural Press.

Smout, T. C. (ed.) (1997), *Scottish Woodland History*, Edinburgh: Scottish Cultural Press.

Smout, T. C. (2000), *Nature Contested: Environmental History in Scotland and Northern England since 1600*, Edinburgh: Edinburgh University Press.

Smout, T. C. (ed.) (2003), *People and Woods in Scotland: A History*, Edinburgh: Edinburgh University Press.

Smout, T. C. (2005), 'Oak as a commercial crop in the eighteenth and nineteenth centuries', *Botanical Journal of Scotland* 57 (1): 107–14.

Smout, T. C. (2006), 'The pinewoods and human use, 1600–1900', *Forestry* 79 (3): 341–9.

Smout, T. C., A. R. MacDonald and F. Watson (2005), *A History of the Native Woodlands of Scotland 1500–1920*, Edinburgh: Edinburgh University Press.

Steven, H. M. and A. Carlisle (1959), *The Native Pinewoods of Scotland*, Edinburgh: Oliver & Boyd.

Stiven, R. and K. Holl (2004), *Wood Pasture*, Perth: Scottish Natural Heritage.

Swanson, G., D. Campbell and H. Armstrong (2008), *Estimating Deer Abundance in Woodlands: The Combination Plot Technique*, Forestry Commission Bulletin 128, Edinburgh: Forestry Commission.

Tansley, A. G. (1939), *The British Islands and their Vegetation*, Cambridge: Cambridge University Press.

Thomas, P. and J. Packham (2007), *Ecology of Woodlands and Forests: Description, Dynamics and Diversity*, Cambridge: Cambridge University Press.

Thompson, R. (2004), *Predicting Site Suitability for Natural Colonisation: Upland Birchwoods and Native Pinewoods in Northern Scotland*, Forestry Commission Information Note 54, Edinburgh: Forestry Commission.

Thompson, R. (2005), *Thinning in Atlantic Oakwoods: Assessing Options at the Stand Scale*, Munlochy: Highland Birchwoods.

Thompson, R. N., J. W. Humphrey, R. Harmer and R. Ferris (2003), *Restoration of Native Woodland on Ancient Woodland Sites*, Forestry Commission Practice Guide, Edinburgh: Forestry Commission.

Tipping, R. (1994), 'The form and fate of Scotland's woodlands', *Proceedings of the Society of Antiquaries of Scotland* 124: 1–54.

Tipping, R. (2008), 'Blanket peat in the Scottish Highlands: timing, cause, spread and the myth of environmental determinism', *Biodiversity and Conservation* 17 (9): 2,097–113.

Tipping, R. and A. Davies (2006), 'Long-term woodland dynamics in West Glen Affric, northern Scotland', *Forestry* 79 (3): 351–9.

Tittensor, R. M. (1970), 'History of the Loch Lomond oakwoods', *Scottish Forestry* 24: 100–18.

Tolkien, J. R. R. (1955), *The Return of the King*, London: George Allen & Unwin.

Towers, W., J. Hall, A. Hester, A. Malcolm and D. Stone (2004), *The Potential for Native Woodland in Scotland: The Native Woodland Model*, Perth: Scottish Natural Heritage.

UKWAS (2011), *The UK Woodland Assurance Standard*, 3rd edn (as amended to November 2011), Edinburgh: UKWAS.

van Andel, J. and J. Aronson (2012), *Restoration Ecology: The New Frontier*, 2nd edn, Chichester: Wiley-Blackwell.

Vera, F. W. M. (2000), *Grazing Ecology and Forest History*, Wallingford: CABI.

Walker, G. J. and K. J. Kirby (1989), *Inventories of Ancient, Long-Established and Semi-Natural Woodland for Scotland*, Research and Survey in Nature Conservation 22, Peterborough: Nature Conservancy Council.

Warren, C. (2002), *Managing Scotland's Environment*, Edinburgh: Edinburgh University Press.

Watts, K., J. W. Humphrey, M. Griffiths, C. Quine and D. Ray (2005), *Evaluating Biodiversity in Fragmented Landscapes: Principles*, Forestry Commission Information Note 73, Edinburgh: Forestry Commission.

West, R. G. (1970), 'Pleistocene history of the British flora', in D. Walker and R. G. West (eds), *Studies in the Vegetational History of the British Isles*, Cambridge: Cambridge University Press, pp. 1–12.

West, R. G. (1980), 'Pleistocene forest history in East Anglia', *New Phytologist* 85: 571–622.

Whitbread, A. M. (1990), 'How relevant is the identification of ancient woodland to woodland conservation in the upland counties of Great Britain?', *Quarterly Journal of Forestry* 84: 29–36.

White, J. (1998), *Estimating the Age of Large and Veteran Trees in Britain*, Forestry Commission Information Note 12, Edinburgh: Forestry Commission.

Willis, J., J. McIntyre, P. Quelch and R. Thompson (2008), 'Practical application of the Sunart Oakwoods management models with low impact harvesting techniques', *Scottish Forestry* 62 (1): 10–15.

Wilson, S. McG. (2006), 'The European beech in Scotland: history, distribution and ecological potential', *Scottish Forestry* 60 (4): 4–13.

Wilson, S. McG. (2007), 'The selection of tree species for forestry in Scotland: strategic arguments in favour of maintaining diversity', *Scottish Forestry* 61 (4): 3–12.

Wilson, S. McG. (2009), 'A new inventory of aspen (*Populus tremula* L.) populations in Caithness and Sutherland', *Scottish Forestry* 63 (4): 7–12.

Wilson, S. McG. (2010), 'The European beech (*Fagus sylvatica* L.) in Great Britain: ecological status, silviculture and management of genetic resources', *Communicationes Instituti Forestalis Bohemicae* 25: 122–40.

Wilson, S. McG. (2011a), 'Productive conifers in the riparian buffer zone: any case for the defence?', *Scottish Forestry* 65 (4): 14–18.

Wilson, S. McG. (2011b), *Using Alternative Conifer Species for Productive Forestry in Scotland*, Edinburgh: Forestry Commission Scotland.

Wilson, S. McG. (2012), 'Retaining timber potential after PAWS restoration', *Quarterly Journal of Forestry* 106 (2): 105–18.

Wilson, S. McG. (2013a), 'Cattle grazing in Scottish woodlands: experiences, opportunities and challenges', *Scottish Forestry* 67 (1): 26–33.

Wilson, S. McG. (2013b), 'Adoption of alternative silvicultural systems in Great Britain: a review', *Quarterly Journal of Forestry* 107 (4): 279–93.

Wood, R. F. (1955), *Studies of the North-West American Forests in Relation to Silviculture in Great Britain*, Forestry Commission Bulletin 25, London: HMSO.

Woodland Trust (2005), *The Conservation and Restoration of Plantations on Ancient Woodland Sites*, Grantham: Woodland Trust.

Worrell, R. (1995), 'European aspen (*Populus tremula* L.): a review with particular reference to Scotland', *Forestry* 68 (2): 93–105 and 68 (3): 231–43.

Worrell, R. (1999), *The Birch Woodland Management Handbook*, Munlochy: Highland Birchwoods.

Worrell, R. (2014), 'Long-distance colonisation of oak dispersed by jays in Highland Scotland: a review of dispersal of acorns by the Eurasian jay', *Scottish Forestry* 68 (1): 18–30.

Worrell, R. and D. C. Malcolm (1998), 'Anomalies in the distribution of silver birch (*Betula pendula* Roth) in Scotland', *Botanical Journal of Scotland* 50: 1–10.

Yalden, D. W. (2002), The History of British Mammals (Poyser Natural History), London: T. & A. D. Poyser Ltd/Academic Press.

Index